PREFACE

Welcome to "Advanced Java" Java has evolved significantly since its inception, becoming one of the most popular programming languages for a good reason. This book aims to take you beyond the basics of Java, introducing advanced concepts, techniques, and tools to help you become a proficient Java developer. Whether you're new to Java or an experienced developer looking to enhance your skills, this book will be your guide. We will cover a diverse range of topics, from advanced object-oriented programming and concurrency to database connectivity, web development, and modern Java frameworks.

Our objective is to do more than just teach you how to write Java code; we want to help you become a Java craftsman or craftswoman, capable of creating complex, efficient, and elegant software solutions. You'll gain the knowledge and practical experience needed to confidently address real-world challenges. The journey begins with advanced object-oriented programming principles and design patterns, where you'll learn to design your software for scalability, maintainability, and flexibility using industry-standard practices.

Concurrency is a critical aspect of modern software development, and this book will delve into multithreading, synchronization, and concurrent data structures, providing you with the tools to write high-performance, parallelized applications. Mastering database connectivity is essential for any Java developer. You'll learn to work with databases, including advanced SQL queries, JDBC, and connection pooling, enabling you to build robust, data-driven applications.

Web development is another fundamental component of modern Java programming. You'll explore technologies like Servlets, JSP, and Java Server Faces (JSF), and we'll introduce the Spring Framework, a comprehensive toolset for developing enterprise-level applications. Throughout the book, we'll emphasize best practices, coding standards, and design guidelines to help you write not only functional but also maintainable and elegant code. You'll learn how to leverage tools and libraries to enhance your productivity and streamline your development process.

As you embark on this journey into "Advanced Java," remember that mastering any craft requires time and practice. Java is a versatile and powerful tool, and with dedication and persistence, you can unlock its full potential. We encourage you to engage with the hands-on exercises and embrace the challenges that advanced Java programming presents. By the end of this book, we hope you'll have expanded not only your technical skills but also your mindset as a software developer.

Let's begin this adventure together and explore the world of "Advanced Java".

Table of Contents

CHAPTER 1 - Network Basics and Socket Overview

1.1 Introduction to Networking

Networking serves as a gateway into the realm of networking within the context of Java programming, focusing on advanced concepts and techniques for building robust, scalable, and secure networked applications.
This introductory section lays the groundwork for understanding the fundamental principles, tools, and practices essential for leveraging Java's powerful networking capabilities. Java, renowned for its platform independence, versatility, and extensive standard library, provides comprehensive support for networking through its built-in APIs (Application Programming Interfaces). These APIs enable developers to create a wide range of networked applications, from simple client-server interactions to complex distributed systems.

At the heart of Java's networking capabilities lies the java.net package, which offers classes and interfaces for implementing various networking protocols, handling socket communications, and managing network resources. Understanding the java.net package is crucial for harnessing the full potential of Java's networking capabilities.
Introduction to Networking for Advanced Java include
Socket Programming: Socket programming forms the foundation of network communication in Java. Sockets facilitate communication between client and server applications by establishing connections and transmitting data streams. Understanding socket programming allows developers to create networked applications that can exchange data reliably and efficiently.
TCP/IP and UDP Protocols: Java supports both TCP/IP (Transmission Control Protocol/Internet Protocol) and UDP (User Datagram Protocol), two fundamental networking protocols used for communication over the internet. TCP/IP provides reliable, connection-oriented communication, while UDP offers lightweight, connectionless communication. Mastery of these protocols enables developers to choose the most suitable approach for their networking needs.
Concurrency and Multithreading: Networking applications often require concurrent handling of multiple client connections and asynchronous communication. Java's multithreading capabilities, facilitated by the java.lang.Thread class and the java.util.concurrent package, allow developers to implement scalable and responsive networked applications that can handle concurrent tasks efficiently.
Security and Encryption: Network security is paramount in today's interconnected world. Java provides robust support for implementing security measures such as encryption, authentication, and secure communication protocols (e.g., SSL/TLS). Understanding how to incorporate security features into Java networking applications helps protect sensitive data and prevent unauthorized access.
Remote Method Invocation (RMI): RMI is a Java-specific technology for enabling communication between distributed Java objects over a network. By leveraging RMI, developers can create distributed applications where objects residing on different machines can interact seamlessly. Understanding RMI empowers developers to build distributed systems with ease.
Web Services and APIs: Java offers extensive support for developing web services and APIs (Application Programming Interfaces) using technologies such as Java EE (Enterprise Edition) and RESTful web services. These technologies enable the creation of interoperable, scalable, and loosely coupled networked applications that can integrate seamlessly with other systems and platforms.

1.1.1 Network Layers Overview

In an "Advanced Java Networking", a comprehensive understanding of network layers is vital for developers aiming to build high-performance, scalable, and efficient networked applications. This section provides an in-depth overview of the layered architecture of modern networking protocols, emphasizing the OSI (Open Systems Interconnection) model and its relevance to Java networking.
The OSI model serves as a conceptual framework for understanding how communication protocols interact within a networked environment. It consists of seven layers, each responsible for specific functions and abstraction levels, facilitating modular design, interoperability, and ease of implementation. By understanding the OSI model, developers can design robust and flexible networking solutions that adhere to industry standards and best practices.

The following is a breakdown of the OSI model layers and their relevance to advanced Java networking:

7 LAYERS OF THE OSI MODEL	
APPLICATION	END USER LAYER HTTP, FTP, IRC, SSH, DNS
PRESENTATION	SYNTAX LAYER SSL, SSH, IMAP, FTP, MPEG, JPEG
SESSION	SYNCH & SEND TO PORT API'S, SOCKETS, WINSOCK
TRANSPORT	END-TO-END CONNECTIONS TCS, UDP
NETWORK	PACKETS IP, ICMP, IPSEC, IGMP
DATA LINK	FRAMES ETHERNET, PPP, SWITCH, BRIDGE
PHYSICAL	PHYSICAL STRUCTURE COAX, FIBER, WIRELESS

Figure 1.1

Physical Layer

This layer deals with the physical transmission of data over the network medium, including electrical signals, voltage levels, and physical connectors.

In advanced Java networking, developers may interact with physical layer concepts indirectly through network interface controllers (NICs) and low-level hardware interactions, though most interactions occur at higher layers of abstraction.

Data Link Layer

The data link layer is responsible for framing data into packets, error detection, and media access control (MAC) addressing.

Advanced Java networking applications often rely on data link layer protocols such as Ethernet for local network communication. Java libraries abstract away low-level details, allowing developers to focus on higher-level functionality.

Network Layer

The network layer facilitates routing of packets between different networks, addressing, and congestion control.

Advanced Java networking may involve interactions with network layer protocols such as IP (Internet Protocol) and routing algorithms. Java provides APIs for socket programming and network configuration, enabling developers to implement network layer functionalities within their applications.

Transport Layer

This layer ensures reliable and efficient end-to-end communication between hosts, handling flow control, error recovery, and segmentation.

In advanced Java networking, developers commonly utilize transport layer protocols such as TCP (Transmission Control Protocol) and UDP (User Datagram Protocol) for communication between applications. Java's java.net package offers classes and interfaces for socket programming and transport layer interactions.

Session Layer

The session layer establishes, maintains, and terminates communication sessions between applications, providing synchronization and checkpointing mechanisms.

Advanced Java networking may involve session layer functionalities implemented through application protocols and middleware frameworks. Java's concurrency utilities and network APIs enable developers to manage communication sessions effectively within their applications.

Presentation Layer
This layer handles data representation, encryption, and compression, ensuring compatibility between different systems.
In advanced Java networking, developers may utilize presentation layer concepts indirectly through data serialization, encryption libraries, and protocol negotiation mechanisms. Java provides APIs for data manipulation and conversion, facilitating interoperability between heterogeneous systems.

Application Layer
The application layer provides network services directly to end-users, including file transfer, email, web browsing, and remote access.
Advanced Java networking involves the development of application layer protocols, APIs, and services using Java EE (Enterprise Edition), web frameworks, and middleware technologies. Java libraries and frameworks simplify the development of networked applications, allowing developers to focus on application logic and functionality.

1.1.2 Understanding Network Protocols

Before we touch upon Java-specific classes, it's essential to understand the protocols that govern communication between devices. The most widely used protocol suite is TCP/IP, which stands for Transmission Control Protocol/Internet Protocol. TCP/IP ensures reliable, ordered, and error-checked delivery of a stream of bytes between applications running on hosts communicating over an IP network.
Network protocols serve as the foundation of communication in computer networks, enabling devices to exchange data seamlessly and reliably. These protocols define various aspects of communication, including addressing, data encapsulation, error detection and correction, flow control, and security. By understanding network protocols, developers can design, implement, and troubleshoot networked applications effectively, ensuring compatibility, reliability, and security.
Key aspects of understanding network protocols for an advanced Java audience include:
TCP/IP Protocol Suite
The TCP/IP (Transmission Control Protocol/Internet Protocol) suite is the foundation of modern networking, governing communication across the internet and many private networks.
In advanced Java networking, developers interact extensively with TCP/IP protocols, particularly TCP for reliable, connection-oriented communication and UDP for lightweight, connectionless communication.
Java's networking APIs, such as the java.net package, provide comprehensive support for implementing TCP/IP-based applications, including socket programming, IP addressing, and protocol-specific configurations.

HTTP and HTTPS Protocols
HTTP (Hypertext Transfer Protocol) and its secure counterpart HTTPS are application layer protocols used for transmitting data over the World Wide Web.
Advanced Java networking often involves building web applications and services that communicate using HTTP/HTTPS protocols. Java frameworks like Spring and JAX-RS facilitate the development of web-based applications, handling HTTP request/response cycles, session management, and security features.
Java provides libraries for HTTP client and server implementations, enabling developers to integrate web functionality into their applications seamlessly.

FTP and SFTP Protocols
FTP (File Transfer Protocol) and SFTP (SSH File Transfer Protocol) are used for transferring files between systems over a network.
Advanced Java networking may involve implementing FTP/SFTP clients or servers for automated file transfers. Java libraries like Apache Commons Net and JSch provide support for FTP/SFTP operations, simplifying the development of file transfer applications.

SMTP and IMAP Protocols
SMTP (Simple Mail Transfer Protocol) and IMAP (Internet Message Access Protocol) are used for sending and retrieving email messages, respectively.
Advanced Java networking may include integrating email functionality into applications, such as sending automated emails or processing incoming messages. JavaMail API provides comprehensive support for

SMTP, IMAP, and POP3 (Post Office Protocol) operations, allowing developers to build robust email applications.

DNS Protocol

DNS (Domain Name System) resolves domain names to IP addresses, facilitating hostname resolution on the internet.

Advanced Java networking may involve DNS-related tasks, such as resolving domain names programmatically or implementing DNS client/server functionality. Java's networking APIs provide support for DNS resolution and hostname manipulation, enabling developers to interact with DNS services effectively.

Security Protocols (SSL/TLS)

SSL (Secure Sockets Layer) and its successor TLS (Transport Layer Security) are cryptographic protocols used for securing communication over a network.

Advanced Java networking often requires implementing secure communication using SSL/TLS protocols. Java's javax.net.ssl package provides APIs for SSL/TLS configuration, certificate management, and secure socket communication, ensuring data confidentiality and integrity.

1.2 Socket Communication

Socket communication is a key concept in network programming, enabling data exchange between applications running on different systems across a network. In advanced Java, socket communication involves a more in-depth understanding of various protocols, threading, and performance considerations. A socket is an endpoint for communication between two machines. In Java, the java.net package provides two main classes for socket programming:

Socket for client-side communication.

ServerSocket for server-side communication.

Basic Socket Programming

Creating a Server Socket

```
ServerSocket serverSocket = new ServerSocket(portNumber);
Socket clientSocket = serverSocket.accept(); // Waits for a client connection
```

Creating a Client Socket

```
Socket socket = new Socket("hostname", portNumber);
```

Communication Streams

```
// For reading from the socket
BufferedReader in = new BufferedReader(new InputStreamReader(clientSocket.getInputStream()));
// For writing to the socket
PrintWriter out = new PrintWriter(clientSocket.getOutputStream(), true);
```

1.3 TCP/IP Client Sockets with Socket

TCP/IP client sockets in Java are used to establish a connection to a server over the network, allowing for data exchange between the client and server. Here's a comprehensive guide to creating and using TCP/IP client sockets with the Socket class in Java.

Setting Up a TCP/IP Client Socket

Import Required Packages

```
import java.io.*;
import java.net.*;
```

Creating a Client Socket

```
String serverAddress = "localhost"; // or the server's IP address
int portNumber = 12345; // the server's port number
try (Socket socket = new Socket(serverAddress, portNumber)) {
  // Connection established
} catch (IOException e) {
  e.printStackTrace();
}
```

1. Setting Up Input and Output Streams

```
try (Socket socket = new Socket(serverAddress, portNumber);
   PrintWriter out = new PrintWriter(socket.getOutputStream(), true);
```

```
    BufferedReader in = new BufferedReader(new InputStreamReader(socket.getInputStream()))) {
   // Communication logic here
} catch (IOException e) {
   e.printStackTrace();
}
```

Communication Logic

```
try (Socket socket = new Socket(serverAddress, portNumber);
    PrintWriter out = new PrintWriter(socket.getOutputStream(), true);
    BufferedReader in = new BufferedReader(new InputStreamReader(socket.getInputStream()));
    BufferedReader stdIn = new BufferedReader(new InputStreamReader(System.in))) {
   String userInput;
   System.out.println("Type a message: ");
   while ((userInput = stdIn.readLine()) != null) {
      out.println(userInput); // Send to server
      System.out.println("Server response: " + in.readLine()); // Receive from server
   }

} catch (IOException e) {
   e.printStackTrace();
}
```

Complete TCP/IP Client Example

Here's a complete example of a TCP/IP client that connects to a server, sends user input, and prints the server's response.

```
import java.io.*;
import java.net.*;
public class TCPClient {
   public static void main(String[] args) {
      String serverAddress = "localhost"; // or the server's IP address
      int portNumber = 12345; // the server's port number
      try (Socket socket = new Socket(serverAddress, portNumber);
          PrintWriter out = new PrintWriter(socket.getOutputStream(), true);
          BufferedReader in = new BufferedReader(new InputStreamReader(socket.getInputStream()));
          BufferedReader stdIn = new BufferedReader(new InputStreamReader(System.in))) {
         System.out.println("Connected to the server at " + serverAddress + " on port " + portNumber);
         String userInput;
         System.out.println("Type a message (type 'bye' to quit): ");
         while ((userInput = stdIn.readLine()) != null) {
            if ("bye".equalsIgnoreCase(userInput)) {
               break; // Exit the loop if the user types 'bye'
            }
            out.println(userInput); // Send to server
            System.out.println("Server response: " + in.readLine()); // Receive from server
         }
         System.out.println("Client disconnected.");
      } catch (IOException e) {
         e.printStackTrace();
      }
   }
}
```

1.4 TCP/IP Server Sockets

Creating a TCP/IP server socket in Java involves setting up a server that listens for incoming client connections on a specific port. Once a connection is established, the server can communicate with the client using input and output streams. Here's a detailed explanation of how to create and use TCP/IP server sockets with the Server Socket and Socket classes in Java.

Setting Up a TCP/IP Server Socket

1. Import Required Packages

```
import java.io.*;
import java.net.*;
```

2. Creating a Server Socket

```
int portNumber = 12345; // The server's port number

try (ServerSocket serverSocket = new ServerSocket(portNumber)) {
    System.out.println("Server is listening on port " + portNumber);
    while (true) {
        Socket clientSocket = serverSocket.accept(); // Waits for a client connection
        new ClientHandler(clientSocket).start(); // Handle the client connection in a new thread
    }
} catch (IOException e) {
    e.printStackTrace();
}
```

3. Handling Client Connections

```
class ClientHandler extends Thread {
    private Socket clientSocket;
    public ClientHandler(Socket socket) {
        this.clientSocket = socket;
    }
    @Override
    public void run() {
        try (PrintWriter out = new PrintWriter(clientSocket.getOutputStream(), true);
             BufferedReader in = new BufferedReader(new InputStreamReader(clientSocket.getInputStream()))) {
            String inputLine;
            while ((inputLine = in.readLine()) != null) {
                System.out.println("Received: " + inputLine);
                out.println("Echo: " + inputLine); // Echo the received message
            }
        } catch (IOException e) {
            e.printStackTrace();
        }
    }
}
```

Complete TCP/IP Server Example

Here's a complete example of a TCP/IP server that listens for client connections and echoes received messages back to the clients.

```
import java.io.*;
import java.net.*;
public class TCPServer {
    public static void main(String[] args) {
        int portNumber = 12345; // The server's port number
        try (ServerSocket serverSocket = new ServerSocket(portNumber)) {
            System.out.println("Server is listening on port " + portNumber);
            while (true) {
                Socket clientSocket = serverSocket.accept(); // Waits for a client connection
                System.out.println("New client connected");
                new ClientHandler(clientSocket).start(); // Handle the client connection in a new thread
            }
        } catch (IOException e) {
            e.printStackTrace();
        }
    }
}
```

```
class ClientHandler extends Thread {
    private Socket clientSocket;
    public ClientHandler(Socket socket) {
        this.clientSocket = socket;
    }
    @Override
    public void run() {
        try (PrintWriter out = new PrintWriter(clientSocket.getOutputStream(), true);
             BufferedReader in = new BufferedReader(new InputStreamReader(clientSocket.getInputStream()))) {
            String inputLine;
            while ((inputLine = in.readLine()) != null) {
                System.out.println("Received: " + inputLine);
                out.println("Echo: " + inputLine); // Echo the received message
            }
        } catch (IOException e) {
            e.printStackTrace();
        }
    }
}
```

1.5 Datagrams in Java

Datagrams in Java are a means of implementing connectionless network communication using the User Datagram Protocol (UDP). Unlike TCP, which establishes a connection and ensures reliable data transfer, UDP sends data packets, called datagrams, without establishing a connection, making it faster but less reliable. Java provides two primary classes for working with datagrams. DatagramPacket and DatagramSocket. The DatagramPacket class encapsulates data, destination IP address, and port number into a packet that can be sent or received. It supports creating packets from byte arrays and extracting data from received packets. The DatagramSocket class is responsible for sending and receiving these datagram packets. A DatagramSocket can be bound to a specific port, enabling it to listen for incoming packets or send packets to a specified address and port. This makes datagrams ideal for applications that require fast, lightweight communication without the overhead of connection management, such as online gaming, real-time systems, and broadcasting messages to multiple clients. Although UDP does not guarantee delivery, order, or error checking, its simplicity and speed are advantageous in scenarios where timely delivery is more critical than reliability. In essence, datagrams in Java provide a straightforward and efficient mechanism for handling network communication in time-sensitive applications.

Java provides the java.net package, which contains the necessary classes to create and manipulate datagrams. Here is an overview of the primary classes involved

DatagramSocket: This class represents a socket for sending and receiving datagram packets.

DatagramPacket: This class represents a datagram packet, which contains data either to be sent or received.

Sending and Receiving Datagrams

Sending a Datagram

To send a datagram, you create a DatagramSocket and a DatagramPacket. Here's an example

```
import java.net.DatagramPacket;
import java.net.DatagramSocket;
import java.net.InetAddress;
public class DatagramSender {
    public static void main(String[] args) {
        try {
            // Create a socket to send the datagram
            DatagramSocket socket = new DatagramSocket();
            // The message to be sent
            String message = "Hello, this is a test message";
            byte[] buffer = message.getBytes();
            // The IP address of the receiver
            InetAddress receiverAddress = InetAddress.getByName("localhost");
            // Create a packet with the data, the receiver's address, and port number
```

```
        DatagramPacket packet = new DatagramPacket(buffer, buffer.length, receiverAddress, 9876);
        // Send the packet
        socket.send(packet);
        // Close the socket
        socket.close();
      } catch (Exception e) {
        e.printStackTrace();
      }
    }
}
```

Receiving a Datagram

To receive a datagram, you also create a DatagramSocket and a DatagramPacket, but you need to specify the port number to listen on:

```
import java.net.DatagramPacket;
import java.net.DatagramSocket;
public class DatagramReceiver {
    public static void main(String[] args) {
      try {
        // Create a socket to receive the datagram on port 9876
        DatagramSocket socket = new DatagramSocket(9876);
        // Create a buffer to hold the incoming data
        byte[] buffer = new byte[1024];
        // Create a packet to receive the data into
        DatagramPacket packet = new DatagramPacket(buffer, buffer.length);
        // Receive the packet
        socket.receive(packet);
        // Convert the received data to a string
        String receivedMessage = new String(packet.getData(), 0, packet.getLength());
        System.out.println("Received message: " + receivedMessage);
        // Close the socket
        socket.close();
      } catch (Exception e) {
        e.printStackTrace();
      }
    }
}
```

Key Points

No Connection Required: Unlike TCP, UDP does not establish a connection before sending data, which makes it faster but less reliable.

Data Loss: Packets sent via UDP may be lost or arrive out of order.

Broadcast and Multicast: UDP supports broadcasting (sending data to all devices in a subnet) and multicasting (sending data to multiple specific devices).

Advanced Usage

For more advanced usage, you might need to handle scenarios such as:

Handling Timeouts: Setting timeouts on the socket to avoid blocking indefinitely.

Fragmentation and Reassembly: Handling larger messages that need to be split across multiple datagrams.

Security: Implementing security measures to ensure data integrity and authenticity.

Here's an example of setting a timeout

```
socket.setSoTimeout(5000); // Set a timeout of 5 seconds
```

1.6 InetAddress

The InetAddress class represents an IP address, which can be either IPv4 or IPv6. It provides methods to resolve hostnames to IP addresses and vice versa, enabling developers to handle network operations. Key functionalities include getByName() to resolve hostnames, getLocalHost() for the local machine's address, and getAllByName() for multiple addresses associated with a hostname. InetAddress also supports checking reachability with isReachable(). By abstracting the complexities of raw IP addresses, InetAddress facilitates efficient network programming, including establishing socket connections and managing network interfaces.
Code: InetAddress ip = InetAddress.getByName("www.example.com");
Core Features and Methods
Obtaining InetAddress Objects

By Hostname: Resolves the hostname to its corresponding IP address.
InetAddress address = InetAddress.getByName("www.example.com");
This method performs a DNS lookup and may throw UnknownHostException if the hostname cannot be resolved.
By IP Address**:** Creates an InetAddress object from a byte array representing the raw IP address.
byte[] ip = {127, 0, 0, 1}; // IPv4 address for localhost
InetAddress address = InetAddress.getByAddress(ip);
For IPv6, the byte array length should be 16.
By Local Host**:** Retrieves the IP address of the local machine.
InetAddress localAddress = InetAddress.getLocalHost();
This method may throw UnknownHostException if the local host name cannot be resolved into an address.
All IP Addresses for a Hostname**:** Retrieves all IP addresses associated with a hostname.
InetAddress[] addresses = InetAddress.getAllByName("www.example.com");

Commonly Used Methods
getHostName(): Returns the hostname associated with the IP address.
String hostname = address.getHostName();

getCanonicalHostName()**:** Returns the fully qualified domain name (FQDN) for the IP address.
String canonicalHostname = address.getCanonicalHostName()

getHostAddress()**:** Returns the textual representation of the IP address.
String ipString = address.getHostAddress();

getAddress()**:** Returns the raw IP address as a byte array.
byte[] ipAddress = address.getAddress();

Advanced Usage Examples

1. Resolving Hostnames and IP Addresses

```
import java.net.InetAddress;
public class InetAddressExample {
public static void main(String[] args) {
      try {
         InetAddress address = InetAddress.getByName("www.example.com");
         System.out.println("Hostname: " + address.getHostName());
         System.out.println("Canonical Hostname: " + address.getCanonicalHostName());
         System.out.println("IP Address: " + address.getHostAddress());
      } catch (Exception e) {
         e.printStackTrace();
      }
   }
}
```

2. Handling Multiple IP Addresses

When dealing with services that might have multiple IP addresses (for load balancing or redundancy), you can retrieve all associated addresses:

```
import java.net.InetAddress;
```

```java
public class MultipleIPAddressesExample {
   public static void main(String[] args) {
      try {
         InetAddress[] addresses = InetAddress.getAllByName("www.google.com");
         for (InetAddress address : addresses) {
            System.out.println("IP Address: " + address.getHostAddress());
         }
      } catch (Exception e) {
         e.printStackTrace();
      }
   }
}
```

InetAddress and Network Programming

Example: Connecting to a Server

The InetAddress class is often used in conjunction with sockets to specify the target address for a connection.

```java
import java.net.InetAddress;
import java.net.Socket;
public class ClientExample {
   public static void main(String[] args) {
      try {
         InetAddress serverAddress = InetAddress.getByName("www.example.com");
         Socket socket = new Socket(serverAddress, 80);
         // Use the socket for communication
         socket.close();
      } catch (Exception e) {
         e.printStackTrace();
      }
   }
}
```

Handling IPv4 and IPv6 Addresses

The InetAddress class seamlessly handles both IPv4 and IPv6 addresses. Java will automatically resolve and use the appropriate type based on the network configuration and address provided.

Example: Checking Address Type

```java
import java.net.InetAddress;
import java.net.Inet6Address;
import java.net.Inet4Address;
public class IPAddressTypeExample {
   public static void main(String[] args) {
      try {
         InetAddress address = InetAddress.getByName("www.google.com");
         if (address instanceof Inet6Address) {
            System.out.println("This is an IPv6 address.");
         } else if (address instanceof Inet4Address) {
            System.out.println("This is an IPv4 address.");
         } else {
            System.out.println("Unknown IP address type.");
         }
      } catch (Exception e) {
         e.printStackTrace();
      }
   }
}
```

Reverse DNS Lookup

Performing a reverse DNS lookup can help find the hostname associated with an IP address.

```
import java.net.InetAddress;
public class ReverseDNSLookupExample {
   public static void main(String[] args) {
      try {
         InetAddress address = InetAddress.getByName("8.8.8.8");
         System.out.println("Hostname: " + address.getHostName());
      } catch (Exception e) {
         e.printStackTrace();
      }
   }
}
```

Network Interface Interaction

InetAddress can be used with the NetworkInterface class to get detailed information about the network interfaces on a machine.

Example: Network Interface Details

```
import java.net.InetAddress;
import java.net.NetworkInterface;
import java.util.Enumeration;
public class NetworkInterfaceExample
 {
   public static void main(String[] args) {
      try {
         Enumeration<NetworkInterface> interfaces = NetworkInterface.getNetworkInterfaces();
         while (interfaces.hasMoreElements()) {
            NetworkInterface networkInterface = interfaces.nextElement();
            System.out.println("Interface: " + networkInterface.getName());
            Enumeration<InetAddress> addresses = networkInterface.getInetAddresses();
            while (addresses.hasMoreElements()) {
               InetAddress address = addresses.nextElement();
               System.out.println("  Address: " + address.getHostAddress());
            }
         }
      }
          catch (Exception e)
          {
         e.printStackTrace();
      }
   }
}
```

Socket Communication in Practice

When a client and a server communicate over a network using sockets, the typical sequence of steps is as follows:

1. Server creates a ServerSocket and binds it to a specific port number.
2. Server invokes the accept() method of ServerSocket to wait for client requests.
3. Client creates a Socket and attempts to connect to the server's IP address and port number.
4. Server's accept() method returns a new Socket object that is connected to the client's socket.
5. Data is read from and written to the socket's input and output streams.
6. Both client and server close their socket connections once communication is complete.

1.7 URLs and URL Connection

In Java, a URL (Uniform Resource Locator) is the address of a resource on the Internet. It not only tells you the location of that resource but also how to retrieve it. A URL is composed of several parts: the protocol, the host, the port (optional), the path, and the query string (optional).

1.7.1 The URL Class

The URL (Uniform Resource Locator) class in Java is part of the java.net package and represents a URL, which is a pointer to a "resource" on the World Wide Web. The resource can be something as simple as a file or a directory, or it can be a reference to a more complicated object, such as a query to a database or a search engine. Once you have a URL object, you can retrieve various components of the URL, like the protocol, host, port, and file path, using the appropriate methods provided by the class.

URL Class Structure

A typical URL has the following structure protocol://hostname:port/path?query#fragment

Where:

- protocol: The protocol to use (e.g., http, https, ftp).
- hostname: The domain name or IP address of the server.
- port: The port number on the server (optional, default for HTTP is 80).
- path: The file or resource to retrieve.
- query: The query string (optional, used for passing parameters).
- fragment: The reference to a section of the resource (optional).

Key Methods of the URL Class

Creating a URL

```
URL url = new URL("http://www.example.com:80/docs/resource1.html?name=Network#DOWNLOADING");
```

Getting URL Components

```
String protocol = url.getProtocol(); // "http"
String host = url.getHost();        // "www.example.com"
int port = url.getPort();          // 80 (returns -1 if no port is specified)
String path = url.getPath();        // "/docs/resource1.html"
String query = url.getQuery();      // "name=Network"
String fragment = url.getRef();     // "DOWNLOADING"
```

Opening a Connection

```
URLConnection connection = url.openConnection();
```

1.7.2 The URLConnection Class

The URLConnection class represents a communication link between the application and a URL. It is an abstract class that provides methods to interact with the resource at the URL. This includes methods for reading from and writing to the resource, as well as setting request properties and getting response headers.

To interact with the resource pointed to by a URL, Java uses the URLConnection class, which represents a communication link between the application and a URL. Instances of this class can be used both to read from and write to the resource referred to by the URL.

Common Usage of URLConnection

Opening a Connection

```
URL url = new URL("http://www.example.com");
URLConnection connection = url.openConnection();
connection.connect();  // Optional, implicitly called by getInputStream()
```

Reading from a URLConnection

The URLConnection class provides input and output streams. If you want to read data from a URL, you can do so through the input stream obtained from the URLConnection.

Code-

```
InputStream inputStream = urlConnection.getInputStream();
BufferedReader reader = new BufferedReader(new InputStreamReader(inputStream));
String inputLine;
while ((inputLine = reader.readLine()) != null) {
   System.out.println(inputLine);
}
reader.close();
```

The above code snippet opens a stream and reads from the URL line by line.

Writing to a URLConnection

To send data to a URL, you would write to the URLConnection's output stream. However, before writing, you must configure the URLConnection to allow output

Code-

```
urlConnection.setDoOutput(true);
DataOutputStream out = new DataOutputStream(urlConnection.getOutputStream());
out.writeBytes("parameter1=value1&parameter2=value2");
out.flush();
out.close();
```

Setting Request Properties

You can set various request properties on a URLConnection, such as setting request methods (GET, POST, etc.), setting request headers, and so on.

Code-

```
urlConnection.setRequestMethod("GET");
urlConnection.setRequestProperty("Content-Type", "application/x-www-form-urlencoded");
```

Handling URLConnection Responses

You can also read response codes and messages from the URLConnection to determine if the request was successful.

Code-

```
int responseCode = urlConnection.getResponseCode();
String responseMessage = urlConnection.getResponseMessage();
```

Exercise

Exercise 1 – MCQ

1. What is a socket in network programming?
a) A protocol for secure data transmission
b) A hardware component for network connections
c) An endpoint for communication between two machines
d) A type of network cable
2. Which of the following is true about TCP/IP sockets?
a) They do not guarantee message delivery.
b) They transmit data in an unencrypted format.
c) They provide a connection-oriented, reliable stream of data.
d) They are primarily used for broadcasting messages.
3. Which method is used to connect a client socket to a server socket?
a) bind()
b) connect()
c) listen()
d) accept()
4. In Java, which class is used to create a client socket?
a) ServerSocket
b) Socket
c) DatagramSocket
d) URL
5. Which method is used by a server to listen for incoming client connections?
a) connect()
b) bind()
c) accept()
d) listen()
6. Which of the following is required to create a ServerSocket in Java?
a) The client's IP address
b) The server's IP address
c) The port number the server will listen on
d) The protocol (TCP or UDP) to use
7. What is a Datagram in Java networking?

a) connection-oriented packet
b) A secure data transmission method
c) A small packet of information sent over the network
d) A high-speed data transfer protocol
8. Which class is used for sending and receiving datagram packets in Java?
a) DatagramPacket
b) DatagramSocket
c) Socket
d) ServerSocket
9. Which of the following methods is used to retrieve the IP address of a hostname?
a) InetAddress.getByName()
b) InetAddress.getLocalHost()
c) URL.getHost()
d) URLConnection.getIP()
10. What does the InetAddress class represent in Java networking?
a) A TCP/IP protocol
b) b) A URL's domain name
c) An IP address
d) A physical network interface

Exercise 2 -True False

1. A socket is a software endpoint that establishes bidirectional communication between a server and one or more clients.
2. TCP/IP client sockets can only send data after a connection has been established with a server socket.
3. The ServerSocket class is used to create a client socket that can request to connect to a server.
4. Datagram sockets are used for connectionless socket programming and are based on the UDP protocol.
5. The InetAddress class in Java is used to work with both IPv4 and IPv6 addresses.
6. A single instance of InetAddress can represent both a hostname and its corresponding IP address.
7. URLConnection is a direct subclass of URL and is used to send and receive data over the web.
8. It's possible to specify a timeout value for a connection attempt made by a client socket.
9. Server sockets automatically accept incoming connections without any method invocation needed by the programmer.
10. URLs and URLConnections support both HTTP and HTTPS protocols for data transmission.

Exercise 3- Fill in the blanks

1. In Java, a ________ is an endpoint for communication between two machines.
2. The ________ class is used to create a client socket that connects to a server in a TCP/IP network.
3. In server-side programming, the ________ class is used to listen for incoming connection requests from clients.
4. The ________ class in Java is used for sending and receiving datagram packets over a network.
5. The ________ class provides methods to get the IP address of a hostname.
6. __________ is used to convert human-readable domain names to IP addresses.
7. The __________ protocol is responsible for dynamically assigning IP addresses to devices on a network.
8. The process of converting domain names to IP addresses is facilitated by __________.
9. The process of closing a socket connection in Java is accomplished using the __________ method of the Socket class.
10. A __________ is a unique identifier associated with each application running on a host and using a network connection.

Exercise 4 – Match case

1. Used for connection-oriented communication
2. Represents a URL in Java
3. Listens for incoming connections on a specified port
4. Sends and receives packets of information

A. DatagramSocket
B. ServerSocket

C. URL
D. Socket

Exercise 5 – One word answer
1. What Java class is used for creating datagram sockets for sending and receiving UDP packets?
2. Which method of the URL class is used to establish a connection to the resource referred by the URL?

Exercise 6 – Small answer
1. How do you retrieve the IP address of a host name using Java?
2. Describe how to send a GET request to a web server and read the response using Java.

Exercise 7 – Long answer
1. Explain the process of establishing a TCP connection between a client and a server in Java, including the steps for setting up the server to listen for connections and how the client initiates the connection. Detail the role of the ServerSocket and Socket classes in this process.
2. Describe how to implement a simple chat application using UDP sockets in Java. Outline the steps necessary for sending and receiving messages between a client and a server, including the creation of DatagramSocket objects, the construction and handling of DatagramPacket objects for sending and receiving messages, and the considerations for ensuring communication reliability in the inherently unreliable UDP protocol.

Answers:
Exercise 1: 1) c 2) c 3) b 4) b 5) c 6) c 7) c 8) b 9) a 10) c
Exercise 2: 1) True 2) True 3) False 4) True 5) True 6) False 7) False 8) True 9) False 10) True
Exercise 3: 1) socket 2) Socket 3) ServerSocket 4) DatagramSocket 5) InetAddress 6) DNS 7) DHCP (Dynamic Host Configuration Protocol) 8) DNS (Domain Name System) 9) Close() 10) port number
Exercise 4: 1 - D. Socket 2 - C. URL 3 - B. ServerSocket 4 - A. DatagramSocket
Exercise 5: 1) DatagramSocket 2) openConnection

Online Resources

Online Practice Paper
Link: https://forms.gle/p1ZvDdS6PGg7WSpg8
QR Code:

YouTube Video Link

Link: https://www.youtube.com/playlist?list=PLzlh_31VWEFrVCJw3kRCEX-irsYWE6lxR
QR Code:

CHAPTER 2 - JDBC Programming

2.1 The JDBC Connectivity Model

The JDBC (Java Database Connectivity) model is a crucial aspect of advanced Java programming, facilitating interaction between Java applications and a wide range of databases. JDBC provides a standardized API for database-independent connectivity, ensuring that Java programs can access data stored in relational databases in a seamless and efficient manner.

JDBC is an API that enables Java applications to execute SQL statements, retrieve results, and propagate changes back to the database. It supports a variety of SQL operations, including querying, updating, and managing data, as well as database metadata. The JDBC API is designed to provide a common interface for database access, regardless of the underlying database management system (DBMS).

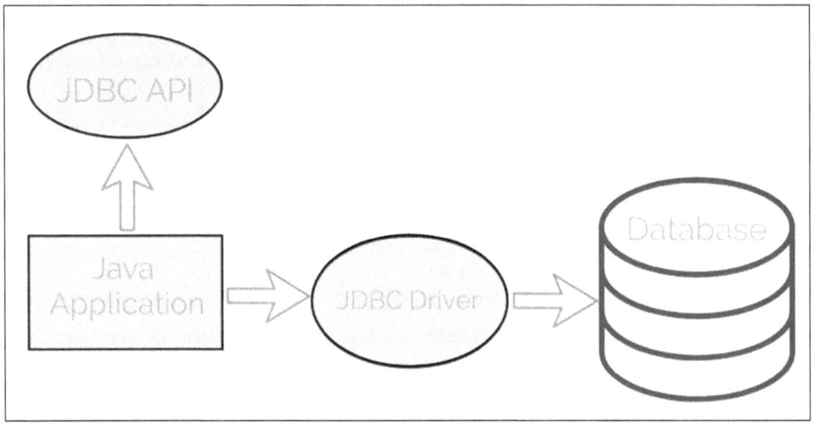

Figure 2.1

2.1.1 Components of the JDBC Connectivity Model

The JDBC Connectivity Model comprises several components that work together to enable connectivity between Java applications and a wide range of databases.

JDBC API

The JDBC API provides the application-to-JDBC Manager connection. This API includes two major sets of interfaces

i). The java.sql package contains classes and interfaces for the core JDBC API.

ii). The javax.sql package includes interfaces and classes for advanced features such as connection pooling, distributed transactions, and rowset operations.

JDBC Driver Manager

The Driver Manager is a very important part of the JDBC Connectivity Model. It can establish a connection between a Java application and the JDBC drivers. The Driver Manager is responsible for keeping track of the drivers that are available and handling requests from application to the appropriate drivers.

The DriverManager class manages a list of database drivers and establishes a connection to the database. It tries to connect to the database using the drivers listed in its internal registry.

```
Connection connection = DriverManager.getConnection(url, username, password);
```

JDBC Test Suite

This is a suite of tests that a JDBC driver must pass to ensure that the driver complies with the JDBC API.

The JDBC Test Suite consists of a series of tests designed to verify that JDBC drivers conform to the JDBC API. These tests cover a wide range of functionalities, including connection management, SQL statement execution, transaction handling, and error handling. The primary goal is to ensure that a JDBC driver can interact with a database in a consistent and predictable manner.

Components of the JDBC Test Suite

Setup and Configuration

Configuration files to specify database connection details, such as URL, username, and password.
Scripts to initialize and clean up the test database environment.
Connection Tests
Tests to validate the driver's ability to establish, maintain, and close connections.
Verification of connection properties, such as auto-commit mode and isolation levels.
Statement Tests
Tests for executing various types of SQL statements, including SELECT, INSERT, UPDATE, and DELETE.
Verification of Statement, PreparedStatement, and CallableStatement functionalities.
Transaction Tests
Tests to verify transaction management, including commit, rollback, and savepoints.
Checking behaviour under different isolation levels.
ResultSet Tests
Tests for retrieving and navigating through result sets.
Verification of cursor movement, data type retrieval, and updatability.
Metadata Tests
Tests to validate database and result set metadata retrieval.
Verification of DatabaseMetaData and ResultSetMetaData functionalities.
Error Handling Tests
Tests to ensure proper handling and reporting of SQL exceptions and warnings.
Verification of the driver's ability to handle various error scenarios gracefully.
Performance Tests
Benchmark tests to measure the performance of the driver under different workloads.
Stress tests to evaluate the driver's stability under high load conditions.

JDBC-ODBC Bridge

The JDBC-ODBC Bridge is a driver provided by the Java Development Kit (JDK) that allows Java applications to connect to databases via the Open Database Connectivity (ODBC) interface. This bridge driver translates JDBC method calls into ODBC function calls, enabling connectivity between Java applications and databases that support ODBC.

The JDBC-ODBC Bridge is known as the Type 1 JDBC driver. It is a native code driver that requires the ODBC driver to be installed on the client machine. The bridge was provided primarily to facilitate legacy database access and to allow developers to connect to databases that did not have a pure Java JDBC driver available.

Architecture

The architecture of the JDBC-ODBC Bridge involves several layers
Java Application: The application uses JDBC API to interact with the database.
JDBC-ODBC Bridge Driver: This driver translates JDBC calls into ODBC calls.
ODBC Driver Manager: Manages ODBC drivers and routes ODBC calls to the appropriate database driver.
ODBC Driver: A driver provided by the database vendor that translates ODBC calls into database-specific calls.
Database: The actual database system that processes queries and returns results.

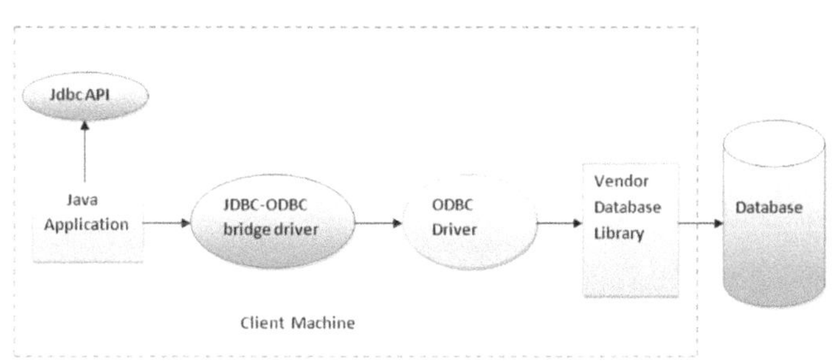

Figure- JDBC-ODBC Bridge Driver

Figure 2.2

Usage
Load the JDBC-ODBC Bridge Driver
```
Class.forName("sun.jdbc.odbc.JdbcOdbcDriver");
```
Establish a Connection
```
String url = "jdbc:odbc:DataSourceName";
Connection connection = DriverManager.getConnection(url, "username", "password");
```
Create a Statement
```
Statement statement = connection.createStatement();
```
Execute a Query
```
ResultSet resultSet = statement.executeQuery("SELECT * FROM tablename");
```
Process the Result Set
```
while (resultSet.next()) {
System.out.println(resultSet.getString("columnname"));
}
```
Close the Connection
```
resultSet.close();
statement.close();
connection.close();
```

Advantages
Legacy Support: The JDBC-ODBC Bridge provides a way to connect to legacy databases that only support ODBC.
Availability: It was included in the JDK, making it readily available for developers.

Limitations
Platform Dependence: The JDBC-ODBC Bridge relies on native code and the ODBC driver, making it platform-dependent.
Performance: Due to the multiple layers of translation, performance can be slower compared to other JDBC driver types.
Security: Native code drivers can pose security risks.
Deprecation: The JDBC-ODBC Bridge was deprecated in JDK 8 and removed in JDK 9, so it is not available in modern Java environments.
Complexity: Requires proper configuration of ODBC data sources, which can be cumbersome.

2.1.2 JDBC Drivers
JDBC drivers are the core of the JDBC Connectivity Model. They are used to connect to the database. There are four types of JDBC drivers:

- Type 1: JDBC-ODBC bridge driver
- Type 2: Native-API/partly Java driver
- Type 3: Net-protocol/all-Java driver
- Type 4: Native-protocol/all-Java driver

Each type has its own advantages and disadvantages, and the choice of driver depends on the specific needs of the application and the environment.

2.1.3 Establishing a Connection
To establish a connection to a database using JDBC, the following steps are typically followed:

Load the Driver: The JDBC driver should be loaded at the beginning of the program by calling Class.forName().
```
Class.forName("com.mysql.jdbc.Driver");
```
Establish a Connection: After loading the driver, a connection should be established by using DriverManager.getConnection().
```
Connection con = DriverManager.getConnection(
  "jdbc:mysql://localhost:3306/yourdatabase", "username", "password");
```
Create a Statement: Once the connection is established, a Statement object should be created to send SQL statements to the database.
```
Statement stmt = con.createStatement();
```

Execute a Query: SQL queries are executed using the Statement object created in the previous step.

```
ResultSet rs = stmt.executeQuery("SELECT * FROM tablename");
```

Process the Results: The results returned by the query should be processed.

```
while(rs.next()){
  // Retrieve by column name
  int id  = rs.getInt("id");
  String name = rs.getString("name");
  // Display values
  System.out.print("ID: " + id);
  System.out.println(", Name: " + name);
}
```

Close the Connection: Finally, it's important to close the ResultSet, Statement, and Connection objects to avoid any memory leaks.

```
rs.close();
stmt.close();
con.close();
```

2.1.4 Handling Exceptions

When dealing with database connections, it is important to handle exceptions properly. JDBC operations throw a SQLException when an error occurs during database access. The SQLException contains information such as a description of the error, an SQLSTATE code, and an error code that is specific to the database.

It is good practice to use try-catch blocks to catch SQLException and perform cleanup in the finally block.

Code-

```
try {
  // Load driver, establish connection, create statement, execute queries
} catch(SQLException se) {
  // Handle errors for JDBC
  se.printStackTrace();
} catch(Exception e) {
  // Handle errors for Class.forName
  e.printStackTrace();
} finally {
  // finally block used to close resources
  try {
    if(stmt!=null) stmt.close();
  } catch(SQLException se2) {
  } // nothing we can do
  try {
    if(con!=null) con.close();
  } catch(SQLException se) {
    se.printStackTrace();
  } // end finally try
}
```

Transaction Management

Transaction management is a critical aspect of database operations, ensuring data integrity and consistency during complex operations. In JDBC (Java Database Connectivity), transaction management allows developers to control the execution of multiple SQL statements as a single unit of work. This means that either all statements execute successfully, or none of them do, thereby maintaining the integrity of the database.

Key Concepts

Atomicity: Ensures that all operations within a transaction are completed; if not, the transaction is aborted.

Consistency: Guarantees that the database remains in a consistent state before and after the transaction.

Isolation: Ensures that transactions are isolated from each other until they are completed.

Durability: Ensures that the results of a completed transaction are permanently stored in the database.

JDBC Transaction Management Steps

Disable Auto-Commit Mode

By default, JDBC uses auto-commit mode, where each SQL statement is committed immediately after execution. For transaction management, auto-commit mode must be disabled i.e.,

```
connection.setAutoCommit(false);
```

Execute SQL Statements

Execute the required SQL statements as part of the transaction.

```
Statement stmt = connection.createStatement();
stmt.executeUpdate("INSERT INTO users (id, name) VALUES (1, 'John')");
stmt.executeUpdate("UPDATE accounts SET balance = balance - 100 WHERE user_id = 1");
```

Commit the Transaction

If all statements execute successfully, commit the transaction to persist the changes.

```
connection.commit();
```

Rollback the Transaction

If any statement fails, rollback the transaction to undo all changes made during the transaction.

```
connection.rollback();
```

Handle Exceptions

Ensure proper handling of exceptions to manage transaction outcomes.

```
try {
   connection.setAutoCommit(false);
   // Execute SQL statements
   connection.commit();
} catch (SQLException e) {
   connection.rollback();
   e.printStackTrace();
} finally {
   connection.setAutoCommit(true);
}
```

2.2 Creating a SQL Query

Once the connection to the database is established, the next step is to execute SQL statements. This is done by creating a Statement or PreparedStatement object.

Using Statement Objects

Create a Statement Object: The Statement object is used to send SQL queries to the database.

Code: Statement stmt = conn.createStatement();

Formulate the SQL Query: Write the SQL query as a String.

Code: String sql = "SELECT * FROM Users";

Using PreparedStatement Objects

PreparedStatement objects are a subclass of Statement that offer performance improvements and are more secure against SQL injection attacks.

Prepare the Statement: Unlike a regular Statement, a PreparedStatement is compiled by the database immediately and can be parameterized.

```
String psql = "SELECT * FROM Users WHERE username = ?";
PreparedStatement pstmt = conn.prepareStatement(psql);
```

Set Parameters: If you have any parameters in your SQL query, set them using the appropriate setter methods.

```
pstmt.setString(1, "johndoe");
```

Getting the Results

After the SQL query is formulated and executed, the next step is to retrieve the results.

Executing the Query

Execute the Query: Use executeQuery() to execute the SQL statement, which returns a ResultSet object for SELECT statements.

```
ResultSet rs = stmt.executeQuery(sql); // For Statement
// or
ResultSet rs = pstmt.executeQuery(); // For PreparedStatement
```

Processing the ResultSet

The ResultSet object represents a database result set, which is usually generated by executing a statement that queries the database.

Iterate Over the Results: Use a while loop to iterate through the ResultSet.

```
while (rs.next()) {
String user = rs.getString("username");
String email = rs.getString("email");
// Process the row.
}
```

Retrieve Column Values: Use getter methods such as getString() or getInt() to retrieve column values from the current row.

```
int id = rs.getInt("id");
```

Handle Exceptions: It is essential to handle SQLException when dealing with result sets.

```
try {
// Execute query and process result set
} catch (SQLException e) {
e.printStackTrace();
// Handle any SQL errors
}
```

Closing Resources

It is crucial to close the ResultSet, Statement, and Connection objects after use to free up database resources.

```
finally {
  try {
    if (rs != null) rs.close();
    if (stmt != null) stmt.close();
    if (pstmt != null) pstmt.close();
    if (conn != null) conn.close();
  } catch (SQLException e) {
    e.printStackTrace();
  }
}
```

2.3 Getting the Results

Once a connection to the database is established and a SQL query has been sent, the next critical step is to retrieve and manipulate the results. This is a core part of database interaction and is essential for any application that needs to display or use data from a database.

Retrieving Data with ResultSet

The retrieval of results from a query is handled by the ResultSet object in JDBC. A ResultSet object maintains a cursor pointing to its current row of data. Initially, the cursor is positioned before the first row. The next() method moves the cursor to the next row, and because it returns false when there are no more rows in the ResultSet object, it can be used in a while loop to iterate through the result set.

Code-

```
Statement stmt = conn.createStatement();
ResultSet rs = stmt.executeQuery("SELECT * FROM Employees");
while (rs.next()) {
  int id = rs.getInt("id");
  String name = rs.getString("name");
  // process each row
}
```

Processing ResultSet Data

To get values from the current row in ResultSet, you can use the various get methods, such as getInt, getString, or getDouble, specifying the column name or the column index as an argument.

Code-

```
int age = rs.getInt(3); // Using column index
String email = rs.getString("email"); // Using column name
```

Handling SQLExceptions

Always include error handling in your database access code to manage exceptions that could occur, such as connectivity issues or query errors.

Code-

```
try {
   // ... execute query and process results
} catch (SQLException e) {
   e.printStackTrace();
   // Handle database access errors
}
```

2.3 Updating Database Data

Updating database data from a Java application is a fundamental operation that is just as important as retrieving data. The JDBC (Java Database Connectivity) API provides Statement and PreparedStatement objects to execute update operations, including INSERT, UPDATE, and DELETE statements. These objects facilitate interaction with the database to modify its content efficiently and securely.

Using Statements

To perform an update using a Statement object, you would use the executeUpdate() method, which returns an integer representing the number of rows affected by the operation.

Code-

```
Statement stmt = conn.createStatement();
int rowsAffected = stmt.executeUpdate("UPDATE Employees SET age = 35 WHERE id = 101");
System.out.println("Rows affected: " + rowsAffected);
```

Using PreparedStatements for Updates

For updates, especially those that take parameters, using a PreparedStatement is more efficient and secure.

Code-

```
String query = "INSERT INTO Employees (name, age, department) VALUES (?, ?, ?)";
PreparedStatement pstmt = conn.prepareStatement(query);
pstmt.setString(1, "John Doe");
pstmt.setInt(2, 30);
pstmt.setString(3, "Human Resources");
int rowsAffected = pstmt.executeUpdate();
System.out.println("Rows inserted: " + rowsAffected);
```

Batch Updates

For operations that involve multiple updates, batch updates can be used for performance optimization.

Code-

```
conn.setAutoCommit(false);
Statement stmt = conn.createStatement();
stmt.addBatch("INSERT INTO Employees VALUES (106, 'Jane', 28)");
stmt.addBatch("UPDATE Employees SET age = 29 WHERE name = 'John'");
stmt.addBatch("DELETE FROM Employees WHERE name = 'Doe'");
int[] count = stmt.executeBatch();
conn.commit();
conn.setAutoCommit(true);
```

Transaction Management

It's important to manage transactions when updating data to ensure data integrity. JDBC allows you to commit or roll back transactions manually.

Code-

```
try {
   conn.setAutoCommit(false);
   // ... perform various updates
   conn.commit(); // Commit transaction
} catch (SQLException e) {
```

```
    if (conn != null) {
      try {
        conn.rollback(); // Rollback transaction on error
      } catch (SQLException ex) {
        ex.printStackTrace();
      }
    }
    e.printStackTrace();
} finally {
    conn.setAutoCommit(true);
}
```

2.5 Error Checking and the SQLException Class

Error checking is an essential aspect of database programming, ensuring that any issues during database operations are detected and handled appropriately. In JDBC (Java Database Connectivity), the SQLException class plays a pivotal role in managing database-related errors. Understanding how to use this class effectively is crucial for developing robust and reliable Java applications that interact with databases.

2.5.1 Error Checking and the SQLException Class

The JDBC API provides the SQLException class to handle errors that occur in the database access layer. This class captures information about database access errors, and developers must understand how to handle these exceptions appropriately to create robust applications.
The SQLException Class
SQLException is a checked exception that extends java.lang.Exception. It provides information about database access errors or other errors that occur while interacting with a database. Here are some key points about the SQLException class:
Hierarchical Nature: SQLException can have a cause, allowing nested exceptions.
Information Provided: It provides detailed information such as the SQL state, error code, and a descriptive message.
Chained Exceptions: Multiple exceptions can be chained together to provide a detailed context for errors.

2.5.2 Understanding SQLException

When a JDBC operation encounters an error, it throws an SQLException. This exception can provide several pieces of information about the error, including:
SQL State: An SQLSTATE value, which is a five-character alphanumeric identifier defined by the SQL standard to indicate the nature of the error.
Error Code: A database-specific error code.
Message: A descriptive message explaining the error.

Key Methods of SQLException
getMessage(): Returns a description of the error.
String message = sqlException.getMessage();
getSQLState(): Returns the SQL state, a five-character string defined by the ANSI SQL standard.
String sqlState = sqlException.getSQLState();
getErrorCode(): Returns the vendor-specific error code.
int errorCode = sqlException.getErrorCode();
getNextException(): Retrieves the next SQLException in the chain.
SQLException nextException = sqlException.getNextException();
printStackTrace(): Prints the stack trace of the SQLException.
sqlException.printStackTrace();

2.5.3 Handling SQLExceptions

Proper handling of SQL exceptions involves catching them in a try-catch block, extracting useful information, and taking appropriate action (e.g., logging the error, rolling back transactions, notifying the user). Here's an example of how to handle SQLException in JDBC

```
import java.sql.Connection;
```

```
import java.sql.DriverManager;
import java.sql.SQLException;
import java.sql.Statement;
public class JDBCErrorHandlingExample {
    public static void main(String[] args) {
        String url = "jdbc:mysql://localhost:3306/mydb";
        String username = "user";
        String password = "password";
        Connection connection = null;
        Statement statement = null;
        try {
            connection = DriverManager.getConnection(url, username, password);
            statement = connection.createStatement();
            // Attempt to execute an SQL statement
            String sql = "INSERT INTO users (id, name, email) VALUES (1, 'John Doe', 'john@example.com')";
            int rowsInserted = statement.executeUpdate(sql);
            System.out.println("Rows inserted: " + rowsInserted);
        } catch (SQLException e) {
            // Handle SQLException
            while (e != null) {
                System.err.println("SQL State: " + e.getSQLState());
                System.err.println("Error Code: " + e.getErrorCode());
                System.err.println("Message: " + e.getMessage());
                e.printStackTrace();
                e = e.getNextException();
            }
        } finally {
            // Close resources
            try {
                if (statement != null) statement.close();
                if (connection != null) connection.close();
            } catch (SQLException e)
              {
                e.printStackTrace();
            }
        }
    }
}
```

Best Practices for SQLException

Use Specific Catch Blocks: Catch specific SQL exceptions if your code can recover from them.

Log the Error Details: Always log the error details to troubleshoot issues effectively.

Clean Up Resources: Ensure that database connections, statements, and result sets are closed properly, ideally in the finally block or using try-with-resources statement.

2.6 The SQLWarning Class

SQLWarning is a subclass of SQLException in the Java Database Connectivity (JDBC) API. While SQLException is used to represent serious errors that occur during database operations, SQLWarning is used to handle warnings that are less severe and do not stop the execution of an application. Warnings typically indicate conditions that might need attention but are not critical enough to halt program execution.

Key Characteristics of SQLWarning

Non-fatal: Unlike SQLException, SQLWarning does not indicate a fatal error. It is used for conditions that are not severe enough to stop the execution.

Chained Warnings: Multiple warnings can be chained together, allowing you to traverse through all the warnings associated with a particular database operation.

Associated with Connection, Statement, and ResultSet: Warnings can be associated with different JDBC objects such as Connection, Statement, and ResultSet.

2.6.1 Understanding SQLWarning

SQLWarnings do not stop the execution of an application, as they are not thrown like exceptions but rather attached to the Connection, Statement, and ResultSet objects. They indicate issues that are not critical but may require attention, such as deprecations, minor data truncations, etc.

Key Methods of SQLWarning

getNextWarning(): Retrieves the next SQLWarning in the chain.

```
SQLWarning nextWarning = sqlWarning.getNextWarning();
```

getMessage(): Returns a description of the warning.

```
String message = sqlWarning.getMessage();
```

getSQLState(): Returns the SQL state of the warning.

```
String sqlState = sqlWarning.getSQLState();
```

getErrorCode(): Returns the vendor-specific error code.

```
int errorCode = sqlWarning.getErrorCode();
```

printStackTrace(): Prints the stack trace of the SQLWarning.

```
sqlWarning.printStackTrace();
```

2.6.2 Retrieving SQLWarnings

To retrieve warnings, you can use the getWarnings method on the Connection, Statement, or ResultSet object. After processing the warning, you should call the clearWarnings method to dismiss it.

```
try {
  // ... JDBC operations
  SQLWarning warning = conn.getWarnings();
  while (warning != null) {
    System.out.println("Message: " + warning.getMessage());
    System.out.println("SQL State: " + warning.getSQLState());
    System.out.println("Error Code: " + warning.getErrorCode());
    warning = warning.getNextWarning();
  }
} catch (SQLException se)
{
  // Handle the SQLException
}
finally {
  try {
    if (conn != null) conn.clearWarnings();
  } catch (SQLException se)
        {
    se.printStackTrace();
  }
}
```

Best Practices for SQLWarning

Check for Warnings: Always check for and process warnings after connection establishment, query execution, and result set retrieval.

Log Warnings: Like errors, warnings should be logged for review.

Clear Warnings: After processing, clear the warnings to prevent old warnings from affecting subsequent operations.

Benefits of Handling SQLWarnings

Awareness of Potential Issues: Handling warnings allows developers to be aware of potential issues in their SQL operations that may not be severe enough to stop execution but could affect the results or performance.

Improved Debugging: Logging warnings can help in debugging and maintaining the application by providing insights into non-critical issues that occur during database interactions.

User Notifications: By handling and possibly notifying users of warnings, applications can provide more transparency and potentially prevent misunderstandings or misuse of the application.
Proactive Issue Resolution: Being aware of and addressing warnings can help in proactively resolving issues that might become severe over time or under different conditions.

Practical Use Cases for SQLWarnings
Data Truncation: A warning might be issued if data is truncated when inserted into a database column with a length limit.
Deprecated Features: Warnings can alert developers to the use of deprecated SQL features or syntax that should be updated.
Connection Issues: Network or connection issues that do not prevent the application from running but could affect performance might generate warnings.
Performance Recommendations: The database might provide warnings with recommendations for query optimizations or performance improvements.

2.1 The Statement Interface

In the context of Java Database Connectivity (JDBC), the Statement interface is used to execute SQL queries against a database. It is a key part of the JDBC API, allowing Java applications to send SQL commands to a database and process the results.
Creating a Statement Object
To create a Statement object, you need to invoke the createStatement method on an active Connection object:
Code-

```
Statement stmt = conn.createStatement();
```

Executing Queries
The Statement object allows you to execute SQL queries using the executeQuery method, which returns a ResultSet object containing the data produced by the query
Code-

```
String query = "SELECT * FROM employees";
ResultSet rs = stmt.executeQuery(query);
```

Executing Update Statements
For SQL commands that modify the database (INSERT, UPDATE, DELETE), use the executeUpdate method, which returns an integer indicating the number of rows affected:
Code-

```
String update = "UPDATE employees SET age = 30 WHERE id = 101";
int rowsAffected = stmt.executeUpdate(update);
```

Handling Exceptions
All operations on a Statement object can throw an SQLException, so they must be used within a try-catch block
Code-

```
try {
  // operations using Statement
} catch (SQLException e)
{
  // handle exception
}
```

1. Closing Statement

It is important to close Statement objects to release database resources
Code: stmt.close();

Key Characteristics of the Statement Interface
Execution of SQL Commands: The Statement interface is used to execute both static SQL queries and SQL commands, such as SELECT, INSERT, UPDATE, and DELETE.
Handling Result Sets: It can handle the results returned by SELECT queries, encapsulated in ResultSet objects.
No Parameters: Unlike PreparedStatement, Statement does not support parameters. It is primarily used for executing static SQL queries without any placeholders.

2.8 PreparedStatement

A PreparedStatement represents a precompiled SQL statement that can be executed multiple times with high efficiency. It is a subclass of Statement and is suitable for executing SQL statements multiple times with different parameters.

Creating a PreparedStatement Object

A PreparedStatement is created by calling the prepareStatement method on a Connection object with the SQL query as an argument

Code-

```
String psql = "INSERT INTO employees (name, age) VALUES (?, ?)";
PreparedStatement pstmt = conn.prepareStatement(psql);
```

Setting Parameters

Before execution, you need to specify the values for the placeholders (denoted by ?) using the appropriate set methods:

Code-

```
pstmt.setString(1, "John Doe");
pstmt.setInt(2, 25);
```

Executing the PreparedStatement

To execute the prepared statement, call executeQuery for SELECT statements or executeUpdate for INSERT, UPDATE, and DELETE statements

Code-

```
int rowsInserted = pstmt.executeUpdate();
```

Closing PreparedStatement

Similar to Statement objects, PreparedStatement objects must be closed after their use:

Code-

```
Pstmt.close();
```

2.8.1 Advantages of PreparedStatement

Precompiled SQL Statements

Efficiency: PreparedStatement objects are precompiled by the database, meaning the SQL query is parsed and compiled only once. This precompilation reduces the overhead of parsing and compiling SQL statements each time they are executed, which can lead to significant performance improvements for repeated execution of the same query.

Reuse: The precompiled SQL statement can be executed multiple times with different parameters, making it more efficient for batch processing and repeated query execution.

SQL Injection Prevention

Security: One of the major advantages of PreparedStatement is its ability to prevent SQL injection attacks. SQL injection is a common attack vector where malicious users can inject arbitrary SQL code through input parameters. PreparedStatement automatically escapes input parameters, ensuring that user-provided data is treated as data and not executable code.

Parameter Binding: By using parameter placeholders (e.g., ?) in the SQL query and setting the values using setter methods (setString, setInt, etc.), PreparedStatement safely handles input values.

Parameterization

Ease of Use: PreparedStatement allows for parameterized queries using placeholders, which can be dynamically set at runtime. This makes the code cleaner and easier to maintain, especially for complex queries.

Flexibility: You can reuse the same PreparedStatement object with different parameter values, simplifying code when executing the same SQL statement multiple times with different data.

Performance Enhancements

Batch Processing: PreparedStatement supports batch processing, where multiple SQL statements can be executed in a single batch. This reduces the number of database round-trips and improves performance.

Caching: Some database systems cache the execution plans of PreparedStatement objects, further enhancing performance by avoiding repeated parsing and optimization.

Improved Readability and Maintainability

Cleaner Code: Using PreparedStatement leads to more readable and maintainable code by separating the SQL logic from the data values. This separation makes the code easier to understand and debug.

Consistent Parameter Handling: With PreparedStatement, parameter values are set consistently using specific setter methods, reducing the risk of errors related to SQL syntax and data type mismatches.

2.8 CallableStatement

In Java JDBC (Java Database Connectivity), a CallableStatement is an interface that extends PreparedStatement. It represents a precompiled SQL statement that can be executed either as a stored procedure or as a callable SQL function. CallableStatement provides a way to call stored procedures, which are stored and managed in the database.

Creating a CallableStatement

To create a CallableStatement object, you call the prepareCall method on a Connection object, passing in the SQL statement to call the stored procedure.

Code:
```
String call = "{ CALL updateEmployeeSalary(?, ?) }";
CallableStatement cstmt = conn.prepareCall(call);
```

In the SQL, the {} braces enclose a call to the stored procedure named updateEmployeeSalary, which takes two parameters.

Setting Parameters

Parameters can be input (set before execution), output (retrieved after execution), or both. Use appropriate set methods for input parameters and registerOutParameter for output parameters.

Code:
```
cstmt.setInt(1, 101); // Set input parameter
cstmt.registerOutParameter(2, Types.DECIMAL); // Register output parameter
```

Executing CallableStatement

To execute the CallableStatement, you can use the execute method. After execution, output parameters can be retrieved using the appropriate get methods.

Code:
```
cstmt.execute();
BigDecimal newSalary = cstmt.getBigDecimal(2); // Retrieve output parameter
```

Exception Handling

As with Statement and PreparedStatement, you must handle exceptions

Code:
```
try {
    // Call stored procedure and retrieve results
} catch (SQLException e) {
    // handle exception
} finally {
    // Clean up resources
    cstmt.close();
}
```

Key Features of CallableStatement

Stored Procedure Execution: The primary purpose of CallableStatement is to execute stored procedures defined in the database. Stored procedures are precompiled SQL statements stored in the database and can perform complex operations.

Parameterization: Like PreparedStatement, CallableStatement supports parameterized queries, allowing you to pass input parameters to the stored procedure.

Output Parameters: Callable procedures can return one or more values, known as output parameters. CallableStatement provides methods to register output parameters and retrieve their values after execution.

Function Calls: CallableStatement can also be used to call SQL functions defined in the database. Functions can return a single value, which can be retrieved using the appropriate getter methods.

Batch Execution: CallableStatement supports batch execution, allowing you to execute multiple stored procedures or function calls in a single batch, improving performance by reducing database round-trips.

Example Usage of CallableStatement

Here's an example demonstrating the use of CallableStatement to call a stored procedure that calculates the total salary of employees in a department

```
import java.sql.CallableStatement;
import java.sql.Connection;
import java.sql.DriverManager;
import java.sql.SQLException;
import java.sql.Types;
public class CallableStatementExample {
```

```
    public static void main(String[] args) {
        String url = "jdbc:mysql://localhost:3306/mydb";
        String username = "user";
        String password = "password";
        try (Connection connection = DriverManager.getConnection(url, username, password)) {
            // Prepare the SQL call to the stored procedure
            String sql = "{CALL calculate_department_salary(?, ?)}"; // Assuming the stored procedure name is
calculate_department_salary
            CallableStatement callableStatement = connection.prepareCall(sql);
            // Set input parameter (department ID)
            callableStatement.setInt(1, 123);
            // Register output parameter (total salary)
            callableStatement.registerOutParameter(2, Types.DOUBLE);
            // Execute the stored procedure
            callableStatement.execute();
            // Retrieve the output parameter value
            double totalSalary = callableStatement.getDouble(2);
            System.out.println("Total salary for department 123: " + totalSalary);
        } catch (SQLException e) {
            e.printStackTrace();
        }
    }
}
```

In this example, calculate_department_salary is assumed to be the name of the stored procedure in the database. The procedure takes the department ID as input and returns the total salary for that department as an output parameter.

2.10 The ResultSet Interface

In Java JDBC (Java Database Connectivity), the ResultSet interface represents a set of rows retrieved from a relational database after executing an SQL query. It provides methods for iterating over the rows, accessing column values, and navigating through the result set. The ResultSet object acts as a cursor that moves forward one row at a time.

Key Features of ResultSet

Row Iteration: The primary purpose of ResultSet is to iterate over the rows returned by a SQL query. It provides methods such as next() to move the cursor to the next row and previous() to move it to the previous row.

Column Access: ResultSet allows access to column values of the current row using methods like getInt(), getString(), getDouble(), etc., which retrieve values based on the column index or column name.

Metadata Retrieval: ResultSet provides metadata about the result set, such as the number of columns, column names, column types, etc. Methods like getMetaData() return a ResultSetMetaData object containing metadata information.

Scrollable and Updatable: Depending on the type of Statement used to create the ResultSet, it can be scrollable (allows moving the cursor back and forth) and updatable (allows modifying the underlying data).

Concurrency Control: ResultSet supports different levels of concurrency control, allowing multiple users to access and manipulate the result set concurrently. The concurrency level is determined by the Statement used to create the ResultSet.

The ResultSet interface represents the result set of a database query. A ResultSet object maintains a cursor pointing to its current row of data and allows for the iterative retrieval of results.

Navigating the ResultSet

After executing a SQL query, you can navigate through the ResultSet using various methods:

next(): Moves the cursor to the next row

previous(): Moves to the previous row (if the result set type allows it)

first(), last(), beforeFirst(), afterLast(): Moves to the specified position (for certain types of result sets)

Retrieving Data from ResultSet

To retrieve column values from the current row, use getter methods such as getInt, getString, or getBoolean, specifying the column name or index.

Code:

```
while (rs.next()) {
    int id = rs.getInt("employee_id");
    String name = rs.getString("employee_name");
    // Process each row
}
```

Updating Data

Some ResultSet objects are updatable, allowing modification of the underlying database data

Code:

```
rs.updateString("employee_name", "John Doe");
rs.updateRow(); // Reflects the update in the database
```

Handling Exceptions

You must handle SQLExceptions when working with ResultSet:

Code:

```
try {
    // Navigate and retrieve data from ResultSet
} catch (SQLException e) {
    // handle exception
}
```

Closing ResultSet

It is crucial to close the ResultSet once you are done with it

Code: rs.close();

Example Usage of ResultSet

Here's an example demonstrating the basic usage of ResultSet to iterate over the rows and retrieve column values

```
import java.sql.Connection;
import java.sql.DriverManager;
import java.sql.ResultSet;
import java.sql.SQLException;
import java.sql.Statement;
public class ResultSetExample {
    public static void main(String[] args) {
        String url = "jdbc:mysql://localhost:3306/mydb";
        String username = "user";
        String password = "password";
        try (Connection connection = DriverManager.getConnection(url, username, password)) {
            Statement statement = connection.createStatement();
            ResultSet resultSet = statement.executeQuery("SELECT * FROM users");
            // Iterate over the result set
            while (resultSet.next()) {
                int id = resultSet.getInt("id");
                String name = resultSet.getString("name");
                String email = resultSet.getString("email");
                System.out.println("ID: " + id + ", Name: " + name + ", Email: " + email);
            }
        } catch (SQLException e) {
            e.printStackTrace();
        }
    }
}
```

In this example, the ResultSet object is obtained by executing a SQL query "SELECT * FROM users". The next() method is used to iterate over each row, and getInt(), getString() methods are used to retrieve column values by column name.

2.10.1 ResultSet Types

In Java JDBC (Java Database Connectivity), the ResultSet interface provides support for different types of result sets, allowing developers to choose the appropriate type based on their specific requirements. The type of ResultSet is determined by the Statement used to create it and can affect characteristics such as scrollability, updatability, and performance.

Here are the commonly used types of ResultSet in Java JDBC

Forward-Only ResultSet (TYPE_FORWARD_ONLY)

This is the default type of ResultSet. It allows the cursor to move forward only, from the first row to the last row, and does not support scrolling backward or jumping to a specific row.

Characteristics

Forward-only result sets are generally faster and consume less memory compared to other types.

They are not suitable for situations where you need to navigate the result set in both forward and backward directions or need random access to specific rows.

Scroll-Sensitive ResultSet (TYPE_SCROLL_SENSITIVE)

Scroll-sensitive result sets allow both forward and backward movement of the cursor and support changes made to the result set by other users or processes while the result set is open.

Characteristics

Any changes made to the data underlying the result set are visible to the result set, even if those changes were made by another user or process.

This type of result set can be useful for applications where data modifications occur frequently and need to be reflected immediately.

Scroll-Insensitive ResultSet (TYPE_SCROLL_INSENSITIVE)

Scroll-insensitive result sets also allow both forward and backward movement of the cursor but do not reflect changes made to the data underlying the result set by other users or processes.

Characteristics

The result set retains its original data regardless of any modifications made to the underlying data by other users or processes.

This type of result set is suitable for situations where data modifications are infrequent, and the application needs to maintain a consistent snapshot of the data.

2.11 Updatable Result Sets

In JDBC, a ResultSet typically represents a database result set, which is a table of data representing a database result query, that is, generated by executing a statement that queries the database. By default, ResultSet objects are read-only. However, JDBC provides a way to create updatable result sets, which allow you to update the database directly through the ResultSet object.

Creating Updatable Result Sets

To create an updatable result set, you need to specify the ResultSet type and concurrency when creating a Statement or PreparedStatement object.

Code:

```
Statement stmt = conn.createStatement(
ResultSet.TYPE_SCROLL_INSENSITIVE,
ResultSet.CONCUR_UPDATABLE
);
```

Updating Rows

Once you have an updatable ResultSet, you can modify the data in the current row and synchronize the updated row with the database.

Code:

```
ResultSct rs − stmt.executeQuery("SELECT * FROM Fmployees WHERE Department='HR'");
while (rs.next()) {
// Assume there is a column in the table named 'Salary'
float salary = rs.getFloat("Salary");
rs.updateFloat("Salary", salary + 1000); // Give a raise of $1000
rs.updateRow(); // This line updates the row in the database
```

```
}
```

Inserting Rows

You can also insert new rows into the database through an updatable result set.

Code:

```
rs.moveToInsertRow(); // Moves cursor to the insert row
rs.updateString("Name", "John Doe");
rs.updateString("Department", "HR");
rs.insertRow(); // Inserts the row to the database
rs.moveToCurrentRow(); // Moves the cursor to the current row
```

Deleting Rows

With an updatable ResultSet, you can also delete rows from the database.

Code:

```
if (rs.getString("Name").equals("John Doe")) {
rs.deleteRow(); // Deletes the current row from the database
}
```

2.11.1 Best Practices and Considerations

Use updatable result sets sparingly, as they can be less performant than standard update operations.

Ensure that the SQL query used to create the ResultSet selects only the necessary columns and rows.

Check the database documentation to understand any limitations or behaviours specific to the database.

2.12 JDBC Types

JDBC provides a set of standard SQL types defined in the java.sql.Types class. Each JDBC type corresponds to a SQL type and is used to identify the type of a column in a ResultSet or to identify the parameter type of a PreparedStatement.

Here are the commonly used JDBC Types

Numeric Types

INTEGER: Represents a 32-bit signed integer.
BIGINT: Represents a 64-bit signed integer.
SMALLINT: Represents a 16-bit signed integer.
DECIMAL: Represents fixed-precision decimal numbers.
DOUBLE: Represents double-precision floating-point numbers.
FLOAT: Represents single-precision floating-point numbers.

Character Types

CHAR: Represents fixed-length character strings.
VARCHAR: Represents variable-length character strings.
LONGVARCHAR: Represents long character strings.
CLOB: Represents Character Large Object data types for large character data.

Binary Types

BINARY: Represents fixed-length binary data.
VARBINARY: Represents variable-length binary data.
LONGVARBINARY: Represents long binary data.
BLOB: Represents Binary Large Object data types for large binary data.

Date and Time Types

DATE: Represents SQL DATE data types.
TIME: Represents SQL TIME data types.
TIMESTAMP: Represents SQL TIMESTAMP data types.

Other Types

BOOLEAN: Represents boolean values.
ARRAY: Represents SQL ARRAY data types.
STRUCT: Represents SQL structured types.
NULL: Represents SQL NULL values.

REF: Represents SQL REF data types.

2.12.1 Commonly Used JDBC Types

INTEGER: Corresponds to SQL INTEGER.
VARCHAR: Corresponds to SQL VARCHAR.
BOOLEAN: Corresponds to SQL BIT or BOOLEAN.
NUMERIC: Corresponds to SQL NUMERIC with full precision.
TIMESTAMP: Corresponds to SQL TIMESTAMP.
BLOB: Corresponds to SQL BINARY LARGE OBJECT.
CLOB: Corresponds to SQL CHARACTER LARGE OBJECT.

2.12.2 Using JDBC Types

When working with PreparedStatement, you need to specify the JDBC type of the parameters.
Code:

```
PreparedStatement pstmt = conn.prepareStatement(
   "INSERT INTO Employees (Name, JoinDate) VALUES (?, ?)"
);
pstmt.setString(1, "John Doe");
pstmt.setTimestamp(2, new Timestamp(System.currentTimeMillis()));
```

In the above example, setString and setTimestamp are used to set the parameters, and the JDBC types are inferred from the method names. For some complex types or when the JDBC type needs to be explicitly specified, you can use setObject.

```
pstmt.setObject(1, "John Doe", Types.VARCHAR);
pstmt.setObject(2, new Timestamp(System.currentTimeMillis()), Types.TIMESTAMP);
```

2.13 Executing SQL Queries

Executing SQL queries in Java involves using the Java Database Connectivity (JDBC) API, which provides a standard interface for interacting with relational databases. Below is a detailed explanation of how to execute SQL queries in Java, including the necessary steps and code examples.

Steps to Execute SQL Queries in Java

Load the JDBC Driver: Ensure that the JDBC driver for the database you are using is available in your classpath and load it.

Establish a Database Connection: Use the DriverManager class to establish a connection to the database using the connection URL, username, and password.

Create a Statement Object: Use the Connection object to create a Statement, PreparedStatement, or CallableStatement object depending on the type of SQL query you want to execute.

Execute the SQL Query: Execute the SQL query using the appropriate method of the Statement object.

Process the Result: If the query returns a result set (e.g., a SELECT statement), process the ResultSet object to retrieve the data. If the query modifies data (e.g., an INSERT, UPDATE, or DELETE statement), process the update count returned by the execution method.

Close the Resources: Close the ResultSet, Statement, and Connection objects to free up resources.

2.13.1 Using Statement Objects

The Statement object is used for simple SQL queries with no parameters. Here's the general process

Create a Statement: After establishing a connection, create a Statement object.

Code:

```
Statement statement = connection.createStatement();
```

Execute the Query: Use executeQuery for SELECT queries, which returns a ResultSet.

Code-

```
ResultSet resultSet = statement.executeQuery("SELECT * FROM employees");
```

Process the Results: Iterate through the ResultSet.

Code:

```
while (resultSet.next()) {
int id = resultSet.getInt("id");
String name = resultSet.getString("name");
// Process each row as needed
```

```
}
```

Close the Statement and ResultSet: To avoid memory leaks and release resources.

Code:

```
resultSet.close();
statement.close();
```

Example of Executing SQL Queries

Below is an example demonstrating how to execute a SELECT query and an UPDATE query in Java using JDBC

```
import java.sql.Connection;
import java.sql.DriverManager;
import java.sql.ResultSet;
import java.sql.SQLException;
import java.sql.Statement;
public class JDBCExample {
  public static void main(String[] args) {
    String url = "jdbc:mysql://localhost:3306/mydb";
    String username = "user";
    String password = "password";
    Connection connection = null;
    Statement statement = null;
    ResultSet resultSet = null;
    try {
      // Step 1: Load the JDBC driver (not needed for newer JDBC versions)
      // Class.forName("com.mysql.cj.jdbc.Driver");
      // Step 2: Establish a database connection
      connection = DriverManager.getConnection(url, username, password);
      // Step 3: Create a Statement object
      statement = connection.createStatement();
      // Step 4: Execute a SELECT query
      String selectSQL = "SELECT * FROM users";
      resultSet = statement.executeQuery(selectSQL);
      // Step 5: Process the ResultSet
      while (resultSet.next()) {
        int id = resultSet.getInt("id");
        String name = resultSet.getString("name");
        String email = resultSet.getString("email");
        System.out.println("ID: " + id + ", Name: " + name + ", Email: " + email);
      }
      // Execute an UPDATE query
      String updateSQL = "UPDATE users SET email = 'newemail@example.com' WHERE id = 1";
      int rowsAffected = statement.executeUpdate(updateSQL);
      System.out.println("Rows updated: " + rowsAffected);
    } catch (SQLException e) {
      e.printStackTrace();
    } finally {
      // Step 6: Close the resources
      try {
        if (resultSet != null) resultSet.close();
        if (statement != null) statement.close();
        if (connection != null) connection.close();
      } catch (SQLException e) {
        e.printStackTrace();
      }
    }
  }
}
```

Explanation of the Code
Loading the JDBC Driver
This step is typically not required for modern JDBC drivers, as the driver is automatically loaded when the connection is established.
Establishing a Database Connection
The DriverManager.getConnection() method is used to establish a connection to the database. The method requires the database URL, username, and password.
Creating a Statement Object
The Connection.createStatement() method is used to create a Statement object for sending SQL statements to the database.
Executing a SELECT Query
The Statement.executeQuery() method is used to execute a SELECT SQL query, which returns a ResultSet object containing the query results.
Processing the ResultSet
The ResultSet.next() method is used to iterate over the rows in the result set. Column values are retrieved using getter methods like getInt(), getString(), etc.
Executing an UPDATE Query
The Statement.executeUpdate() method is used to execute an UPDATE SQL query, which returns the number of rows affected by the query.
Closing the Resources
The ResultSet, Statement, and Connection objects are closed in the finally block to ensure that resources are released properly, even if an exception occurs.

2.13.2 Using PreparedStatement Objects

For queries with parameters or when the query needs to be executed multiple times with different parameters, PreparedStatement is more suitable.
Prepare the Statement: Create a PreparedStatement with parameter placeholders (?).
Code-:

```
PreparedStatement preparedStatement = connection.prepareStatement(
"SELECT * FROM employees WHERE department = ?"
);
```

Set Parameters: Assign values to the placeholders.
Code:

```
preparedStatement.setString(1, "Engineering");
```

2.14 ResultSetMetaData

ResultSetMetaData is an object that can be used to get information about the types and properties of the columns in a ResultSet.
Retrieving ResultSetMetaData
You can retrieve ResultSetMetaData from the ResultSet object:
Code:

```
ResultSetMetaData metaData = resultSet.getMetaData();
```

Using ResultSetMetaData
Once you have the ResultSetMetaData object, you can query it for information about the result set's columns.
Get Column Count: Find out how many columns there are.
Code:

```
int columnCount = metaData.getColumnCount();
```

Get Column Names and Types: Iterate over the columns and retrieve names and types.
Code:

```
for (int i = 1; i <= columnCount; i++) {
String columnName = metaData.getColumnName(i);
String columnType = metaData.getColumnTypeName(i);
// Process column name and type as needed
}
```

Other MetaData: You can also get additional metadata like column precision, scale, schema name, etc.

Code:

```
int precision = metaData.getPrecision(columnIndex);
int scale = metaData.getScale(columnIndex);
String schemaName = metaData.getSchemaName(columnIndex);
```

2.14.1 Importance of ResultSetMetaData

ResultSetMetaData is particularly useful when

You're working with dynamic queries and the structure of the result set is not known at compile time.

You need to write generic code to process result sets from different queries.

2.15 Executing SQL Updates

In JDBC, executing SQL updates allows you to modify the data in a database. This includes creating, updating, and deleting records. SQL updates are performed using the executeUpdate method of Statement or PreparedStatement objects.

2.15.1 Using Statement Objects for Updates

To execute an update using a Statement object

Create a Statement: Obtain a Statement object from an active connection.

Code-

```
Statement statement = connection.createStatement();
```

Execute Update: Use the executeUpdate method for SQL commands that change the database.

Code:

```
String updateSql = "UPDATE employees SET salary = salary + 5000 WHERE department = 'Sales'";
int rowsAffected = statement.executeUpdate(updateSql);
System.out.println("Updated rows: " + rowsAffected);
```

The method returns the number of rows affected by the update.

2.15.2 Using PreparedStatement Objects for Parameterized Updates

For updates that require parameters, a PreparedStatement is more suitable

Prepare the Statement: Include placeholders (?) in the SQL

Code:

```
String updateSql = "UPDATE employees SET salary = ? WHERE department = ?";
PreparedStatement pstmt = connection.prepareStatement(updateSql);
```

Set Parameters: Set the values for the placeholders.

Code:

```
pstmt.setBigDecimal(1, new BigDecimal("5000"));
pstmt.setString(2, "Sales");
```

Execute Update: Execute the update as with a Statement.

Code:

```
int rowsAffected = pstmt.executeUpdate();
System.out.println("Updated rows: " + rowsAffected);
```

2.15.3 Best Practices for SQL Updates

Use PreparedStatement objects for updates with parameters to prevent SQL injection attacks.

Always check the number of rows affected to ensure your update executed as expected.

Use try-with-resources or ensure resources are closed in a finally block.

2.16 Transaction Management

Transaction management is crucial for maintaining the integrity of data. A transaction is a set of operations that must either all succeed or all fail as a unit.

2.16.1 Basic Transaction Steps

Transactions in JDBC follow these steps

Disable Auto-Commit Mode**:** This allows you to control when transactions are committed to the database.

Code:

```
connection.setAutoCommit(false);
```

Execute SQL Commands: Perform one or more SQL updates.
Code:
```
pstmt.setInt(1, newQuantity);
pstmt.setInt(2, productId);
pstmt.executeUpdate();
```
Commit or Rollback: If all operations succeed, commit the transaction. If any operation fails, roll back all changes.
Code:
```
connection.commit();
```
On error
Code:
```
connection.rollback();
```
Restore Default Commit Behaviour: Re-enable auto-commit mode.
Code:
```
connection.setAutoCommit(true);
```

2.16.2 Savepoints

Savepoints allow partial rollbacks within a transaction. You can set a savepoint at a specific point in a transaction and roll back to that savepoint if needed.
Code:
```
Savepoint savepoint1 = connection.setSavepoint("Savepoint1");
// ... perform some updates
try {
   // ... perform more updates
   connection.commit();
} catch (SQLException e) {
   connection.rollback(savepoint1);
   connection.commit();
}
```

2.16.3 Handling Exceptions in Transactions

Proper exception handling is essential in transaction management:
Code:
```
try {
   // Disable auto-commit, execute updates, and commit
} catch (SQLException e) {
   e.printStackTrace();
   try {
      // Attempt to rollback on error
      connection.rollback();
   } catch (SQLException e2) {
      e2.printStackTrace();
   }
} finally {
   // Restore auto-commit mode
   try {
      connection.setAutoCommit(true);
   } catch (SQLException e3) {
      e3.printStackTrace();
   }
}
```

Exercise

Exercise 1- MCQ

1. What does JDBC stand for?
a) Java Database Connectivity
b) Java Development Code
c) Java Data Control
d) Java Database Code
2. Which of these is not a JDBC driver type?
a) Type 1
b) Type 2
c) Type 3
d) Type 5
3. Which method is used to execute a SQL query in JDBC?
a) execute()
b) executeQuery()
c) executeUpdate()
d) runQuery()
4. Connection, Statement, and ResultSet are interfaces in which package?
a) java.sql
b) javax.sql
c) java.database
d) javax.database
5. What does the Connection interface method setAutoCommit(false) do?
a) It starts a new transaction.
b) It commits the current transaction.
c) It disables automatic transaction commits.
d) It enables automatic error handling.
6. Which PreparedStatement method is used to set a null value?
a) setNull()
b) setObject()
c) set()
d) setNullValue()
7. What does the executeUpdate method return?
a) A ResultSet object
b) The number of rows affected
c) A boolean value
d) Nothing
8. Which of these is not a core component of the JDBC architecture?
a) DriverManager
b) JDBC API
c) SQL Editor
d) JDBC Test Suite
9. The CallableStatement interface is used for what purpose in JDBC?
a) To call stored procedures
b) To execute simple SQL statements
c) To update rows in a database
d) To retrieve the result set metadata
10. What does ResultSetMetaData provide?
a) Information about the database
b) Information about the tables in the database
c) Information about the columns in a ResultSet
d) Debugging information for SQL exceptions

Exercise 2 – True/False

1. In Java, the finalize() method is called by the garbage collector when it determines that there are no more references to the object.

2. The HashMap class in Java maintains the insertion order of elements.
3. An abstract class in Java can have both abstract and non-abstract methods.
4. In Java, the == operator can be used to compare two strings for equality.
5. The ArrayList class in Java is synchronized.
6. In Java, the static keyword can be applied to classes.
7. Java supports multiple inheritance through classes.
8. The interface keyword is used to define a contract in Java, which can include abstract methods and static final variables.
9. Java's switch statement can work with the String type.
10. The throw keyword is used to explicitly throw an exception.

Exercise 3: Fill in the blanks

1. In JDBC, the ________ method of the Connection interface is used to create a Statement object for sending SQL statements to the database.
2. The ________ interface is used in JDBC to call stored procedures and functions stored in the database.
3. To execute a select query and return the data in a ResultSet, use the ________ method of the Statement interface.
4. When handling SQL exceptions, the JDBC API provides the ________ class, which offers information on database access errors or other errors.
5. The ________ method of the Connection interface is used to commit all changes made since the previous commit or rollback.
6. JDBC __________ are used to define reusable, portable descriptions of a database.
7. By default, JDBC connections are in __________ mode, meaning each SQL statement is treated as a separate transaction.
8. __________ is a common library used to pool database connections, which can significantly improve performance in applications with high database usage.
9. __________ __________ can be used to handle large amounts of data efficiently by iterating through the results as they are fetched from the database.
10. _________ is used to call stored procedures in a database.

Exercise 4: Match Case

1. Method to roll back changes made during a transaction
2. Used to dynamically prepare SQL statements
3. Catches exceptions related to database access
4. Object used to create a connection to a database

A. SQLException
B. rollback()
C. PreparedStatement
D. Connection

Exercise 5: One word answer

1. What interface in JDBC is used for executing stored procedures?
2. Which method in JDBC is used to commit a transaction?

Exercise 6: Small answer

1. How do you retrieve column names from a ResultSet in JDBC?
2. Describe how to use a PreparedStatement to insert data into a database table in JDBC.

Exercise 7: Long answer

1. Explain the process of managing transactions in JDBC, including how to start a transaction, commit changes, and roll back in case of errors. Discuss the significance of setting the auto-commit mode and how exceptions are handled during a transaction.
2. Describe the steps involved in executing a SQL query using JDBC, from establishing a connection with the database to processing the ResultSet obtained from the query. Include details on the roles of the Connection,

Statement (or PreparedStatement), and ResultSet interfaces in this process, and how resource management is handled to prevent resource leaks.

Answers:
Exercise 1: 1) a 2) d 3) b 4) c 5) a 6) a 7) b 8) c 9) a 10) c
Exercise 2: 1) True 2) False 3) True 4) True 5) False 6) False 7) False 8) True 9) True 10) True
Exercise 3: 1) createStatement 2) CallableStatement 3) executeQuery 4) SQLException 5) commit 6) RowSet 7) auto-commit 8) HikariCP 9) Streaming ResultSets 10) CallableStatement
Exercise 4: 1 - B. rollback() 2 - C. PreparedStatement 3 - A. SQLException 4 - D. Connection
Exercise 5: 1) CallableStatement 2) commit

Online Resources

Online Practice Paper

Link: https://forms.gle/DbWhhgW6MczMDuw99

QR Code:

YouTube Video Link

Link: https://www.youtube.com/playlist?list=PLzlh_31VWEFpAiZLj3UJPkHzZrDjgBcgE

QR Code:

CHAPTER 3 - Introduction of Java EE Overview

3.1 Overview of Java EE

Java EE (Java Platform, Enterprise Edition), now known as Jakarta EE, is a set of specifications that extend the Java SE (Standard Edition) platform to provide a robust, scalable, and secure environment for enterprise-level applications. Java EE, or Java Platform, Enterprise Edition, is a robust platform developed by Sun Microsystems, now owned by Oracle Corporation, for building enterprise-level applications. It provides a set of standardized APIs (Application Programming Interfaces) and runtime environments that simplify the development, deployment, and management of large-scale, distributed applications.

At its core, Java EE extends the capabilities of the Java Platform, Standard Edition (Java SE) by adding libraries, frameworks, and specifications tailored specifically for enterprise-level development. This includes support for building web-based applications, distributed computing, and enterprise integration.

Java EE simplifies the development of large-scale, multi-tiered, distributed, and transactional applications by providing a comprehensive suite of services and APIs.

Key Components of Java EE

Servlets and JavaServer Pages (JSP)

Servlets: Java EE includes support for Servlets, which are Java classes that handle HTTP requests and responses. Servlets are used to build web applications that generate dynamic content.

JSP: JavaServer Pages provide a way to create dynamically generated web pages using HTML, XML, or other document types. JSP pages are compiled into Servlets by the web container.

Enterprise JavaBeans (EJB)

Session Beans: Handle business logic and can be stateless or stateful.

Message-Driven Beans: Handle asynchronous messages from a message queue or topic.

Entity Beans: Represent persistent data and provide an object-relational mapping to the underlying database (deprecated in favor of JPA).

Java Persistence API (JPA)

JPA is a specification for object-relational mapping (ORM) that allows developers to manage relational data in Java applications. It simplifies database interactions by mapping Java objects to database tables.

Java Message Service (JMS)

JMS provides a way to create, send, receive, and read messages in a distributed environment. It allows applications to communicate asynchronously using message queues and topics.

Java Transaction API (JTA)

JTA enables distributed transactions, ensuring data integrity and consistency across multiple resource managers, such as databases and message systems.

Contexts and Dependency Injection (CDI)

CDI provides a powerful set of services for dependency injection, allowing developers to manage the lifecycle and interactions of components in a loosely coupled way.

JavaServer Faces (JSF)

JSF is a framework for building component-based user interfaces for web applications. It simplifies the development of web interfaces by providing reusable UI components and managing the state of these components.

Web Services

JAX-RS: Java API for RESTful Web Services provides a way to create RESTful web services using annotations.

JAX-WS: Java API for XML Web Services provides a way to create SOAP-based web services.

Security

Java EE provides a robust security model that includes authentication, authorization, data integrity, and confidentiality. It supports various security mechanisms, such as role-based access control and SSL/TLS for secure communications.

Interceptors and Filters

Interceptors allow developers to define code that can intercept method calls or lifecycle events in an application. Filters can be used to preprocess and postprocess requests and responses in web applications, providing capabilities like logging, authentication, and data compression.

3.2 Features and Benefits of Java EE

Java EE offers a wide range of features and benefits that make it a preferred choice for enterprise application development:

Portability: Java EE applications are platform-independent, meaning they can run on any Java EE-compatible application server, providing flexibility and reducing vendor lock-in.
Scalability: Java EE supports the development of scalable applications that can handle increased workloads and user demand by leveraging features such as clustering, load balancing, and distributed caching.
Security: Java EE includes built-in security features for protecting applications and data, including authentication, authorization, and encryption mechanisms, ensuring the confidentiality, integrity, and availability of enterprise systems.
Productivity: Java EE provides a rich set of APIs, frameworks, and development tools that streamline the development process, reducing time-to-market and development costs.
Reliability: Java EE applications are known for their stability and robustness, thanks to features such as transaction management, fault tolerance, and error handling mechanisms.
Interoperability: Java EE supports interoperability with other enterprise systems and technologies through standards-based protocols and APIs, enabling seamless integration with existing IT infrastructure.
Community Support: Java EE benefits from a large and active developer community, providing access to resources, documentation, tutorials, and community-driven libraries and frameworks.

3.3 Evolution of Java EE

Java Platform, Enterprise Edition (Java EE), now known as Jakarta EE, is a set of specifications extending the Java SE platform with specifications for enterprise features such as distributed computing and web services. Understanding its evolution helps grasp the improvements, features, and architectural paradigms that have shaped modern enterprise Java applications.
Java EE Beginnings: J2EE
Java 2 Platform, Enterprise Edition (J2EE)
Release Year: 1999
Key Features
Servlets: Introduced to handle web requests and responses.
JavaServer Pages (JSP): Simplified the creation of dynamic web content.

Enterprise JavaBeans (EJB) 1.0: Facilitated development of scalable, transactional, and multi-tier enterprise applications.

Java Database Connectivity (JDBC): Provided standard API for database access.
Goals: Simplified application development with a unified architecture, encouraging modular, reusable, and scalable component development.

Early Evolution: J2EE 1.2 to J2EE 1.4
J2EE 1.2 (1999)
Enhancements
EJB 1.1: Added support for entity beans, container-managed persistence.

JDBC 2.0: Enhanced database connectivity features.

Servlet 2.2 and JSP 1.1: Improved web components.

CORBA support: Enabled interoperability with other languages and systems.

J2EE 1.3 (2001)
New Features
EJB 2.0: Introduced local interfaces, container-managed relationships.
JSP 1.2: Tag library improvements.

Servlet 2.3: Filters and lifecycle event listeners.

Java Message Service (JMS) 1.0: Standardized messaging API for enterprise messaging systems.

J2EE 1.4 (2003)
Web Services
JAX-RPC 1.1: Java API for XML-based RPC.
SAAJ 1.2: SOAP with Attachments API for Java.

JAXR 1.0: Java API for XML Registries.
Component Updates
EJB 2.1: Message-driven beans and web service endpoints.
JSP 2.0: Expression Language (EL) for JSPs.
Focus: Integration of web services and XML support.

Transition to Java EE: Java EE 5 to Java EE 8
Java EE 5 (2006)
Simplification

POJO-based Programming: Plain Old Java Objects made enterprise applications easier to develop.

EJB 3.0: Major simplification with POJO-based EJBs, annotations.

Java Persistence API (JPA) 1.0: Standardized ORM framework.

New Technologies

JSF 1.2: JavaServer Faces for building user interfaces.

JAXB 2.0: Java Architecture for XML Binding.

Annotations: Simplified configuration and reduced XML.

Java EE 6 (2009)
Profiles and Extensibility

Web Profile: Lightweight subset for web applications.
Contexts and Dependency Injection (CDI) 1.0: Improved dependency injection and lifecycle management.

New APIs

JAX-RS 1.1: Simplified RESTful web services.
Servlet 3.0: Asynchronous processing and pluggability.

Pruning: Removal of outdated and less used technologies.

Java EE 7 (2013)
HTML5 and Web Applications
WebSocket 1.0: Full-duplex communication channel over a single TCP connection.
Batch Processing 1.0: Batch processing of jobs.
JSON Processing 1.0: Parsing and generating JSON.
Enhancements
JAX-RS 2.0: Client API, asynchronous processing.

JMS 2.0: Simplified API.

Concurrency Utilities: Managed thread pools.

Java EE 8 (2017)
Cloud and Microservices
JSON Binding (JSON-B) 1.0: Data binding for JSON.
JAX-RS 2.1: Reactive client API, Server-Sent Events (SSE).
Servlet 4.0: HTTP/2 support.

Security API 1.0: Simplified security for applications.
Focus: Enhanced support for modern web standards and cloud-native applications.

Transition to Jakarta EE
Eclipse Foundation Transition
Year: 2017
Reason: Oracle contributed Java EE to the Eclipse Foundation to foster open governance and community-driven development.
Renaming: Java EE became Jakarta EE under the new governance.

Jakarta EE 8 (2019)
Equivalence: Essentially equivalent to Java EE 8 but under the Jakarta EE brand.
Objective: Ensuring compatibility and providing a smooth transition.

Jakarta EE 9 (2020)
Namespace Change: From javax.* to jakarta.* to reflect the new ownership and direction.
Minimal Changes: Focused on rebranding and reorganizing the codebase.

Jakarta EE 9.1 (2021)
Java SE 11 Support: First release to fully support Java SE 11.

Jakarta EE 10 (2022)
Modernization: Introduction of new features and APIs.
Jakarta Data: Simplified data access.

Enhanced CDI: Improved dependency injection and context management.

Modularity: Better support for modular applications.
Focus: Cloud-native development, microservices, and modern enterprise needs.
Modern Era: The Future of Jakarta EE
Upcoming Developments
Microservices and Cloud-Native Architectures: Emphasis on building scalable, resilient, and distributed systems.
Reactive Programming: Support for non-blocking, asynchronous programming models.

Community-Driven Innovations: Increased contributions and innovations driven by the open-source community.

3.4 Java EE Architecture and Components

The architecture of Java EE is based on the concept of tiers, or layers, each responsible for a specific aspect of application functionality. These tiers typically include the client tier, presentation tier, business tier, and data tier. Java EE components are deployed across these tiers to provide various services and functionalities. The key components of Java EE include servlets, JavaServer Pages (JSP), Enterprise JavaBeans (EJB), Java Persistence API (JPA), Java Message Service (JMS), and Java Naming and Directory Interface (JNDI). These components work together to enable the development of robust, scalable, and maintainable enterprise applications.

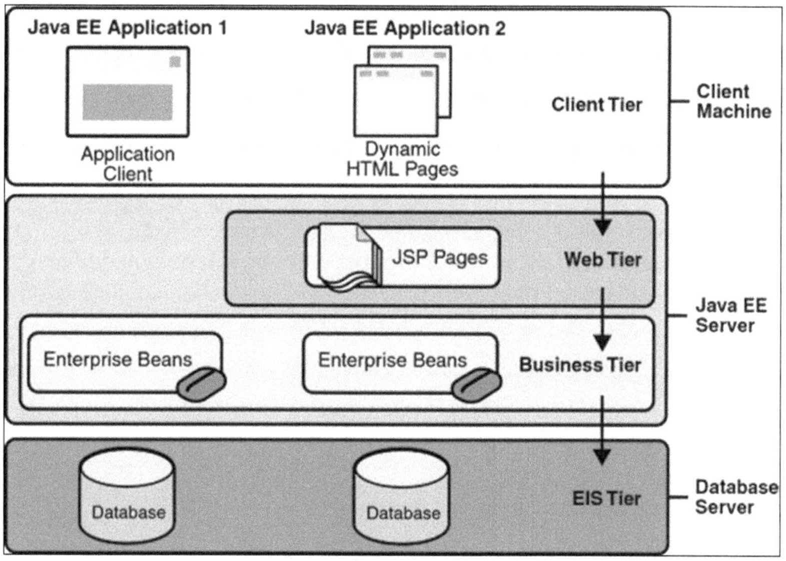

Figure 3.1

Java EE architecture is designed to support distributed, multi-tiered applications. The architecture promotes modularity and reusability, dividing an application into distinct functional layers.
Client Tier
Web Tier
Business Tier
Enterprise Information System (EIS) Tier

Each tier has specific responsibilities and interacts with the others to fulfil the application's requirements.
Client Tier
Role: Interacts directly with the user.
Types:
Web Clients: Use web browsers with HTML, CSS, and JavaScript.
Application Clients: Standalone applications built using JavaFX or Swing.
Mobile Clients: Applications running on mobile devices.
Key Components
HTML/CSS/JavaScript: For creating dynamic and responsive web interfaces.
JavaFX/Swing: For building rich client-side desktop applications.

Web Tier
Role: Manages client requests, processes them, and returns responses.
Technologies
Servlets: Java classes that handle HTTP requests and responses.
JavaServer Pages (JSP): Facilitates the creation of dynamic web content using embedded Java code.
JavaServer Faces (JSF): A component-based UI framework for building user interfaces.
WebSockets: Supports full-duplex communication between the client and server.
Key Components
Servlets
    Definition: Managed by a servlet container, they process incoming requests and generate responses.
    Example: Handling form submissions, managing sessions.
JSP
    Definition: Allows embedding Java code within HTML pages to generate dynamic content.
    Example: Displaying user-specific information on a web page.
JSF
    Definition: Provides reusable UI components and manages user interactions in a component-based manner.
    Example: Creating complex web forms with validation and data binding.

WebSockets

Definition: Enables real-time communication between the client and server.

Example: Chat applications, live updates.

Business Tier

Role: Encapsulates business logic, data access, and processing rules.

Technologies

Enterprise JavaBeans (EJB): Server-side components that manage business logic.

Context and Dependency Injection (CDI): Framework for dependency injection and lifecycle management.

Java Persistence API (JPA): Standardizes data persistence and object-relational mapping (ORM).

Key Components

EJB

Stateless Session Beans

Definition: Perform operations without maintaining client state.

Example: Processing a single client request.

Stateful Session Beans

Definition: Maintain state across multiple client interactions.

Example: Shopping cart management.

Message-Driven Beans

Definition: Handle asynchronous messaging.

Example: Processing messages from a queue.

CDI

Definition: Manages the lifecycle and dependencies of Java objects, promoting loose coupling.

Example: Injecting services into components.

JPA

Definition: Facilitates database operations using ORM, mapping Java objects to database tables.

Example: CRUD operations on database entities.

Enterprise Information System (EIS) Tier

Role: Integrates with enterprise information systems like databases, ERP systems, and legacy systems.

Technologies

Java Database Connectivity (JDBC): Standard API for database access.

Java EE Connector Architecture (JCA): Standard API for connecting to enterprise systems.

Java Transaction API (JTA): Manages transactions across multiple resources.

Key Components

JDBC

Definition: Provides a standard interface to connect and interact with relational databases.

Example: Executing SQL queries, retrieving results.

JCA

Definition: Enables integration with enterprise information systems.

Example: Connecting to an ERP system.

JTA

Definition: Ensures atomicity and consistency of transactions across multiple resources.

Example: Managing distributed transactions involving multiple databases.

Java EE Containers

Containers provide runtime support for various Java EE components, managing their lifecycle, security, and deployment.

Web Container: Manages servlets and JSP execution.

EJB Container: Manages the execution of enterprise beans.

Application Client Container: Manages standalone Java applications.

Applet Container: Manages Java applets in web browsers.

Responsibilities

Lifecycle Management: Creating, initializing, and destroying components.

Security Management: Enforcing security constraints and policies.

Transaction Management: Managing transactions to ensure data consistency.
Resource Management: Handling resources such as database connections and threads.

Integration and Interoperability
Java EE supports various standards and protocols for integration with other systems and services
Web Services: JAX-WS for SOAP-based web services, JAX-RS for RESTful web services.
Messaging: Java Message Service (JMS) for asynchronous communication.
Java Mail: For sending and receiving email.
Java Authentication and Authorization Service (JAAS): For securing applications.

Interoperability Standards
XML and JSON: Data interchange formats.
SOAP and REST: Web service protocols.
CORBA: Middleware for interoperability between different programming languages.

Best Practices and Design Patterns
Model-View-Controller (MVC): Separates application logic, user interface, and control logic.
Dependency Injection: Reduces coupling between components and improves testability.
Singleton: Ensures a class has only one instance and provides a global point of access.
Factory: Creates objects without specifying the exact class of object to be created.
Observer: Allows objects to notify other objects about changes.

Examples
MVC: Using JSF for the presentation layer, EJB for business logic, and JPA for data access.
Dependency Injection: Using CDI to inject services into managed beans.
Singleton: Implementing a cache or configuration manager.
Factory: Creating different types of payment processors based on payment method.
Observer: Implementing event-driven systems where components react to changes.

3.5 Java EE Development and Deployment

Java EE provides a powerful platform for building, packaging, and deploying enterprise applications. This chapter covers the essential tools, processes, and techniques for Java EE development and deployment, focusing on development tools, building and packaging strategies, deployment descriptors, annotations, and deployment on popular Java EE application servers.

Java EE Development Tools and IDEs

Java EE development is facilitated by various Integrated Development Environments (IDEs) and tools that streamline coding, debugging, and deployment processes. Here are some of the most popular tools:

Eclipse IDE for Enterprise Java Developers

Features

Built-in support for Java EE projects.
Tools for developing, debugging, and deploying Java EE applications.
Integration with application servers like GlassFish and WildFly.

Plugins:

Eclipse Web Tools Platform (WTP): Adds support for web and Java EE development.
JBoss Tools: Enhances support for Red Hat JBoss Middleware.

IntelliJ IDEA Ultimate

Features

Comprehensive support for Java EE technologies, including EJB, CDI, JPA, and more.
Advanced coding assistance, refactoring tools, and intelligent code completion.
Integrated application server support for seamless deployment.

Plugins

Database Navigator Provides tools for database development.
JPA Support: Enhances JPA development with visual tools and advanced code assistance.

NetBeans IDE

Features:

Full support for Java EE development, including EJB, web services, and persistence.
Visual web and enterprise application development tools.
Easy integration with application servers like GlassFish.

Plugins

NetBeans Enterprise Pack: Adds advanced Java EE tools.
Hibernate and Spring support: Facilitates development with these popular frameworks.

Building and Packaging Java EE Applications

Building and packaging Java EE applications involves compiling source code, resolving dependencies, and creating deployable artifacts. Here are key aspects of this process:

Build Tools

Apache Maven

Role: Manages project build, reporting, and documentation.
Features: Dependency management, build lifecycle management, plugins for various tasks.
Example: pom.xml configuration file to define project dependencies and build instructions.

Gradle

Role: Flexible build automation tool.
Features: Groovy-based DSL for configuration, incremental builds, rich plugin ecosystem.
Example: build.gradle file to define dependencies and tasks.

Packaging Artifacts

WAR (Web Application Archive)

Usage: Packages web modules (servlets, JSPs, static resources).
Structure
/WEB-INF: Contains deployment descriptor (web.xml), libraries, and classes.
/META-INF: Metadata files.

EAR (Enterprise Application Archive)

Usage: Packages entire Java EE applications, including EJBs, web modules, and other resources.
Structure
/META-INF: Contains deployment descriptor (application.xml).
/lib: Shared libraries.
Other JAR and WAR files: Modules of the enterprise application.

JAR (Java ARchive)

Usage: Packages EJB modules and utility libraries.
Structure
/META-INF: Metadata files, including ejb-jar.xml.

Deployment Descriptors and Annotations

Java EE uses deployment descriptors and annotations to configure application components and resources.

Deployment Descriptors

Definition: XML files that specify configuration and deployment settings for Java EE applications.

Examples

web.xml:

Purpose: Configures web components (servlets, filters, listeners).

Location: /WEB-INF/web.xml.

Example:

```
<web-app>
  <servlet>
    <servlet-name>ExampleServlet</servlet-name>
    <servlet-class>com.example.ExampleServlet</servlet-class>
  </servlet>
  <servlet-mapping>
```

```
    <servlet-name>ExampleServlet</servlet-name>
    <url-pattern>/example</url-pattern>
  </servlet-mapping>
</web-app>
```

ejb-jar.xml:

Purpose: Configures EJB components.
Location: /META-INF/ejb-jar.xml.
Example:

```
<ejb-jar>
  <enterprise-beans>
    <session>
      <ejb-name>ExampleBean</ejb-name>
      <ejb-class>com.example.ExampleBean</ejb-class>
      <session-type>Stateless</session-type>
    </session>
  </enterprise-beans>
</ejb-jar>
```

2. Annotations

Definition: Java metadata used to configure components directly in the code, reducing the need for XML configuration.
Examples:

Servlet Annotation

Example:

```
@WebServlet("/example")
public class ExampleServlet extends HttpServlet {
  protected void doGet(HttpServletRequest request, HttpServletResponse response) throws
ServletException, IOException {
    response.getWriter().write("Hello, World!");
  }
}
```

EJB Annotation

Example:

```
@Stateless
public class ExampleBean {
  public String sayHello() {
    return "Hello, World!";
  }
}
```

Deployment on Java EE Application Servers
Java EE applications are deployed on application servers that provide runtime environments and manage resources.
GlassFish
Overview: Open-source Java EE application server originally developed by Sun Microsystems and now maintained by the Eclipse Foundation.
Deployment Steps
Start GlassFish Server: Run the server using command line or admin console.
Admin Console: Access via http://localhost:4848.
Deploy Application: Use the admin console to upload and deploy WAR/EAR files.
Command Line Deployment: Use asadmin command for deployment: asadmin deploy path/to/your-app.war
Verify Deployment: Access the deployed application via browser or API client.
WildFly (formerly JBoss)
Overview: Community-driven application server by Red Hat, known for its high performance and flexibility.
Deployment Steps

Start WildFly Server: Run the server using command line or admin console.
Admin Console: Access via http://localhost:9990.
Deploy Application: Use the admin console to upload and deploy WAR/EAR files.
Command Line Deployment: Use jboss-cli.sh command for deployment: jboss-cli.sh --connect --command="deploy path/to/your-app.war"
Verify Deployment: Access the deployed application via browser or API client.

3.6 Key Components of Java EE

Servlets: Servlets are Java classes that extend the functionality of web servers to handle requests and generate dynamic content. They run on the server-side and receive requests from clients, process them, and send responses back. Servlets are commonly used in the presentation tier of Java EE applications to handle HTTP requests and responses.

JavaServer Pages (JSP): JSP is a technology that allows developers to create dynamic web pages with embedded Java code. It simplifies the process of building web interfaces by enabling the mixing of static HTML content with dynamic Java code. JSP pages are translated into servlets by the container at runtime, making them part of the presentation tier in Java EE applications.

Enterprise JavaBeans (EJB): EJB is a server-side component model for building distributed, transactional, and scalable enterprise applications. It provides a framework for developing reusable business components that encapsulate business logic and can be accessed remotely by clients. EJBs are typically used in the business tier of Java EE applications to implement complex business processes.

Java Persistence API (JPA): JPA is a Java specification for accessing, persisting, and managing data between Java objects and a relational database. It provides a high-level, object-relational mapping (ORM) framework that allows developers to work with database entities using object-oriented programming concepts. JPA is commonly used in the data tier of Java EE applications to interact with relational databases.

Java Message Service (JMS): JMS is a Java API for sending and receiving asynchronous messages between distributed applications. It provides a standard way for applications to communicate and exchange data in a loosely coupled manner. JMS is often used in Java EE applications for implementing messaging systems, event-driven architectures, and integrating with external systems.

Java Naming and Directory Interface (JNDI): JNDI is a Java API for accessing naming and directory services in a distributed environment. It provides a standard way for Java applications to look up and retrieve objects, such as EJB components, JMS resources, and database connections, from a naming or directory service. JNDI is commonly used in Java EE applications for locating and accessing various resources and components.

JavaMail API: JavaMail API provides a platform-independent and protocol-independent framework for building email and messaging applications in Java EE. It allows developers to send, receive, and manipulate email messages programmatically.

Java Transaction API (JTA): The Java Transaction API (JTA) is a vital component of Java EE, offering a standardized approach to managing transactions within enterprise applications. With JTA, developers can initiate, commit, and rollback transactions programmatically, ensuring data integrity and consistency. JTA coordinates transactions across various resources, including databases and messaging services, and supports distributed transactions across multiple systems. By providing mechanisms for transaction management, monitoring, and recovery, JTA facilitates the development of robust and reliable enterprise applications, allowing for seamless integration with other Java EE components such as Enterprise JavaBeans (EJB) and the Java Persistence API (JPA).

JavaServer Faces (JSF): JavaServer Faces (JSF) is a user interface framework for Java EE, simplifying web application development with reusable UI components and MVC architecture. JSF streamlines UI development by abstracting complex tasks like state management and event handling, enhancing productivity. With its rich component library and lifecycle management, JSF promotes component-based development and reduces code redundancy. It supports server-side processing, making it suitable for enterprise applications. JSF's integration with Java EE technologies like CDI and JPA enables seamless development of scalable, maintainable applications. Overall, JSF empowers developers to build robust, responsive web interfaces efficiently, enhancing user experience in Java EE applications.

Contexts and Dependency Injection (CDI): Contexts and Dependency Injection (CDI) is a key Java EE technology facilitating loosely coupled, modular application development. CDI manages bean lifecycles, enabling dependency injection, reducing boilerplate code, and promoting reusable, maintainable code. With CDI, beans are created within defined contexts, facilitating contextual awareness and scoped Behaviour. It fosters decoupling by allowing components to be easily swapped or extended. CDI promotes code organization, modularity, and testability, enhancing developer productivity. By standardizing dependency injection and providing powerful contextual services, CDI streamlines Java EE application development, promoting robust, flexible architectures for enterprise-grade applications.

Exercise

Exercise 1 – MCQ

1. Java EE is designed for:
a) Building desktop applications
b) Developing single-threaded applications
c) Creating enterprise-level applications
d) Programming microcontrollers
2. Which of the following is a benefit of using Java EE?
a) Low-level thread management
b) Cross-platform compatibility
c) Limited scalability
d) Reduced security features
3. What major change was introduced in Java EE 5?
a) Decrease in the number of APIs
b) Introduction of annotations
c) Removal of EJBs
d) Discouragement of web development
4. Which component in Java EE is responsible for handling requests and responses in a web application?
a) JPA
b) Servlets
c) EJB
d) JMS
5. JSP in Java EE is used for:
a) Messaging between components
b) Creating dynamic web content
c) Mapping Java objects to database tables
d) Naming and directory services
6. Enterprise JavaBeans (EJB) in Java EE are used for:
a) Managing persistent data
b) Simplifying transaction management and security
c) Generating web pages
d) Interchanging messages asynchronously
7. The Java Persistence API (JPA) is a specification for:
a) Asynchronous messaging
b) Object-relational mapping
c) Application integration
d) Remote method invocation
8. Java Message Service (JMS) in Java EE is used for:
a) Data persistence
b) Asynchronous messaging
c) Generating dynamic web content
d) Handling HTTP requests and responses
9. Java Naming and Directory Interface (JNDI) in Java EE is used for:
a) Object-relational mapping
b) Accessing naming and directory services
c) Asynchronous communication
d) Web page generation
10. Which of the following best describes the architecture of Java EE?
a) Monolithic
b) Layered
c) Single-tier
d) Peer-to-peer

Exercise 2 - True/False

1. Java EE stands for Java Platform, Enterprise Edition, which is used for developing large-scale, multi-tiered, scalable, reliable, and secure network applications.
2. Java EE is primarily focused on simplifying app development and improving app performance for desktop environments.
3. One of the main benefits of Java EE is its support for rapid development and deployment of applications.
4. Java EE does not support distributed computing and web services.
5. Java EE was initially called J2EE and was renamed to Java EE in version 5.
6. The latest version of Java EE is Java EE 8, and it has not evolved since its release.
7. Java EE architecture includes a web tier, business tier, and EIS (Enterprise Information Systems) tier.
8. In Java EE architecture, servlets operate in the EIS tier.
9. Servlets are Java programming language objects that dynamically process requests and construct responses.
10. JSP (JavaServer Pages) is a technology that allows software developers to create dynamically generated web pages based on HTML, XML, or other document types.

Exercise 3 - Fill in the blanks

1. Java EE stands for Java Platform, __________ Edition, which is used for developing large-scale, enterprise-level applications.
2. __________ is a technology within Java EE that allows developers to create dynamic web pages using HTML, XML, or other document types.
3. In Java EE, __________ API is used for creating, sending, receiving, and reading messages, enabling communication between different components of an application.
4. The Java Persistence API (JPA) is a specification within Java EE for managing relational data in applications. It is part of the larger __________ specification.
5. Contexts and Dependency Injection (CDI) in Java EE helps to bind together the web tier and transactional tier of the application, and its full form is __________ and Dependency Injection.
6. The _____ pattern is commonly used in Java EE applications to separate the business logic from the presentation layer.
7. _____ (JCA) provides a standard architecture for integrating Java EE applications with enterprise information systems.
8. The __________ file in a WAR package contains the deployment descriptor for web components.
9. The __________ annotation is used to define a servlet component in a Java EE application.
10. The __________ API is used for sending and receiving email in a Java EE application.

Exercise 4: Match Case

1. Java classes for handling HTTP requests and responses in web applications.
2. User interface framework for Java EE, facilitating component-based web development.
3. Standard API for managing transactions in Java EE applications
4. Server-side components providing business logic and services in Java EE applications. (JSF)

A. Java Transaction API (JTA)
B. Servlets
C. Enterprise JavaBeans (EJB)
D. JavaServer Faces

Exercise 5 - One-word answer

1. What Java EE specification is used for managing relational data in applications?
2. Which Java EE API enables real-time, bidirectional communication between a client and a server?

Exercise 6- Small answer

1. Describe the primary purpose of the Servlet technology in Java EE.
2. Explain the role of EJB (Enterprise JavaBeans) in Java EE applications.

Exercise 7 – Long answer

1. Discuss the evolution of Java EE, highlighting the major changes and improvements introduced with each version up to the current edition. Include how these changes have influenced enterprise application development.
2. Explain in detail how Contexts and Dependency Injection (CDI) enhances the development of Java EE applications. Discuss its benefits, how it integrates with other Java EE technologies, and provide examples of its use in application development scenarios.

Answer:
Exercise 1- 1) c 2) b 3) b 4) b 5) b 6) b 7) b 8) b 9) b 10) b
Exercise 2 - 1) True 2) False3) True 4) False 5) True 6) False7) True 8) False 9) True 10) True
Exercise 3 - 1) Enterprise 2) JavaServer Pages (JSP) 3) Java Message Service (JMS) 4) Java EE 5) Contexts 6) Model-View-Controller (MVC) 7) Java Connector Architecture 8) web.xml 9) @WebServlet 10) JavaMail
Exercise 4: 1 - B. Servlets 2 - D. JavaServer Faces (JSF) 3 - A. Java Transaction API (JTA) 4 - C. Enterprise JavaBeans (EJB)
Exercise 5 - 1) JPA (Java Persistence API) 2) WebSocket

Online Resources

Online Practice Paper

Link: https://forms.gle/EFRLye68mJB8KQof7
QR Code:

YouTube Video Link

Link: https://www.youtube.com/playlist?list=PLzlh_31VWEFpuOaJocdor00sKleSYUmnH
QR Code:

CHAPTER 4 - Enterprise Application Development in Java

4.1 Introduction

Developing enterprise applications in Java involves leveraging the features and capabilities provided by Java EE. This includes using frameworks and tools to streamline development, such as Java EE application servers like Apache Tomcat, Wild Fly, or IBM WebSphere. Enterprise application development in Java also involves implementing design patterns and best practices to ensure scalability, reliability, and maintainability. Developers need to understand concepts such as transaction management, security, concurrency, and distributed computing to build effective enterprise applications. Additionally, integrating with external systems and services, such as databases, messaging systems, and web services, is a common requirement in enterprise application development. Overall, Java EE provides a robust foundation for developing enterprise applications that can meet the needs of modern businesses.

Enterprise application development in Java is a cornerstone of modern software engineering, providing robust, scalable, and secure solutions for businesses and organizations. Java, with its platform independence, strong community support, and extensive ecosystem, is ideally suited for building complex enterprise applications that meet the diverse needs of large-scale enterprises. Enterprise applications are typically characterized by their need to support a high number of users, process large volumes of data, and ensure reliable performance and uptime. These applications often include functionalities like transaction management, security, messaging, and web services, all of which are essential for business operations. Java EE (Enterprise Edition), now known as Jakarta EE, provides a comprehensive set of specifications and libraries that cater to these requirements.

One of the fundamental components of Java EE is the Enterprise JavaBeans (EJB) framework, which simplifies the development of large-scale enterprise applications by providing built-in support for transactions, security, concurrency, and remote access. EJBs are used to encapsulate business logic and can be deployed in a distributed environment, ensuring that enterprise applications are both scalable and maintainable. JavaServer Faces (JSF) is another critical component, offering a robust framework for building web-based user interfaces. By using reusable UI components, JSF streamlines the development of dynamic and responsive web applications, enhancing user experience.

The Java Persistence API (JPA) addresses the need for data persistence in enterprise applications. By providing an object-relational mapping (ORM) solution, JPA allows developers to manage database operations using Java objects, reducing the complexity associated with database interactions.

Contexts and Dependency Injection (CDI) in Java EE further enhances modularity and maintainability by managing the lifecycle of components and their dependencies. This allows developers to create loosely coupled applications that are easier to test and maintain. Java Message Service (JMS) provides reliable messaging capabilities, enabling asynchronous communication between different parts of an enterprise application. This is crucial for integrating disparate systems and ensuring that they work together seamlessly.

In conclusion, enterprise application development in Java leverages the extensive capabilities of Java EE/Jakarta EE to build robust, scalable, and maintainable solutions. By using frameworks and APIs like EJB, JSF, JPA, CDI, and JMS, developers can address the complex needs of modern enterprises, ensuring that their applications are secure, efficient, and capable of supporting critical business operations.

4.2 Leveraging Java EE for Enterprise Applications

Java EE (Java Enterprise Edition) is a powerful platform designed for building robust, scalable, and secure enterprise applications. Leveraging Java EE for enterprise development offers numerous benefits, including:

Component-based architecture: Java EE promotes a component-based architecture, allowing developers to build applications using reusable components such as servlets, JavaServer Faces (JSF), Enterprise JavaBeans (EJB), and Java Persistence API (JPA). This promotes modularity, maintainability, and code reusability, essential aspects of enterprise application development.

Scalability: Java EE provides features and APIs that support scalability, enabling applications to handle increasing workloads and user demands. Technologies such as EJBs and clustering support distributed computing, load balancing, and failover, ensuring that applications can scale horizontally as needed.

Security: Security is a critical aspect of enterprise applications, especially when dealing with sensitive data and transactions. Java EE offers robust security mechanisms, including authentication, authorization, encryption, and

secure communication protocols. Developers can leverage features such as Java Authentication and Authorization Service (JAAS) and Java Secure Socket Extension (JSSE) to implement comprehensive security solutions.
Transaction management: Many enterprise applications require support for transactions to ensure data integrity and consistency. Java EE provides a built-in transaction management framework that supports declarative transaction demarcation using annotations or XML configuration. Developers can manage transactions across multiple resources, including databases, message queues, and web services, ensuring ACID (Atomicity, Consistency, Isolation, Durability) properties.
Enterprise integration: Java EE offers a variety of APIs and technologies for integrating with other systems and services, such as Java Message Service (JMS), Java Naming and Directory Interface (JNDI), and Java API for RESTful Web Services (JAX-RS). This enables seamless integration with external systems, legacy applications, and third-party services, facilitating interoperability and data exchange.

4.3 Design Patterns and Best Practices for Enterprise Development

Effective enterprise application development involves applying design patterns and best practices to address common challenges and ensure the scalability, maintainability, and performance of the software. Some key design patterns and best practices for Java EE development include:
Model-View-Controller (MVC): MVC is a widely used architectural pattern for separating concerns in user interface development. In Java EE, frameworks such as JSF (JavaServer Faces) and Spring MVC facilitate the implementation of MVC architecture, promoting modular development and code organization.
Dependency Injection (DI): DI is a design pattern that promotes loose coupling between components by injecting dependencies rather than instantiating them directly. Java EE supports DI through frameworks like CDI (Contexts and Dependency Injection), which simplifies component wiring and promotes reusability and testability.
Service-oriented Architecture (SOA): SOA is an architectural approach that promotes the decomposition of applications into reusable services, which can be accessed and combined to fulfill business requirements. Java EE supports SOA principles through technologies such as JAX-WS (Java API for XML Web Services) and JAX-RS (Java API for RESTful Web Services), enabling the development of service-oriented applications.
Data Access Object (DAO): DAO is a design pattern that encapsulates data access logic in separate classes, promoting separation of concerns and facilitating database interaction. In Java EE, JPA (Java Persistence API) provides a standardized approach to implementing DAOs, allowing developers to perform CRUD (Create, Read, Update, Delete) operations on entities using object-oriented APIs.
Exception handling: Effective exception handling is crucial for robust enterprise applications. Java EE promotes the use of checked exceptions for handling recoverable errors and unchecked exceptions for unrecoverable errors. Additionally, Java EE provides features such as declarative exception handling through annotations and global exception handling mechanisms, improving application robustness and maintainability.

4.4 Integration with External Systems and Services

Enterprise applications often need to integrate with external systems and services, such as databases, messaging systems, web services, and third-party APIs. Java EE provides various technologies and APIs for seamless integration:
Database integration: Java EE supports database integration through JDBC (Java Database Connectivity) and JPA (Java Persistence API). JDBC allows applications to connect to relational databases, execute SQL queries, and process result sets, while JPA provides a higher-level, object-relational mapping (ORM) framework for interacting with databases using entity classes and JPQL (Java Persistence Query Language).
Messaging integration: Java EE offers JMS (Java Message Service) for asynchronous messaging between distributed applications. JMS provides a standard API for producing and consuming messages from message queues or topics, enabling reliable communication and event-driven architectures.
Web services integration: Java EE supports integration with web services using technologies such as JAX-WS (Java API for XML Web Services) and JAX-RS (Java API for RESTful Web Services). JAX-WS allows applications to create and consume SOAP-based web services, while JAX-RS enables the development of RESTful web services using HTTP and JSON/XML payloads.
External API integration: Java EE applications can integrate with third-party APIs using HTTP clients like HttpURLConnection or frameworks such as Apache HttpClient. This allows applications to interact with external services, retrieve data, and perform operations such as authentication, authorization, and data synchronization.
Enterprise resource integration: Java EE provides JNDI (Java Naming and Directory Interface) for accessing enterprise resources such as EJB components, JMS destinations, JDBC data sources, and connection factories.

JNDI enables applications to look up and obtain references to resources configured in the application server or external systems, facilitating resource sharing and reuse.

4.5 Security in Java EE

Security is a critical aspect of enterprise applications, ensuring that data is protected, access is controlled, and communication is secure. Java EE provides a comprehensive set of security mechanisms and APIs to address these needs. These security features help developers implement robust security controls in their applications, protecting them from unauthorized access and various threats.

Security Mechanisms in Java EE

Java EE offers several built-in security mechanisms, including:

Declarative Security: Configured using annotations or deployment descriptors (XML files), declarative security allows developers to define security constraints without writing explicit security code. This approach separates security configuration from business logic.

Programmatic Security: Involves writing explicit security code within the application. Developers can use APIs to perform security checks and enforce security policies dynamically.

Authentication: Verifies the identity of users or systems accessing the application. Java EE supports various authentication mechanisms, such as basic authentication, form-based authentication, and custom authentication modules.

Authorization: Determines whether an authenticated user or system has the necessary permissions to access a resource or perform an action. Java EE uses role-based access control (RBAC) to manage authorization.

Transport Layer Security (TLS): Ensures secure communication between clients and servers by encrypting data transmitted over the network. Java EE applications can be configured to use TLS for secure communication.

Security Realms: Define a database of users, groups, and roles used for authentication and authorization. Security realms can be configured in the application server to manage security information.

Authentication and Authorization

Authentication: Authentication in Java EE can be configured using annotations or deployment descriptors. Common authentication methods include:

Basic Authentication: Uses a simple username and password dialog.

Form-Based Authentication: Provides a customizable login form for user authentication.

Digest Authentication: A more secure form of authentication that hashes credentials before transmission.

Custom Authentication: Developers can implement custom authentication mechanisms using JAAS (Java Authentication and Authorization Service).

Authorization: Authorization is typically managed using roles. Roles represent a set of permissions associated with a user or group. Java EE supports role-based access control (RBAC), which simplifies authorization management.

Declarative Authorization: Roles and access permissions are defined in annotations or deployment descriptors.

Example using annotations

```
@RolesAllowed({"ADMIN", "USER"})
public void someMethod() {
    // Method implementation
}
```

Example using deployment descriptors (web.xml or ejb-jar.xml)

```
<security-role>
    <role-name>ADMIN</role-name>
</security-role>
<security-role>
    <role-name>USER</role-name>
</security-role>
```

Programmatic Authorization: Developers can check user roles dynamically using security APIs

```
if (request.isUserInRole("ADMIN")) {
   // Perform admin-specific operations
}
```

Securing Web Applications

Securing web applications in Java EE involves several practices:

Defining Security Constraints

Use deployment descriptors to define which resources require authentication and what roles are allowed access.

Example in web.xml

```
<security-constraint>
   <web-resource-collection>
      <web-resource-name>Protected Area</web-resource-name>
      <url-pattern>/protected/*</url-pattern>
   </web-resource-collection>
   <auth-constraint>
      <role-name>USER</role-name>
   </auth-constraint>
</security-constraint>
```

Configuring Authentication Methods

Specify the authentication method in the deployment descriptor.

Example in web.xml

```
<login-config>
   <auth-method>FORM</auth-method>
   <form-login-config>
      <form-login-page>/login.html</form-login-page>
      <form-error-page>/error.html</form-error-page>
   </form-login-config>
</login-config>
```

Using HTTPS

Ensure that sensitive data is transmitted securely by configuring the web application to use HTTPS.
Configure the application server to use TLS/SSL.

Input Validation and Sanitization

Protect against injection attacks (e.g., SQL injection, XSS) by validating and sanitizing user inputs.

Session Management

Use secure cookies and set appropriate session timeout values to protect user sessions.

Error Handling

Customize error pages to avoid exposing sensitive information.

Role-Based Access Control (RBAC)

RBAC is a method for restricting access to authorized users based on their roles. In Java EE, roles are defined and associated with users, and permissions are granted based on these roles.

Defining Roles

Roles can be defined in deployment descriptors or using annotations.

Example in web.xml

```
<security-role>
        <role-name>ADMIN</role-name>
</security-role>
<security-role>
        <role-name>USER</role-name>
</security-role>
```

Assigning Roles to Users

Roles are assigned to users in the application server's security realm.

Role-Based Authorization

Access to resources and operations is controlled based on user roles.
Example using annotations:

```
@RolesAllowed("ADMIN")
public void adminMethod() {
   // Admin-specific implementation
}
@RolesAllowed({"ADMIN", "USER"})
public void commonMethod() {
   // Common implementation for both roles
}
```

By leveraging the security features in Java EE, developers can create secure, robust, and compliant enterprise applications. These security mechanisms help ensure that applications are protected against unauthorized access and other security threats, safeguarding sensitive data and maintaining user trust.

4.6 Enterprise Application Design Patterns

Design patterns are proven solutions to common problems encountered in software design. They provide a template for how to solve a problem in a way that is efficient, reusable, and maintainable. In enterprise application development, design patterns help manage complexity, improve code readability, and promote best practices.
Overview of Design Patterns
Design patterns in enterprise applications can be broadly categorized into three types:
Creational Patterns: Deal with object creation mechanisms, trying to create objects in a manner suitable to the situation.
Structural Patterns: Deal with object composition, forming larger structures from individual objects.
Behavioural Patterns: Deal with communication between objects and how they interact.
Enterprise applications often employ a combination of these patterns to address various architectural concerns, ensuring scalability, maintainability, and robustness.

4.6.1 MVC (Model-View-Controller) Pattern

The MVC pattern separates an application into three interconnected components:
Model: Represents the application's data and business logic. It directly manages the data, logic, and rules of the application.
View: Represents the presentation layer, displaying the data to the user. It retrieves data from the model and displays it to the user.
Controller: Acts as an intermediary between the model and the view. It receives user input from the view, processes it (often updating the model), and returns the output display to the view.

In Java EE, MVC is commonly implemented using frameworks like JavaServer Faces (JSF) or Spring MVC
Model: JavaBeans, JPA entities.
View: JSP, Facelets (for JSF), or Thymeleaf.
Controller: Servlets, Managed Beans (for JSF), or Spring Controllers.

Example

```
// Model: A simple POJO representing a User
public class User {
   private String username;
   private String email;
   // Getters and setters
}
// Controller: A servlet handling user registration
@WebServlet("/register")
public class RegisterServlet extends HttpServlet {
   protected void doPost(HttpServletRequest request, HttpServletResponse response) throws ServletException,
IOException {
      String username = request.getParameter("username");
      String email = request.getParameter("email");
      User user = new User();
```

```
        user.setUsername(username);
        user.setEmail(email);
        // Add business logic and update the model
        // Forward to view
        request.setAttribute("user", user);
        request.getRequestDispatcher("/WEB-INF/views/registrationSuccess.jsp").forward(request, response);
    }
}
// View: JSP displaying registration success
<!-- /WEB-INF/views/registrationSuccess.jsp -->
<html>
<body>
    <h2>Registration Successful</h2>
    <p>Welcome, ${user.username}!</p>
</body>
</html>
```

4.6.2 DAO (Data Access Object) Pattern

The DAO pattern abstracts and encapsulates all access to the data source. The DAO manages the connection with the data source to obtain and store data. It provides a separation between the data persistence logic and the business logic of the application.

Benefits

Encapsulation**:** Hides the details of the data access from the business logic.

Maintenance: Changes to data access logic do not affect business logic.

Testability: Easier to mock data access for unit testing.

Example

```
// DAO Interface
public interface UserDao {
    void saveUser(User user);
    User findUserById(int id);
}
// DAO Implementation
public class UserDaoImpl implements UserDao {
    private EntityManager entityManager;
    public UserDaoImpl(EntityManager entityManager) {
        this.entityManager = entityManager;
    }
    @Override
    public void saveUser(User user) {
        entityManager.persist(user);
    }
    @Override
    public User findUserById(int id) {
        return entityManager.find(User.class, id);
    }
}
```

4.6.3 Service Locator Pattern

The Service Locator pattern is used to decouple the service consumers from the concrete classes of the services they use. It provides a central registry where services can be looked up.

Benefits

Decoupling**:** Reduces the dependency of clients on the concrete implementations of services.

Centralized Management: Simplifies service access and management.

Example

```
// Service Locator
public class ServiceLocator {
```

```
    private static InitialContext context;
    static {
        try {
            context = new InitialContext();
        } catch (NamingException e) {
            e.printStackTrace();
        }
    }
    public static <T> T getService(String jndiName) {
        try {
            return (T) context.lookup(jndiName);
        } catch (NamingException e) {
            throw new RuntimeException(e);
        }
    }
}
// Usage in Business Logic
public class UserService {
    private UserDao userDao;
    public UserService() {
        this.userDao = ServiceLocator.getService("java:global/myApp/UserDaoImpl");
    }
    public void registerUser(User user) {
        userDao.saveUser(user);
    }
}
```

Testing and Debugging

Effective testing and debugging are crucial for the development of reliable enterprise applications. Java EE provides various tools and techniques to facilitate these processes.

Testing

Unit Testing: JUnit is commonly used for unit testing individual components. Mocking frameworks like Mockito can simulate dependencies.

Integration Testing**:** Arquillian allows testing Java EE components in a real runtime environment, ensuring that they work together correctly.

Functional Testing: Tools like Selenium can automate end-to-end testing of web applications.

Example of Unit Testing with JUnit and Mockito:

```
@RunWith(MockitoJUnitRunner.class)
public class UserServiceTest {
    @Mock
    private UserDao userDao;
    @InjectMocks
    private UserService userService;
    @Test
    public void testRegisterUser() {
        User user = new User();
        user.setUsername("testUser");
        user.setEmail("test@example.com");
        userService.registerUser(user);
        verify(userDao).saveUser(user);
    }
}
```

Debugging

Integrated Development Environments (IDEs)**:** IDEs like Eclipse and IntelliJ IDEA provide powerful debugging tools, allowing developers to set breakpoints, inspect variables, and step through code.

Logging: Using frameworks like SLF4J with Logback or Log4j helps track application Behaviour and diagnose issues.
Profiling: Tools like VisualVM and YourKit can profile applications to identify performance bottlenecks and memory leaks.

4.7.1 Unit Testing with Junit

Unit testing is the process of testing individual components of an application in isolation to ensure that each part functions correctly. JUnit is a widely-used testing framework in Java that provides annotations and assertions to facilitate the creation and execution of unit tests.

Key Features of JUnit
Annotations: JUnit uses annotations to denote test methods and setup/teardown methods.
@Test: Marks a method as a test method.
@BeforeEach: Runs before each test method.
@AfterEach: Runs after each test method.
@BeforeAll: Runs once before all test methods.
@AfterAll: Runs once after all test methods.

Assertions: JUnit provides a set of assertion methods to test expected outcomes.
assertEquals(expected, actual): Asserts that two values are equal.
assertTrue(condition): Asserts that a condition is true.
assertFalse(condition): Asserts that a condition is false.
assertNotNull(object): Asserts that an object is not null.
Example:

```
import static org.junit.jupiter.api.Assertions.*;
import org.junit.jupiter.api.BeforeEach;
import org.junit.jupiter.api.Test;
public class CalculatorTest {
    private Calculator calculator;
    @BeforeEach
    public void setUp() {
        calculator = new Calculator();
    }
    @Test
    public void testAdd() {
        assertEquals(5, calculator.add(2, 3));
    }
    @Test
    public void testSubtract()
 {
        assertEquals(1, calculator.subtract(3, 2));
    }
}
```

4.7.2 Integration Testing with Arquillian

Integration testing verifies that different components of an application work together as expected. Arquillian is a testing framework that extends JUnit to enable integration testing of Java EE applications in a real runtime environment.
Key Features of Arquillian
Container Management: Arquillian can deploy tests to various containers (e.g., JBoss, GlassFish, TomEE) to ensure the application behaves correctly in different environments.

Test Enrichment**:** Arquillian can inject dependencies into test classes, such as EJBs, CDI beans, and JPA entities.

Deployment**:** Arquillian manages the packaging and deployment of test archives to the container.
Example

```
import static org.junit.Assert.assertNotNull;
import javax.inject.Inject;
import org.jboss.arquillian.container.test.api.Deployment;
import org.jboss.arquillian.junit.Arquillian;
import org.jboss.shrinkwrap.api.ShrinkWrap;
import org.jboss.shrinkwrap.api.spec.JavaArchive;
import org.junit.Test;
import org.junit.runner.RunWith;
@RunWith(Arquillian.class)
public class UserServiceTest
{
  @Inject
  private UserService userService;
  @Deployment
  public static JavaArchive createDeployment() {
    return ShrinkWrap.create(JavaArchive.class)
            .addClasses(UserService.class, User.class)
            .addAsManifestResource("META-INF/persistence.xml", "persistence.xml");
  }
  @Test
  public void testRegisterUser() {
    User user = new User("john.doe", "john.doe@example.com");
    userService.registerUser(user);
    assertNotNull(user.getId());
  }
}
```

4.7.3 Debugging Techniques and Tools

Debugging is the process of identifying and resolving bugs in software. Effective debugging techniques and tools are crucial for maintaining code quality and reliability.

Techniques

Breakpoints: Set breakpoints in the code to pause execution and inspect the state of the application.

Step Execution: Step through code line by line to observe the flow of execution.

Variable Inspection: Inspect the values of variables at different points in the program.

Logging: Use logging frameworks (e.g., SLF4J, Logback) to record application Behaviour and identify issues.

Exception Handling: Analyze stack traces and exception messages to pinpoint the source of errors.

Tools

Integrated Development Environments (IDEs): IDEs like Eclipse, IntelliJ IDEA, and NetBeans provide powerful debugging tools, including visual breakpoints, variable inspection, and step execution.

Logging Frameworks: SLF4J, Logback, and Log4j help log application events and errors for post-mortem analysis.

Profilers: Tools like VisualVM, YourKit, and JProfiler can profile applications to detect performance issues, memory leaks, and thread contention.

Performance Tuning and Profiling

Performance tuning involves optimizing the performance of an application to meet desired benchmarks. Profiling is the process of analyzing an application's runtime Behaviour to identify bottlenecks.

Steps in Performance Tuning

Identify Performance Goals: Define clear performance goals and metrics (e.g., response time, throughput).

Profile the Application: Use profiling tools to gather data on CPU usage, memory consumption, and I/O operations.

Analyze Results: Identify bottlenecks and areas for improvement based on profiling data.

Optimize Code: Refactor code, optimize algorithms, and improve resource management.

Monitor Performance: Continuously monitor application performance in production to ensure that optimizations are effective.

Profiling Tools
VisualVM: A visual tool integrating command-line JDK tools for profiling and monitoring Java applications.

YourKit: A comprehensive profiler for analyzing CPU and memory usage, as well as performance bottlenecks.

JProfiler: A powerful profiler for analyzing performance, memory leaks, and threading issues in Java applications.

4.8 Deployment and Packaging

Deployment and packaging involve preparing and distributing an application for execution in a target environment.
Packaging
WAR (Web Application Archive): Used to package web applications. Contains web components (e.g., Servlets, JSPs), libraries, and configuration files.
EAR (Enterprise Application Archive): Used to package enterprise applications. Contains multiple modules, including WARs, EJB JARs, and resource adapters.
JAR (Java Archive): Used to package Java libraries and standalone applications. Contains compiled classes, resources, and metadata.

Deployment
Deployment Descriptors: XML files (e.g., web.xml, ejb-jar.xml) that define configuration and deployment settings for Java EE components.
Application Servers: Java EE application servers (e.g., GlassFish, WildFly, TomEE) provide runtime environments for deploying and managing enterprise applications.
Continuous Integration/Continuous Deployment (CI/CD): CI/CD pipelines automate the build, test, and deployment process, ensuring that applications are consistently and reliably deployed.
Example of Deployment Descriptor (web.xml):

```
<web-app>
  <display-name>MyApp</display-name>
  <servlet>
    <servlet-name>MyServlet</servlet-name>
    <servlet-class>com.example.MyServlet</servlet-class>
  </servlet>
  <servlet-mapping>
    <servlet-name>MyServlet</servlet-name>
    <url-pattern>/myServlet</url-pattern>
  </servlet-mapping>
  <welcome-file-list>
    <welcome-file>index.html</welcome-file>
  </welcome-file-list>
</web-app>
```

Example CI/CD Pipeline:
Source Control: Code is checked into a version control system (e.g., Git).
Build: A build tool (e.g., Maven, Gradle) compiles the code and packages it into a deployable artifact (WAR, EAR).
Test: Automated tests (unit, integration) are run to ensure code quality.
Deploy: The artifact is deployed to a staging environment for further testing, then to production if tests pass.

4.8.1 Packaging Java EE Applications (WAR, EAR)

Packaging is a critical step in Java EE application development, where the code and resources are bundled into deployable units.

WAR (Web Application Archive)

A WAR file is used to package web components such as Servlets, JSPs, HTML files, JavaScript, and other resources required by web applications.

Structure of a WAR File

```
MyApp.war
│
├── META-INF/
│   └── MANIFEST.MF
│
├── WEB-INF/
│   ├── web.xml
│   ├── classes/
│   │   └── com/example/ (compiled Java classes)
│   ├── lib/
│   │   └── (library JAR files)
│   └── (additional configuration files)
│
├── index.html
├── styles.css
└── script.js
```

Key Points

WEB-INF/web.xml**:** The deployment descriptor for the web application, specifying configuration settings like Servlets, filters, listeners, and security constraints.

WEB-INF/classes**:** Contains compiled Java classes.

WEB-INF/lib**:** Contains JAR files of libraries required by the web application.

EAR (Enterprise Application Archive)

An EAR file is used to package enterprise applications that may include multiple modules like web modules (WAR), EJB modules (JAR), and resource adapters (RAR).

Structure of an EAR File

```
MyApp.ear
│
├── META-INF/
│   └── application.xml
│
├── MyApp.war
├── MyEJBModule.jar
└── lib/
    └── (library JAR files)
```

Key Points

META-INF/application.xml: The deployment descriptor for the enterprise application, defining the modules included in the EAR and their configurations.

lib: Contains shared libraries accessible to all modules within the EAR.

Deployment Descriptors and Annotations

Deployment descriptors and annotations are used to configure Java EE applications. They provide metadata to the container about how components should be deployed and managed.

Deployment Descriptors

Deployment descriptors are XML files that describe configuration information for Java EE components. They are used in WAR and EAR files.

Example of web.xml (for a WAR file):

```
<web-app>
  <display-name>MyWebApp</display-name>
  <servlet>
    <servlet-name>MyServlet</servlet-name>
    <servlet-class>com.example.MyServlet</servlet-class>
  </servlet>
  <servlet-mapping>
    <servlet-name>MyServlet</servlet-name>
    <url-pattern>/myServlet</url-pattern>
  </servlet-mapping>
  <welcome-file-list>
    <welcome-file>index.html</welcome-file>
  </welcome-file-list>
</web-app>
```

Example of application.xml (for an EAR file):

```
<application>
  <display-name>MyEnterpriseApp</display-name>
  <module>
    <web>
      <web-uri>MyWebApp.war</web-uri>
      <context-root>/myapp</context-root>
    </web>
  </module>
  <module>
    <ejb>MyEJBModule.jar</ejb>
  </module>
</application>
```

Annotations

Annotations provide a way to specify configuration metadata directly in Java code, making it more concise and easier to maintain.

Example of Annotations in Servlets:

```
import javax.servlet.annotation.WebServlet;
import javax.servlet.http.HttpServlet;
import javax.servlet.http.HttpServletRequest;
import javax.servlet.http.HttpServletResponse;

@WebServlet("/myServlet")
public class MyServlet extends HttpServlet {
  protected void doGet(HttpServletRequest request, HttpServletResponse response) {
    // Handle GET request
  }
}
```

Example of Annotations in EJBs:

```
import javax.ejb.Stateless;
@Stateless
public class MyBean {
  public void businessMethod() {
    // Business logic
  }
}
```

4.8.2 Deploying Applications to Application Servers

Deploying a Java EE application involves transferring the packaged application (WAR or EAR) to an application server, where it can be executed and managed.
Common Java EE Application Servers
GlassFish: An open-source application server originally developed by Sun Microsystems.
WildFly: An open-source application server formerly known as JBoss AS.
TomEE: A lightweight application server based on Apache Tomcat with Java EE support.

Deployment Process
Prepare the Application Package: Ensure the application is correctly packaged as a WAR or EAR file.
Transfer the Package to the Server: This can be done using the server's administration console, command-line tools, or automated scripts.
Deploy the Application: Use the server's deployment mechanisms to deploy the package. The server will extract the package, configure the application, and make it available for use.
Example with GlassFish (using asadmin CLI):

```
asadmin deploy --name MyApp MyApp.war
```

4.8.3 Continuous Integration and Deployment (CI/CD)

CI/CD is a set of practices and tools designed to automate the process of building, testing, and deploying applications. It ensures that code changes are automatically integrated, tested, and deployed to production, leading to faster and more reliable software delivery.

Continuous Integration (CI)
CI involves automatically integrating code changes from multiple developers into a shared repository several times a day. Each integration is verified by an automated build and tests to detect errors early.
Tools for CI
Jenkins: An open-source automation server for building, testing, and deploying code.
Travis CI: A cloud-based CI service for GitHub projects.
GitLab CI: Integrated CI/CD for GitLab repositories.
Example CI Pipeline (Jenkinsfile):

```
pipeline {
  agent any
  stages {
    stage('Build') {
      steps {
        sh 'mvn clean package'
      }
    }
    stage('Test') {
      steps {
        sh 'mvn test'
      }
    }
    stage('Deploy') {
      steps {
        sh 'asadmin deploy --name MyApp target/MyApp.war'
      }
    }
  }
}
```

Continuous Deployment (CD)
CD extends CI by automatically deploying every code change that passes the tests to a production environment. It ensures that the application is always in a deployable state.
Steps in a CD Pipeline
Build: Compile the code and package it into deployable artifacts.
Test: Run automated tests to validate the code.

Deploy: Automatically deploy the application to a staging environment for further testing, and then to production if tests pass.

Example CD Pipeline (GitLab CI/CD):

```
stages:
  - build
  - test
  - deploy

build:
  stage: build
  script:
    - mvn clean package
test:
  stage: test
  script:
    - mvn test

deploy:
  stage: deploy
  script:
    - asadmin deploy --name MyApp target/MyApp.war
  only:
    - master
```

By implementing CI/CD, development teams can ensure that their Java EE applications are continuously integrated, tested, and deployed with minimal manual intervention, leading to improved efficiency, reliability, and faster delivery of new features and bug fixes.

Case Studies and Real-World Examples

Case Study: E-Commerce Application

Overview: An e-commerce application enables users to browse products, add items to a shopping cart, and complete purchases. The application must handle a high volume of transactions, ensure data consistency, and provide a smooth user experience.

Components

User Interface: Implemented with JavaServer Faces (JSF) or Thymeleaf, providing a rich and dynamic user interface.

Business Logic: Managed by Enterprise JavaBeans (EJB) for transaction management, inventory control, and order processing.

Persistence Layer: Uses Java Persistence API (JPA) for database interactions, ensuring data consistency and integrity.

Web Services: RESTful web services (JAX-RS) to support mobile applications and third-party integrations.

Key Challenges

Scalability: Ensuring the application can handle high traffic, especially during peak times like sales events.

Security: Protecting user data and preventing unauthorized access.

Transaction Management: Ensuring atomicity, consistency, isolation, and durability (ACID properties) during complex transactions like order processing.

Solution

Scalability: Implemented caching with Ehcache and load balancing with Apache HTTP Server.

Security: Utilized Java EE security mechanisms, including JAAS for authentication and role-based access control (RBAC) for authorization.

Transaction Management: Used container-managed transactions with EJB to ensure robust transaction handling.

Outcome: The application successfully managed high traffic and complex transactions, providing a seamless shopping experience. Implementing best practices in security and transaction management ensured data integrity and user trust.

Case Study: Banking System

Overview: A banking system handles customer accounts, transactions, loans, and other financial services. The system must be highly secure, reliable, and capable of processing a large number of transactions.

Components

User Interface: A web-based interface built with JSF or Angular for customer interaction.

Business Logic: EJBs handle core banking operations such as fund transfers, account management, and loan processing.

Persistence Layer: JPA for database interactions, ensuring transactional integrity.

Web Services: SOAP-based web services (JAX-WS) for integration with external financial institutions.

Key Challenges

Data Security: Protecting sensitive financial data from breaches.

Reliability: Ensuring continuous availability and fault tolerance.

Regulatory Compliance: Adhering to financial regulations and standards.

Solution

Data Security: Implemented encryption for data at rest and in transit, and used Java EE security features to enforce strict access controls.

Reliability: Deployed the application in a clustered environment with failover mechanisms and regular backups.

Regulatory Compliance: Ensured the application met standards like PCI DSS and implemented auditing features.

Outcome: The banking system delivered a secure, reliable, and compliant solution. Customers experienced high availability and secure transactions, reinforcing trust in the banking services.

Lessons Learned and Best Practices

Modular Architecture: Breaking down applications into modular components (e.g., using microservices) enhances maintainability and scalability.

Security: Incorporating security best practices from the start, including encryption, authentication, and authorization, is crucial for protecting sensitive data.

Scalability: Designing for scalability, such as using load balancers, caching, and clustering, ensures the application can handle increased load without performance degradation.

Transaction Management: Proper transaction management using EJB and JPA ensures data consistency and integrity, especially in complex transactions.

Testing: Comprehensive testing, including unit, integration, and performance tests, helps identify and resolve issues early in the development cycle.

Continuous Integration/Continuous Deployment (CI/CD): Automating the build, test, and deployment process reduces errors and accelerates the release cycle.

Documentation and Training: Maintaining thorough documentation and providing training for development and operations teams promotes better understanding and smoother operation.

Future of Enterprise Java Development

Microservices Architecture: Moving towards microservices allows for more scalable and resilient applications. Java frameworks like Spring Boot and Jakarta EE MicroProfile facilitate this transition.

Cloud-Native Development: Increasing adoption of cloud-native development practices and platforms (e.g., Kubernetes, Docker) enables more efficient deployment, scaling, and management of Java EE applications.

Serverless Computing: Leveraging serverless architectures (e.g., AWS Lambda, Azure Functions) for specific tasks can reduce infrastructure management overhead and cost.

Enhanced Security: Continued focus on security with advancements in encryption, threat detection, and secure coding practices to protect against evolving threats.

AI and Machine Learning Integration: Integrating AI and machine learning capabilities into Java EE applications to provide smarter, more personalized experiences.

Improved Developer Experience: Enhanced tools and frameworks (e.g., Jakarta EE, Quarkus) that simplify development, increase productivity, and reduce time to market.

Adoption of DevOps Practices: Wider adoption of DevOps practices to streamline development, deployment, and operations, ensuring continuous delivery and faster iteration cycles.

Exercise

Exercise 1 – MCQ

1. What is the primary focus of Java EE in enterprise application development?
a) Desktop application development
b) Web and enterprise application development
c) Mobile application development
d) Standalone console applications
2. Which component in Java EE is used for creating dynamic web content?
a) JDBC
b) EJB
c) JSP
d) JMS
3. What pattern is commonly used in Java EE for separating business logic from user interface?
a) Singleton
b) MVC (Model-View-Controller)
c) Observer
d) Factory
4. Which Java EE technology is used for database operations and object-relational mapping?
a) JPA
b) JMS
c) JNDI
d) Servlet
5. How does Java EE support distributed computing and services integration?
a) Through JSP
b) Through EJB
c) Through Servlets
d) Through JDBC
6. Which design pattern is NOT directly associated with Java EE?
a) DAO (Data Access Object)
b) Factory
c) Template method
d) Dependency Injection
7. What is the role of JMS in Java EE?
a) Data persistence
b) Message-driven communication
c) Synchronous data access
d) Web page rendering
8. Which of the following is a benefit of using Java EE for enterprise application development?
a) Limited scalability
b) Platform independence
c) Reduced security
d) High coupling
9. What technology does Java EE use for RESTful web services?
a) JSP
b) EJB
c) JMS
d) JAX-RS
10. Which of the following best describes the use of CDI in Java EE?
a) Messaging service
b) Dependency management and integration
c) Web page design
d) Data persistence

Exercise 2 – True/False

1. In Java EE, the Model-View-Controller (MVC) design pattern is implemented using Servlets, JSP, and EJB.
2. Enterprise JavaBeans (EJB) are primarily used for front-end user interface development.
3. The Java API for WebSocket enables synchronous communication in Java EE applications.
4. Java EE provides built-in support for integrating with external systems using JAX-RS for RESTful web services.
5. The Decorator pattern is a common design pattern used in Java EE to add new functionality to existing objects at runtime.
6. Java EE's Contexts and Dependency Injection (CDI) can only be used within the web tier of an application.
7. The Java Transaction API (JTA) enables distributed transactions that span multiple databases and systems.
8. JavaServer Faces (JSF) is a component-based MVC framework that simplifies the development of user interfaces in Java EE.
9. Microservices architecture is discouraged in Java EE due to its monolithic nature.
10. The Singleton design pattern in Java EE ensures that a class has only one instance and provides a global point of access to it.

Exercise 3 – Fill in the blanks

1. In Java EE, the _________ API is used for creating RESTful web services.
2. _________ beans in Java EE are used for defining business logic that can be executed without maintaining any client state.
3. The design pattern that ensures only one instance of a class is created in a Java EE application is called the _________ pattern.
4. For database access and object-relational mapping, Java EE applications typically use the _________ API.
5. The Java EE specification that allows applications to perform distributed transactions across multiple resources is known as the _________.
6. _______ is a design pattern that separates the presentation layer from the business logic layer in an application.
7. The ______ framework is used for building component-based user interfaces for web applications.
8. The _______ annotation in a servlet class specifies the URL pattern that the servlet will respond to.
9. A _______ file is used to package enterprise applications that may include multiple modules like web and EJB modules.
10. _______is a set of services that help manage the lifecycle of stateful components in Java EE applications.

Exercise 4 – Match Case

1. Simplifies construction of user interfaces
2. Used for creating RESTful web services
3. Manages relational data and object-relational mapping
4. Enables distributed transactions across multiple resources

A. JPA
B. JSF
C. JAX-RS
D. JTA

Exercise 5- One word answer

1. Which Java EE API is utilized for the development of SOAP-based web services?
2. What is the name of the Java EE framework that simplifies the construction of user interfaces for web applications?

Exercise 6 – Small answer

1. What are some key advantages of leveraging Java EE for enterprise application development?
2.Can you discuss a design pattern commonly used in Java EE for enterprise development and explain its significance?

Exercise 7- Long answer

1. Explain the role of Java EE in enterprise application development, highlighting its features and components.
2. Delve into the scalability and performance benefits offered by Java EE, including features like clustering, load balancing, and connection pooling.

Answers-

Exercise 1 – 1) B 2) C 3) B 4) A 5) B 6) C 7) B 8) B 9) D 10) B

Exercise 2 – 1) True 2) False 3) False 4) True 5) True 6) False 7) True 8) True 9) False 10) True

Exercise 3 – 1) JAX-RS 2) Stateless session 3) Singleton 4) JPA (Java Persistence API) 5) JTA (Java Transaction API) 6) Model-View-Controller (MVC) 7) Java Server Faces 8) @WebServlet 9) EAR (Enterprise Application Archive) 10) Contexts and Dependency Injection

Exercise 4- 1- B.JSF 2- C.JAX-RS 3- A.JPA 4- D.JTA

Exercise 5 – 1) JAX-WS 2) JSF

Online Resources

Online Practice Paper

Link: https://forms.gle/1dVqBZ4UM6HAnLU18

QR Code:

YouTube Video Link

Link: https://www.youtube.com/playlist?list=PLzlh_31VWEFokCbKSWCTyPylh8zmCWzTr

QR Code:

CHAPTER 5 - Building and Deploying JAR and WAR Files

5.1 Introduction

In the world of Java development, mastering the art of building and deploying Java Archive (JAR) and Web Application Archive (WAR) files is crucial for efficiently distributing and deploying applications. JAR files serve as the foundation for packaging compiled Java classes, libraries, and resources into a single file, making application distribution seamless and manageable. On the other hand, WAR files are specifically designed for web applications, encapsulating the web application resources, including Servlets, JSPs, HTML files, and associated metadata, for deployment to a Java EE (Enterprise Edition) server. This chapter aims to demystify the processes of building and deploying both JAR and WAR files, providing developers with the essential knowledge to streamline their development workflow, ensure smooth deployments, and ultimately, deliver robust Java and web applications.

In the landscape of Java development, packaging applications into deployable units is a pivotal step in the software development lifecycle. This process is essential for ensuring that Java applications can be easily distributed, deployed, and executed across different environments. Among the most commonly used packaging formats in Java are JAR (Java Archive) and WAR (Web Application Archive) files. Understanding how to effectively build and deploy these files is crucial for any Java developer aiming to create robust and scalable applications.

JAR Files

Java Archive (JAR) files are the standard packaging format for Java applications, libraries, and components. They encapsulate Java classes, resources, and metadata into a single compressed file. JAR files are versatile and widely used, making them suitable for a variety of Java projects, including standalone applications, libraries, and executable JARs.

Building a JAR file involves compiling Java source code into bytecode and packaging it along with resources (such as images, configuration files, and libraries) into a JAR file using tools like Apache Maven or Gradle. Once built, JAR files can be executed using the Java Virtual Machine (JVM) or included as dependencies in other Java projects.

WAR Files

Web Application Archive (WAR) files are specifically designed for packaging Java web applications. They contain the components required to deploy a web application, including servlets, JSPs (JavaServer Pages), HTML pages, CSS stylesheets, JavaScript files, and configuration files. WAR files are typically deployed to Java EE application servers like Apache Tomcat, WildFly, or GlassFish.

Creating a WAR file involves organizing the web application's directory structure according to Java EE specifications and packaging it into a WAR file. The deployment descriptor (web.xml) defines the configuration settings for the web application, such as servlet mappings, filters, and security constraints.

Deployment

Once JAR or WAR files are built, they can be deployed to various environments, including development, testing, staging, and production. Deployment involves transferring the packaged application to the target environment and configuring the application server to run the application. This process may include setting up database connections, configuring security settings, and defining resource contexts.

In this advanced Java book, we will delve into the intricacies of building, configuring, and deploying JAR and WAR files. We will explore best practices, tools, and techniques for streamlining the development and deployment process, enabling you to build robust, scalable, and maintainable Java applications. Whether you are a seasoned Java developer or just beginning your journey, mastering the art of building and deploying JAR and WAR files is essential for Java application development success.

5.2 Building JAR Files: Compiling Java Source Code, Packaging Resources

Java Archive (JAR) files are essential for distributing Java applications. They encapsulate compiled Java classes, associated metadata, and resources (like images and text files) into a single file. Understanding how to build JAR files is crucial for Java developers, as it facilitates application deployment and sharing. This chapter covers the process of compiling Java source code and packaging resources into a JAR file, providing a comprehensive guide for students and new developers.

5.2.1 Compiling Java Source Code

Before a Java application can be packaged into a JAR file, its source code must first be compiled into bytecode. This is accomplished using the Java Compiler (javac). The compiler checks the source code for errors and, if none are found, generates .class files containing the bytecode that the Java Virtual Machine (JVM) can execute.

5.2.2 Step-by-Step Compilation Process

Organize Your Source Files: Ensure that your Java source files are organized in a way that reflects their package structure. For example, a file MyClass.java in the package com.example.app should be located in a directory com/example/app.

Use the javac Command: Navigate to the root directory of your source files and run the javac command, specifying the path to your source files. For instance:

Code: javac com/example/app/MyClass.java

This command compiles MyClass.java and any other classes it depends on.

Deal with Dependencies: If your application depends on external libraries, include them in the classpath using the -classpath option:

Code: javac -classpath "path/to/libraries/*" com/example/app/MyClass.java

5.2.3 Packaging Resources into a JAR File

After compilation, the next step is packaging the .class files and any necessary resources (images, configuration files, etc.) into a JAR file. This is done using the jar tool included with the JDK.

Creating a JAR File

Prepare Your Manifest File (optional): A manifest file is a special file in a JAR that specifies entry points and other metadata. Create a text file named MANIFEST.MF with the following line to specify your application's entry point (if your application is executable)

Code: Main-Class: com.example.app.MainClass

Place this file in a directory named META-INF.

Use the jar Command: To create a JAR file, use the jar command with the cfm option, specifying the name of the JAR file you want to create, the path to the manifest file, and the root directory of the compiled classes and resources

Code: jar cfm MyApplication.jar META-INF/MANIFEST.MF -C bin/ .

Here, -C bin/ . tells the jar tool to add the contents of the bin/ directory (where your compiled .class files and resources are located) to the JAR file.

Verify Your JAR File: After creating the JAR file, you can verify its contents using the jar tf command

Code: jar tf MyApplication.jar

This command lists the files packaged inside MyApplication.jar, allowing you to ensure that all necessary components are included.

Building JAR files is a fundamental skill for Java developers. By compiling Java source code and packaging it along with necessary resources, developers can easily distribute their applications. Remember, the key steps involve organizing your source code, compiling it with javac, and then using the jar tool to package the compiled code and resources into a JAR file.

Building WAR Files: Assembling Web Application Resources, Packaging

Building WAR files involves assembling the necessary resources and components of a web application into a structured format that can be deployed to a Java EE application server.

5.3.1 Introduction to WAR Files

Web Application Archive (WAR) files are a fundamental aspect of deploying web applications in the Java ecosystem. They allow developers to package Servlets, JavaServer Pages (JSPs), Java classes, XML files, JavaScript files, and other resources into a single, deployable unit. This topic delves into the process of assembling web application resources and packaging them into WAR files. By understanding how to build WAR files, developers can efficiently deploy web applications to any Servlet/JSP container, such as Apache Tomcat or Jetty. Building WAR files involves assembling the necessary resources and components of a web application into a structured format that can be deployed to a Java EE application server. This process is crucial for preparing web applications for deployment and ensures that all required files, such as servlets, JSPs (JavaServer Pages), HTML pages, CSS stylesheets, JavaScript files, and configuration files, are properly organized and included.

Here's a detailed explanation of the steps involved in building WAR files

Assembling Web Application Resources

Before creating a WAR file, it's essential to organize the web application's directory structure according to Java EE specifications.

The web application directory typically includes folders for static resources (e.g., HTML, CSS, JavaScript), dynamic content (e.g., JSPs), configuration files (e.g., web.xml), and Java classes.

Each resource should be placed in the appropriate directory within the web application structure to ensure proper functioning and accessibility.

Packaging Resources into WAR Format

Once the web application resources are organized, they need to be packaged into a WAR file.

A WAR file is essentially a compressed archive (similar to a ZIP file) that contains all the necessary files and directories required for the web application to run.

The WAR file follows a specific structure mandated by Java EE specifications, which includes directories like WEB-INF and META-INF.

Creating Deployment Descriptor (web.xml)

The deployment descriptor (web.xml) is a crucial component of a Java web application. It provides configuration settings and metadata required by the application server to deploy and run the web application.

The web.xml file contains elements that define servlets, servlet mappings, filters, listeners, security constraints, error pages, and other configuration details.

Developers need to create or configure the web.xml file according to the requirements of the web application, specifying servlets, URL patterns, initialization parameters, and other settings.

Using Build Tools

Build tools like Apache Maven, Gradle, or Ant can automate the process of building WAR files.

These tools simplify the process by automatically compiling source code, copying resources, generating deployment descriptors, and packaging everything into a WAR file.

Developers can define the project structure, dependencies, and build configurations in the project's build script (e.g., pom.xml for Maven) to customize the build process.

Validating and Testing

Before deploying the WAR file to an application server, it's essential to validate its contents and test its functionality.

Developers should ensure that all required resources are included in the WAR file, the deployment descriptor is correctly configured, and the application behaves as expected.

Testing may involve running the application locally on a servlet container (e.g., Apache Tomcat) or using automated testing frameworks to verify its behaviour.

5.3.2 Understanding WAR File Structure

Understanding the structure of a WAR (Web Application Archive) file is essential for developing, deploying, and maintaining Java web applications. A WAR file is a standard packaging format for Java web applications and contains all the necessary components required for deployment to a Java EE application server. Let's delve into the details of the WAR file structure.

META-INF Directory

The META-INF directory is located at the root of the WAR file and contains metadata information about the application.

Within META-INF, you may find

MANIFEST.MF: This file contains metadata about the WAR file itself, such as version information, dependencies, and entry points for the application.

context.xml: Optionally, some application servers may include a context.xml file here, which defines context configuration for the web application.

WEB-INF Directory

The WEB-INF directory is also located at the root of the WAR file and contains configuration files and classes that are essential for the web application.

Within WEB-INF, you typically find

web.xml**:** The deployment descriptor for the web application. This XML file contains configuration settings for servlets, filters, listeners, security constraints, error pages, and other web application components.

classes: This directory contains compiled Java classes (e.g., servlets, utility classes) that are part of the web application.

lib: This directory contains JAR files (Java libraries) that are used by the web application. These JAR files may contain third-party libraries or custom code.
lib-provided: Some application servers may support this directory, which contains JAR files that are provided by the server environment. These JARs are typically available at runtime but are not packaged with the application.
Static Resources
The root directory of the WAR file may contain various static resources, such as HTML files, CSS stylesheets, JavaScript files, images, and other assets required by the web application.
These resources are accessible directly via the web server and are typically served without processing by the application server.
Dynamic Resources
Dynamic resources, such as JSP (JavaServer Pages) files, are typically located within the root directory or in subdirectories of the WAR file.
JSP files contain HTML markup mixed with Java code and are processed by the application server to generate dynamic content for web pages.
These files are compiled into servlets by the application server during deployment or runtime.
Other Configuration Files
Depending on the specific requirements of the web application and the technologies used, other configuration files may be included in the WAR file.
Examples include Spring configuration files (e.g., applicationContext.xml), Hibernate configuration files (e.g., hibernate.cfg.xml), or any other framework-specific configuration files.

5.3.3 Assembling Web Application Resources

Assembling web application resources involves organizing and preparing the various components that make up a Java web application. This process is crucial for ensuring that all necessary files, such as HTML pages, CSS stylesheets, JavaScript files, server-side code (e.g., servlets, JSPs), configuration files, and libraries, are properly structured and included in the application.
Here's a detailed explanation of the steps involved in assembling web application resources
Identifying Application Components
The first step in assembling web application resources is to identify the components required for the application. This includes determining the types of content the application will serve, such as static HTML pages, dynamic web pages generated by server-side code, and resources like images, stylesheets, and scripts.
Creating Directory Structure
Once the components are identified, developers create a directory structure to organize the resources. The structure typically follows best practices and conventions to ensure clarity and maintainability.
Common directories include
WEB-INF: Contains configuration files and classes that are essential for the web application.
WEB-INF/classes: Contains compiled Java classes.
WEB-INF/lib: Contains JAR files (Java libraries) used by the application.
static: Contains static resources like HTML pages, images, stylesheets, and JavaScript files.
WEB-INF/views: Contains dynamic web pages (e.g., JSP files) used for generating HTML content dynamically.
Organizing Static Resources
Static resources, such as HTML pages, images, stylesheets, and JavaScript files, are placed in the appropriate directories within the project structure.
HTML pages may be organized based on their functionality or purpose, such as login.html, home.html, about.html, etc.
CSS stylesheets and JavaScript files may be grouped together based on their role in the application (e.g., styles.css, scripts.js).
Creating Dynamic Web Pages
Dynamic web pages, such as JSP (JavaServer Pages) files, are created to generate HTML content dynamically based on data or logic.
JSP files contain a mixture of HTML markup and Java code, allowing developers to embed dynamic content within static HTML templates.
Developers write server-side code in JSP files to interact with databases, process user input, and generate dynamic content for web pages.
Configuring Deployment Descriptor

The deployment descriptor (web.xml) is configured to define the structure of the web application, specify servlet mappings, filters, listeners, and other configuration settings.
Developers define servlet mappings to map URL patterns to servlet classes, configure session management, specify error pages, and define security constraints.
Including Libraries and Dependencies
External libraries and dependencies required by the application are included in the project structure.
JAR files containing third-party libraries or custom code are placed in the WEB-INF/lib directory.
Testing and Validation
Once the resources are assembled, developers test and validate the application to ensure that all components are functioning as expected.
Testing may involve running the application locally on a servlet container (e.g., Apache Tomcat) and verifying its Behaviour in different scenarios.

5.3.4 Packaging into a WAR File

Once your application's resources are correctly organized, you can package everything into a WAR file using the Java Archive Tool (jar), included in the JDK, or build tools like Maven or Gradle.
Using the jar Tool
Navigate to the root directory of your web application.
Run the following command
Code: jar -cvf myapp.war *
This command packages the current directory's contents into myapp.war.
Using Maven
Define your project as a web application in the pom.xml with <packaging>war</packaging>.
Run the following Maven command
Code: mvn package
Maven builds the WAR file based on the project structure and dependencies defined in pom.xml.
Using Gradle
Apply the war plugin in your build.gradle file.
Configure your project's web application specifics as needed.
Run the command
Code: gradle build
Gradle assembles the WAR file based on the project's configuration.
Building WAR files is an integral part of developing and deploying Java web applications. By carefully assembling web application resources and packaging them into WAR files, developers can ensure that their applications are ready for deployment on any Java EE-compatible server.

Deploying JAR Files: Executing Standalone Applications

Deploying JAR files involves making standalone Java applications accessible and executable on various platforms. These applications are packaged into JAR (Java Archive) files, which contain compiled Java classes, resources, and metadata necessary for execution. Deploying JAR files typically involves distributing them to end-users and ensuring they can run the applications on their systems.

5.4.1 Introduction to JAR Files

Deploying Java applications in the form of Java Archive (JAR) files is a common practice for distributing standalone applications. A JAR file bundles the application's classes, libraries, and resources into a single file, making it easy to distribute and execute. This chapter provides a detailed guide on deploying JAR files for executing standalone applications, covering everything from the basics of JAR file structure to the execution process, ensuring students grasp the essential concepts clearly.
Here's a detailed explanation of deploying JAR files, focusing on executing standalone applications
Packaging the Application into a JAR File
Before deployment, the Java application needs to be packaged into a JAR file using tools like Apache Maven, Gradle, or manually using the jar command.
The JAR file contains compiled Java classes, resources (such as images, configuration files), and a manifest file (META-INF/MANIFEST.MF) that includes metadata about the JAR file, such as version information, main class, and dependencies.
Distribution to End-Users

Once the JAR file is created, it needs to be distributed to end-users who want to run the application.
Distribution methods vary depending on the deployment scenario and target audience. It can include direct downloads from a website, distribution via email, or packaging with software distribution platforms.
Execution on End-User Systems
End-users can execute the standalone Java application by double-clicking on the JAR file or using the command line.
On most systems, double-clicking the JAR file launches the application if the system is configured to associate JAR files with the Java Runtime Environment (JRE).
Alternatively, users can run the JAR file from the command line using the java command followed by the -jar option and the name of the JAR file (java -jar myapp.jar).
Handling Dependencies
Standalone Java applications may depend on external libraries or JAR files. These dependencies should be packaged with the application or made available to the application at runtime.
One common approach is to include the required libraries within the JAR file's lib directory. When the application runs, it can load classes from these libraries as needed.
Ensuring Platform Compatibility
Developers should ensure that the standalone Java application is compatible with the target platforms and environments where it will be deployed.
This includes verifying compatibility with different operating systems, Java Runtime Environment (JRE) versions, and hardware architectures.
Testing and Quality Assurance
Before deployment, thorough testing and quality assurance should be performed to ensure that the application functions correctly on various platforms and in different environments.
Testing may involve running the application on different operating systems, testing with different JRE versions, and verifying functionality and performance.
Providing User Documentation and Support
Along with deploying the JAR file, it's essential to provide user documentation and support resources to help end-users install, configure, and use the application effectively.
Documentation may include installation instructions, usage guidelines, troubleshooting tips, and contact information for technical support.

5.4.2 Understanding JAR File Structure

Before diving into deployment, it's crucial to understand the structure of a JAR file. A JAR file is essentially a zip file that includes a META-INF directory. This directory contains a manifest file (MANIFEST.MF), which can specify configuration data for the Java Virtual Machine (JVM), including the entry point of the application (the class with the main method).
Understanding the structure of a JAR (Java Archive) file is essential for Java developers as well as JAR files are the standard packaging format for Java applications, libraries, and components. They encapsulate Java classes, resources, and metadata into a single compressed file, making it easier to distribute and deploy Java software. Let's explore the components and organization of a JAR file in detail.
Overall Structure
A JAR file is essentially a ZIP file with a .jar extension. It can be opened and manipulated using standard ZIP file utilities.
Internally, a JAR file consists of multiple entries, including directories, files, and metadata.
Manifest File (META-INF/MANIFEST.MF)
The manifest file is a special metadata file located in the META-INF directory within the JAR file.
It contains information about the contents of the JAR file, including version information, dependencies, main class, and other attributes.
The manifest file follows a specific format defined by the Java Archive (JAR) File Specification.
Directory Structure
Similar to a file system, a JAR file can contain directories (folders) and files organized in a hierarchical structure.
Directories within the JAR file are used to organize related resources, such as Java packages, configuration files, and other assets.
Java Classes (.class files)
The primary contents of a JAR file are compiled Java class files (*.class files) containing bytecode instructions that can be executed by the Java Virtual Machine (JVM).

These class files are organized according to the package structure defined in the Java source code.
Each class file represents a compiled Java class or interface and may contain methods, fields, constructors, and other elements.
Resources
In addition to Java classes, a JAR file can contain various types of resources, such as images, XML files, property files, configuration files, and other non-code assets.
Resources are typically stored in the JAR file alongside the compiled Java classes, organized within directories based on their usage or purpose.
External Dependencies (Optional)
A JAR file may include dependencies on external libraries or JAR files required by the application.
These dependencies can be packaged within the JAR file's lib directory or referenced externally using the Java classpath.
Packaging Tools and Build Systems
JAR files are typically created using packaging tools such as the jar command-line tool provided by the Java Development Kit (JDK), Apache Maven, or Gradle.
Build systems and IDEs automate the process of creating JAR files as part of the software development lifecycle.

5.4.3 Preparing Your Application for Deployment

Preparing your application for deployment involves a series of steps to ensure that your software is ready to be released to end-users or deployed to production environments. This process encompasses various tasks, including testing, optimization, configuration, and documentation. Let's delve into the details of preparing your application for deployment in an advanced Java book.
Code Refactoring and Optimization
Before deployment, it's crucial to refactor and optimize your codebase to improve performance, scalability, and maintainability.
This may involve refactoring complex or redundant code, optimizing algorithms, improving database queries, and eliminating performance bottlenecks.
Optimization techniques such as caching, lazy loading, and database indexing can also be applied to enhance application performance.
Unit Testing and Test Automation
Comprehensive unit testing is essential to ensure that individual components of your application behave as expected.
Develop unit tests using frameworks like JUnit, TestNG, or Mockito to validate the functionality of classes and methods.
Implement test automation to streamline the testing process and ensure consistent test coverage across different modules and functionalities.
Integration Testing
Integration testing verifies that different components of your application work together seamlessly.
Test integration points such as database interactions, API calls, and third-party integrations to validate end-to-end functionality.
Use tools like Arquillian or Spring Boot Test for integration testing in Java EE applications.
Security Testing
Security testing is essential to identify and mitigate vulnerabilities in your application.
Conduct security assessments, vulnerability scans, and penetration testing to uncover security flaws such as SQL injection, cross-site scripting (XSS), and authentication bypass vulnerabilities.
Implement security best practices such as input validation, output encoding, and proper authentication and authorization mechanisms.
Configuration Management
Proper configuration management ensures that your application behaves consistently across different environments.
Externalize configuration settings such as database credentials, API keys, and environment-specific parameters to configuration files or environment variables.
Use tools like Spring Boot's application.properties or application.yml files for centralized configuration management.
Documentation

Comprehensive documentation is essential for users, administrators, and developers to understand and use your application effectively.
Document installation instructions, configuration settings, usage guidelines, API endpoints, and troubleshooting procedures.
Provide API documentation using tools like Swagger or Javadoc to document code structure, classes, methods, and parameters.
Packaging and Dependency Management
Package your application into a deployable format such as a JAR (Java Archive) or WAR (Web Application Archive) file.
Manage dependencies using build tools like Apache Maven or Gradle to ensure that all required libraries and dependencies are included in the deployment package.
Define build profiles for different environments (e.g., development, testing, production) to manage environment-specific configurations and dependencies.
Continuous Integration and Deployment (CI/CD)
Implement CI/CD pipelines to automate the build, testing, and deployment processes.
Use CI/CD tools like Jenkins, GitLab CI, or Travis CI to automate code integration, testing, and deployment to production environments.
Configure automated deployment scripts to deploy your application to staging and production environments with minimal manual intervention.

To deploy a Java application as a JAR file, follow these preparatory steps
Compile Your Application: Ensure all .java files are compiled into .class files. Use the Java compiler (javac) for this purpose.
Organize Resources: Besides .class files, your application might use resources like images, configuration files, or external libraries. Make sure these are organized within your project structure, typically in a resources directory.
Create a Manifest File: Although optional, creating a custom manifest file allows you to specify the application's entry point. Here's a simple manifest example:
Code**:** Main-Class: com.example.MainApp **(**Save this as a text file, typically named MANIFEST.MF)

5.4.4 Packaging the Application into a JAR File

Packaging the application into a JAR (Java Archive) file is a fundamental step in Java development, especially for distributing standalone applications or libraries. A JAR file packages all the necessary components of a Java application into a single archive, making it easier to distribute, deploy, and execute across different environments. Let's explore the process of packaging an application into a JAR file in detail.
Compilation and Build Process
Before packaging, the Java source code needs to be compiled into bytecode (.class files) using a Java compiler (e.g., javac).
The compiled class files, along with resources such as images, configuration files, and other assets, are organized within the project directory structure.
Defining Manifest Attributes (Optional)
The JAR file may include a manifest file (META-INF/MANIFEST.MF) that contains metadata about the contents of the JAR file.
Manifest attributes specify information such as the main class, version number, vendor, and dependencies of the application.
Developers can create a custom manifest file or let the build tool generate it automatically.
Using Build Tools
Build tools like Apache Maven, Gradle, or Ant simplify the process of creating JAR files by automating the build and packaging tasks.
Developers define the project structure, dependencies, and build configurations in the project's build script (e.g., pom.xml for Maven, build.gradle for Gradle) to customize the build process.
Build tools compile the source code, copy resources, generate the manifest file, and package everything into a JAR file with a specified name and version.
Creating JAR File Manually (Optional)
Developers can also create JAR files manually using the jar command-line tool provided by the Java Development Kit (JDK).

The jar tool allows developers to specify options and parameters to customize the packaging process, including specifying the main class, including or excluding specific files, and setting compression level.
For example, the command jar cvf myapp.jar -C <project_directory> creates a JAR file named myapp.jar containing all files and directories in the specified project directory.
Including Dependencies
If the application depends on external libraries or JAR files, developers need to ensure that these dependencies are included in the JAR file.
Dependencies can be packaged within the JAR file's lib directory or referenced externally using the Java classpath.
Validating and Testing
Once the JAR file is created, it's essential to validate its contents and test the application to ensure that it behaves as expected.
Developers can run the application locally by executing the JAR file using the java -jar command and verify its functionality, behaviour, and performance.
Versioning and Distribution
Developers should follow versioning best practices to track changes and releases of the application.
Distribute the JAR file to end-users or other developers through distribution channels such as websites, package repositories, or software distribution platforms.

With your application compiled and resources organized, you can now package it into a JAR file. If you have a custom manifest file, include it using the jar tool provided with the JDK
Code: jar cfm MyApp.jar META-INF/MANIFEST.MF -C bin/ .
In this command:
cfm indicates that you're creating a JAR file, specifying a manifest file.
MyApp.jar is the name of the JAR file you're creating.
META-INF/MANIFEST.MF is the path to your custom manifest file.
-C bin/ . tells the jar tool to change to the bin/ directory and include all files (.) in the JAR.
If you don't need a custom manifest, you can omit the manifest path
Code: jar cf MyApp.jar -C bin/ .

5.4.5 Deploying and Executing the JAR File
Deploying and executing a JAR (Java Archive) file involves making the Java application packaged within the JAR file available for execution on various platforms. This process is essential for distributing standalone Java applications or libraries and ensuring that end-users can run the application seamlessly.
Let's explore the detailed steps for deploying and executing a JAR file
Distribution of the JAR File
The first step is to distribute the JAR file to end-users or other developers who want to execute the Java application.
Distribution methods may include direct downloads from a website, distribution via email, or packaging with software distribution platforms.
Java Runtime Environment (JRE) Installation
End-users need to have a compatible Java Runtime Environment (JRE) installed on their system to execute the JAR file.
If the JRE is not already installed, users can download and install it from the official Java website or through package managers on their operating system.
Executing the JAR File
End-users can execute the JAR file using the Java command-line tool (java) provided by the Java Development Kit (JDK).
To execute the JAR file, users open a terminal or command prompt, navigate to the directory containing the JAR file, and run the following command: java -jar myapp.jar
Replace myapp.jar with the name of the JAR file you want to execute. This command launches the Java application contained within the JAR file.
Setting the Classpath (Optional)
If the JAR file depends on external libraries or JAR files that are not packaged within the JAR file itself, users need to set the classpath to include these dependencies.
Users can specify the classpath using the -cp or -classpath option followed by a list of directories or JAR files containing the required dependencies.

Passing Command-Line Arguments (Optional)
Java applications packaged within JAR files can accept command-line arguments when executed.
Users can pass arguments to the application by including them after the JAR file name in the command-line execution, separated by spaces.
GUI Applications (Optional)
If the Java application is a graphical user interface (GUI) application, executing the JAR file typically launches the application's main GUI window.
Users interact with the application through the graphical user interface, which provides features, functionality, and user interaction.
Troubleshooting and Error Handling
During execution, users may encounter errors or exceptions that need to be addressed.
Developers can provide error handling mechanisms within the application to gracefully handle errors, display meaningful error messages, and guide users through troubleshooting steps.
Logging and Debugging (Optional)
Developers can include logging and debugging functionality within the application to help diagnose and troubleshoot issues encountered during execution.
Logging frameworks like Log4j or java.util.logging can be used to log informative messages, warnings, errors, and debug information.
Documentation and User Support
Provide documentation and user support resources to help users understand how to execute and use the application effectively.
Documentation may include installation instructions, usage guidelines, troubleshooting tips, and contact information for technical support.

Once your JAR file is ready, deploying and executing the standalone application is straightforward. Ensure the target system has a compatible Java Runtime Environment (JRE) installed. To run the application, use the java command followed by the -jar option and the JAR file name
Code: java -jar MyApp.jar
This command instructs the JVM to launch the application defined in the JAR file's manifest file. If your application depends on external libraries not included within the JAR, you might need to specify the classpath using the -cp or -classpath option along with the -jar option.

Best Practices for Deploying JAR Files
Test on Multiple Platforms: If your application is intended for different operating systems, test the JAR file on all target platforms to ensure compatibility.
Use a Build Tool: Tools like Maven or Gradle can automate the compilation, packaging, and dependency management of your Java projects, making the deployment process more efficient.
Keep Security in Mind: Ensure your application does not expose sensitive information and complies with security best practices, especially if it processes user data.
Deploying Java applications as JAR files simplifies distribution and execution, making it an essential skill for Java developers.

Deploying WAR Files: Deploying Web Applications to Java EE Application Servers
Deploying WAR (Web Application Archive) files involves packaging and deploying Java web applications to Java EE (Enterprise Edition) application servers.

5.5.1 Introduction
Deploying Web Application Archive (WAR) files to Java EE (Enterprise Edition) application servers is a pivotal process in the development and distribution of web applications. WAR files package web application resources, including Servlets, Java Server Pages (JSPs), HTML files, scripts, and Java classes, into a single deployable unit. This chapter elucidates the process of deploying WAR files onto Java EE application servers, ensuring a clear understanding for students by detailing each step involved, from preparation to execution.
WAR files encapsulate all the necessary resources, such as servlets, JavaServer Pages (JSPs), Java classes, and static content, required to run a web application. Here's a detailed explanation of deploying WAR files to Java EE application servers

Understanding the WAR File Structure: A WAR file has a specific directory structure that includes the following components
WEB-INF/: Contains the web application deployment descriptor (web.xml), the application's configuration files, and server-side classes and libraries.
web.xml: Deployment descriptor file that defines servlets, servlet mappings, filters, listeners, and other configuration settings.
classes/: Directory containing compiled Java classes.
lib/: Directory containing JAR files required by the web application.
META-INF/: Contains metadata about the web application.
Static Resources: HTML, CSS, JavaScript files, and images used by the web application.
Creating and Packaging the WAR File: Use a build tool like Apache Maven, Gradle, or the jar command to create a WAR file. Below are examples using Maven and Gradle.
Using Maven
Define the project in a pom.xml file and specify the war packaging type.
Use the Maven command to package the application: mvn clean package
Using Gradle
Define the project in a build.gradle file and apply the war plugin.
Use the Gradle command to package the application: gradle clean build
Preparing the Application Server: Before deploying the WAR file, ensure that the Java EE application server (such as Apache Tomcat, GlassFish, WildFly) is installed and configured properly.
Example: Setting up Apache Tomcat
Download and install Apache Tomcat.
Configure Tomcat by editing configuration files such as server.xml and context.xml if necessary.
Start the Tomcat server using the provided startup scripts (e.g., startup.sh for Unix/Linux or startup.bat for Windows).
Deploying the WAR File: There are several methods to deploy a WAR file to a Java EE application server: Using the Application Server's Management Console:
Access the application server's web-based management console (e.g., Tomcat Manager, GlassFish Admin Console).
Navigate to the deployment section.
Upload the WAR file through the web interface and deploy it.
Copying the WAR File to the Deployment Directory
Copy the WAR file directly to the application server's deployment directory (e.g., webapps directory in Tomcat).
The application server automatically detects the WAR file and deploys it.
Using Command Line Tools
Some application servers provide command-line tools for deploying applications.
For example, to deploy a WAR file to GlassFish using asadmin: asadmin deploy myapp.war
Verifying the Deployment
After deploying the WAR file, verify that the web application is running correctly.
Access the application using a web browser by navigating to the URL where the application is hosted (e.g., http://localhost:8080/myapp).
Configuration and Environment Setup
Configure environment-specific settings, such as database connections, external services, and application properties.
Use context parameters in web.xml or external configuration files to manage environment-specific configurations.
Monitoring and Managing the Application
Use the application server's management console to monitor the health and performance of the deployed application.
Configure logging and monitoring tools to track application performance, errors, and usage.
Undeploying and Updating Applications
To undeploy an application, use the management console or remove the WAR file from the deployment directory.
To update an application, undeploy the existing version and deploy the new version of the WAR file.

5.5.2 Understanding WAR Files and Java EE Servers

In the realm of Java enterprise development, WAR (Web Application Archive) files and Java EE (Enterprise Edition) servers are critical components for deploying and running web applications. This section aims to provide a detailed understanding of WAR files and their deployment on Java EE servers for an advanced Java book.

Understanding WAR Files

A WAR file is a packaged collection of web components such as servlets, JavaServer Pages (JSPs), Java classes, HTML files, and other resources. It follows a standardized directory structure that the Java EE application servers recognize and utilize to deploy and manage web applications.

Key Components of a WAR File

WEB-INF Directory: This is the most crucial directory within a WAR file. It contains:

web.xml: The deployment descriptor file that defines servlets, servlet mappings, filter configurations, listeners, and other web application settings.

classes/: This directory contains compiled Java class files.

lib/: Contains JAR files that the web application depends on.

web.xml: The deployment descriptor file that configures the application.

META-INF Directory: Contains metadata about the archive itself. This directory includes:

MANIFEST.MF: A manifest file that provides metadata about the JAR/WAR file such as version, class-path, etc.

Static Resources: These include HTML files, CSS, JavaScript, images, and other static content accessible directly by the clients.

Example Directory Structure of a WAR File

```
myapp.war
|-- META-INF/
|   |-- MANIFEST.MF
|-- WEB-INF/
|   |-- web.xml
|   |-- classes/
|   |   |-- com/
|   |   |   |-- example/
|   |   |       |-- MyServlet.class
|   |-- lib/
|       |-- dependency.jar
|-- index.html
|-- styles.css
|-- script.js
```

Java EE Servers

Java EE servers (also known as application servers) provide the runtime environment for Java web applications. They manage the lifecycle of web components, handle security, transaction management, resource pooling, and provide other enterprise-level services. Some popular Java EE servers include Apache Tomcat, GlassFish, WildFly (formerly JBoss), and WebLogic.

Key Features of Java EE Servers

Servlet Container: Manages the lifecycle of servlets, JSPs, and handles HTTP requests and responses.

EJB Container: Manages Enterprise JavaBeans (EJBs), which are used for building modular and reusable business logic components.

Resource Management: Handles database connections, message queues, and other resource pooling.

Security: Provides mechanisms for authentication, authorization, and secure communication.

Transaction Management: Ensures data consistency and integrity through transaction management.

Deploying WAR Files to Java EE Servers

Deploying a WAR file involves placing it into the deployment directory of the Java EE server and configuring any necessary server-specific settings. Here's a detailed step-by-step guide for deploying WAR files

Step 1: Packaging the WAR File

Use a build tool like Apache Maven, Gradle, or the jar command to create a WAR file.

Ensure that the web.xml file is correctly configured and all necessary resources are included.

Step 2: Preparing the Application Server

Install and configure the Java EE server. Each server has its setup process, typically involving downloading the server package, extracting it, and configuring environment variables.

Start the server using provided scripts (e.g., startup.sh for Unix/Linux or startup.bat for Windows).

Step 3: Deploying the WAR File
Via Management Console: Most Java EE servers provide a web-based management console for deploying applications.
Access the console (e.g., Tomcat Manager, GlassFish Admin Console).
Upload the WAR file and deploy it through the interface.
Copying to Deployment Directory: Simply copy the WAR file to the server's deployment directory (e.g., webapps in Tomcat).
The server will automatically detect and deploy the WAR file.
Using Command Line Tools: Some servers provide command-line tools for deployment.
For example, to deploy a WAR file to GlassFish using asadmin: asadmin deploy myapp.war

Step 4: Verifying the Deployment
After deployment, access the application via a web browser to ensure it is running correctly.
Navigate to the application URL (e.g., http://localhost:8080/myapp).
Configuration and Environment Setup
Proper configuration is crucial for the successful deployment and operation of a web application. This includes setting up environment-specific properties, database connections, and external services.
Environment Variables: Use environment variables to configure sensitive information such as database credentials and API keys.
Configuration Files: Externalize configuration settings in properties files or XML files.
Context Parameters: Define context parameters in web.xml to manage environment-specific configurations.
Monitoring and Managing the Application
Java EE servers offer tools and interfaces to monitor and manage deployed applications. This includes
Logging: Configure logging to track application Behaviour and diagnose issues.
Performance Monitoring: Use server-provided tools or external monitoring tools to track application performance and resource usage.
Security Management: Implement and manage security policies, user roles, and permissions.
Updating and Undeploying Applications
Updating: To update an application, undeploy the existing version and deploy the new WAR file.
Undeploying: Use the management console or remove the WAR file from the deployment directory to undeploy an application.

5.5.3 Preparing Your Application for Deployment

Preparing your application for deployment is a critical phase in the software development lifecycle. It ensures that the application is production-ready, stable, and performs well under expected load conditions. This section provides a detailed guide on how to prepare your Java application for deployment, focusing on best practices, testing, optimization, and configuration.
Code Refactoring and Optimization
Code Cleanup: Refactor your code to improve readability, maintainability, and performance. Remove any unused code, libraries, and dependencies.
Performance Optimization: Optimize critical sections of your code, focusing on efficient algorithms, reducing I/O operations, and optimizing database queries.
Profiling: Use profiling tools like VisualVM or JProfiler to identify and address performance bottlenecks in your application.
Comprehensive Testing
Unit Testing: Ensure thorough unit test coverage for all critical components using frameworks like JUnit or TestNG.
Integration Testing: Validate the interaction between different modules and services. Tools like Arquillian can help with integration testing in Java EE environments.
System Testing: Perform end-to-end testing to ensure the entire system works as expected, including all integrated components.
Regression Testing: Run a full suite of tests to ensure that recent changes have not introduced new bugs.
User Acceptance Testing (UAT): Involve end-users to test the application in an environment that simulates production to ensure it meets their requirements.

Security Testing
Vulnerability Scanning: Use tools like OWASP ZAP or Burp Suite to scan your application for common security vulnerabilities, such as SQL injection, XSS, and CSRF.
Penetration Testing: Conduct manual penetration tests to uncover and address security weaknesses.
Security Best Practices: Implement secure coding practices, such as input validation, output encoding, and proper authentication and authorization mechanisms.
Configuration Management
Externalize Configuration: Store configuration settings outside the codebase to allow changes without modifying the code. Use properties files, YAML files, or environment variables for configuration.
Environment-Specific Configurations: Manage different configurations for development, testing, and production environments. Tools like Spring Boot Profiles can help manage these configurations.
Secrets Management: Securely manage sensitive information such as database credentials, API keys, and encryption keys using tools like HashiCorp Vault or AWS Secrets Manager.
Documentation
Code Documentation: Ensure that your code is well-documented with clear comments and annotations.
User Documentation: Provide comprehensive user guides, installation instructions, and usage documentation.
API Documentation: Use tools like Swagger or Javadoc to generate documentation for your APIs, making it easier for other developers to understand and use your services.
Packaging and Dependency Management
Build Tools: Use build tools like Maven or Gradle to manage dependencies and automate the build process.
Dependency Management: Ensure all required libraries and dependencies are specified in your build configuration (pom.xml for Maven, build.gradle for Gradle).
Artifact Versioning: Follow semantic versioning for your artifacts to track changes and compatibility.
Continuous Integration and Deployment (CI/CD)
CI/CD Pipelines: Implement CI/CD pipelines to automate the build, test, and deployment processes. Tools like Jenkins, GitLab CI, or Travis CI can help set up CI/CD pipelines.
Automated Testing: Integrate automated testing into your CI/CD pipeline to ensure that code changes do not break the application.
Deployment Automation: Use tools like Ansible, Chef, or Kubernetes to automate the deployment process and ensure consistency across different environments.
Performance Tuning and Profiling
Load Testing: Use tools like Apache JMeter or Gatling to simulate load conditions and measure application performance.
Performance Profiling: Profile the application to identify performance hotspots and optimize resource usage.
Resource Allocation: Configure appropriate resource limits (CPU, memory, disk space) based on profiling results to ensure optimal performance.
Logging and Monitoring
Logging: Implement robust logging mechanisms using frameworks like Log4j, SLF4J, or java.util.logging to capture application events and errors.
Monitoring: Set up monitoring tools like Prometheus, Grafana, or New Relic to track application performance, health, and usage metrics in real-time.
Alerts: Configure alerts for critical issues or performance degradation to enable timely intervention and resolution.
Deployment Readiness Checklist
Environment Setup: Ensure that the target environment (servers, databases, networks) is properly configured and ready for deployment.
Backup and Rollback: Create backups of the current production environment and have a rollback plan in place in case the deployment needs to be reverted.
Final Testing: Perform a final round of testing in a staging environment that closely resembles the production setup.

5.5.4 Deploying WAR Files

Deploying WAR (Web Application Archive) files is a critical aspect of Java EE (Enterprise Edition) application development. A WAR file packages web components such as servlets, JavaServer Pages (JSPs), Java classes, and static content, and is deployed to a Java EE application server to run web applications. This section provides a detailed guide on deploying WAR files for an advanced Java audience.

Preparing the WAR File

A WAR file follows a specific directory structure that the Java EE server uses to deploy the web application. Key components include:

WEB-INF Directory: Contains the deployment descriptor (web.xml), server-side classes, and libraries.

web.xml: Specifies servlet configurations, servlet mappings, filters, listeners, and other web application settings.

classes/: Contains compiled Java class files.

lib/: Contains JAR files required by the application.

META-INF Directory: Contains metadata about the web application.

MANIFEST.MF: Provides metadata about the WAR file, such as version and class-path.

Static Resources: HTML, CSS, JavaScript files, images, and other static content.

Example Directory Structure:

```
myapp.war
|-- META-INF/
|   |-- MANIFEST.MF
|-- WEB-INF/
|   |-- web.xml
|   |-- classes/
|   |   |-- com/
|   |   |   |-- example/
|   |   |       |-- MyServlet.class
|   |-- lib/
|       |-- dependency.jar
|-- index.html
|-- styles.css
|-- script.js
```

Creating the WAR File

Use a build tool like Apache Maven, Gradle, or the jar command to package your web application into a WAR file.

Using Maven

Define the project in a pom.xml file with war packaging.

Package the application

mvn clean package

Using Gradle

Define the project in a build.gradle file with the war plugin.

Package the application

gradle clean build

Setting Up the Application Server

Ensure the Java EE application server is installed and configured. Popular servers include Apache Tomcat, GlassFish, WildFly (formerly JBoss), and WebLogic.

Example: Setting Up Apache Tomcat

Download and install Apache Tomcat.

Configure Tomcat by editing configuration files such as server.xml and context.xml if needed.

Start the Tomcat server using the provided scripts (e.g., startup.sh for Unix/Linux or startup.bat for Windows).

Deploying the WAR File

Access the server's management console (e.g., Tomcat Manager, GlassFish Admin Console).

Navigate to the deployment section.

Upload the WAR file and deploy it through the web interface.

Copying to the Deployment Directory

Copy the WAR file to the server's deployment directory (e.g., webapps in Tomcat).

The server automatically detects and deploys the WAR file.

Using Command Line Tools

Some servers provide command-line tools for deployment.

For example, to deploy a WAR file to GlassFish using asadmin: asadmin deploy myapp.war

Verifying the Deployment

After deployment, verify that the web application is running correctly.

Access the application using a web browser at the application's URL (e.g., http://localhost:8080/myapp).
Configuring the Environment
Environment-Specific Configurations: Manage different configurations for development, testing, and production environments. Use context parameters in web.xml or external configuration files.
Database Connections: Configure database connections and data sources in the server's configuration files.
Logging: Configure logging using frameworks like Log4j, SLF4J, or java.util.logging to capture application logs.
Monitoring and Managing the Application
Logging: Implement robust logging mechanisms to track application events and errors.
Monitoring: Set up monitoring tools to track application performance, health, and usage metrics in real-time. Use tools like Prometheus, Grafana, or New Relic.
Alerts: Configure alerts for critical issues or performance degradation to enable timely intervention and resolution.
Updating and Undeploying Applications
Updating: To update an application, undeploy the existing version and deploy the new WAR file.
Undeploying: Use the management console or remove the WAR file from the deployment directory to undeploy an application.
Example: Undeploying in Tomcat:
Access the Tomcat Manager.
Locate the application in the list of deployed applications.
Click the "Undeploy" button next to the application.

5.5.5 Best Practices for Deployment

Deploying Java EE applications effectively is crucial to ensure they run smoothly, securely, and efficiently in production environments. Here are some best practices for deployment, tailored for advanced Java developers:
Automate the Deployment Process
CI/CD Pipelines: Implement Continuous Integration and Continuous Deployment (CI/CD) pipelines using tools like Jenkins, GitLab CI, or Travis CI. Automation reduces manual errors and ensures consistency across deployments.
Build Automation: Use build tools like Maven or Gradle to automate the process of building, packaging, and deploying your applications.
Configuration Management
Externalize Configuration: Keep configuration settings outside the codebase. Use environment variables, properties files, or configuration servers (like Spring Cloud Config) to manage settings.
Environment-Specific Configurations: Maintain separate configurations for development, testing, staging, and production environments to avoid issues caused by environment-specific settings.
Security Best Practices
Secure Sensitive Data: Manage sensitive information such as database credentials, API keys, and encryption keys securely using tools like HashiCorp Vault or AWS Secrets Manager.
TLS/SSL: Ensure that all communication between clients and servers is encrypted using TLS/SSL.
Access Control: Implement strict access control policies, ensuring that only authorized personnel can deploy or modify applications.
Testing
Automated Testing: Integrate automated testing into your CI/CD pipeline to ensure code quality and functionality. This includes unit tests, integration tests, and end-to-end tests.
Performance Testing: Conduct performance tests using tools like JMeter or Gatling to ensure the application can handle expected load and stress conditions.
Security Testing: Perform regular security testing, including vulnerability scanning and penetration testing, to identify and mitigate potential security issues.
Monitoring and Logging
Centralized Logging: Implement centralized logging using tools like ELK Stack (Elasticsearch, Logstash, Kibana) or Splunk to collect and analyze logs from all application components.
Real-Time Monitoring: Use monitoring tools such as Prometheus, Grafana, or New Relic to monitor application performance, availability, and health in real-time.
Alerts and Notifications: Set up alerts for critical issues and performance anomalies to enable prompt responses.
Resource Management
Resource Allocation: Allocate resources (CPU, memory, disk) appropriately based on profiling and load testing results to ensure optimal performance.

Scalability: Design your application to be horizontally scalable, allowing it to handle increased load by adding more instances.

Database Management

Migrations: Use database migration tools like Liquibase or Flyway to manage database schema changes in a controlled and versioned manner.

Backups: Regularly back up your database and ensure that backup and restore processes are tested and reliable.

Blue-Green Deployment

Minimize Downtime: Use blue-green deployment strategies to minimize downtime during deployments. This involves maintaining two identical production environments (blue and green) and switching traffic between them during deployments.

Rollback Strategy

Plan for Rollbacks: Have a rollback plan in place in case a deployment introduces critical issues. Ensure that your CI/CD pipeline supports rolling back to previous stable versions of the application.

Documentation

Deployment Documentation: Maintain detailed documentation of the deployment process, including prerequisites, configuration settings, and steps for deployment and rollback.

Runbooks: Create runbooks for handling common issues and incidents to assist the operations team in troubleshooting and resolving problems quickly.

Compliance and Auditing

Compliance Checks: Ensure your deployment process complies with relevant regulations and standards, such as GDPR, HIPAA, or PCI-DSS.

Audit Trails: Maintain audit trails for all deployment activities to track changes and identify who deployed what and when.

User Feedback and Iteration

Collect Feedback: Gather feedback from users and stakeholders after deployments to identify areas for improvement.

Continuous Improvement: Continuously iterate on your deployment process based on feedback and lessons learned from previous deployments.

Exercise

Exercise 1 - MCQ

1. What is the purpose of a JAR file in Java?
a) To compress image files
b) To collect Java class files and associated metadata and resources
c) To enhance the performance of Java applications
d) To provide additional security features for Java applications
2. Which command is used to create a JAR file?
a) Javac
b) jar
c) Java
d) javap
3. What does WAR stand for in the context of Java web applications?
a) Web Archive
b) Web Application Resources
c) Web Assembly Resources
d) Wide Area Network
4. Which of the following is true about WAR files?
a) They are used to package desktop applications.
b) They can only include HTML and CSS files.
c) They include Java class files, JSPs, libraries, and static web resources.
d) They are not deployable on Java EE application servers.
5. What is the first step in building a JAR file?
a) Packaging resources
b) Compiling Java source code
c) Creating a manifest file
d) Testing the application

6. Which file is crucial for specifying an entry point in a JAR file?
a) CLASSPATH file
b) MANIFEST.MF
c) build.xml
d) application.properties
7. What is the main difference between JAR and WAR files?
a) JAR files are larger.
b) WAR files are used for web applications.
c) JAR files cannot include XML files.
d) WAR files cannot include Java class files.
8. In the context of WAR files, what is the standard directory for servlet classes?
a) /src
b) /WEB-INF/classes
c) /lib
d) /META-INF
9. How can you deploy a JAR file as a standalone application?
a) By running it through a web server
b) By executing the java command with the JAR file as an argument
c) By uploading it to a Java EE application server
d) By converting it to a WAR file first
10. Which of the following tools can be used to build WAR files?
a) Maven
b) Notepad
c) Windows Explorer
d) Microsoft Word

Exercise 2 -True/False
1. A JAR file can include both Java class files and resource files such as images and text files.
2. WAR files are exclusively used for desktop applications.
3. The javac command is used to create JAR files from compiled Java classes.
4. A WAR file can be deployed to a Java EE application server to run a web application.
5. The MANIFEST.MF file cannot specify the main class in a JAR file.
6. JAR files are used to distribute Java libraries and frameworks.
7. Servlet classes and JSPs are stored in the WEB-INF/classes directory inside a WAR file.
8.To deploy a WAR file, you must manually extract its contents into the application server's deployment directory.
9. Maven can be used to automate the process of building both JAR and WAR files.
10. The web.xml file is optional in Servlet 3.0 and newer web applications.

Exercise 3 - Fill in the blanks
1. To compile Java source code into bytecode, the ______ command is used before packaging into a JAR file.
2. A JAR file's manifest file, which can specify the application's entry point, is located in the ______ directory.
3. The standard directory for placing JSPs, HTML files, and CSS in a WAR file is the ______ directory.
4. To deploy a standalone application packaged as a JAR, the java -jar command is followed by the ______.
5. In a Maven project, the file that defines the project's build configuration, including its dependencies, is named ______.
6. The ________ manifest file is a special file contained within a JAR that can define various metadata about the JAR file.
7. A typical web.xml file includes elements such as <servlet>, <servlet-mapping>, and <______>.
8. The Jib plugin for Maven and Gradle can be used to build optimized Docker images for Java applications without needing a ________ file.
9. Continuous Integration/Continuous Deployment (CI/CD) pipelines often use tools like Jenkins, Travis CI, or GitHub Actions to automate the process of building, testing, and ________ JAR and WAR files.
10. In Apache Tomcat, the conf/server.xml file is used to configure various settings, including ________ and ports.

Exercise 4- Match Case

1. Deploy a web application using WAR
2. Standard directory for Java source code
3. Command to execute an executable JAR
4. Location for application properties in a Maven project

A. src/main/java
B. java -jar
C. Java EE application server
D. src/main/resources

Exercise 5 - One word answer
1. What is the file extension for Java Archive files?
2. What is the Maven build phase that generates the packaged application?

Exercise 6 - Small answer
1. What is the primary purpose of the MANIFEST.MF file in a JAR archive?
2. How does Maven facilitate the building of WAR files for web applications?

Exercise 7- Long answer
1. Explain the process of deploying a WAR file to a Java EE application server. Include the steps from building the WAR file to accessing the deployed application.
2. Describe the role of Maven in building and managing Java projects, specifically focusing on how it handles dependencies and simplifies the build process for both JAR and WAR files.

Answer
Exercise 1- 1) b, 2) b, 3) a, 4) c, 5) b, 6) b, 7) b, 8) b, 9) b, 10) a
Exercise 2 – 1) True 2) False 3) False 4) True 5) False 6) True 7) True 8) False 9) True 10) True
Exercise 3 -1) javac 2) META-INF 3) src/main/webapp 4) JAR file name 5) pom.xml 6) MANIFEST.MF 7) welcome-file-list 8) Dockerfile 9) deploying, 10) connectors
Exercise 4 - 1 – C. Java EE application server 2 – A. src/main/java 3 – B. java -jar 4 – D. src/main/resources
Exercise 5- 1) jar 2) package

Online Resources

Online Practice Paper

Link: https://forms.gle/4bfqqAKSv2Yrb65v8
QR Code:

YouTube Video Link

Link: https://www.youtube.com/playlist?list=PLzlh_31VWEFpMZfsWV2xV3X89dvL3CFJd
QR Code:

CHAPTER 6 - Basics of Web Application Development

6.1 Introduction

Web application development is a cornerstone of modern software engineering, enabling the creation of applications accessible over the Internet through web browsers. It encompasses a broad range of practices and technologies, integrating various disciplines such as front-end development, back-end development, database management, and deployment processes.

Front-End Development

The front-end of a web application, also known as the client-side, is what users interact with directly. It involves the design and development of the user interface (UI) and user experience (UX). Key technologies for front-end development include HTML, CSS, and JavaScript.

HTML (Hyper Text Markup Language): This is the standard markup language used to create the structure of web pages. HTML elements form the building blocks of web pages, allowing developers to embed text, images, and other media.

CSS (Cascading Style Sheets): CSS is used to style and layout web pages. It allows developers to apply styles, such as colours, fonts, and spacing, to HTML elements, ensuring that web pages are visually appealing and consistent across different devices.

JavaScript: This is a powerful scripting language that enables interactive and dynamic behaviour on web pages. JavaScript can manipulate HTML and CSS, handle events, validate forms, and interact with web APIs to fetch or send data asynchronously.

Modern front-end development often utilizes frameworks and libraries like React, Angular, and Vue.js, which help manage the complexity of building dynamic and responsive user interfaces.

Back-End Development

The back-end, or server-side, of a web application handles the logic, database interactions, user authentication, and data processing. It is responsible for receiving requests from the front-end, processing them, and sending appropriate responses.

Server-Side Languages: Popular languages for back-end development include Java, Python, Ruby, PHP, and JavaScript (Node.js). Each of these languages has its frameworks and libraries to streamline development, such as Spring Boot for Java, Django for Python, and Express for Node.js.

Databases: Databases are used to store and manage data. They can be relational (SQL) like MySQL, PostgreSQL, and Oracle, or non-relational (NoSQL) like MongoDB and Cassandra. The choice of database depends on the application's requirements, such as the need for complex queries or scalability.

APIs (Application Programming Interfaces): APIs enable communication between different parts of a web application or with external services. RESTful APIs and Graph QL are common approaches for structuring these communications.

Full-Stack Development

Full-stack development refers to the ability to work on both the front-end and back-end parts of a web application. Full-stack developers have a comprehensive understanding of the entire web development process, allowing them to build and maintain entire web applications.

Development Tools and Practices

Several tools and practices are essential for effective web application development

Version Control: Systems like Git enable developers to track changes in code, collaborate with others, and manage different versions of the application.

Development Environments: Integrated Development Environments (IDEs) like Visual Studio Code, IntelliJ IDEA, and WebStorm provide features like syntax highlighting, debugging, and code completion.

Testing: Automated testing tools and frameworks such as JUnit, Selenium, and Jest help ensure that web applications are reliable and perform well.

Deployment: Deployment involves making a web application available on the internet. This process can involve web servers (like Apache and Nginx), cloud services (like AWS, Azure, and Google Cloud), and containerization technologies (like Docker and Kubernetes).

6.2 What is a Web Application?

A web application is a software application that runs on a web server and can be accessed via a web browser. Unlike traditional desktop applications, which are launched by your operating system, web applications must be accessed through a network, often the internet. In the context of advanced Java programming, developing web applications involves understanding and using several key technologies and frameworks that facilitate the creation, deployment, and management of these applications.

Key Components of a Web Application

Client-Side Technologies

HTML (HyperText Markup Language): The standard language for creating web pages and web applications.

CSS (Cascading Style Sheets): Used for describing the presentation of a document written in HTML.

JavaScript: A scripting language that enables interactive web pages.

Server-Side Technologies

Java Servlets: Java programming language classes that dynamically process requests and construct responses. They run on the server side.

JavaServer Pages (JSP): A technology that allows for the creation of dynamically generated web pages based on HTML, XML, or other document types.

JavaServer Faces (JSF): A Java framework for building user interfaces for web applications.

Spring Framework: A comprehensive framework that supports the creation of web applications, with features like dependency injection, aspect-oriented programming, and integration with various data access technologies.

Hibernate: An ORM (Object-Relational Mapping) tool that simplifies data handling in Java applications by mapping Java objects to database tables.

Web Servers and Application Servers

Apache Tomcat: An open-source implementation of the Java Servlet, JavaServer Pages, and Java Expression Language technologies.

Jetty: A lightweight and scalable web server and servlet container.

JBoss EAP: A Java EE-based application server used for building, deploying, and hosting highly-transactional Java applications and services.

GlassFish: An open-source application server for the Java EE platform.

Databases

Relational Databases: MySQL, PostgreSQL, Oracle Database.

NoSQL Databases: MongoDB, Cassandra, CouchDB.

Architecture of a Web Application

A typical web application follows a multi-tiered architecture that separates the user interface, business logic, and data storage.

Presentation Tier (Client-Side): This is the front-end part of the application that the user interacts with directly. It includes HTML, CSS, and JavaScript.

Application Tier (Server-Side): This layer contains the business logic of the application. It is implemented using Java Servlets, JSP, JSF, or Spring MVC.

Data Tier (Database): This layer manages data storage and retrieval. It interacts with the application tier through JDBC (Java Database Connectivity) or ORM frameworks like Hibernate.

Lifecycle of a Web Application

Request Handling: The web server receives a request from the client.

Processing: The server processes the request using servlets, JSP, or other server-side technologies.

Response Generation: The server generates a response (HTML, JSON, XML, etc.) and sends it back to the client.

Rendering: The client's browser renders the response for the user to view and interact with.

Security Considerations

Security is a crucial aspect of web application development. Common security practices include:

Authentication and Authorization: Ensuring users are who they claim to be and have permission to access resources.

Encryption: Using HTTPS to secure data transmission between the client and server.

Input Validation: Preventing injection attacks (e.g., SQL injection, XSS) by validating and sanitizing user inputs.

Advanced Topics
RESTful Web Services: Building scalable web services using REST principles, which involve using HTTP methods (GET, POST, PUT, DELETE) to operate on resources.
Microservices Architecture: Breaking down a monolithic application into smaller, independent services that communicate over HTTP.
WebSockets: Enabling real-time communication between the client and server over a single, long-lived connection.
Asynchronous Processing: Using Java EE features like JMS (Java Message Service) and EJB (Enterprise JavaBeans) to handle background tasks and improve application responsiveness.

Example: A Simple Web Application Using Java Servlets and JSP
Directory Structure

```
webapp/
  WEB-INF/
    web.xml
    classes/
    lib/
  index.jsp
  login.jsp
  welcome.jsp
```

web.xml (Deployment Descriptor)

```
<web-app>
    <servlet>
        <servlet-name>LoginServlet</servlet-name>
        <servlet-class>com.example.LoginServlet</servlet-class>
    </servlet>
    <servlet-mapping>
        <servlet-name>LoginServlet</servlet-name>
        <url-pattern>/login</url-pattern>
    </servlet-mapping>
</web-app>
```

```
package com.example;
import java.io.IOException;
import javax.servlet.ServletException;
import javax.servlet.annotation.WebServlet;
import javax.servlet.http.HttpServlet;
import javax.servlet.http.HttpServletRequest;
import javax.servlet.http.HttpServletResponse;
@WebServlet("/login")
public class LoginServlet extends HttpServlet {
    protected void doPost(HttpServletRequest request, HttpServletResponse response)
            throws ServletException, IOException {
        String username = request.getParameter("username");
        String password = request.getParameter("password");
        if ("admin".equals(username) && "password".equals(password)) {
            request.getRequestDispatcher("welcome.jsp").forward(request, response);
        } else {
            response.sendRedirect("login.jsp");
        }
    }
}
```

login.jsp

```
<!DOCTYPE html>
<html>
<head>
   <title>Login</title>
</head>
<body>
   <form action="login" method="post">
      Username: <input type="text" name="username"><br>
      Password: <input type="password" name="password"><br>
      <input type="submit" value="Login">
   </form>
</body>
</html>
```

welcome.jsp:

```
<!DOCTYPE html>
<html>
<head>
   <title>Welcome</title>
</head>
<body>
   <h1>Welcome, admin!</h1>
</body>
</html>
```

Key Characteristics

Accessibility

Web applications are designed to be platform-independent. They can be accessed from any device with a web browser, regardless of the underlying operating system, whether it's Windows, macOS, Linux, or mobile operating systems like Android and iOS. This cross-platform accessibility makes web applications highly versatile and convenient for users.

User Interface

The front-end of a web application is developed using a combination of HTML, CSS, and JavaScript

HTML (HyperText Markup Language) provides the basic structure of the web application.

CSS (Cascading Style Sheets) is used to control the layout and presentation, ensuring that the application is visually appealing and consistent.

JavaScript adds interactivity and dynamic behaviour, enabling features like form validation, asynchronous content updates (AJAX), and enhanced user experiences without the need to reload the page.

Modern front-end development often utilizes frameworks and libraries like React, Angular, and Vue.js, which simplify the process of building complex, interactive user interfaces.

Client-Server Architecture

Web applications operate on a client-server model

Client-Side (Front-End): Runs on the user's browser, handling the presentation and user interaction. The client sends requests to the server and processes the responses to update the UI.

Server-Side (Back-End): Runs on the web server, handling business logic, database interactions, and processing client requests. Common server-side languages include Java, Python, Ruby, PHP, and JavaScript (Node.js).

The server-side component processes incoming requests, interacts with databases, performs computations, and sends responses back to the client-side, which then updates the user interface accordingly.

Interactivity

Modern web applications are designed to be interactive and responsive, providing a user experience similar to that of desktop applications. This is achieved through the use of advanced front-end technologies and practices, such as:

Single Page Applications (SPAs): These applications load a single HTML page and dynamically update content as the user interacts with the app. Frameworks like React and Angular are commonly used to build SPAs.

Progressive Web Apps (PWAs): These are web applications that use modern web capabilities to deliver an app-like experience. They can work offline, send push notifications, and be installed on the user's device.

Data Management
Web applications often require data storage and retrieval. This is managed through databases, which can be either relational (SQL) like MySQL, PostgreSQL, and Oracle, or non-relational (NoSQL) like MongoDB and Cassandra. The choice of database depends on the application's requirements, such as the need for complex queries, scalability, and data structure.
Deployment
Deployment of web applications involves making the application available on a web server, which can be hosted on-premises or in the cloud (e.g., AWS, Azure, Google Cloud). The deployment process often includes:
Version Control: Systems like Git manage source code changes and facilitate collaboration among developers.
Continuous Integration and Continuous Deployment (CI/CD): These pipelines automate the process of testing, building, and deploying the application, ensuring rapid and reliable updates.
Containerization: Tools like Docker and orchestration platforms like Kubernetes help manage application deployment, scaling, and management in a consistent and reproducible environment.

Examples
Common examples of web applications include
Email Services: Such as Gmail and Outlook.
Online Banking: Platforms that allow users to manage their bank accounts online.
Social Media: Websites like Facebook, Twitter, and Instagram.
E-Commerce: Platforms like Amazon and eBay.
Productivity Tools: Applications like Google Docs, Trello, and Slack.

1.3 Understanding Web Clients and Servers

Web Clients
A web client is an application that communicates with a web server over a network. Web browsers are the most common type of web client, but other types include mobile apps and command-line tools.
Key Technologies and Concepts:
HTML (HyperText Markup Language): The standard language for creating and structuring web pages.
CSS (Cascading Style Sheets): Used for styling and layout of web pages.
JavaScript: A scripting language that enables interactive features and dynamic content.
AJAX (Asynchronous JavaScript and XML): Allows web pages to be updated asynchronously by exchanging data with a web server behind the scenes.
Frameworks and Libraries
React: A JavaScript library for building user interfaces.
Angular: A TypeScript-based open-source front-end web application platform.
Vue.js: A progressive JavaScript framework for building user interfaces.

Example: A Simple HTML and JavaScript Client:

```
<!DOCTYPE html>
<html>
<head>
  <title>Simple Web Client</title>
  <script>
    function fetchData() {
      fetch('http://example.com/data')
        .then(response => response.json())
        .then(data => {
          document.getElementById('content').innerHTML = data.message;
        });
    }
  </script>
</head>
<body>
  <button onclick="fetchData()">Fetch Data</button>
  <div id="content"></div>
</body>
</html>
```

This example demonstrates how a simple HTML page can fetch and display data from a server using JavaScript.

Web Servers

A web server handles incoming requests from clients, processes them, and returns the appropriate response. In Java web development, the server-side typically manages business logic, data processing, and database interactions.

Key Technologies and Concepts

Servlets: Java classes that handle HTTP requests and responses.
JSP (JavaServer Pages): Enables embedding Java code in HTML to generate dynamic web content.

Frameworks

Spring MVC: Part of the Spring Framework, it follows the Model-View-Controller (MVC) design pattern.
JavaServer Faces (JSF): A Java framework for building component-based user interfaces for web applications.

Application Servers

Apache Tomcat: An open-source implementation of Java Servlet, JSP, and WebSocket technologies.
Jetty: A highly scalable and flexible web server and servlet container.
JBoss EAP: An enterprise-grade application server for building, deploying, and hosting highly-transactional Java applications and services.
GlassFish: An open-source application server for the Java EE platform.

Example: A Java Servlet Handling a GET Request
web.xml (Deployment Descriptor)

```
<web-app>
   <servlet>
      <servlet-name>DataServlet</servlet-name>
      <servlet-class>com.example.DataServlet</servlet-class>
   </servlet>
   <servlet-mapping>
      <servlet-name>DataServlet</servlet-name>
      <url-pattern>/data</url-pattern>
   </servlet-mapping>
</web-app>
```

DataServlet.java

```
package com.example;
import java.io.IOException;
import javax.servlet.ServletException;
import javax.servlet.annotation.WebServlet;
import javax.servlet.http.HttpServlet;
import javax.servlet.http.HttpServletRequest;
import javax.servlet.http.HttpServletResponse;
import org.json.JSONObject;
@WebServlet("/data")
public class DataServlet extends HttpServlet {
   protected void doGet(HttpServletRequest request, HttpServletResponse response)
         throws ServletException, IOException {
      response.setContentType("application/json");
      JSONObject json = new JSONObject();
      json.put("message", "Hello, World!");
      response.getWriter().write(json.toString());
   }
}
```

In this example, the DataServlet processes a GET request to the /data endpoint and returns a JSON response.

Client-Server Communication

Web clients and servers communicate using the HTTP protocol. This communication follows a request-response model

Request Methods
GET: Retrieve data from the server.
POST: Send data to the server to create or update a resource.
PUT: Update an existing resource on the server.
DELETE: Remove a resource from the server.
Request-Response Cycle
The client sends an HTTP request to the server.
The server processes the request, executes business logic, interacts with databases if necessary, and generates a response.
The server sends the HTTP response back to the client, which then renders the response to the user.

Example Request-Response Cycle
Client Request (HTTP GET)

```
GET /data HTTP/1.1
Host: example.com
```

Server Response (HTTP Response)

```
HTTP/1.1 200 OK
Content-Type: application/json
{
  "message": "Hello, World!"
}
```

Java Technologies for Web Development
Servlets: Core Java classes for handling HTTP requests and responses.
JSP (JavaServer Pages): Allows embedding Java code within HTML to create dynamic web pages.
JavaServer Faces (JSF): A framework for building component-based user interfaces for web applications.
Spring Framework
Spring MVC: A part of the Spring Framework that follows the Model-View-Controller design pattern for building web applications.
Spring Boot: Simplifies the setup and development of new Spring applications.
JAX-RS: Java API for creating RESTful web services.

6.4 Key Components of Web Applications

Web applications consist of multiple layers and components, each playing a crucial role in delivering a seamless user experience and ensuring robust application performance. In advanced Java development, understanding these components in detail is essential for designing and building sophisticated web applications.
Client-Side Technologies
HTML (HyperText Markup Language)
Role: Structures the content of web pages.
Features: Elements like <div>, <span>, <p>, and semantic elements like <header>, <footer>, <article>, etc.
CSS (Cascading Style Sheets)
Role: Styles HTML elements to enhance the visual presentation.
Features: Selectors, properties (e.g., color, font-size, margin), and layout models (e.g., Flexbox, Grid).
JavaScript
Role: Adds interactivity and dynamic Behaviour to web pages.
Features: DOM manipulation, event handling, asynchronous programming with Promises and async/await, and integration with APIs.
AJAX (Asynchronous JavaScript and XML)
Role: Allows web pages to be updated asynchronously without reloading.
Features: XMLHttpRequest, Fetch API, and JSON for data interchange.
Frameworks and Libraries
React: A JavaScript library for building user interfaces with components.
Angular: A platform and framework for building single-page client applications using HTML and TypeScript.
Vue.js: A progressive framework for building user interfaces with a simple and flexible API.
Server-Side Technologies
Java Servlets

Role: Handle client requests and generate responses.

Features: Lifecycle methods (init, service, destroy), request and response handling, and session management.

JavaServer Pages (JSP)

Role: Allows embedding Java code in HTML to create dynamic web pages.

Features: Directives (<%@ ... %>), scriptlets (<% ... %>), and JSP tags (<jsp:include>, <jsp:forward>).

JavaServer Faces (JSF)

Role: A component-based framework for building user interfaces.

Features: Managed beans, facelets, component libraries, and event handling.

Spring Framework

Spring MVC

Role: Implements the Model-View-Controller design pattern.

Features: DispatcherServlet, controllers, models, views, and form handling.

Spring Boot

Role: Simplifies Spring application development.

Features: Auto-configuration, embedded servers (Tomcat, Jetty), and starter dependencies.

Hibernate

Role: An ORM (Object-Relational Mapping) tool for database operations.

Features: Entity mapping, HQL (Hibernate Query Language), and session management.

Application Servers:

Apache Tomcat: A servlet container for running Java servlets and JSP.

Jetty: A lightweight web server and servlet container.

JBoss EAP: An enterprise-grade application server for Java EE applications.

GlassFish: An open-source application server for Java EE.

Data Tier

Relational Databases

Examples: MySQL, PostgreSQL, Oracle Database.

Features: SQL for querying and managing data, ACID properties, and transactional support.

NoSQL Databases

Examples: MongoDB, Cassandra, CouchDB.

Features: Schema-less data models, horizontal scaling, and flexibility in handling unstructured data.

Java Database Connectivity (JDBC)

Role: Provides an API for connecting and executing queries on databases.

Features: Connection management, statement execution (Statement, PreparedStatement), and result set processing.

JPA (Java Persistence API)

Role: A specification for managing relational data in Java applications.

Features: Annotations (@Entity, @Table, @Id), entity lifecycle management, and JPQL (Java Persistence Query Language).

Web Servers and Application Servers

Web Servers

Role: Handle HTTP requests and serve static content (HTML, CSS, JavaScript, images).

Examples: Apache HTTP Server, Nginx.

Application Servers

Role: Provide an environment to run web applications, manage resources, and offer services like transaction management and security.

Examples: Apache Tomcat, Jetty, JBoss EAP, GlassFish.

Security Components

Authentication and Authorization

Role: Verify user identity and control access to resources.

Technologies: Spring Security, JAAS (Java Authentication and Authorization Service).

Encryption

Role: Secure data transmission and storage.

Technologies: SSL/TLS for HTTPS, JCE (Java Cryptography Extension).

Input Validation and Sanitization

Role: Prevent security vulnerabilities like SQL injection and XSS (Cross-Site Scripting).

Technologies: Validation frameworks (Hibernate Validator), encoding libraries (OWASP ESAPI).

Additional Components
RESTful Web Services:
Role: Build scalable web services using REST principles.
Technologies: JAX-RS (Jersey, RESTEasy), Spring REST.
Microservices Architecture
Role: Decompose applications into smaller, independently deployable services.
Technologies: Spring Cloud, Docker, Kubernetes.
Asynchronous Processing
Role: Handle long-running tasks without blocking server resources.
Technologies: Async servlets, JMS (Java Message Service), WebSockets.

Example: A Complete Web Application Architecture
Directory Structure

```
webapp/
  WEB-INF/
    web.xml
    classes/
    lib/
  index.jsp
  login.jsp
  welcome.jsp
src/
  main/
    java/
      com/
        example/
          controller/
            LoginServlet.java
          model/
            User.java
          service/
            UserService.java
          repository/
            UserRepository.java
resources/
  application.properties
  static/
    css/
      styles.css
    js/
      scripts.js
  templates/
    login.html
    welcome.html
```

web.xml

```
<web-app>
    <servlet>
        <servlet-name>LoginServlet</servlet-name>
        <servlet-class>com.example.controller.LoginServlet</servlet-class>
    </servlet>
    <servlet-mapping>
        <servlet-name>LoginServlet</servlet-name>
        <url-pattern>/login</url-pattern>
    </servlet-mapping>
</web-app>
```

LoginServlet.java

```
package com.example.controller;
import java.io.IOException;
import javax.servlet.ServletException;
import javax.servlet.annotation.WebServlet;
import javax.servlet.http.HttpServlet;
import javax.servlet.http.HttpServletRequest;
import javax.servlet.http.HttpServletResponse;
import com.example.service.UserService;
@WebServlet("/login")
public class LoginServlet extends HttpServlet {
   private UserService userService = new UserService();
   protected void doPost(HttpServletRequest request, HttpServletResponse response)
         throws ServletException, IOException {
      String username = request.getParameter("username");
      String password = request.getParameter("password");
      if (userService.authenticate(username, password)) {
         request.getRequestDispatcher("welcome.jsp").forward(request, response);
      } else {
         response.sendRedirect("login.jsp");
      }
   }
}
```

UserService.java

```
package com.example.service;
import com.example.model.User;
import com.example.repository.UserRepository;
public class UserService {
   private UserRepository userRepository = new UserRepository();
   public boolean authenticate(String username, String password) {
      User user = userRepository.findByUsername(username);
      return user != null && user.getPassword().equals(password);
   }
}
```

UserRepository.java

```
package com.example.repository;
import com.example.model.User;
import java.util.HashMap;
import java.util.Map;
public class UserRepository {
   private static Map<String, User> users = new HashMap<>();
   static {
      users.put("admin", new User("admin", "password"));
   }
   public User findByUsername(String username) {
      return users.get(username);
   }
}
```

User.java

```
package com.example.model;
public class User {
   private String username;
```

```
    private String password;
    public User(String username, String password) {
        this.username = username;
        this.password = password;
    }
    public String getUsername() {
        return username;
    }
    public String getPassword() {
        return password;
    }
}
```

This example illustrates a basic web application structure with user authentication functionality. It highlights the integration of various components, including servlets, JSP, a service layer, and a repository for data management.

6.5 HTTP Protocol Basics

The HyperText Transfer Protocol (HTTP) is the foundation of any data exchange on the Web and it is a protocol used for transmitting hypertext requests and information between servers and clients. Understanding HTTP is crucial for advanced Java developers as it is the basis for web communication. This section delves into the core concepts, methods, and statuses of HTTP, providing a comprehensive guide for Java web development.

HTTP is an application-layer protocol used primarily for distributed, collaborative, hypermedia information systems. It follows a client-server model where the client sends requests and the server returns responses.

6.5.1 The Nature of HTTP

HTTP is a stateless protocol that operates as a request-response system. This means each request from a client to a server is independent; the server does not retain session information between requests. Here's a breakdown of the key concepts

Stateless Protocol: HTTP is inherently a stateless protocol, meaning that each request from a client to a server is independent, and the server does not retain any state information between different requests. Here's a deeper look into what this entails:

Independence of Requests: Each HTTP request is self-contained and must carry all the information needed for the server to fulfill it. The server does not remember previous requests from the same client.

Scalability: Statelessness allows servers to handle a large number of requests efficiently because there is no need to maintain session information between requests. This simplifies server design and can enhance performance and scalability.

Challenges: Statelessness can complicate scenarios where continuous interaction or session tracking is required, such as user authentication, shopping carts, or complex transactions.

Request-Response Model: HTTP operates on a simple, yet powerful, request-response model. Here's a detailed look at this model

Client-Server Architecture: In the HTTP model, a client (usually a web browser or other HTTP client) sends a request to the server. The server, which hosts the website or web application, processes this request and returns a response.

Request: The client initiates communication by sending an HTTP request to the server. This request contains:

Request Line: Includes the HTTP method (e.g., GET, POST), the URI (Uniform Resource Identifier), and the HTTP version.

Headers: Provide metadata about the request, such as User-Agent, Accept, Content-Type, etc.

Body: Optional, typically used with methods like POST and PUT to send data to the server.

Example of a GET request:

```
GET /index.html HTTP/1.1
Host: example.com
User-Agent: Mozilla/5.0
Accept: text/html
```

Response: The server processes the request and sends back an HTTP response. This response contains

Status Line: Includes the HTTP version, status code (e.g., 200 OK, 404 Not Found), and a reason phrase.

Headers: Provide metadata about the response, such as Content-Type, Content-Length, etc.

Body: The actual content, such as HTML, JSON, or other data.

Example of an HTTP response:

```
HTTP/1.1 200 OK
Content-Type: text/html
Content-Length: 138
<html>
<head><title>Example</title></head>
<body><h1>Hello, World!</h1></body>
</html>
```

6.5.2 Components of HTTP Requests and Responses

HTTP Requests comprise several parts: HTTP requests typically consist of the following components

Request Line: The first line of an HTTP request, which includes the HTTP method, the resource identifier (URI), and the HTTP version.

Example: GET /index.html HTTP/1.1

Headers: Headers provide additional information about the request, such as the user agent, content type, cookies, and more. They are key-value pairs separated by a colon.

Example:

Host: www.example.com
User-Agent: Mozilla/5.0
Accept: text/html,application/xhtml+xml,application/xml;q=0.9,image/webp,*/*;q=0.8

Body: The optional body of the request contains data being sent to the server, typically used with methods like POST, PUT, and PATCH.

Example (POST request body):

username=user&password=pass123

HTTP Responses contain: HTTP responses consist of the following components

Status Line: The first line of an HTTP response, which includes the HTTP version, the status code, and a reason phrase.

Example: HTTP/1.1 200 OK

Headers: Similar to request headers, response headers provide additional information about the response, such as content type, content length, server information, and more.

Example:

Content-Type: text/html
Content-Length: 1024
Server: Apache

Body: The body of the response contains the actual content being sent from the server to the client. This can be HTML for web pages, JSON for API responses, binary data, or any other type of content.

Example (HTML response body):

```
<!DOCTYPE html>
<html>
<head>
<title>Example Page</title>
</head>
<body>
<h1>Hello, World!</h1>
</body>
</html>
```

Advanced Concepts in HTTP Requests and Responses

Content Negotiation**:** Clients and servers can negotiate the content type and encoding using headers like Accept and Content-Type.

Conditional Requests: Clients can include headers like If-Modified-Since or If-None-Match to perform conditional GET requests, reducing bandwidth usage.

Authentication: HTTP provides various mechanisms for authentication, such as Basic Authentication, Digest Authentication, and Token-based Authentication.

Compression: Both requests and responses can be compressed using algorithms like gzip or deflate to reduce bandwidth usage and improve performance.

Chunked Transfer Encoding: Allows the server to send the response in chunks, which is useful for large responses or when the content length is not known in advance.

Caching: Clients and servers can use caching mechanisms to store and reuse responses, reducing latency and bandwidth usage.

Redirection: Servers can issue redirection responses (status codes 3xx) to instruct clients to retrieve a resource from a different location.

6.5.3 Understanding HTTP Methods

Understanding HTTP methods is crucial for advanced Java developers building web applications and APIs. HTTP methods define the actions that clients can perform on resources hosted on a web server. Here's an in-depth explanation of common HTTP methods

Common HTTP Methods

GET: The GET method requests data from a specified resource. It should only retrieve data and should not have any side effects on the server. GET requests can be cached, bookmarked, and shared. They should be idempotent, meaning that making the same request multiple times should produce the same result.

Example: Retrieving information about a user profile. GET /users/123 HTTP/1.1

POST: The POST method submits data to be processed to a specified resource. It can create a new resource, update existing resources, or perform other state-changing operations on the server. POST requests are not idempotent, meaning that making the same request multiple times may result in different outcomes.

Example: Creating a new user profile.

```
POST /users HTTP/1.1
Content-Type: application/json
{"name": "John Doe", "email": "john@example.com"}
```

PUT: The PUT method replaces all current representations of the target resource with the uploaded content. If the resource does not exist, PUT can create it. PUT requests are idempotent, meaning that making the same request multiple times has the same effect as making it once.

Example: Updating an existing user profile.

```
PUT /users/123 HTTP/1.1
Content-Type: application/json
{"name": "Jane Doe", "email": "jane@example.com"}
```

DELETE: The DELETE method removes the specified resource from the server. After a successful DELETE request, the resource should no longer be available. DELETE requests are idempotent, meaning that making the same request multiple times has the same effect as making it once.

Example: Deleting a user profile.

```
DELETE /users/123 HTTP/1.1
```

PATCH: The PATCH method is used to apply partial modifications to a resource. It is typically used to update specific fields of an existing resource without replacing the entire resource. PATCH requests are not guaranteed to be idempotent.

Example: Updating only the email address of a user profile.

```
PATCH /users/123 HTTP/1.1
Content-Type: application/json
{"email": "updated_email@example.com"}
```

HEAD: The HEAD method is similar to GET, but it only retrieves the headers of the response without the body. It is often used to check the status of a resource or to retrieve metadata about a resource without downloading the entire content.
Example: Checking if a resource exists without downloading it.
HEAD /users/123 HTTP/1.1
OPTIONS: The OPTIONS method is used to describe the communication options for the target resource. It can be used to retrieve information about the supported methods, headers, and other capabilities of a server.
Example: Checking the allowed methods for a resource.
OPTIONS /users/123 HTTP/1.1

Using HTTP Methods in Java
Java developers can use various libraries and frameworks to work with HTTP methods:
Using HttpURLConnection: A built-in Java class for making HTTP requests. It provides methods like setRequestMethod to specify the HTTP method.
Using Apache HttpClient: A popular third-party library for sending HTTP requests and processing responses. It provides classes like HttpGet, HttpPost, HttpPut, etc., to work with different HTTP methods.
Using Java 11+ HttpClient: The java.net.http.HttpClient class introduced in Java 11 provides a modern API for working with HTTP requests. It offers methods like GET, POST, PUT, etc., to specify the HTTP method.

Status Codes

Understanding HTTP status codes is essential for advanced Java developers working with web applications and APIs. HTTP status codes provide information about the result of a client's request to the server. Here's a comprehensive explanation of common HTTP status codes:

Common HTTP Status Codes

1xx - Informational

100 Continue: The server has received the initial part of the request and is waiting for the client to send the remainder.
101 Switching Protocols: The server has received and is responding to a request to switch protocols, such as upgrading to WebSockets.

2xx - Success

200 OK: The request was successful. The response depends on the request method; for GET requests, the resource is returned.
201 Created: The request has been fulfilled, resulting in the creation of a new resource.
204 No Content: The server successfully processed the request, but there is no content to return.

3xx - Redirection

301 Moved Permanently: The requested resource has been permanently moved to a new location, and the client should update its bookmarks or links.
302 Found: The requested resource has been temporarily moved to a different location. The client should use the new URL for future requests.
304 Not Modified: The client's cached copy of the resource is still valid, and the server has not modified it since the last request.

4xx - Client Error

400 Bad Request: The server could not understand the request due to invalid syntax or other client-side errors.
401 Unauthorized: The request requires user authentication. The client must provide valid credentials.
403 Forbidden: The server understood the request, but the client is not allowed to access the requested resource.

5xx - Server Error

500 Internal Server Error: A generic error message indicating that something went wrong on the server's end.
502 Bad Gateway: The server received an invalid response from an upstream server while trying to fulfill the request.
503 Service Unavailable: The server is currently unable to handle the request due to temporary overloading or maintenance.

Using Status Codes in Java

Java developers can handle HTTP status codes when working with web applications and APIs using various libraries and frameworks:

Using HttpURLConnection: The HttpURLConnection class in Java provides methods like getResponseCode() to retrieve the status code from an HTTP response.

Example:

```
HttpURLConnection connection = (HttpURLConnection) url.openConnection();
int statusCode = connection.getResponseCode();
```

Using Apache HttpClient: The CloseableHttpResponse object returned by Apache HttpClient's request methods contains methods like getStatusLine() to retrieve the status line, from which the status code can be extracted.

Example:

```
CloseableHttpClient client = HttpClients.createDefault();
HttpGet request = new HttpGet("http://example.com");
CloseableHttpResponse response = client.execute(request);
int statusCode = response.getStatusLine().getStatusCode();
```

Using Java 11+ HttpClient: The HttpResponse object returned by Java 11+ HttpClient's request methods contains methods like statusCode() to retrieve the status code directly.

Example:

```
    HttpClient client = HttpClient.newHttpClient();
    HttpRequest request = HttpRequest.newBuilder()
      .uri(URI.create("http://example.com"))
      .build();
    HttpResponse<String> response = client.send(request, HttpResponse.BodyHandlers.ofString());
    int statusCode = response.statusCode();
```

1.6 Introduction to HTML

HTML (Hypertext Markup Language) is the standard language used to create and design web pages. Understanding HTML is fundamental for advanced Java developers building web applications and APIs. Here's an introduction to HTML:

HTML is a markup language used to structure and present content on the World Wide Web. It consists of a series of elements (tags) that define the structure and semantics of a web page's content. Web browsers interpret HTML code and render it as visual or audible web pages.

Key Concepts in HTML

Elements and Tags

Elements: HTML documents are made up of elements, each represented by an opening tag, content, and closing tag. Elements can also be self-closing.

Example

```
<p>This is a paragraph element.</p>
```

Tags: Tags are used to mark the beginning and end of HTML elements. They are enclosed in angle brackets (<>). Some tags, like <br> for line breaks, are self-closing.

Example

```
<h1>Heading 1</h1>
```

Attributes

Attributes provide additional information about an element and are specified within the opening tag. They are comprised of a name and a value, separated by an equal sign (=).

Example:

```
<a href="https://www.example.com">Visit Example</a>
```

Common HTML Elements

Headings: <h1> to <h6> for defining different levels of headings.

Paragraphs: <p> for defining paragraphs of text.

Links: <a> for creating hyperlinks to other pages or resources.

Images: <img> for embedding images into the page.

Lists: <ul>, <ol>, <li> for creating unordered and ordered lists.

Tables: <table>, <tr>, <td> for creating tabular data.

6.6.1 Basics of HTML

HTML documents are the building blocks of the web, defining the structure of web pages using markup. HTML elements are represented by tags, written using angle brackets. Most elements have an opening tag and a closing tag, with the content in between.

6.6.2 Structure of an HTML Document

An HTML document consists of several elements that define its structure, content, and presentation. Here's an overview of the main components

Document Type Declaration (<!DOCTYPE>)

The <!DOCTYPE> declaration specifies the document type and version of HTML being used. It ensures that the web browser renders the document correctly.

Example:

```
<!DOCTYPE html>
```

HTML Element (<html>)

The <html> element is the root element of the HTML document. It wraps all the content on the page.

Example:

```
<!DOCTYPE html>
<html lang="en">
<head>
<title>Document Title</title>
</head>
<body>
<!-- Content goes here -->
</body>
</html>
```

Head Element (<head>)

The <head> element contains meta-information about the document, such as the title, character encoding, and links to external resources like stylesheets and scripts.

Example:

```
<head>
<meta charset="UTF-8">
<title>Document Title</title>
<link rel="stylesheet" href="styles.css">
<script src="script.js"></script>
</head>
```

Title Element (<title>)

The <title> element specifies the title of the document, which appears in the browser's title bar or tab.

Example:

```
<title>Document Title</title>
```

Body Element (<body>)

The <body> element contains the visible content of the HTML document, including text, images, links, and other elements.

Example:

```
<body>
<h1>Hello, World!</h1>
<p>This is a paragraph.</p>
</body>
```

Heading Elements (<h1> to <h6>)
Heading elements define headings of different levels, with <h1> being the highest level and <h6> being the lowest level.
Example:

```
<h1>Main Heading</h1>
<h2>Subheading</h2>
```

Paragraph Element (<p>)
The <p> element defines a paragraph of text.
Example:

```
<p>This is a paragraph.</p>
```

Other Elements
Other common elements include links (<a>), images (<img>), lists (<ul>, <ol>, <li>), tables (<table>, <tr>, <td>), forms (<form>,
<input>,
<button>), and more.
Code

```
<!DOCTYPE html>
<html>
<head>
  <title>Page Title</title>
</head>
<body>
  <h1>My First Heading</h1>
  <p>My first paragraph.</p>
</body>
</html>
```

<!DOCTYPE html>: Declares the document type and version of HTML.
<html>: The root element of an HTML page.
<head>: Contains meta-information about the document, like its title.
<title>: Specifies the title of the document, shown in the browser's title bar or page's tab.
<body>: Contains the content of the document, such as text, images.

6.7 TCP/IP port and URL

TCP/IP (Transmission Control Protocol/Internet Protocol) is the suite of communication protocols used to connect devices on the internet. Ports are virtual endpoints for communication in TCP/IP networks. Each port is associated with a specific service or process on a device. Here are some key points about TCP/IP ports:
Port Number: Ports are identified by a numeric value ranging from 0 to 65535. Ports from 0 to 1023 are reserved for well-known services (e.g., HTTP on port 80, HTTPS on port 443), while ports from 1024 to 49151 are registered for various applications, and ports from 49152 to 65535 are dynamic or private ports.
Port Types
Well-Known Ports: Ports commonly associated with specific services. For example, port 80 is typically used for HTTP, port 443 for HTTPS, port 25 for SMTP (Simple Mail Transfer Protocol), etc.

Registered Ports: Ports that have been registered with the Internet Assigned Numbers Authority (IANA) for specific applications or services.

Dynamic/Private Ports: Ports that are not assigned to any specific service and can be used dynamically by applications as needed.
Port Usage: Ports facilitate communication between different applications or services over a network. When a client communicates with a server, it specifies the destination port to connect to the desired service.

URL (Uniform Resource Locator)
A URL is a reference or address used to locate a resource on the internet. It consists of several components that specify the protocol, domain name (or IP address), port (optional), path, query parameters, and fragment identifier. Here's a breakdown of the components of a URL
Protocol: Specifies the protocol used to access the resource, such as HTTP, HTTPS, FTP, etc.

Domain Name (or IP Address): Specifies the hostname or IP address of the server hosting the resource.

Port: (Optional) Specifies the port number to connect to on the server. If not specified, the default port for the protocol is used (e.g., port 80 for HTTP, port 443 for HTTPS).

Path: Specifies the path to the resource on the server's filesystem. It represents the location of the resource within the server's directory structure.

Query Parameters: (Optional) Used to pass data to the server as part of the URL. Query parameters are separated from the path by a question mark (?) and separated from each other by an ampersand (&).

Fragment Identifier: (Optional) Specifies a specific section or anchor within the resource. Fragment identifiers are preceded by a hash (#) symbol.

Using Ports and URLs in Java
Java provides various APIs and libraries for working with TCP/IP ports and URLs. For example:
The java.net.Socket class allows Java applications to create client-side TCP/IP connections to servers on specific ports.
The java.net.ServerSocket class allows Java applications to listen for incoming TCP/IP connections on specific ports and handle them appropriately.
The java.net.URL class allows Java applications to parse and manipulate URLs, making it easy to work with web resources.

6.7.1 What are TCP/IP Ports?
TCP/IP ports are virtual endpoints used by the Transmission Control Protocol (TCP) and the User Datagram Protocol (UDP) to facilitate communication between devices over a network. In TCP/IP networking, ports serve as gateways for incoming and outgoing data transmissions, allowing multiple services or processes to operate concurrently on a single device. Here's a detailed explanation of TCP/IP ports:
Key Points about TCP/IP Ports
Port Number: Each TCP/IP port is identified by a unique number ranging from 0 to 65535. This range is divided into three categories:
Well-Known Ports (0-1023): Reserved for standard services and protocols. For example, port 80 is used for HTTP, port 443 for HTTPS, port 22 for SSH, etc.
Registered Ports (1024-49151): Assigned to specific services by the Internet Assigned Numbers Authority (IANA) upon request from organizations or vendors.
Dynamic/Private Ports (49152-65535): Available for use by applications and services dynamically. These ports are commonly used for client-side connections.
Multiplexing: TCP/IP ports enable multiplexing, allowing multiple network services or processes to share a single IP address. Each port serves as a unique identifier for a specific service or application running on a device.
Client-Server Communication: In client-server communication, the client initiates a connection to a specific port on the server to access a particular service or resource. The server listens for incoming connections on specific ports and responds accordingly.

Connection-Oriented Protocol (TCP): TCP is a connection-oriented protocol that establishes a reliable, bi-directional communication channel between two endpoints. TCP/IP ports are associated with TCP connections, which provide features such as error detection, flow control, and reliable data transmission.

Connectionless Protocol (UDP): UDP is a connectionless protocol that allows data to be transmitted without establishing a dedicated connection. UDP ports are used for applications that prioritize speed and efficiency over reliability, such as real-time streaming and online gaming.

Using TCP/IP Ports in Java
In Java, developers can work with TCP/IP ports using various networking APIs provided by the java.net package.
For example:
The java.net.Socket class represents a client-side TCP socket, allowing Java applications to establish connections to remote servers on specific ports.

The java.net.ServerSocket class represents a server-side TCP socket, enabling Java applications to listen for incoming connections on specific ports and accept them.

The java.net.DatagramSocket class facilitates communication via UDP, allowing Java applications to send and receive datagrams (UDP packets) to and from specific ports.

6.7.1.1 How TCP/IP Ports Work

TCP/IP ports play a crucial role in facilitating communication between devices over a network using the Transmission Control Protocol (TCP) and the User Datagram Protocol (UDP). Understanding how TCP/IP ports work is essential for advanced Java developers building networked applications. Let's dive into the workings of TCP/IP ports.

How TCP/IP Ports Work
Addressing Endpoints: In a TCP/IP network, each device is identified by its IP address. However, an IP address alone is not sufficient to determine which application or service running on the device should receive incoming data. TCP/IP ports address this by providing an additional layer of addressing, allowing multiple services to operate concurrently on a single device.
Port Numbers: TCP/IP ports are identified by numeric values ranging from 0 to 65535. These port numbers are divided into three ranges:
Well-Known Ports (0-1023): Reserved for standard services and protocols. For example, port 80 is used for HTTP, port 443 for HTTPS, port 22 for SSH, etc.
Registered Ports (1024-49151): Assigned to specific services by the Internet Assigned Numbers Authority (IANA) upon request.
Dynamic/Private Ports (49152-65535): Available for use by applications and services dynamically.
Connection Establishment: In TCP, the client initiates a connection to a specific port on the server by sending a SYN (synchronize) packet. The server responds with a SYN-ACK (synchronize-acknowledge) packet, indicating that it is willing to establish a connection. Finally, the client sends an ACK (acknowledge) packet to confirm the connection establishment. Once the connection is established, data can be exchanged bidirectionally between the client and server.
Data Transmission: After the TCP connection is established, data can be transmitted between the client and server. Each packet of data contains the source and destination port numbers, allowing the receiving device to determine which application or service should handle the data.
Connection Termination: In TCP, connections are terminated using a handshake process. Either the client or server can initiate the termination by sending a FIN (finish) packet. The other party responds with an ACK packet, acknowledging the termination request. Once both parties have acknowledged the termination, the connection is closed.
UDP Communication: Unlike TCP, UDP is a connectionless protocol that does not require a handshake process to establish connections. Instead, UDP packets contain source and destination port numbers, allowing data to be transmitted without establishing a dedicated connection. UDP is commonly used for applications that prioritize speed and efficiency over reliability, such as real-time streaming and online gaming.
Using TCP/IP Ports in Java
In Java, developers can work with TCP/IP ports using the java.net package, which provides classes like Socket, ServerSocket, and DatagramSocket for TCP and UDP communication. These classes allow Java applications to establish connections, listen for incoming connections, and send/receive data over specific ports.

6.7.1.2 Significance in Web Applications

The significance of web applications in advanced Java development is immense, considering the widespread use of the internet and the demand for dynamic, interactive online experiences. Here are some key aspects highlighting the significance of web applications in the context of advanced Java development:

Global Reach

Web applications can be accessed from anywhere with an internet connection, providing a global reach for businesses and services. Advanced Java developers can leverage this reach to develop applications that cater to a worldwide audience, expanding their market and user base.

Cross-Platform Compatibility

Web applications are platform-independent and can run on any device with a web browser, including desktops, laptops, tablets, and smartphones. Advanced Java developers can utilize Java technologies like Servlets, JSP, and Spring to build responsive, cross-platform web applications that adapt to different screen sizes and resolutions.

Scalability

Web applications can scale horizontally by adding more servers to handle increasing traffic and user load. Advanced Java developers can design scalable architectures using technologies like Spring Boot, microservices, and cloud platforms to ensure that their applications can handle growing demands without compromising performance or reliability.

Rich User Interfaces

Modern web applications feature rich user interfaces with interactive elements, animations, and real-time updates. Advanced Java developers can use front-end frameworks like Angular, React, or Vue.js, along with Java-based backend services, to create visually appealing and engaging user experiences.

Integration Capabilities

Web applications can integrate with other systems and services using APIs (Application Programming Interfaces), allowing seamless data exchange and interoperability. Advanced Java developers can use Java frameworks like Spring Integration or Apache Camel to build integrations with external systems, databases, and third-party APIs.

Security

Security is a critical aspect of web applications, especially those handling sensitive data or transactions. Advanced Java developers can implement robust security measures using techniques like encryption, authentication, authorization, and input validation to protect against common web application vulnerabilities such as SQL injection, cross-site scripting (XSS), and CSRF (Cross-Site Request Forgery).

Continuous Delivery

Web applications can benefit from continuous integration and continuous delivery (CI/CD) pipelines, enabling rapid and automated deployment of updates and new features. Advanced Java developers can use tools like Jenkins, Docker, and Kubernetes to automate the build, test, and deployment processes, ensuring faster time-to-market and improved agility.

6.7.2 What is a URL?

A URL (Uniform Resource Locator) is a reference or address used to locate a resource on the internet. It serves as a standardized way to specify the location of web pages, files, documents, and other resources. URLs are fundamental to web browsing and are used extensively in web development. Here's a breakdown of the components of a URL

Components of a URL

Protocol: The protocol specifies the communication protocol used to access the resource. Common protocols include:

HTTP: Hypertext Transfer Protocol, used for accessing web pages.

HTTPS: Secure Hypertext Transfer Protocol, a secure version of HTTP.

FTP: File Transfer Protocol, used for transferring files.

SMTP: Simple Mail Transfer Protocol, used for sending emails.

File: Accessing files on a local or remote file system.

Domain Name (or IP Address): The domain name or IP address identifies the server hosting the resource. Domain names are human-readable names associated with IP addresses (e.g., example.com), while IP addresses are numerical addresses (e.g., 192.0.2.1) used to identify devices on the internet.

Port: (Optional) The port number specifies the communication port on the server to connect to. If not specified, the default port for the protocol is used (e.g., port 80 for HTTP, port 443 for HTTPS).

Path: The path specifies the location of the resource on the server's filesystem. It represents the hierarchical structure of directories leading to the resource.

Query Parameters: (Optional) Query parameters are used to pass data to the server as part of the URL. They are separated from the path by a question mark (?) and separated from each other by an ampersand (&). Query parameters are typically used in GET requests to specify search criteria or parameters for dynamic content generation.
Fragment Identifier: (Optional) The fragment identifier specifies a specific section or anchor within the resource. It is preceded by a hash (#) symbol and is commonly used in web pages to link to specific sections of a document.
Example URL: Here's an example of a URL with all its components:
https://www.example.com:8080/path/to/resource?param1=value1&param2=value2#section2
Protocol: HTTPS
Domain Name: www.example.com
Port: 8080
Path: /path/to/resource
Query Parameters: param1=value1, param2=value2
Fragment Identifier: section2

Using URLs in Advanced Java Development
In advanced Java development, URLs are used extensively for
Accessing resources from external servers or APIs.
Constructing links within web applications.
Passing parameters and data between client and server.
Redirecting users to specific pages or sections.
Handling routing and navigation within web frameworks.

6.8 Web Container

In the landscape of Java web development, the concept of a web container (or servlet container) is central to deploying and managing web applications. A web container provides an environment for Java components such as Servlets, JavaServer Pages (JSP), and JavaServer Faces (JSF) to execute. This chapter explores the necessity of web containers, their roles, and how they empower developers to build dynamic, scalable, and robust web applications.

6.8.1 What is a Web Container?

a web container, also known as a servlet container or a web server, is a runtime environment responsible for managing the execution of web applications based on Java Servlets, JavaServer Pages (JSP), and other Java EE (Enterprise Edition) technologies. Web containers provide a platform for deploying, running, and managing web applications, handling HTTP requests and responses, and managing the lifecycle of servlets and JSP pages. Here's a detailed explanation of what a web container is and how it works.

Key Characteristics of a Web Container
Servlet Lifecycle Management: Web containers manage the lifecycle of servlets, including their initialization, execution, and destruction. Servlets are Java classes that handle HTTP requests and generate dynamic content for web applications.
Request Handling: Web containers receive HTTP requests from clients (such as web browsers) and route them to the appropriate servlet or JSP page based on the request URL and mapping configurations.
Response Processing: After servlets or JSP pages generate dynamic content, the web container formats the content into HTTP responses and sends them back to the clients.
Multi-Threading Support: Web containers handle multiple concurrent requests from clients by using multi-threading. Each incoming request is typically processed by a separate thread to ensure responsiveness and scalability.
Deployment and Configuration: Web containers provide tools and APIs for deploying web applications, configuring servlet mappings, defining security constraints, managing resources (such as database connections and JNDI resources), and configuring runtime parameters.
Integration with Java EE Technologies: Web containers are often part of Java EE application servers, which provide additional services and APIs for enterprise-level applications, such as transaction management, messaging, security, and distributed computing.

Examples of Web Containers:
Apache Tomcat: Tomcat is a lightweight, open-source web container developed by the Apache Software Foundation. It is widely used for deploying Java web applications and is known for its simplicity and ease of use.
Jetty: Jetty is another popular open-source web container developed by the Eclipse Foundation. It is lightweight, embeddable, and highly scalable, making it suitable for a wide range of applications, from small embedded systems to large-scale enterprise deployments.
IBM WebSphere Application Server: WebSphere is a commercial Java EE application server developed by IBM. It includes a robust web container along with additional enterprise-level features for building and deploying mission-critical applications.
Oracle WebLogic Server: WebLogic is another commercial Java EE application server developed by Oracle. It provides a high-performance web container along with advanced features for scalability, reliability, and security.

Advantages of Using a Web Container
Portability: Web containers provide a standardized runtime environment for Java web applications, ensuring portability across different platforms and operating systems.
Scalability: Web containers support multi-threading and can handle large numbers of concurrent requests, making them suitable for scalable web applications.
Simplicity: Web containers abstract away many of the complexities of web application development, allowing developers to focus on writing business logic rather than managing low-level networking and HTTP protocols.

6.8.2 The Need for Web Containers

The need for web containers arises from the requirements of deploying, managing, and executing Java-based web applications efficiently. Web containers, also known as servlet containers or web servers, fulfill this need by providing a runtime environment specifically designed for hosting web applications built using Java Servlets, JavaServer Pages (JSP), and related technologies. Here's a breakdown of why web containers are essential:
Servlet Lifecycle Management
Web containers manage the lifecycle of servlets, including their initialization, execution, and destruction. Servlets are Java classes that handle HTTP requests and generate dynamic content for web applications. By providing a structured environment for managing servlets, web containers ensure efficient resource utilization and consistent Behaviour across different servlet instances.
Request Handling
Web containers are responsible for receiving HTTP requests from clients (such as web browsers) and routing them to the appropriate servlet or JSP page based on the request URL and mapping configurations. They handle various types of requests, including GET, POST, PUT, DELETE, and others, and ensure that each request is processed correctly according to the application's configuration.
Response Processing
After servlets or JSP pages generate dynamic content in response to incoming requests, web containers format the content into HTTP responses and send them back to the clients. They handle HTTP headers, cookies, session management, and other aspects of the response generation process to ensure compliance with web standards and optimal performance.
Multi-Threading Support
Web containers handle multiple concurrent requests from clients by using multi-threading. Each incoming request is typically processed by a separate thread, allowing the container to handle high loads and maintain responsiveness even under heavy traffic. Multi-threading support is essential for building scalable web applications that can serve large numbers of users simultaneously.
Deployment and Configuration
Web containers provide tools and APIs for deploying web applications, configuring servlet mappings, defining security constraints, managing resources (such as database connections and JNDI resources), and configuring runtime parameters. They simplify the deployment and management of web applications, allowing developers to focus on writing business logic rather than dealing with low-level infrastructure concerns.
Integration with Java EE Technologies
Web containers are often part of Java EE application servers, which provide additional services and APIs for enterprise-level applications. They integrate seamlessly with other Java EE technologies such as Enterprise JavaBeans (EJB), Java Persistence API (JPA), Java Messaging Service (JMS), and Java Transaction API (JTA), allowing developers to build complex, distributed applications with ease.

Examples of Web Containers
Apache Tomcat: One of the most popular web containers, known for its performance, flexibility, and configuration options.
Jetty: A lightweight container and server with a small footprint, often used for embedded systems and microservices.
GlassFish: An open-source application server that includes a web container and supports the full Java EE platform for enterprise applications.

6.8.3 Integrating Web Containers in Development

Integrating web containers into the development process is crucial for advanced Java developers working on web applications. It involves setting up and configuring the web container environment to streamline the development, testing, and deployment of Java-based web applications. Here's how you can integrate web containers into your development workflow:
Choose a Web Container
Select a web container that meets your requirements based on factors such as performance, scalability, ease of use, community support, and compatibility with your application's technologies. Popular web containers for Java web development include Apache Tomcat, Jetty, and embedded containers provided by Java EE application servers like WildFly and Apache TomEE.
Configure Development Environment
Set up your development environment to include the selected web container. Install the web container software and configure it to work with your IDE (Integrated Development Environment), build tools, and other development tools. Configure the necessary settings such as port numbers, context paths, and deployment directories to match your development environment.
Develop Web Applications
Use your preferred Java web framework (such as Spring MVC, JavaServer Faces, or Struts) to develop web applications. Write servlets, JSP pages, filters, listeners, and other components as needed. Organize your project structure and dependencies according to best practices to ensure maintainability and scalability.
Testing
Test your web applications locally by deploying them to the integrated web container in your development environment. Use tools like JUnit, Selenium, and JMeter for unit testing, integration testing, and load testing. Verify that your application behaves as expected and meets the functional and non-functional requirements.
Debugging
Use the debugging capabilities of your IDE to troubleshoot and debug issues in your web application code. Set breakpoints, inspect variables, and step through code execution to identify and fix bugs. Take advantage of logging frameworks like Log4j or SLF4J to log useful information for debugging purposes.
Continuous Integration
Integrate your web application development process with a continuous integration (CI) system such as Jenkins, Travis CI, or CircleCI. Configure automated build and test pipelines to ensure that changes to your application are tested and validated automatically whenever code is committed to the version control repository.
Deployment
Prepare your web application for deployment to production environments. Package your application into WAR (Web ARchive) files and deploy them to standalone web containers or Java EE application servers. Configure deployment settings such as connection pools, security settings, and environment-specific configurations.
Monitoring and Maintenance
Monitor the performance and health of your deployed web applications using monitoring tools and frameworks such as JMX (Java Management Extensions), Prometheus, and Grafana. Monitor server metrics, application logs, and user experience to identify and address performance bottlenecks and issues proactively.

Web containers play a vital role in Java web development, offering a standardized, efficient, and secure environment for deploying web applications. By abstracting the complexities of network communication, session management, and security, web containers allow developers to focus on creating dynamic content and business logic, thereby accelerating development cycles and enhancing application quality.

Exercise

Exercise 1 – MCQ

1. What is the primary purpose of a web container?

a) To store web pages
b) To manage and execute web applications
c) To secure network connections
d) To design user interfaces
2. What does HTTP stand for in the context of web communication?
a) Hyperlink Text Transfer Protocol
b) Hyper Transfer Text Protocol
c) Hypertext Transfer Protocol
d) High-Tech Transfer Protocol
3. What is the function of a URL in web communication?
a) It defines the layout of a web page
b) It specifies the address of a web resource
c) It encrypts data during transmission
d) It manages user authentication
4. Which protocol is used for transmitting data over the internet?
a) FTP
b) TCP/IP
c) SMTP
d) UDP
5. What is the basic unit of communication in the HTTP protocol?
a) Packet
b) Message
c) Segment
d) Frame
6. What does HTML stand for in web development?
a) Hyperlink Text Markup Language
b) Hypertext Markup Language
c) High-Tech Markup Language
d) Hyper Transfer Markup Language
7. What defines the structure and content of a web page?
a) CSS
b) JavaScript
c) HTML
d) XML
8. What is a characteristic of a web application?
a) It runs only on desktop computers
b) It requires installation like traditional software
c) It can be accessed through a web browser
d) It cannot interact with databases
9. What does TCP/IP stand for in network communication?
a) Transmission Control Protocol/Internet Protocol
b) Transmission Control Program/Internet Program
c) Telecommunication Control Protocol/Internet Protocol
d) Telecommunication Control Program/Internet Program
10. What is the role of web clients in web communication?
a) To host websites
b) To request and display web resources
c) To manage databases
d) To secure network connections

Exercise 2 – True/False

1. A Web Container is a physical storage device for web pages.
2. URL stands for Universal Resource Locator.
3. HTTP is a stateful protocol.
4. TCP/IP Ports are used to identify specific applications or services on a computer.
5. HTML is a programming language.

6. Web clients initiate requests to web servers.
7. A web application is a software application that runs locally on a user's computer.
8. Integrating Web Containers in development involves deploying web applications to production servers.
9. Web Containers are only needed for developing complex web applications.
10. Understanding web clients and servers is not essential for web development.

Exercise 3 – Fill in the blanks
1. In a URL, the protocol component specifies the __________ used to access the resource.
2. HTML stands for Hypertext Markup __________.
3. Web servers respond to client requests by sending __________ back to the client.
4. TCP/IP Ports are identified by __________ numbers.
5. A web application is a software program designed to run on a __________ and interact with users through a web browser.
6. __ is a stateless protocol, meaning each request from a client to a server is independent and not reliant on previous requests.
7. The ___ layer of a web application interacts with data sources such as databases, external APIs, or file systems to retrieve and store data.
8. The ___ layer of a web application contains the core application logic, including data processing, validation, and business rules.
9. Web applications often follow the ___ architecture, where the presentation layer (UI), business logic, and data access layer are separated.
10. The ___ refers to the server-side logic and resources responsible for processing client requests and generating responses.

Exercise 4 – Match case
1. HTML
2. URL
3. HTTP
4. Web Server

A. Specifies the address of a web resource.
B. Defines the structure and content of a web page.
C. Protocol used for transmitting data over the internet.
D. Software that responds to client requests over the internet.

Exercise 5 – One-word answer
1. What is HTTP?
2. What does URL stand for?

Exercise 6 – Small answer
1. What is the role of a web server in serving web pages?
2. What is the purpose of TCP/IP Ports in networking?

Exercise 7- Long answer
1. Describe the process of how a web browser retrieves a web page from a web server and displays it to the user.
2. Explain the significance of HTTP in web communication and how it works.

Answer-
Exercise 1 – 1) b 2) c 3) b 4) b 5) b 6) b 7) c 8) a 9) a 10) b
Exercise 2 – 1) False 2) True 3) False 4) True 5) False 6) True 7) False 8) False 9) True 10) False
Exercise 3 – 1) protocol 2) Language 3) data 4) numeric 5) server 6) HTTP 7) data access 8) business logic 9) MVC 10) server-side
Exercise 4 – 1 – B. Defines the structure and content of a web page. 2 – A. Specifies the address of a web resource 3 – C. Protocol used for transmitting data over the internet 4 – D. Software that responds to client requests over the internet.
Exercise 5 – 1) Protocol 2) Locator

Online Resources

Online Practice Paper

Link: https://forms.gle/NhbzndzP51BDHdJj9
QR Code:

YouTube Video Link

Link: https://www.youtube.com/playlist?list=PLzlh_31VWEFrYDrcJYl6fw8TfqdUoi_Q4
QR Code:

CHAPTER 7 - Web Container and Web Application Project Setup

7.1 Setting up Tomcat Container

Apache Tomcat serves as one of the most popular open-source Java Servlet containers, offering a "pure Java" HTTP web server environment for Java code to run. It is an implementation of the Java Servlet, JavaServer Pages (JSP), and Java Expression Language (EL) technologies. This chapter guides you through setting up the Tomcat container for web application development, ensuring you have a solid foundation for deploying and managing Java web applications.

Apache Tomcat serves as a robust and popular open-source web server and servlet container, widely used in advanced Java development for hosting Java-based web applications. Here's an in-depth explanation of what Apache Tomcat serves for in advanced Java development:

Servlet Container: Tomcat serves as a servlet container, providing a runtime environment for executing Java Servlets, JavaServer Pages (JSP), and other Java EE (Enterprise Edition) components. Servlets are Java classes that handle HTTP requests and generate dynamic content, while JSP pages allow for the creation of dynamic web pages using HTML-like syntax mixed with Java code.

Web Server: Tomcat also functions as a standalone web server, capable of serving static and dynamic content to clients over the HTTP protocol. It can handle HTTP requests, serve static files (HTML, CSS, JavaScript, images), and execute dynamic content generated by servlets and JSP pages.

Development and Testing: In the context of advanced Java development, Tomcat serves as a development and testing environment for building and testing Java-based web applications locally. Developers can deploy their applications to Tomcat running on their local machines, test them in a controlled environment, and debug issues efficiently using tools and IDEs.

Production Deployment: Tomcat is widely used for deploying Java-based web applications to production environments. It provides a stable and scalable platform for hosting web applications in production, offering features such as connection pooling, session management, security, and clustering for high availability.

Integration with Java EE Technologies: Tomcat integrates seamlessly with other Java EE technologies and frameworks, allowing developers to build complex, enterprise-level applications. It supports features such as JDBC (Java Database Connectivity) for database access, JNDI (Java Naming and Directory Interface) for resource lookup, JTA (Java Transaction API) for transaction management, and JMX (Java Management Extensions) for monitoring and management.

Embeddability: Tomcat is embeddable in Java applications, allowing developers to embed the Tomcat servlet container directly into their applications. This feature enables the creation of self-contained, standalone applications that include a web server and servlet container, making deployment and distribution more manageable.

Community Support: Tomcat has a large and active community of developers, users, and contributors who provide extensive documentation, tutorials, and support forums. The vibrant community ensures that Tomcat remains up-to-date, well-maintained, and compatible with the latest Java standards and technologies.

7.1.1 Downloading and Installing Tomcat

Downloading and installing Apache Tomcat is a straightforward process, essential for advanced Java developers who want to work with Java-based web applications. Here's a step-by-step guide to downloading and installing Tomcat:

Download Tomcat

Visit the official Apache Tomcat website at https://tomcat.apache.org/.

Navigate to the "Download" section.

Choose the latest stable version of Tomcat suitable for your operating system (Windows, Linux, macOS).

Select the appropriate distribution format (ZIP or TAR.GZ) for your operating system.

Extract the Tomcat Archive

Once the download is complete, locate the downloaded Tomcat archive file.

Extract the contents of the archive to a directory on your local machine. You can use any unzip utility or command-line tool to extract the contents.

Choose a location where you have to write permissions and where Tomcat can be easily accessed.

Set Environment Variables (Optional)
Optionally, you can set up environment variables to simplify the use of Tomcat commands and scripts.
Set the CATALINA_HOME environment variable to the directory where Tomcat is installed.
Add the bin directory within the Tomcat installation directory to the PATH environment variable to run Tomcat scripts from any location.

Start Tomcat
Navigate to the bin directory within the Tomcat installation directory.
Execute the startup.sh script (for Unix-based systems) or startup.bat script (for Windows) to start the Tomcat server.
The Tomcat server will start, and you should see log messages indicating that the server has started successfully.
Verify Installation
Open a web browser and navigate to http://localhost:8080. This URL accesses the default Tomcat homepage.
If Tomcat is running correctly, you should see the Tomcat homepage, which provides information about the server and links to documentation and management tools.
You can also access the Tomcat Manager web application at http://localhost:8080/manager, where you can deploy and manage web applications.
Stop Tomcat
To stop the Tomcat server, navigate to the bin directory within the Tomcat installation directory.
Execute the shutdown.sh script (for Unix-based systems) or shutdown.bat script (for Windows) to stop the Tomcat server.
The server will shut down, and you should see log messages indicating that the server has stopped.

7.1.2 Configuring Tomcat

Configuring Apache Tomcat is a crucial step in setting up the environment for advanced Java development. Configuration allows developers to tailor Tomcat to their specific needs, optimize performance, enhance security, and integrate with other systems. Here's a guide on configuring Tomcat for advanced Java development:
Server Configuration
server.xml: This is the main configuration file for Tomcat. It includes settings for the server, connectors, hosts, and other global configurations. Key configurations include:
Define the ports for HTTP and HTTPS connectors.
Configure server behaviours such as thread pool settings, connection timeouts, and compression settings.
Define virtual hosts for serving multiple domains.
Connector Configuration:
Configure HTTP and HTTPS connectors to listen on specific ports.
Customize connector settings such as protocol, SSL/TLS settings, and connection timeouts.
Context Configuration
context.xml: This file defines settings for individual web applications (contexts) deployed on Tomcat. Key configurations include:
Configure context-specific resources such as data sources, JMS (Java Message Service) connections, and JNDI (Java Naming and Directory Interface) resources.
Specify context parameters and environment variables.
Define session management settings, such as session timeout and persistence options.
Logging Configuration
logging.properties: Tomcat uses JULI (Java Utility Logging Implementation) for logging. Customize logging settings in this file to control logging Behaviour, log levels, and log output destinations.
Security Configuration
Security Realms**:** Configure security realms for authentication and authorization. Tomcat supports various realms, including JDBCRealm, JNDIRealm, and DataSourceRealm, which allow authentication against databases, LDAP servers, and other systems.
SSL/TLS Configuration**:** Secure Tomcat connections with SSL/TLS encryption. Configure SSL certificates, keystore settings, cipher suites, and protocol versions in the connector configuration.
Performance Tuning
Thread Pool Configuration: Adjust thread pool settings to optimize server performance. Configure parameters such as maximum threads, accept count, and thread priority based on anticipated workload and hardware resources.

Cache Configuration: Enable caching to improve application performance. Configure cache settings for static resources, servlet sessions, and web content using built-in caching mechanisms or external caching solutions.
Monitoring and Management
JMX Configuration: Enable JMX (Java Management Extensions) monitoring for Tomcat. Configure JMX settings in catalina.properties to expose Tomcat's management interfaces for monitoring and management tools.
Management Interfaces**:** Configure access to Tomcat's management interfaces, such as the Tomcat Manager and Host Manager applications. Define user roles, access controls, and security constraints in the tomcat-users.xml file.
Customization and Extensions
Custom Contexts: Customize individual web application contexts by creating context-specific configuration files in the conf/Catalina/localhost directory.
External Libraries and Resources**:** Configure additional libraries, resources, and dependencies required by web applications. Place JAR files in the lib directory or define classpaths in context-specific configuration files.
Code**:**

```
<tomcat-users>
<role rolename="manager-gui"/>
<user username="admin" password="password" roles="manager-gui"/>
</tomcat-users>
```

Restart Tomcat and navigate to http://localhost:8080/manager/html to access the Tomcat Web Manager.

7.1.3 Deploying a Web Application to Tomcat

Deploying a web application to Apache Tomcat is a crucial step in the development and deployment process for advanced Java developers. Tomcat provides a straightforward mechanism for deploying Java-based web applications, typically in the form of WAR (Web ARchive) files. Here's a step-by-step guide on deploying a web application to Tomcat:

Build the Web Application

Before deploying, ensure that your web application is properly built and packaged. Typically, Java web applications are packaged as WAR files, which contain all the necessary files and resources required to run the application.

Access the Tomcat Web Application Manager

Open a web browser and navigate to the Tomcat Manager web application. The URL is usually http://localhost:8080/manager.

Log in using the username and password configured in the tomcat-users.xml file. By default, the username is admin and the password is admin.

Upload the WAR File

In the Tomcat Manager interface, locate the "WAR file to deploy" section.

Click the "Choose File" button and select the WAR file of your web application from your local file system.

Click the "Deploy" button to upload and deploy the WAR file to Tomcat.

Monitor Deployment Status

Once the WAR file is uploaded, Tomcat begins deploying the web application. You can monitor the deployment progress and status in the Tomcat Manager interface. Tomcat displays deployment messages and indicates whether the deployment was successful or if any errors occurred.

Access the Deployed Web Application

Once the deployment is complete, you can access the deployed web application using its context path.

The context path is typically the name of the WAR file (minus the .war extension) or a custom context path defined in the deployment descriptor (web.xml).

Open a web browser and navigate to http://localhost:8080/context-path to access the deployed web application, replacing context-path with the actual context path of your application.

Test the Web Application

Verify that the deployed web application functions as expected. Test its various features, functionalities, and interactions to ensure that everything works correctly.

Monitor the application for any errors, exceptions, or unexpected behaviour. Use browser developer tools, server logs, and application logs to troubleshoot and debug issues if necessary.

Undeploying the Web Application (Optional)

If you need to undeploy the web application from Tomcat:

Access the Tomcat Manager web application.
Locate the web application in the list of deployed applications.
Click the "Undeploy" button next to the web application to remove it from Tomcat.

7.2 Creating a Servlets JSP project in Eclipse

Developing web applications in Java often involves working with Servlets and JavaServer Pages (JSP). Eclipse, with its rich set of features and integrations, provides an excellent environment for building, testing, and deploying these applications.

7.2.1 Creating a Servlets JSP Project in Eclipse

Creating a Servlets/JSP project in Eclipse is a common task for advanced Java developers who are building web applications. Eclipse provides robust support for Java EE development, including tools for creating, editing, debugging, and deploying servlets and JSP pages. Here's a step-by-step guide to creating a Servlets/JSP project in Eclipse:

Open Eclipse
Launch the Eclipse IDE on your computer. If you haven't installed Eclipse yet, download it from the official Eclipse website (https://www.eclipse.org/) and install it following the provided instructions.

Create a New Dynamic Web Project
Go to the "File" menu and select "New" -> "Dynamic Web Project".
In the "New Dynamic Web Project" dialog, enter a name for your project, such as "ServletJSPProject".
Choose the target runtime for your project. If you haven't configured a runtime environment yet, click on "New Runtime" to configure one (e.g., Apache Tomcat).
Optionally, specify the project layout, context root, and other project settings.
Click "Finish" to create the project.

Add Servlets
Right-click on the project name in the "Project Explorer" view and select "New" -> "Servlet".
Enter a name for the servlet class, such as "MyServlet", and click "Next".
Specify the package name (e.g., "com.example.servlets") and the URL mapping for the servlet (e.g., "/hello"), then click "Next".
Optionally, choose to generate methods like doGet() and doPost(), then click "Finish".

Write Servlet Code
Open the newly created servlet class (MyServlet.java) and write the Java code to handle HTTP requests. Here's a simple example:

```
package com.example.servlets;
import java.io.IOException;
import javax.servlet.ServletException;
import javax.servlet.annotation.WebServlet;
import javax.servlet.http.HttpServlet;
import javax.servlet.http.HttpServletRequest;
import javax.servlet.http.HttpServletResponse;
@WebServlet("/hello")
public class MyServlet extends HttpServlet {
protected void doGet(HttpServletRequest request, HttpServletResponse response) throws ServletException,
IOException {
response.getWriter().println("Hello from Servlet!");
}
}
```

Add JSP Pages
Right-click on the "WebContent" folder in the project and select "New" -> "JSP".
Enter a name for the JSP file, such as "hello.jsp", and click "Finish".

Write JSP Code:
Open the newly created JSP file (hello.jsp) and write HTML markup mixed with JSP code. Here's a simple example:

```
<!DOCTYPE html>
<html>
```

```
<head>
<title>Hello JSP</title>
</head>
<body>
<h1>Hello from JSP!</h1>
</body>
</html>
```

Run and Test the Project

Right-click on the project name in the "Project Explorer" view and select "Run As" -> "Run on Server".

Choose the server (e.g., Apache Tomcat) on which you want to run the project and click "Finish".

Eclipse will deploy the project to the selected server and open a web browser to display the application.

Access the servlet by navigating to http://localhost:8080/ServletJSPProject/hello and the JSP page by navigating to http://localhost:8080/ServletJSPProject/hello.jsp.

7.2.2 Configuring Servlet and JSP API Dependencies

Configuring Servlet and JSP API dependencies is essential when setting up a Java web project in an IDE like Eclipse. Servlet and JSP APIs are part of the Java EE (Enterprise Edition) specification and provide the foundation for building web applications. Here's how you can configure these dependencies in Eclipse:

Adding Servlet and JSP APIs

Using a Build Tool (Recommended):

If you're using a build tool like Maven or Gradle, add dependencies for Servlet and JSP APIs in the project's pom.xml (for Maven) or build.gradle (for Gradle) file. These tools automatically download the required dependencies and manage them for you.

Using Maven or Gradle (Recommended)

For projects managed by Maven or Gradle, dependencies can be easily added by updating the pom.xml or build.gradle file, respectively.

Maven: Add the following dependencies to your pom.xml

Code:

```
<dependencies>
  <!-- Servlet API -->
  <dependency>
    <groupId>javax.servlet</groupId>
    <artifactId>javax.servlet-api</artifactId>
    <version>4.0.1</version>
    <scope>provided</scope>
  </dependency>
  <!-- JSP API -->
  <dependency>
    <groupId>javax.servlet.jsp</groupId>
    <artifactId>javax.servlet.jsp-api</artifactId>
    <version>2.3.3</version>
    <scope>provided</scope>
  </dependency>
</dependencies>
```

Gradle: Add the dependencies in your build.gradle:

Code:

```
dependencies {
  providedCompile 'javax.servlet:javax.servlet-api:4.0.1'
  providedCompile 'javax.servlet.jsp:javax.servlet.jsp-api:2.3.3'
}
```

Manually Adding JAR Files:

If you're not using a build tool, you can manually add the Servlet and JSP API JAR files to your project's build path.

Download the Servlet and JSP API JAR files from a reliable source, such as the Apache Tomcat website or Maven Central Repository.

In Eclipse, right-click on your project in the "Project Explorer" view and select "Properties".

In the project properties window, navigate to "Java Build Path" -> "Libraries" tab -> "Add External JARs".

Select the downloaded Servlet API JAR file (e.g., servlet-api.jar) and JSP API JAR file (e.g., jsp-api.jar) and click "Open" or "OK" to add them to the build path.

Verifying Dependencies:
After adding the Servlet and JSP API dependencies, verify that they are correctly configured in your project.
Check the project's build path to ensure that the Servlet and JSP API JAR files are listed under the "Referenced Libraries" section.
If you're using a build tool, verify that the dependencies are correctly specified in the project configuration file (pom.xml for Maven, build.gradle for Gradle).

Using Servlet and JSP APIs:
Once the Servlet and JSP APIs are configured in your project, you can start using them to develop web applications:
Create servlet classes to handle HTTP requests and generate dynamic content.
Write JSP pages to create the user interface and generate dynamic HTML content.
Use servlet and JSP APIs to interact with HTTP request and response objects, manage sessions, and perform other web-related tasks.

7.2.3 Manually Configuring in Eclipse
Manually configuring Servlet and JSP dependencies in Eclipse involves adding the necessary JAR files to the project's build path. This approach is suitable if you're not using a build tool like Maven or Gradle. Here's how you can manually configure Servlet and JSP dependencies in Eclipse:
Download Servlet and JSP API JAR Files
Visit a reliable source to download the Servlet and JSP API JAR files. You can get them from the Apache Tomcat website or Maven Central Repository.
Ensure you download the versions compatible with your project and servlet container (e.g., Apache Tomcat).
Add JAR Files to the Project's Build Path
Open Eclipse IDE and navigate to the Java perspective.
Right-click on your project in the "Project Explorer" view and select "Properties" from the context menu.
In the project properties window, go to "Java Build Path".
Switch to the "Libraries" tab.
Click on the "Add External JARs..." button.
Navigate to the directory where you downloaded the Servlet and JSP API JAR files, select them, and click "Open" or "OK".
Verify Configuration
After adding the JAR files, they should appear under the "Referenced Libraries" section in the "Libraries" tab of the project properties window.
Ensure there are no errors or warnings related to missing Servlet or JSP classes in your project.
If there are any errors, double-check that you've added the correct JAR files and versions.
Using Servlet and JSP APIs
Once the Servlet and JSP APIs are configured in your project, you can start using them to develop web applications:
Create servlet classes to handle HTTP requests and generate dynamic content.
Write JSP pages to create the user interface and generate dynamic HTML content.
Use servlet and JSP APIs to interact with HTTP request and response objects, manage sessions, and perform other web-related tasks.

7.3 Web Application Project Structure

The structure of a web application project in Java typically follows a standardized layout to maintain organization, readability, and scalability. Here's a detailed explanation of the common components and directories you'll find in a typical web application project structure:

src (Source) Directory

Java Source Code: Contains the Java source code files for servlets, filters, listeners, and other backend components.

Example: src/com/example/servlets/MyServlet.java

WebContent (or webapp, web) Directory

WEB-INF Directory

web.xml: Deployment descriptor file for configuring servlets, filters, welcome pages, and other web application settings. (Optional for Servlet 3.0+)

lib Directory: Contains third-party libraries (JAR files) required by the application.

classes Directory: Contains compiled Java classes (.class files) if not using a build tool like Maven or Gradle.

Static Resources Directory

css Directory: Contains CSS files.

js Directory: Contains JavaScript files.

images Directory: Contains image files (e.g., PNG, JPEG).

JSP Pages Directory

Contains JavaServer Pages (JSP) files for generating dynamic HTML content.

Example: WebContent/index.jsp, WebContent/user/profile.jsp

Other Static Files

Any other static files such as HTML, XML, or property files.

META-INF (Meta-Information) Directory (Optional)

Contains meta-information files such as MANIFEST.MF for specifying metadata about the application (e.g., version, main class).

WEB-INF (Web Information) Directory

lib Directory: Contains JAR files (libraries) required by the application.

classes Directory: Contains compiled Java classes (.class files) for servlets, filters, listeners, and other backend components.

web.xml: Deployment descriptor file for configuring servlets, filters, welcome pages, and other web application settings. (Mandatory for Servlet 2.5 and earlier)

build (or target) Directory (Optional)

Contains compiled Java classes, JAR files, and other artifacts generated during the build process.

Example Project Structure:

```
MyWebApp
│
├── src
│   └── com
│       └── example
│           └── servlets
│               └── MyServlet.java
│
└── WebContent
    ├── WEB-INF
    │   ├── lib
    │   │   └── servlet-api.jar
    │   └── web.xml
    │
    ├── css
    │   └── styles.css
    │
    ├── js
    │   └── script.js
    │
```

```
├── images
│   └── logo.png
│
├── index.jsp
└── user
    └── profile.jsp
```

7.3.1 Creating Servlets and JSPs

Creating Servlets and JSPs is a fundamental aspect of Java web development. Servlets handle server-side logic, processing requests, and generating responses, while JSPs are used to create dynamic web pages by embedding Java code within HTML. Here's how you can create Servlets and JSPs:

Creating Servlets

Create a Servlet Class

In your Java web project, create a new Java class that extends javax.servlet.http.HttpServlet.

Implement the doGet() or doPost() method to handle HTTP GET or POST requests, respectively.

You can also override other methods like doPut(), doDelete(), init(), and destroy() as needed.

Define Servlet Mapping

Configure the servlet mapping in the deployment descriptor (web.xml or using annotations for Servlet 3.0+).

Specify the URL pattern that maps to your servlet class.

Example

```
<servlet>
<servlet-name>MyServlet</servlet-name>
<servlet-class>com.example.MyServlet</servlet-class>
</servlet>
<servlet-mapping>
<servlet-name>MyServlet</servlet-name>
<url-pattern>/myservlet</url-pattern>
</servlet-mapping>
```

Creating JSPs

Create a JSP File

In your web project, create a new JSP file with a .jsp extension.

Write HTML markup and embed Java code using JSP syntax between <% %> or <%= %> tags.

Write JSP Code

Use JSP expressions (<%= %>), scriptlets (<% %>), and declarations (<%! %>) to write Java code within the JSP.

Access request parameters, session attributes, and other objects implicitly available in JSPs (e.g., request, session, out).

Include External Resources

Include external resources such as CSS files, JavaScript files, or other JSP files using HTML tags like <link>, <script>, or <jsp:include>.

Deploying JSPs

JSP files are automatically compiled into Java servlets the first time they are accessed by a client.

No additional configuration is required for deploying JSPs, as they are part of the web application's deployment.

Example:

```java
// MyServlet.java
package com.example;
import java.io.*;
import javax.servlet.*;
import javax.servlet.http.*;
public class MyServlet extends HttpServlet {
   protected void doGet(HttpServletRequest request, HttpServletResponse response)
         throws ServletException, IOException {
      response.setContentType("text/html");
      PrintWriter out = response.getWriter();
      out.println("<html><body>");
```

```
        out.println("<h1>Hello from Servlet!</h1>");
        out.println("</body></html>");
    }
}
```

Jsp

```
<!-- index.jsp -->
<!DOCTYPE html>
<html>
<head>
  <title>My JSP</title>
</head>
<body>
  <h1>Hello from JSP!</h1>
</body>
</html>
```

7.4 Configuring Servlet JSP API Dependencies

In the development of web applications using Java, Servlets and JavaServer Pages (JSP) are essential components that allow for dynamic content generation and request handling. To effectively build and deploy web applications that utilize these technologies, developers must configure their projects with the necessary Servlet and JSP API dependencies. This section will guide you through the process of configuring these dependencies, ensuring that your Java web applications can leverage the full power of Servlets and JSP.

7.4.1 Understanding Servlet and JSP APIs

Understanding Servlet and JSP APIs is essential for Java web development. These APIs provide the foundation for building dynamic and interactive web applications. Here's a brief explanation of Servlet and JSP APIs:

Servlet API

Servlets are Java classes that extend the functionality of a web server to generate dynamic content and handle client requests. The Servlet API provides a set of interfaces and classes for writing servlets. Key components of the Servlet API include:

javax.servlet.Servlet Interface

All servlets must implement this interface.

Defines methods for initializing the servlet, processing requests, and destroying the servlet.

javax.servlet.http.HttpServlet Class

A convenient base class for writing HTTP servlets.

Extends javax.servlet.GenericServlet and provides methods for handling HTTP-specific requests (e.g., doGet(), doPost()).

Servlet Lifecycle Methods

init(): Called by the container to initialize the servlet.

service(): Called to process client requests.

destroy(): Called by the container before removing the servlet instance.

HTTP Servlet Request and Response

javax.servlet.http.HttpServletRequest: Represents an HTTP request from a client.

javax.servlet.http.HttpServletResponse: Represents an HTTP response returned to the client.

JSP API

JavaServer Pages (JSP) is a technology used to create dynamic web pages by embedding Java code within HTML. The JSP API provides a set of classes and interfaces for writing JSPs. Key components of the JSP API include:

Implicit Objects

Objects available within JSPs without explicit declaration.

Examples include request, session, out (for writing output), and application.

JSP Directives

page: Defines attributes for the entire JSP page (e.g., import statements, content type).

include: Includes content from another resource (e.g., HTML, JSP) during translation.

JSP Scripting Elements
<% %>: Scriptlet tag for embedding Java code.
<%= %>: Expression tag for evaluating and outputting Java expressions.
<%! %>: Declaration tag for declaring variables and methods.
JSP Standard Actions
<jsp:include>: Includes content from another resource during request processing.
<jsp:forward>: Forwards the request to another resource.
<jsp:useBean>: Instantiates and accesses JavaBeans components.
Setting Up Dependencies
The configuration of Servlet and JSP API dependencies varies depending on your project's build tool. The most common tools in Java web development are Maven and Gradle.

7.4.2 Maven Configuration

Configuring Maven for a Java project involves setting up the pom.xml (Project Object Model) file to manage dependencies, build configuration, and project metadata. Here's a detailed explanation of Maven configuration:
Project Structure
Ensure your project follows the standard Maven directory structure:

```
project-root
│
├── src
│   ├── main
│   │   ├── java      (Java source files)
│   │   └── resources (Non-Java resources)
│   └── test
│       ├── java      (Test source files)
│       └── resources (Test resources)
└── pom.xml
```

pom.xml Configuration

Project Metadata: Define project coordinates (groupId, artifactId, version), name, description, and other metadata.
Dependencies: Declare dependencies required by your project.
Build Configuration: Define build settings, plugins, and goals.

Example pom.xml:

```
<project xmlns="http://maven.apache.org/POM/4.0.0"
      xmlns:xsi="http://www.w3.org/2001/XMLSchema-instance"
      xsi:schemaLocation="http://maven.apache.org/POM/4.0.0
                  http://maven.apache.org/xsd/maven-4.0.0.xsd">
   <modelVersion>4.0.0</modelVersion>
   <!-- Project coordinates -->
   <groupId>com.example</groupId>
   <artifactId>my-project</artifactId>
   <version>1.0.0</version>
   <name>My Project</name>
   <description>A Maven-based Java project</description>

   <!-- Dependencies -->
   <dependencies>
      <!-- Servlet API -->
      <dependency>
         <groupId>javax.servlet</groupId>
         <artifactId>javax.servlet-api</artifactId>
         <version>4.0.1</version>
         <scope>provided</scope>
      </dependency>
      <!-- Other dependencies -->
```

```
    </dependencies>

    <!-- Build Configuration -->
    <build>
      <plugins>
        <!-- Maven Compiler Plugin -->
        <plugin>
          <groupId>org.apache.maven.plugins</groupId>
          <artifactId>maven-compiler-plugin</artifactId>
          <version>3.8.1</version>
          <configuration>
            <source>1.8</source>
            <target>1.8</target>
          </configuration>
        </plugin>
        <!-- Other plugins -->
      </plugins>
    </build>
</project>
```

Key Elements

- <dependencies>: Contains dependencies required by the project.
- <build>: Contains build configuration settings and plugins.
- <groupId>: Unique identifier for the project's group.
- <artifactId>: Unique identifier for the project's artifact (JAR, WAR).
- <version>: Project version.
- <scope>: Specifies the visibility of a dependency (e.g., compile, provided, test).

Dependency Management

Use <dependencies> section to declare dependencies required by your project. Maven downloads these dependencies from a repository such as Maven Central Repository.

For the Servlet API, include:

```
<dependency>
   <groupId>javax.servlet</groupId>
   <artifactId>javax.servlet-api</artifactId>
 <version>4.0.1</version>
   <scope>provided</scope>
</dependency>
```

For the JSP API, include:

```
<dependency>
   <groupId>javax.servlet.jsp</groupId>
   <artifactId>javax.servlet.jsp-api</artifactId>
   <version>2.3.3</version>
   <scope>provided</scope>
</dependency>
```

Build Configuration

- Define build settings, such as source and target compatibility, in the <build> section.
- Use plugins (e.g., Maven Compiler Plugin) to customize build process.

The 'provided' scope is used because the server at runtime typically provides these APIs. This prevents them from being included in your WAR file, reducing its size and avoiding potential conflicts.

7.4.3 Gradle Configuration

Configuring Gradle for a Java project involves setting up the build.gradle file to define project structure, dependencies, and build tasks. Here's a detailed explanation of Gradle configuration:

Project Structure

Ensure your project follows the standard Gradle directory structure:

project-root

```
│
├── src
│   ├── main
│   │   ├── java     (Java source files)
│   │   └── resources (Non-Java resources)
│   └── test
│       ├── java     (Test source files)
│       └── resources (Test resources)
└── build.gradle
```

build.gradle Configuration

Project Metadata: Define project coordinates (group, version, description), plugins, and repositories.

Dependencies: Declare dependencies required by your project.

Build Tasks: Define custom build tasks, source and target compatibility settings.

Example build.gradle:

```
plugins {
   id 'java'
}
group 'com.example'
version '1.0.0'
repositories
 {
   mavenCentral()
}
dependencies {
   // Servlet API
   implementation 'javax.servlet:javax.servlet-api:4.0.1'
   // Other dependencies
}
sourceCompatibility = '1.8'
targetCompatibility = '1.8'
```

Key Elements

plugins: Defines plugins applied to the project (e.g., Java plugin).

group: Group identifier for the project.

version: Project version.

repositories: Specifies repositories to resolve dependencies (e.g., Maven Central).

dependencies: Contains dependencies required by the project.

implementation: Specifies the configuration for dependencies that are required to compile the main source set.

sourceCompatibility, targetCompatibility: Specifies Java source and target compatibility.

Dependency Management

Use the dependencies block to declare dependencies required by your project. Gradle resolves these dependencies from repositories such as Maven Central.

Add the Servlet and JSP API dependencies in your dependencies block:

```
dependencies {
   providedCompile 'javax.servlet:javax.servlet-api:4.0.1'
   providedCompile 'javax.servlet.jsp:javax.servlet.jsp-api:2.3.3'
}
```

Build Tasks

Use sourceCompatibility and targetCompatibility to specify Java source and target compatibility.

Define custom tasks and configure build settings as needed.

Similar to Maven, the providedCompile configuration is used to indicate that these dependencies are provided by the container at runtime.

7.5 Project Structure and Deployment Descriptors

Project Structure and Deployment Descriptors are crucial aspects of Java web applications, defining how the application is organized and configured for deployment. Let's explore each:

Project Structure

A well-organized project structure enhances readability, maintainability, and scalability. Here's a typical structure for a Java web application:

```
project-root
│
├── src
│   ├── main
│   │   ├── java          (Java source files)
│   │   ├── resources     (Non-Java resources)
│   │   └── webapp        (Web application resources)
│   │       ├── WEB-INF
│   │       │   ├── lib       (JAR files)
│   │       │   ├── classes   (Compiled Java classes)
│   │       │   └── web.xml   (Deployment descriptor)
│   │       └── static      (Static resources: CSS, JS, images)
│   └── test
│       ├── java          (Test source files)
│       └── resources     (Test resources)
└── pom.xml (or build.gradle)   (Build configuration)
```

src/main/java: Contains Java source files.
src/main/resources: Contains non-Java resources (e.g., properties files, XML configurations).
src/main/webapp: Contains web application resources.
WEB-INF/lib: Contains third-party JAR files.
WEB-INF/classes: Contains compiled Java classes.
WEB-INF/web.xml: Deployment descriptor.
static: Contains static resources (e.g., CSS, JavaScript, images).
src/test: Contains test source files and resources.
pom.xml (or build.gradle): Defines project dependencies and build configuration.

Deployment Descriptor (web.xml):

The deployment descriptor (web.xml) is a configuration file required for Java EE web applications. It contains metadata about the application, including servlets, filters, listeners, and initialization parameters. Here's a basic example:

```xml
<?xml version="1.0" encoding="UTF-8"?>
<web-app xmlns="http://xmlns.jcp.org/xml/ns/javaee"
        xmlns:xsi="http://www.w3.org/2001/XMLSchema-instance"
        xsi:schemaLocation="http://xmlns.jcp.org/xml/ns/javaee
                    http://xmlns.jcp.org/xml/ns/javaee/web-app_4_0.xsd" version="4.0">
    <!-- Servlet Mapping -->
    <servlet>
        <servlet-name>MyServlet</servlet-name>
        <servlet-class>com.example.MyServlet</servlet-class>
    </servlet>
    <servlet-mapping>
        <servlet-name>MyServlet</servlet-name>
        <url-pattern>/myservlet</url-pattern>
    </servlet-mapping>

    <!-- Welcome File -->
    <welcome-file-list>
        <welcome-file>index.jsp</welcome-file>
    </welcome-file-list>

</web-app>
```

<servlet>: Declares a servlet and its corresponding class.
<servlet-mapping>: Maps a URL pattern to a servlet.
<welcome-file-list>: Defines default welcome files for the application.

Testing and Validation

Testing and validation are critical aspects of software development, ensuring that the application behaves as expected, meets requirements, and performs reliably. In advanced Java development, various techniques and tools are employed for testing and validation. Here's an overview:

Testing
Unit Testing
JUnit: A popular Java testing framework for writing and running unit tests.
Write test cases to validate individual components (classes, methods) of the application.
Use assertions to verify expected behaviour and outcomes.
Integration Testing
Test interactions between different components/modules of the application.
Verify the integration and communication between various parts of the system.
Functional Testing
Test the functionality of the application from an end-user perspective.
Use tools like Selenium for automated testing of web applications.
Verify user interactions, UI elements, and application workflows.
Performance Testing
Measure the performance characteristics of the application.
Identify bottlenecks, memory leaks, and performance issues.
Tools like JMeter, Gatling, or Apache Benchmark can be used for load testing.
Security Testing
Test the application for vulnerabilities and security risks.
Identify potential security flaws, such as injection attacks, cross-site scripting (XSS), and authentication bypass vulnerabilities.
Tools like OWASP ZAP, Burp Suite, or Nessus can be used for security testing.

Validation
Input Validation
Validate user input to prevent injection attacks (e.g., SQL injection, XSS).
Sanitize and validate input data before processing or storing it.
Data Validation
Ensure that data meets specific criteria, such as format, range, or constraints.
Validate data integrity and consistency.
Form Validation
Validate form submissions to ensure that required fields are filled, data is in the correct format, and meets validation rules.
Business Logic Validation
Validate business rules and logic to ensure that the application behaves correctly.
Verify that business processes and workflows are implemented correctly.

Tools
JUnit: for unit testing.
Selenium WebDriver: for automated browser testing.
JMeter: for performance testing.
Hamcrest: for writing expressive assertions
OWASP ZAP, Burp Suite: for security testing.
Mockito: for mocking dependencies in unit tests.
AssertJ: for writing expressive assertions.
Gatling: for performance testing.
Code Coverage Tools (e.g., JaCoCo, Cobertura): for measuring test coverage.

7.6 Web application project structure

Understanding the structure of a web application project is crucial for both new and experienced developers venturing into the world of Java web development.
A well-defined project structure not only facilitates the development process but also enhances maintainability, scalability, and collaboration. This chapter delves into the standard structure of a Java web application, focusing on the organization of files and directories, and how this structure supports the application's deployment and execution.

7.6.1 Standard Project Structure

A typical Java web application follows a specific directory layout, primarily dictated by the Servlet API and widely adopted conventions. This structure helps in segregating the application's components, making it easier to manage and deploy.

```
project-root
│
├── src
│   ├── main
│   │   ├── java          (Java source files)
│   │   ├── resources     (Non-Java resources)
│   │   └── webapp        (Web application resources)
│   │       ├── WEB-INF
│   │       │   ├── lib       (Third-party libraries)
│   │       │   ├── classes   (Compiled Java classes)
│   │       │   └── web.xml   (Deployment descriptor)
│   │       └── static    (Static resources: CSS, JS, images)
│   └── test
│       ├── java          (Test source files)
│       └── resources     (Test resources)
├── target                (Compiled output, generated artifacts)
└── pom.xml (or build.gradle)   (Build configuration)
```

Let's break down each component of the standard project structure:
src Directory
src/main/java: Contains Java source files.
src/main/resources: Contains non-Java resources (e.g., properties files, XML configurations).
src/main/webapp: Contains web application resources.
WEB-INF/lib: Contains third-party JAR files.
WEB-INF/classes: Contains compiled Java classes.
WEB-INF/web.xml: Deployment descriptor.
static: Contains static resources (e.g., CSS, JavaScript, images).
src/test Directory
src/test/java: Contains test source files (e.g., JUnit test cases).
src/test/resources: Contains test resources (e.g., test configurations, mock data).
target Directory
Contains compiled output, generated artifacts, and test reports.
This directory is generated during the build process and is typically excluded from version control.
pom.xml (or build.gradle) File
Defines project metadata, dependencies, and build configuration.
pom.xml is used for Maven projects, while build.gradle is used for Gradle projects.

Benefits
Organization: The structured layout makes it easy to locate and manage project components.
Separation of Concerns: The separation of main and test sources ensures clean separation between production and test code.
Convention over Configuration: Following a standard project structure simplifies project setup and maintenance.

Exercise

Exercise 1 – MCQ

1. Which step is involved in setting up Tomcat container?
a) Deploying a Web Application to Tomcat
b) Downloading and Installing Tomcat
c) Creating a Servlets JSP project in Eclipse
d) Configuring Servlet and JSP API Dependencies
2. What is the purpose of deploying a web application to Tomcat?
a) Configuring Servlet JSP API Dependencies
b) Manually Configuring in Eclipse
c) Project Structure and Deployment Descriptors
d) Hosting the application on a web server for access
3. Which tool is commonly used for creating Servlets JSP projects?
a) Tomcat
b) Eclipse
c) Apache HTTP Server
d) NetBeans
4. What is the first step in configuring Servlet and JSP API Dependencies?
a) Downloading Tomcat
b) Creating a web application project
c) Configuring deployment descriptors
d) Configuring servlet and JSP libraries
5. Which aspect is addressed in the project structure of a web application?
a) Servlet configuration
b) JSP API Dependencies
c) Deployment descriptors
d) Organizing files and directories
6. What is the main purpose of configuring servlet and JSP API dependencies?
a) To enable access control
b) To manage session handling
c) To ensure compatibility with Tomcat
d) To include necessary libraries for servlet and JSP development
7. Which step is essential for manually configuring a web application project in Eclipse?
a) Downloading Tomcat
b) Creating a servlet
c) Importing necessary libraries
d) Configuring deployment descriptors
8. What is the function of deployment descriptors in a web application project?
a) To define project structure
b) To manage database connections
c) To configure application settings
d) To specify URL mappings for servlets
9. What is included in the web application project structure?
a) Servlet container
b) JSP API libraries
c) HTML files
d) Configuration files and resource directories
10. Which step is not involved in the process of downloading and installing Tomcat?
a) Extracting the downloaded file
b) Setting up environment variables
c) Configuring servlet and JSP dependencies
d) Starting the Tomcat server

Exercise 2 – True/False

1. Downloading and Installing Tomcat is the final step in setting up the Tomcat container.
2. Deploying a Web Application to Tomcat involves copying the application files to the Tomcat webapps directory.
3. Creating a Servlets JSP project in Eclipse requires installing the necessary dependencies manually.
4. Configuring Servlet and JSP API Dependencies ensures that the required libraries are included in the project.
5. Manually Configuring in Eclipse involves setting up Tomcat within the Eclipse IDE.
6. Project Structure and Deployment Descriptors define the layout of a web application and its settings.
7. Web application project structure typically includes only servlets and JSP files.
8. Configuring Servlet JSP API Dependencies involves specifying the version of Tomcat to use.
9. Deployment Descriptors are optional configuration files for a web application.
10. Setting up Tomcat Container is only necessary for deploying Java applications.

Exercise 3 – Fill in the blanks
1. In Tomcat, the __________ directory is where web applications are deployed.
2. When deploying a web application to Tomcat, the application's files are typically placed in the __________ directory.
3. Eclipse is commonly used as an __________ for developing Java web applications.
4. Configuring Servlet and JSP API Dependencies ensures that the necessary __________ are included in the project.
5. Web application project structure includes directories for storing __________, JSP files, and configuration files.
6. Web containers manage the ___ of servlets, including initialization, request processing, and destruction.
7. After building the project using a build tool like Maven or Gradle, the web application can be deployed to a ___ for testing and production deployment.
8. Web containers include an embedded ___ to handle incoming HTTP requests from clients.
9. A ___ is a runtime environment for executing Java servlets, JavaServer Pages (JSP), and other Java web components.
10. Servlets and JSPs are stored in the ___ directory within the project structure.

Exercise 4 – Match Case
1. Servlet Container
2. Server.xml
3. WAR File
4. Catalina

A. A packaged web application that can be deployed to Tomcat.
B. The Tomcat servlet engine responsible for processing requests.
C. Main configuration file in Tomcat where server settings are defined.
D. Handles the execution of Java Servlets and JSP pages.

Exercise 5– One word answer
1.What does HTML stand for?
2. What is a URL?

Exercise 6 – Small answer
1. What is CSS?
2. What is a browser?

Exercise 7 – Long answer
1. What are the components of a URL and how does it work?
2. How does a web server work?

Answer-
Exercise 1 – 1) b 2) d 3) b 4) d) 5) d 6) d 7) c 8) c 9) d 10) c
Exercise 2 – 1) False 2) True 3) False 4) True 5) True 6) True 7) False 8) False 9) False 10) False

Exercise 3 – 1) webapps 2) webapps 3) IDE (Integrated Development Environment) 4) libraries 5) servlets 6) lifecycle 7) web container 8) HTTP server 9) web container 10) src/main/java
Exercise 4 – 1 – D. Handles the execution of Java Servlets and JSP pages. 2 – C. Main configuration file in Tomcat where server settings are defined 3 – A. A packaged web application that can be deployed to Tomcat 4 – B. The Tomcat servlet engine responsible for processing requests.
Exercise 5– 1) Hypertext Markup Language 2) Locator

Online Resources

Online Practice Paper

Link: https://forms.gle/e1zXHwr3aeCiWf4c9
QR Code:

YouTube Video Link

Link: https://www.youtube.com/playlist?list=PLzlh_31VWEFrXjFY5rN0-s5xYEApWMbVW
QR Code:

CHAPTER 8 - Servlets

8.1 Introduction to Servlets

Servlets are an integral part of Java EE (Enterprise Edition) and provide a powerful mechanism for developing server-side programs that extend the capabilities of web servers. They offer a component-based, platform-independent method for building web-based applications, without the performance limitations of CGI programs.
Servlets are Java components designed to extend the capabilities of web servers by generating dynamic content and handling client requests. They execute server-side logic, allowing developers to create interactive and data-driven web applications. Servlets operate within a Java Servlet container, which manages their lifecycle and provides the necessary infrastructure for communication with clients over the HTTP protocol.
One of the key features of servlets is their ability to process client requests and generate dynamic responses based on application logic. They can handle various types of requests, such as form submissions, AJAX calls, or RESTful API requests, and produce different types of responses, including HTML, XML, JSON, or binary data.
The lifecycle of a servlet consists of several stages, including initialization, request handling, response generation, and destruction. Servlets are initialized when they are first loaded into memory by the servlet container and can handle multiple client requests concurrently, thanks to their multi-threaded execution model.
Servlets interact with clients through the Servlet API, which provides interfaces and classes for handling HTTP requests and responses. Servlets can access request parameters, session attributes, and other HTTP headers to process incoming requests and generate appropriate responses.
Overall, servlets are a fundamental technology for Java web development, offering versatility, performance, and integration capabilities. They play a crucial role in building dynamic and scalable web applications and are an essential topic for developers venturing into advanced Java web development.

8.1.1 The Role of Servlets in Web Applications

Servlets play a pivotal role in the architecture of web applications, serving as the backbone for server-side processing and interaction with clients. Here's an explanation of the role of servlets in web applications:

Handling Client Requests

Servlets are responsible for processing client requests received by the web server. They act as endpoints for incoming HTTP requests, allowing web applications to respond to user interactions such as form submissions, button clicks, or URL requests.

Generating Dynamic Content

Servlets dynamically generate content to be sent back to clients as HTTP responses. They can generate HTML pages, XML documents, JSON data, or any other type of content based on the application's business logic and data.

Implementing Business Logic

Servlets encapsulate the core business logic of web applications. They perform tasks such as data validation, processing user input, executing business rules, and interacting with databases or external services to fulfill client requests.

Managing Sessions and State

Servlets can manage user sessions and maintain state information across multiple requests. They can store session attributes, manage session expiration, and handle session tracking mechanisms to provide a personalized and interactive user experience.

Integrating with Other Components

Servlets seamlessly integrate with other components of the Java EE ecosystem, such as JavaServer Pages (JSP), JavaBeans, Enterprise JavaBeans (EJB), and JDBC (Java Database Connectivity). They work together with these components to create robust and scalable web applications.

Implementing Security Measures

Servlets can implement security measures to protect web applications from unauthorized access and malicious attacks. They can enforce authentication, authorization, and data encryption to ensure the confidentiality, integrity, and availability of sensitive information.

Facilitating Communication

Servlets facilitate communication between clients and other parts of the web application, such as business logic components, data access layers, or external services. They act as intermediaries, processing incoming requests, coordinating interactions, and orchestrating responses.

8.2 Servlet Code Structure

The structure of a servlet code follows a specific pattern mandated by the Servlet API. Here's an explanation of the typical structure of a servlet code:

Import Statements

The servlet code begins with import statements to import necessary classes and packages from the Servlet API and any other dependencies required by the servlet.

```
import javax.servlet.*;
import javax.servlet.http.*;
import java.io.*;
```

Servlet Declaration

Next, you declare the servlet class by extending the HttpServlet class provided by the Servlet API. You also need to override the doGet() or doPost() method (or both) to handle incoming HTTP GET or POST requests.

```
public class MyServlet extends HttpServlet {
// Override doGet() or doPost() method
protected void doGet(HttpServletRequest request, HttpServletResponse response)
throws ServletException, IOException {
// Servlet logic for handling GET requests
}
}
```

Servlet Initialization

If your servlet needs to perform initialization tasks when it is first loaded into memory by the servlet container, you can override the init() method.

```
public void init() throws ServletException {
// Initialization tasks
}
```

Request Handling

Inside the doGet() or doPost() method, you write the logic to handle incoming HTTP requests. You typically access request parameters, session attributes, and other HTTP headers to process the request and generate an appropriate response.

```
protected void doGet(HttpServletRequest request, HttpServletResponse response)
        throws ServletException, IOException {
    // Access request parameters
    String paramValue = request.getParameter("paramName");
    // Access session attributes
    HttpSession session = request.getSession();
    Object attributeValue = session.getAttribute("attributeName");
    // Generate response
    response.setContentType("text/html");
    PrintWriter out = response.getWriter();
    out.println("<html><body>");
    out.println("<h1>Hello, World!</h1>");
    out.println("</body></html>");
}
```

Servlet Destruction

If your servlet needs to perform cleanup tasks before it is removed from service by the servlet container, you can override the destroy() method.

```
public void destroy() {
    // Cleanup tasks
}
```

Basic Servlet Example

```
import java.io.*;
import javax.servlet.*;
import javax.servlet.http.*;
public class MyFirstServlet extends HttpServlet {
public void doGet(HttpServletRequest request, HttpServletResponse response)
  throws ServletException, IOException {
    // Set the response message's MIME type
    response.setContentType("text/html;charset=UTF-8");
    // Write the response message to the client
    PrintWriter out = response.getWriter();
    try {
      out.println("<!DOCTYPE html>"); // HTML 5
      out.println("<html><head>");
      out.println("<meta http-equiv='Content-Type' content='text/html; charset=UTF-8'>");
      out.println("<title>My First Servlet</title></head>");
      out.println("<body>");
      out.println("<h1>Hello, World!</h1>"); // says Hello
      out.println("</body>");
      out.println("</html>");
    } finally
{
      out.close(); // Always close the output writer
    }
  }
}
```

Explanation

Imports

The servlet imports necessary classes from javax.servlet and javax.servlet.http packages.

Class Declaration: The servlet class MyFirstServlet extends HttpServlet, making it a servlet capable of handling HTTP requests.

Overriding doGet(): This method is overridden to provide the implementation for handling GET requests. It takes HttpServletRequest and HttpServletResponse objects as parameters.

Setting Content Type: The response's MIME type is set to "text/html" to inform the client that the response is HTML.

Sending Response: The servlet uses a PrintWriter retrieved from the HttpServletResponse object to send HTML content back to the client.

Deploying a Servlet

To deploy a servlet, you need to compile the class and package it into a web application archive (WAR) file or directly place it in the appropriate directory of a web container (like Apache Tomcat). The servlet must also be declared and mapped to a URL pattern in the web application's web.xml deployment descriptor or through annotations in the servlet code.

8.3 HTTP Methods

HTTP methods, also known as HTTP request methods, are the verbs that clients (e.g., web browsers) use to communicate with web servers. Each HTTP method has a specific purpose and behaviour, allowing clients to perform different actions on resources identified by URLs. Here's a detailed explanation of commonly used HTTP methods:

GET

Purpose: Used to request data from a specified resource.

Behaviour: The GET method retrieves data from the server without altering it. It is idempotent, meaning multiple identical requests should have the same effect as a single request.

Examples: Retrieving a web page, fetching user information from a database.

POST
Purpose: Used to submit data to be processed to a specified resource.
Behaviour: The POST method sends data to the server in the request body. It is not idempotent, meaning repeated requests may have different effects each time.
Examples: Submitting a form, uploading a file, creating a new resource on the server.
PUT
Purpose: Used to replace or update a resource on the server.
Behaviour: The PUT method sends data to the server to replace the specified resource entirely or create it if it does not exist. It is idempotent, meaning repeated identical requests should have the same effect as a single request.
Examples Updating user profile information, uploading a new version of a file.
DELETE
Purpose: Used to delete a specified resource from the server.
Behaviour: The DELETE method requests the server to remove the specified resource. It is idempotent, meaning repeated identical requests should have the same effect as a single request.
Examples: Deleting a user account, removing a file from a server.
PATCH
Purpose: Used to apply partial modifications to a resource.
Behaviour: The PATCH method is similar to PUT but only updates the specified fields of the resource, leaving other fields unchanged. It is not guaranteed to be idempotent.
Examples: Updating specific fields of a user profile, modifying attributes of an entity.
HEAD
Purpose: Similar to GET but retrieves only the response headers, not the response body.
Behaviour: The HEAD method is used to obtain metadata about the requested resource without transferring the actual data. It is typically used to check the status of a resource or verify its existence.
Examples: Checking the last modification date of a resource, verifying the content type of a file.
OPTIONS
Purpose: Used to describe the communication options for the target resource.
Behaviour: The OPTIONS method requests information about the communication options available for the target resource, such as supported HTTP methods and available request headers.
Examples: Cross-origin resource sharing (CORS) preflight requests, discovering available API endpoints.
Understanding when to use each HTTP method allows developers to design more effective and semantic web services, adhering to the principles of RESTful architecture when applicable

8.4 Servlet Lifecycle

The lifecycle of a servlet is managed by the servlet container in which the servlet has been deployed. Understanding this lifecycle is crucial for developing efficient and effective servlets.
Loading and Instantiation
Process: The servlet container loads the servlet class, usually on the first request to the servlet, but it can also load it when the server starts if configured to do so.
Instantiation: After loading the servlet class, the container creates an instance of the servlet.
Initialization
Loading: When a servlet is first accessed or when the servlet container starts up, it loads the servlet class into memory.
Instantiation: The servlet container creates an instance of the servlet by calling its no-argument constructor.
Initialization: After instantiation, the servlet container initializes the servlet by calling its init() method. This method is invoked only once during the servlet's lifecycle and is used to perform any initialization tasks, such as setting up resources, establishing database connections, or loading configuration parameters.
Request Handling
Client Request: When a client sends an HTTP request to the servlet, the servlet container invokes the appropriate method (doGet(), doPost(), doPut(), etc.) based on the type of request.
Service Method: The servlet's service() method acts as the central dispatcher for handling client requests. It receives the request and response objects as parameters and determines which specific method (doGet(), doPost(), etc.) to call based on the request's HTTP method (GET, POST, PUT, DELETE, etc.).

Processing Request: Inside the appropriate method (doGet(), doPost(), etc.), the servlet processes the client's request, retrieves necessary data, performs business logic, and generates an appropriate response.

Response Generation

HTTP Response: After processing the client's request, the servlet constructs an HTTP response containing the desired content (HTML, XML, JSON, etc.) and any necessary headers (content type, status code, etc.).

Sending Response: The servlet sends the response back to the client by writing it to the response output stream obtained from the HttpServletResponse object.

Destruction

Shutdown or Unloading: When the servlet container shuts down or decides to remove the servlet from service (e.g., due to lack of usage), it calls the servlet's destroy() method.

Cleanup: The destroy() method allows the servlet to perform any necessary cleanup tasks, such as closing database connections, releasing resources, or saving state information.

Garbage Collection: After the destroy() method is called, the servlet instance becomes eligible for garbage collection, and the memory occupied by the servlet is reclaimed by the JVM.

Lifecycle Methods

init(): Initializes the servlet and is called by the servlet container during servlet initialization.

service(): Handles client requests and dispatches them to the appropriate doXXX() method based on the request's HTTP method.

doGet(), doPost(), etc.: Methods for handling specific types of HTTP requests (GET, POST, etc.). These methods are called by the service() method.

destroy(): Performs cleanup tasks and is called by the servlet container before removing the servlet from service.

8.5 Servlet Context and Servlet Config

Servlet Context and Servlet Config are important components in the Java Servlet API that provide servlets with access to configuration parameters, initialization parameters, and application-wide resources. Here's a detailed explanation of Servlet Context and Servlet Config

Servlet Context

Definition: Servlet Context represents the entire web application and provides a way for servlets to communicate with the servlet container.

Scope: Servlet Context is global to the entire web application and remains consistent across all servlets and requests within the same application.

Accessing Servlet Context: Servlets can access the Servlet Context using the getServletContext() method inherited from the GenericServlet class or the getServletContext() method of the ServletConfig object.

Functionality

Initialization Parameters: Servlet Context can store initialization parameters defined in the deployment descriptor (web.xml) and make them available to servlets.

Attributes: Servlet Context can store and share attributes (key-value pairs) across servlets within the same application. Attributes can be set, retrieved, and removed using methods like setAttribute(), getAttribute(), and removeAttribute().

Resource Access: Servlet Context provides methods to access application-wide resources such as files, database connections, JNDI resources, and other servlets.

Event Handling: Servlet Context can listen for application-level events, such as context initialization and destruction, using Servlet Context Listeners (ServletContextListener).

Servlet Config

Definition: Servlet Config provides servlets with access to initialization parameters specific to that servlet and allows them to retrieve configuration information from the deployment descriptor.

Scope: Servlet Config is specific to each servlet and provides configuration parameters that are relevant only to that servlet.

Initialization Parameters: Servlet Config allows servlets to access initialization parameters defined in the deployment descriptor (web.xml) using methods like getInitParameter() and getInitParameterNames().

Accessing Servlet Context: Servlet Config provides a reference to the Servlet Context, allowing servlets to access application-wide resources and attributes.

Functionality

Initialization Parameters: Servlet Config allows servlets to retrieve initialization parameters specific to that servlet, enabling customization and configuration of servlet Behaviour.
Access to Servlet Context: Servlet Config provides access to the Servlet Context, enabling servlets to share information and resources with other servlets within the same application.

Relationship Between Servlet Context and Servlet Config
Servlet Config within Servlet Context: Each servlet has its own Servlet Config instance, which is obtained from the Servlet Context during servlet initialization.
Sharing Information: Servlet Config allows servlets to access Servlet Context attributes and resources, enabling communication and resource sharing between servlets within the same application.
Customization: Servlet Config allows servlets to customize their Behaviour by providing access to initialization parameters specific to that servlet, while Servlet Context provides access to application-wide configuration parameters.
Understanding the distinction and proper use of ServletContext and ServletConfig is fundamental for effectively managing configuration data within Java web applications, enabling servlets to behave dynamically based on the provided initialization parameters.

8.6 Forwarding and Redirection of Requests

In web applications, controlling the flow of requests and responses is essential. Servlets provide two mechanisms for this purpose: Request Forwarding and Response Redirection. Each serves a different use case in navigating between resources within a web application.
Request Forwarding
Request forwarding in Java servlets is a mechanism that enables the servlet container to transfer control and data from one servlet to another servlet, JSP, or resource within the same web application. It allows servlets to collaborate and share data seamlessly, facilitating modular and maintainable web application development. Let's delve into the mechanism, usage, and implementation of request forwarding in detail:
Mechanism
Client Request: The client sends an HTTP request to the servlet container, typically targeting a specific servlet.
Servlet Processing: The servlet container determines the appropriate servlet to handle the request based on the request URL or other criteria.
Forwarding: The servlet that receives the request can decide to forward the request to another resource within the same web application.
Forwarding Process: The servlet obtains a RequestDispatcher object for the target resource using getRequestDispatcher() method. It then calls the forward() method of the RequestDispatcher, passing the request and response objects.
Target Resource Processing: The forwarded request is processed by the target resource (servlet, JSP, or HTML file). The target resource can access request attributes set by the forwarding servlet and generate a response accordingly.
Response Generation: The target resource generates a response, which is sent back to the client through the same request cycle.
Usage
Collaborative Processing: Request forwarding is used when multiple servlets or resources need to collaborate to process a single client request.
Data Sharing: It allows servlets to share data (request attributes) and control flow within the same web application.

Implementation
Forwarding Servlet (Example: FirstServlet):

```
import javax.servlet.*;
import javax.servlet.http.*;
import java.io.*;
public class FirstServlet extends HttpServlet {
  protected void doGet(HttpServletRequest request, HttpServletResponse response)
        throws ServletException, IOException {
    // Prepare data or perform business logic
    String message = "Data prepared in FirstServlet";
```

```
        // Set data as request attribute
        request.setAttribute("message", message);
        // Get RequestDispatcher for SecondServlet
        RequestDispatcher dispatcher = request.getRequestDispatcher("/SecondServlet");
        // Forward request to SecondServlet
        dispatcher.forward(request, response);
    }
}
```

Target Servlet (Example: SecondServlet):

```
import javax.servlet.*;
import javax.servlet.http.*;
import java.io.*;
public class SecondServlet extends HttpServlet {
    protected void doGet(HttpServletRequest request, HttpServletResponse response)
            throws ServletException, IOException {
        // Get data from request attribute set by FirstServlet
        String message = (String) request.getAttribute("message");
        // Set content type
        response.setContentType("text/html");
        // Write response
        PrintWriter out = response.getWriter();
        out.println("<html><body>");
        out.println("<h1>Message from FirstServlet: " + message + "</h1>");
        out.println("</body></html>");
    }
}
```

1. Response Redirection

Response redirection in Java servlets is a mechanism used to instruct the client's browser to send a new request to a different URL. It allows servlets to redirect users to other resources within the same or different web applications. Let's explore the mechanism, usage, and implementation of response redirection in detail:

Mechanism

Client Request: The client sends an HTTP request to the servlet container, targeting a specific servlet or resource.

Servlet Processing: The servlet processes the client's request and determines that a redirection response is required.

Redirection Response: The servlet sends an HTTP redirection response to the client's browser, typically with a status code of 3xx (e.g., 302 Found, 307 Temporary Redirect).

Redirect Location: The redirection response includes the URL of the target resource to which the client should send a new request.

Client's Browser: Upon receiving the redirection response, the client's browser automatically sends a new request to the specified URL.

New Request Cycle: The servlet container processes the new request from the client's browser, and the requested resource generates a response accordingly.

Usage

URL Changes: Redirecting users to a different URL is useful when a resource has moved permanently or temporarily to a new location.

External Resources: Redirecting users to resources on different servers or domains enables integration with external services or applications.

Implementation

Redirection Servlet (Example: LoginServlet):

```
import javax.servlet.*;
import javax.servlet.http.*;
import java.io.*;
```

```java
public class LoginServlet extends HttpServlet {
  protected void doPost(HttpServletRequest request, HttpServletResponse response)
      throws ServletException, IOException {
    // Perform login validation
    boolean isLoggedIn = true; // Assuming login is successful
    if (isLoggedIn) {
      // Redirect to welcome.jsp
      response.sendRedirect("welcome.jsp");
    } else {
      // Show error message
      response.setContentType("text/html");
      PrintWriter out = response.getWriter();
      out.println("<html><body>");
      out.println("<h1>Login Failed</h1>");
      out.println("</body></html>");
    }
  }
}
```

welcome.jsp (Target Resource):

```jsp
<%@ page language="java" contentType="text/html; charset=UTF-8" pageEncoding="UTF-8"%>
<!DOCTYPE html>
<html>
<head>
  <meta charset="UTF-8">
  <title>Welcome</title>
</head>
<body>
  <h1>Welcome User!</h1>
  <!-- Display user-specific content -->
</body>
</html>
```

Exercise

Exercise 1 - MCQ

1. What is a Servlet?
a) A Java class that extends the capabilities of servers.
b) A static HTML page.
c) A client-side JavaScript program.
d) A database management tool.
2. Which interface must a servlet implement to handle requests?
a) Runnable
b) HttpServlet
c) ActionListener
d) Remote
3. Which method is called by the servlet container to signal that a servlet is being placed into service?
a) init()
b) start()
c) service()
d) run()
4. Which HTTP method is idempotent?
a) GET
b) POST
c) PUT
d) Both a and c
5. What is the purpose of the doPost() method in a servlet?

a) To handle GET requests
b) To handle POST requests
c) To initialize servlet
d) To destroy the servlet
6. What is Servlet Context?
a) A configuration object for a specific servlet
b) An interface that provides servlet configuration information
c) A shared space that all servlets in the same web application can access
d) None of the above
7. Which method is used to forward a request from a servlet to another resource?
a) sendRedirect()
b) forward()
c) redirectTo()
d) transfer()
8. What does the ServletConfig interface provide?
a) Initialization parameters for a servlet
b) A reference to the ServletContext
c) Methods to communicate with the servlet container
d) All of the above
9. What is the difference between forwarding and redirection in servlets?
a) Forwarding occurs on the client-side, while redirection occurs on the server-side.
b) Forwarding occurs on the server-side, while redirection occurs on the client-side.
c) There is no difference; both are the same.
d) Forwarding sends data, while redirection cannot send data.
10. Which lifecycle method is called once when the servlet is no longer needed?
a) init()
b) service()
c) destroy()
d) finalize()

Exercise 2 - True/False

1. A servlet must be a direct or indirect subclass of the HttpServlet class.
2. The doGet() method is used to handle POST requests.
3. Servlets are initialized each time they receive a request.
4. The init() method is called only once during the lifecycle of a servlet.
5. Servlets can directly write to the response output stream using the getWriter() method of the response object.
6. The service() method is responsible for dispatching requests to the servlet's doGet() or doPost() methods, among others.
7. A servlet's destroy() method is called before the servlet is removed from memory.
8. HTTP GET requests should be used to submit sensitive information.
9. ServletConfig parameters are shared across all servlets in a web application.
10. Servlets can be configured using annotations or through the web.xml deployment descriptor.

Exercise 3 - Fill in the blanks

1. The ________ method of the HttpServlet class is used to handle GET requests.
2. Servlet lifecycle begins with the ________ method and ends with the ________ method.
3. To maintain session between client requests, servlets commonly use ________.
4. ________ allows servlets to forward a request to another resource within the same application.
5. The configuration object passed to a servlet during initialization is known as ________.
6. Servlets can be configured in the __________ file using servlet mappings, initialization parameters, and other settings.
7. Servlets can access request parameters, headers, and other information using methods provided by the __________ object.
8. The __________ method in a servlet is called by the container to process client requests.
9. Servlets are deployed and run within a __________, which is a container for servlets and manages their lifecycle.

10. The __________ method in a servlet is called by the container to initialize the servlet instance.

Exercise 4 – Match Case

1. Method to send a server error response
2. Annotation for servlet initialization parameters
3. Method to obtain the ServletContext object
4. Used to define a listener for servlet events

A. getServletContext()
B. @WebListener
C. sendError()
D. @WebInitParam

Exercise 5 – One word answer

1. What method is used to retrieve form data sent through an HTTP POST request in servlets?
2. What mechanism is commonly used to track a user's session in servlets?

Exercise 6 – Small answer

1. What HTTP status code indicates a successful HTTP request?
2. Which annotation is used to define a servlet in Java EE without using the web.xml file?

Exercise 7 – Long answer

1. Describe the servlet lifecycle, including each stage from when it is first loaded until it is destroyed.
2. Explain the difference between forwarding and redirection in the context of servlets, including when each is used.

Answer-

Exercise 1 – 1) a 2) b 3) a 4) d 5) b 6) c 7) b 8) d 9) b 10) c
Exercise 2 – 1) True 2) False 3) False 4) True 5) True 6) True 7) True 8) False 9) False 10) True
Exercise 3 – 1) doGet 2) init, destroy 3) cookies or HttpSession 4) RequestDispatcher 5) ServletConfig 6) web.xml 7) HttpServletRequest 8) service() 9) servlet container 10) init()
Exercise 4 - 1 – C. sendError() 2 – D. @WebInitParam 3 – A. getServletContext() 4 – B. @WebListener
Exercise 5 – 1) getParameter 2) HttpSession

Online Resources

Online Practice Paper

Link: https://forms.gle/KCd3wxQJ35RS4MjMA
QR Code:

YouTube Video Link

Link: https://www.youtube.com/playlist?list=PLzlh_31VWEFqc1WrGhl0GA26b13vgs3YK
QR Code:

CHAPTER 9 - Session Management

9.1 Understanding Sessions

In the context of web development, particularly when dealing with advanced Java technologies such as Java Servlets and JavaServer Pages (JSP), understanding the concept of sessions and how session information is passed between the client and the server is crucial. This knowledge is foundational for creating dynamic, interactive web applications that can maintain state across multiple page requests. This chapter aims to provide a comprehensive explanation of sessions, how they work, and the mechanisms used for session information passing, ensuring clarity and ease of understanding for students.

9.1.1 What is a Session?

In web development, a session is a fundamental concept that allows web servers to maintain stateful communication with clients over multiple requests. It enables the server to associate data with a specific client and retain information about the client's interactions with the web application throughout a browsing session.

At its core, a session is established when a client makes an initial request to the server, typically through a web browser. The server assigns a unique identifier, known as a session ID, to the client, which is often stored as a cookie in the client's browser. This session ID serves as a means of tracking and identifying the client's session as they navigate through the web application.

Sessions play a crucial role in enabling stateful Behaviour in otherwise stateless HTTP protocol. By maintaining session state, web applications can personalize user experiences, track user interactions, and facilitate various functionalities such as user authentication, shopping cart management, and workflow tracking.

One of the primary functionalities of sessions is to store data associated with a particular client. This data can include user preferences, authentication credentials, shopping cart items, and other relevant information. The server retains this session data for the duration of the session, allowing it to be accessed and updated as the client interacts with the web application.

Sessions also have a defined lifespan, after which they may expire or be invalidated. Session expiration can occur due to user inactivity, explicit logout actions, or based on server-side configuration. Session management mechanisms often include features to prevent session fixation, session hijacking, and ensure the secure transmission of session identifiers to mitigate security risks.

Overall, sessions are a foundational component of web development, enabling stateful communication between web servers and clients. Understanding session management mechanisms and their implementation is essential for building robust, secure, and user-friendly web applications in Java and other web development frameworks.

Functionality

Stateful Communication: Sessions enable stateful communication between a web server and a client by maintaining information about the client's interactions with the server across multiple requests.

Client Identification: Each session is associated with a unique identifier, known as the session ID, which is typically stored as a cookie on the client's browser or appended to URLs.

Data Storage: Sessions allow the server to store data associated with a particular client, such as user preferences, authentication credentials, shopping cart items, or any other relevant information.

Session Tracking: The server uses the session ID to track and identify each client's session, allowing it to retrieve and update session data as the client interacts with the web application.

Expiration: Sessions have a defined lifespan, after which they may expire or be invalidated. Session expiration can occur after a period of inactivity, upon user logout, or based on server-side configuration.

Security: Session management mechanisms often include security features such as session fixation prevention, session hijacking prevention, and secure transmission of session identifiers to protect against unauthorized access.

Usage

User Authentication: Sessions are commonly used to track user authentication status and store user credentials or access tokens during a user's logged-in session.

Personalization: Sessions allow web applications to personalize user experiences by storing user preferences, settings, and browsing history across multiple requests.

Shopping Carts: E-commerce applications use sessions to maintain shopping cart data, allowing users to add, modify, and view items in their cart during a browsing session.

Workflow Management: Sessions facilitate workflow management by maintaining the state of multi-step processes or transactions, such as online forms or checkout processes.

Implementation

Session Tracking Mechanisms: Sessions can be tracked using various mechanisms, including cookies, URL rewriting, hidden form fields, or custom HTTP headers.

Server-Side Storage: Session data is typically stored on the server-side in memory, in a database, or in persistent storage such as files or caches.

Session Management APIs: Most web development frameworks provide session management APIs that abstract the complexities of session handling and provide convenient methods for storing, retrieving, and invalidating session data.

9.1.2 Why Use Sessions?

Using sessions in web development offers several advantages that enhance the functionality, security, and user experience of web applications. Here's a detailed explanation of why sessions are commonly used:

Stateful Communication

Sessions enable stateful communication between web servers and clients by allowing the server to maintain information about the client's interactions with the web application over multiple requests.

Without sessions, HTTP, being a stateless protocol, would require re-authentication and re-submission of data with every request, leading to a less seamless user experience.

Data Persistence

Sessions allow web servers to persist data associated with a particular client across multiple requests.

This data can include user preferences, authentication credentials, shopping cart items, and any other information relevant to the user's session.

Personalization

Sessions facilitate personalized user experiences by storing user-specific data and settings.

Web applications can tailor content, recommendations, and functionality based on the user's preferences and past interactions stored in the session.

User Authentication

Sessions are commonly used to track user authentication status and maintain session data related to logged-in users.

Once authenticated, session data can include user roles, permissions, and access tokens, allowing the server to enforce security policies and provide personalized content.

Shopping Cart Management

E-commerce applications utilize sessions to manage shopping cart data across multiple requests.

Users can add, remove, and modify items in their shopping cart during a browsing session, with the session retaining the cart's state until checkout.

Workflow Management

Sessions help manage multi-step processes or transactions by maintaining the state of user interactions.

Online forms, checkout processes, and other workflows can retain user input and progress, allowing users to resume where they left off without losing data.

Security Enhancements

Session management mechanisms include features to prevent session fixation, session hijacking, and other security vulnerabilities.

Session expiration, secure transmission of session identifiers, and validation of session data help mitigate security risks and protect user information.

Improved Performance

By reducing the need for repeated authentication and data submission, sessions contribute to a smoother user experience and improved performance.

Users can navigate seamlessly through the application without interruptions, enhancing overall satisfaction and engagement.

How Sessions Work

Sessions work by establishing a stateful communication between a web server and a client (typically a web browser) and maintaining information about the client's interactions with the web application over multiple requests. Here's a detailed explanation of how sessions work in web development:

Session Initialization

When a client (e.g., a web browser) makes an initial request to the server, the server creates a new session or retrieves an existing session associated with the client.

The server generates a unique identifier for the session, known as the session ID. This session ID is typically stored as a cookie in the client's browser or appended to URLs.

Session Tracking

Once initialized, the session is associated with the client through the session ID. The client includes the session ID in subsequent requests to the server, allowing the server to identify and track the client's session.

Session tracking mechanisms include cookies, URL rewriting, hidden form fields, or custom HTTP headers, depending on the configuration and capabilities of the server and client.

Data Storage

Sessions allow the server to store data associated with a particular client, such as user preferences, authentication credentials, shopping cart items, and other relevant information.

Session data is typically stored on the server-side in memory, in a database, or in persistent storage such as files or caches.

Session Lifecycle

The session has a defined lifespan, after which it may expire or be invalidated. Session expiration can occur due to user inactivity, explicit logout actions, or based on server-side configuration.

Session management mechanisms often include features to control session expiration, such as setting session timeout values and implementing session invalidation logic.

Data Retrieval and Update

During the client's session, the server can retrieve and update session data as needed based on the client's interactions with the web application.

Servlets, JSPs, or other server-side components can access session data using APIs provided by the servlet container, such as the HttpSession interface in Java servlets.

Session Termination

When the client's session ends (e.g., due to logout or session expiration), the server may invalidate the session and release associated resources.

Session termination may involve cleaning up session data, removing session identifiers from the client's browser, and performing any necessary cleanup tasks on the server-side.

Security Considerations

Sessions play a crucial role in web application security by managing user authentication, enforcing access control policies, and protecting sensitive data.

Session management mechanisms include features to prevent session fixation, session hijacking, and other security vulnerabilities, such as secure transmission of session identifiers and validation of session data.

9.2 Session Information Passing between Client and Server

Session information passing between a client and a server involves the transmission of data associated with a user's session from the client (typically a web browser) to the server and vice versa. This process allows the server to maintain stateful communication with the client and retain information about the user's interactions with the web application. Here's a detailed explanation of how session information is passed between the client and server:

Session Initialization

When a client makes an initial request to the server, the server creates a new session or retrieves an existing session associated with the client.

The server generates a unique identifier for the session, known as the session ID, which is used to identify and track the client's session.

Session ID Transmission

Once initialized, the session ID is transmitted to the client through various mechanisms, such as cookies, URL rewriting, hidden form fields, or custom HTTP headers.

Cookies are the most common mechanism for transmitting session IDs, as they are automatically included in subsequent requests to the server.

Client-Side Storage

The client stores the session ID locally, typically as a cookie in the web browser's cookie storage.

Cookies are automatically included in HTTP requests sent to the server, allowing the server to identify and associate the requests with the client's session.

Session Data Transmission

During the client's session, the server stores and updates session data associated with the session ID.

Session data can include user preferences, authentication credentials, shopping cart items, and any other information relevant to the user's session.

Server-Side Storage

Session data is stored on the server-side, typically in memory, in a database, or in persistent storage such as files or caches.

The server uses the session ID to retrieve and update session data as needed based on the client's interactions with the web application.

Session Termination

When the client's session ends (e.g., due to logout or session expiration), the server may invalidate the session and release associated resources.

Session termination involves cleaning up session data, removing session identifiers from the client's browser, and performing any necessary cleanup tasks on the server-side.

Security Considerations

Session information passing involves security considerations to protect sensitive data and prevent security vulnerabilities such as session fixation and session hijacking.

Secure transmission of session identifiers, validation of session data, and implementing proper session management mechanisms are essential for ensuring the security of session information.

Cookies

Cookies are small pieces of data that are stored on the client-side (typically in the user's web browser) and are used to persistently store information about the user's interaction with a website. In advanced Java web development, cookies play a crucial role in session management, user authentication, personalization, and tracking user behaviour. Here's a detailed explanation of cookies

Functionality

Persistent Data Storage: Cookies allow web servers to store small amounts of data on the client-side, which persists across multiple requests and sessions.

Session Management: Cookies are commonly used to manage sessions by storing unique session identifiers (session IDs) that enable the server to identify and associate subsequent requests with the correct session.

User Authentication: Cookies are used to store authentication tokens or credentials, allowing users to remain authenticated across multiple requests without having to re-enter their credentials.

Personalization: Cookies enable websites to personalize user experiences by storing user preferences, settings, and browsing history, allowing the website to tailor content and recommendations based on the user's preferences.

Tracking and Analytics: Cookies are often used for tracking user Behaviour, such as the pages visited, links clicked, and actions taken on the website. This data can be used for analytics, advertising, and website optimization purposes.

Implementation

Creating Cookies: Cookies are created by the server and sent to the client's browser as part of an HTTP response. The server sets one or more cookie headers containing key-value pairs of data to be stored in the cookie.

Storing Cookies: Once received, the client's browser stores the cookies locally. Cookies are typically stored as text files on the client's device, with each cookie associated with a specific domain and path.

Sending Cookies: With each subsequent HTTP request to the same domain, the client's browser automatically sends any relevant cookies associated with that domain in the request headers.

Accessing Cookies: On the server-side, web applications can access cookies sent by the client's browser using server-side programming languages such as Java. This allows the server to retrieve and process the data stored in the cookies.

Updating and Deleting Cookies: Cookies can be updated or deleted by the server by sending updated cookie headers with new values or by setting expiration dates to delete cookies.

Security Considerations

Data Privacy: Cookies may contain sensitive information, so it's essential to store only necessary data in cookies and avoid storing sensitive information such as passwords or credit card details.

Secure Transmission: When transmitting cookies over HTTP connections, it's crucial to use secure HTTPS connections to encrypt the data and prevent eavesdropping or interception.

Session Security: Session cookies should have short lifespans and be securely managed to prevent session hijacking or fixation attacks.

URL Rewriting

URL rewriting is a technique used in web development to dynamically modify URLs of web pages or resources in a web application. This technique allows web developers to append or modify query parameters in URLs, enabling session management, tracking user behaviour, and implementing other functionalities. Here's a detailed explanation of URL rewriting:

Functionality

Session Management: URL rewriting is commonly used for session management in web applications. Instead of using cookies to store session IDs, the server embeds the session ID directly into URLs. This allows the server to track sessions without relying on cookies.

Tracking User Behaviour: URL rewriting can be used to track user behaviour by appending unique identifiers or tracking parameters to URLs. This data can be used for analytics, advertising, or personalization purposes.

Dynamic URL Generation: URL rewriting allows web developers to dynamically generate URLs with specific parameters based on user input, application state, or other factors. This enables the creation of user-friendly and SEO-friendly URLs.

Stateful Communication: URL rewriting enables stateful communication between web servers and clients by including session identifiers or other state information directly in URLs. This allows the server to maintain state across multiple requests without relying on cookies or other client-side storage mechanisms.

Implementation

Appending query parameters: URL rewriting involves appending query parameters to URLs using the delimiter followed by key value pairs separated by & symbols. For example:
http://example.com/page?param1=value1&param2=value2.

Embedding Session IDs: To implement session management using URL rewriting, the server embeds the session ID directly into URLs. For example: http://example.com/page?sessionid=123456789.

Dynamic URL Generation: Web applications generate URLs dynamically by constructing URLs based on application logic, user input, or other factors. Server-side scripting languages such as JavaServer Pages (JSP), Servlets, or PHP are commonly used to generate dynamic URLs.

Handling Rewritten URLs: On the server-side, web applications parse rewritten URLs to extract query parameters and process requests accordingly. Server-side programming languages such as Java or PHP provide APIs for handling URL parameters and processing requests.

Security Considerations

Session Security: When using URL rewriting for session management, it's essential to ensure the security of session IDs to prevent session hijacking or fixation attacks. Session IDs should be securely generated, transmitted over secure connections (HTTPS), and invalidated after a certain period or upon logout.

Data Privacy: URL rewriting may expose sensitive information, such as session IDs or user-specific data, in URLs. It's crucial to avoid including sensitive information in URLs or encrypting sensitive data to protect user privacy.

Hidden Form Fields

Hidden form fields are HTML form fields that are not displayed to the user in the web browser but are still submitted along with other form data when the form is submitted. These hidden fields are used to pass information between web pages or to store data temporarily on the client side. Here's a detailed explanation of hidden form fields:

Functionality

Data Passing: Hidden form fields allow web developers to pass data between web pages or components without displaying it to the user. This data can include session identifiers, user preferences, or any other information needed for processing the form.

State Management: Hidden form fields can be used to maintain state information between requests, such as the current page state, user actions, or application context. This helps in preserving user input or application state across multiple interactions.

Security: Hidden form fields can be used to store sensitive data or tokens securely on the client side, reducing the risk of exposing sensitive information to malicious users or attackers.

Client-Side Data Storage: Hidden form fields provide a mechanism for storing temporary data on the client side, which can be accessed and manipulated using JavaScript or other client-side scripting languages.

Implementation

HTML Syntax: Hidden form fields are created using the <input type="hidden"> element in HTML. This element creates a hidden input field that is not displayed in the web browser.

Setting Field Values: Hidden form fields can have default values set by the server or dynamically generated values set by client-side scripting languages. These values are submitted along with other form data when the form is submitted.

Accessing Hidden Fields: Hidden form fields can be accessed and manipulated using JavaScript or other client-side scripting languages. This allows developers to dynamically update hidden field values based on user actions or application logic.

Example

```
<form action="submit.php" method="post">
<input type="hidden" name="session_id" value="123456789">
<input type="hidden" name="action" value="update">
<!-- Other form fields -->
<button type="submit">Submit</button>
</form>
```

In this example, two hidden form fields (session_id and action) are included in the form. When the form is submitted, these hidden fields are sent along with other form data to the server-side script specified in the form's action attribute.

Security Considerations

Sensitive Data: Avoid storing sensitive information in hidden form fields, as this data can be accessed and manipulated by users or attackers using browser developer tools or client-side scripting.

Data Integrity: Hidden form fields can be modified by users or attackers, so it's essential to validate and sanitize form data on the server side to ensure data integrity and prevent injection attacks.

SSL Sessions

SSL (Secure Sockets Layer) sessions, also known as TLS (Transport Layer Security) sessions, are cryptographic protocols used to establish secure communication channels between a client and a server over the Internet. SSL/TLS sessions provide encryption, data integrity, and authentication mechanisms to protect sensitive information transmitted between the client and server. Here's a detailed explanation of SSL sessions:

Functionality

Encryption: SSL/TLS sessions encrypt data transmitted between the client and server, ensuring that it cannot be intercepted or tampered with by unauthorized parties. Encryption algorithms such as AES (Advanced Encryption Standard) are commonly used to secure data.

Data Integrity: SSL/TLS sessions provide mechanisms to ensure the integrity of transmitted data, preventing tampering or modification during transit. Message authentication codes (MACs) or cryptographic hash functions are used to verify data integrity.

Authentication: SSL/TLS sessions enable mutual authentication between the client and server, ensuring that both parties can verify each other's identities. This prevents man-in-the-middle attacks and establishes trust in the communication channel.

Session Establishment: SSL/TLS sessions begin with a handshake process, during which the client and server negotiate cryptographic parameters, exchange cryptographic keys, and verify each other's identities. Once the handshake is complete, a secure communication channel is established.
Session Resumption: SSL/TLS sessions support session resumption mechanisms, allowing clients and servers to resume previously established sessions without repeating the full handshake process. This improves performance and reduces latency for subsequent connections.

Implementation

SSL/TLS Protocol: SSL/TLS sessions are implemented using cryptographic protocols such as SSL 3.0, TLS 1.0, TLS 1.1, TLS 1.2, and TLS 1.3. These protocols define the rules and procedures for secure communication between clients and servers.
Certificates: SSL/TLS sessions rely on digital certificates issued by trusted certificate authorities (CAs) to authenticate the identities of clients and servers. Certificates contain public keys used for encryption and digital signatures to verify authenticity.
Key Exchange: SSL/TLS sessions use key exchange algorithms such as RSA (Rivest-Shamir-Adleman), Diffie-Hellman, or Elliptic Curve Cryptography (ECC) to securely exchange cryptographic keys during the handshake process.
Encryption Algorithms: SSL/TLS sessions support various encryption algorithms, including symmetric encryption algorithms (e.g., AES) for encrypting data and asymmetric encryption algorithms (e.g., RSA) for key exchange and digital signatures.
Session Management: SSL/TLS sessions are managed by clients and servers, which maintain session state information, cryptographic parameters, and session keys. Session tickets or session identifiers are used to resume sessions.

Security Considerations

Certificate Trust: SSL/TLS sessions rely on trusted certificate authorities (CAs) to issue valid certificates. It's essential to ensure that certificates are issued by reputable CAs and that certificate chains are properly validated.
Cipher Suites: SSL/TLS sessions support various cipher suites, each with different security properties and performance characteristics. It's crucial to use secure cipher suites and avoid deprecated or vulnerable algorithms.
Key Management: SSL/TLS sessions require secure key management practices to protect cryptographic keys from unauthorized access or disclosure. Key rotation, key storage, and key lifecycle management are essential considerations.

Best Practices for Session Management

Certainly! Effective session management is critical for maintaining security and usability in web applications. Here are some best practices for session management in advanced Java web development:

Use HTTPS

Always use HTTPS (HTTP over SSL/TLS) to encrypt data transmitted between clients and servers. This prevents eavesdropping and tampering of sensitive information, including session IDs and user data.

Generate Secure Session IDs

Generate cryptographically secure session IDs using strong random number generators. Ensure that session IDs are sufficiently long and unpredictable to prevent session prediction and brute-force attacks.

Transmit Session IDs Securely

Transmit session IDs securely over HTTPS connections to prevent interception or sniffing by attackers. Avoid exposing session IDs in URLs, as they may be logged in browser history or server logs.

Implement Session Expiration

Set appropriate session timeout values to expire inactive sessions and release server resources. Consider factors such as application sensitivity and user behaviour when determining session timeout durations.

Invalidate Sessions Properly

Invalidate sessions securely upon logout or when the user's session expires. Ensure that session data is properly cleared from server-side storage and that session IDs are no longer valid for subsequent requests.

Store Session Data Securely

Store session data securely on the server side to prevent unauthorized access or tampering by attackers. Use server-side storage mechanisms such as memory, databases, or distributed caches to store session data.

Implement Session Revocation
Implement mechanisms to revoke or invalidate specific sessions in case of suspected compromise or unauthorized access. This may involve maintaining a blacklist of revoked session IDs or implementing session revocation tokens.

Protect Session Cookies
Set secure attributes for session cookies, such as the "Secure" and "HttpOnly" flags, to prevent session hijacking and cross-site scripting (XSS) attacks. Ensure that session cookies are only transmitted over secure HTTPS connections and are inaccessible to client-side scripts.

Implement Cross-Site Request Forgery (CSRF) Protection
Implement CSRF protection mechanisms, such as synchronizer tokens or double-submit cookies, to prevent attackers from exploiting session state to perform unauthorized actions on behalf of authenticated users.

Monitor and Audit Session Activity
Monitor session activity, including login attempts, session creations, and session expirations, to detect suspicious behaviour or potential security incidents. Implement logging and auditing mechanisms to track session-related events.

Educate Users on Session Security
Educate users on session security best practices, such as logging out after each session, avoiding sharing session IDs or URLs, and recognizing signs of session hijacking or phishing attacks.

9.3 Session Management Mechanisms: Cookies, Rewriting

In the realm of advanced Java web development, understanding the mechanisms for session management is crucial for building robust, user-friendly applications. This chapter delves into two primary methods of session management: cookies and URL rewriting. These techniques enable web applications to maintain state across multiple requests in the inherently stateless HTTP protocol. We aim to provide a detailed explanation of both mechanisms, ensuring students grasp their workings, advantages, and potential pitfalls.

Cookies
Cookies are small pieces of data that a server sends to the client's browser, which the browser then stores and sends back with subsequent requests to the same server. Cookies are a fundamental tool for session management in web applications, allowing servers to identify returning users and maintain session states.

How Cookies Work for Session Management
Cookies play a fundamental role in session management for web applications, allowing developers to maintain state information between the client (browser) and server across multiple requests. Here's how cookies work for session management in advanced Java web development

Cookie Creation
When a web server responds to a client's HTTP request, it can include one or more cookies in the response headers. Cookies are small pieces of data (key-value pairs) generated by the server and sent to the client's browser to store temporary information.

Cookie Storage
Once received, the client's browser stores the cookies locally on the user's device.
Cookies are typically stored as text files in the browser's cookie storage, associated with the domain of the website that set them.

Cookie Transmission
With each subsequent HTTP request to the same domain, the client's browser automatically includes any relevant cookies associated with that domain in the request headers.
This allows the server to identify and associate the request with the client's session or user context.

Session Identification
Cookies are commonly used for session management by storing session identifiers (session IDs) on the client side.
When a user logs in or starts a new session, the server generates a unique session ID and sends it to the client's browser as a cookie.
Subsequent requests from the same client include the session ID cookie, allowing the server to identify and maintain the user's session state.

Session Data Storage
In addition to session IDs, cookies can also store other session-related data, such as user preferences, authentication tokens, or shopping cart items.
This data is typically encrypted or encoded to prevent tampering or unauthorized access by users or attackers.
Expiration and Deletion
Cookies can have expiration dates set by the server, after which they are automatically deleted from the client's browser.
Session cookies, which are used for session management, are often set to expire when the user closes the browser or after a certain period of inactivity.
Cookies can also be explicitly deleted by the server or client-side scripts when they are no longer needed.
Security Considerations
It's essential to secure cookies to prevent security vulnerabilities such as session hijacking or cross-site scripting (XSS) attacks.
Secure attributes, such as the "Secure" and "HttpOnly" flags, should be set for session cookies to ensure they are transmitted securely over HTTPS connections and are inaccessible to client-side scripts.
Session cookies should have short lifespans and be securely managed to mitigate the risk of session fixation or session replay attacks.

Advantages of Using Cookies
State Persistence: Cookies enable web applications to maintain state information between the client and server across multiple requests. This persistence allows for personalized user experiences, such as remembering user preferences or maintaining shopping cart items.
Session Management: Cookies are commonly used to manage user sessions by storing session identifiers (session IDs) on the client side. This allows servers to identify and associate requests with the correct session, facilitating features like user authentication and authorization.
Cross-Site Communication: Cookies provide a mechanism for cross-site communication, allowing websites to share data and maintain consistency across multiple domains or subdomains. This is useful for implementing single sign-on (SSO) solutions or integrating third-party services.
Efficiency: Cookies are lightweight and efficient for transferring small amounts of data between the client and server. Unlike other methods such as URL rewriting or hidden form fields, cookies are automatically included in HTTP requests and responses, reducing overhead and latency.
Customization: Cookies offer flexibility in terms of customization, allowing developers to set various attributes such as expiration dates, domain restrictions, and secure flags. This flexibility enables fine-grained control over how cookies are managed and utilized in web applications.
Browser Compatibility: Cookies are widely supported by web browsers and are compatible with various client-side technologies, making them a reliable choice for session management across different platforms and devices.
Scalability: Cookies scale well with the size and complexity of web applications, allowing developers to manage sessions for large numbers of concurrent users efficiently. This scalability is essential for high-traffic websites and enterprise-level applications.
Security: While cookies have security considerations, such as protecting against session hijacking or XSS attacks, they can be made secure with proper configuration and management. Secure attributes like the "HttpOnly" and "Secure" flags help mitigate security risks associated with cookies.

9.3.1 Considerations

When using cookies for session management in advanced Java web development, there are several important considerations to keep in mind to ensure security, privacy, and compliance with regulations. Here are some key considerations:
Security
Secure attributes: Set secure attributes like the "Secure" and "HttpOnly" flags to protect cookies from being intercepted or tampered with by attackers.
Encryption: Consider encrypting sensitive data stored in cookies to prevent unauthorized access or disclosure.
Session hijacking: Implement mechanisms to mitigate the risk of session hijacking attacks, such as rotating session IDs or using session tokens with short lifespans.
Privacy
Data minimization: Only store necessary information in cookies and avoid storing sensitive or personally identifiable information (PII) whenever possible.

Consent: Obtain user consent before storing cookies that track user Behaviour or preferences, especially for cookies used for advertising or analytics purposes.

Cookie policies: Provide clear and accessible information about cookie usage in your privacy policy and cookie banner, including details about the types of cookies used, their purpose, and how users can manage or opt out of cookies.

Compliance

GDPR compliance: Ensure compliance with the General Data Protection Regulation (GDPR) by obtaining explicit consent from users before storing cookies that collect personal data, providing mechanisms for users to manage their cookie preferences, and honoring user requests to opt out of tracking.

CCPA compliance: Comply with the California Consumer Privacy Act (CCPA) by providing a "Do Not Sell My Personal Information" link or opt-out mechanism for cookies used for targeted advertising purposes.

Cross-Site Tracking

Consider the implications of third-party cookies and cross-site tracking on user privacy and security. Be transparent about the use of third-party cookies and provide users with options to opt out of cross-site tracking.

Expiration and Lifespan

Set appropriate expiration dates and lifespans for cookies to balance usability with security. Session cookies should expire when the browser is closed or after a short period of inactivity, while persistent cookies should have longer expiration dates based on the application's requirements.

User Experience

Balance the need for session management with user convenience and experience. Minimize the use of intrusive cookie banners or pop-ups, and provide users with clear and accessible options to manage their cookie preferences.

Testing and Monitoring

Regularly test and monitor cookie usage in your web application to identify any security vulnerabilities, privacy concerns, or compliance issues. Implement logging and auditing mechanisms to track cookie-related events and activities.

URL Rewriting

URL rewriting is an alternative session management technique used when cookies are disabled or undesirable. It involves appending the session ID to the URL of each request that the client makes.

How URL Rewriting Works

URL rewriting is a technique used in web development to modify or manipulate URLs dynamically, typically to maintain session state or improve search engine optimization (SEO). In advanced Java web development, URL rewriting is commonly used for session management. Here's how URL rewriting works

Session Identification: When a user visits a website for the first time or starts a new session, the server generates a unique session identifier (session ID) for that user. This session ID is typically stored on the server side, but URL rewriting allows it to be included in URLs.

Appending Session ID to URLs: With URL rewriting, the server includes the session ID in the URLs of subsequent web pages visited by the user. This is achieved by appending a query parameter, usually named "sessionID" or similar, to each URL.

Link Modification: Whenever the server generates links to other pages within the website, it modifies the URLs to include the session ID. This ensures that the session context is preserved as the user navigates through the website.

Example

Original URL: http://example.com/page

Rewritten URL: http://example.com/page?sessionID=abc123

Handling Requests: When the user clicks on a link or submits a form with a rewritten URL, the browser includes the session ID as a query parameter in the HTTP request. The server extracts the session ID from the request and associates it with the user's session.

Session Management: Once the session ID is associated with the user's session, the server can use it to retrieve session data and maintain state information for that user across multiple requests.

Expiration and Cleanup: Session IDs generated through URL rewriting are typically set to expire after a certain period of inactivity or when the user closes the browser. The server may also clean up expired session data periodically to free up resources.

Security Considerations

Ensure that session IDs generated through URL rewriting are sufficiently random and unpredictable to prevent session prediction attacks.
Use secure HTTPS connections to transmit URLs with session IDs to prevent interception or tampering by attackers.

Advantages of URL Rewriting
URL rewriting offers several advantages in advanced Java web development, particularly for session management and search engine optimization (SEO). Here's a detailed explanation of the advantages of URL rewriting:
Session Management
State Preservation: URL rewriting allows web applications to preserve session state by embedding session identifiers (session IDs) directly into URLs. This enables users to navigate through a website while maintaining their session context, even if cookies are disabled or not supported.
Compatibility: URL rewriting is compatible with all web browsers and client-side technologies, making it a reliable method for session management across various platforms and devices.
Scalability: URL rewriting scales well with the size and complexity of web applications, allowing developers to manage sessions for large numbers of concurrent users efficiently.
Search Engine Optimization (SEO)
Readable URLs: URL rewriting enables developers to create clean, descriptive, and user-friendly URLs that accurately reflect the content and structure of web pages. This improves usability and accessibility for both users and search engines.
Keyword Inclusion: By incorporating relevant keywords and phrases into rewritten URLs, developers can enhance the visibility and ranking of web pages in search engine results pages (SERPs). This improves organic traffic and helps attract more visitors to the website.
Canonicalization: URL rewriting can be used to implement canonical URLs, which specify the preferred version of a web page to search engines. This helps prevent duplicate content issues and ensures that search engines index and rank the correct version of the page.
Flexibility and Customization
Dynamic Content: URL rewriting enables developers to generate dynamic URLs with specific parameters based on user input, application state, or other factors. This allows for personalized and context-sensitive content delivery.
Session Tracking: URL rewriting provides flexibility in session tracking by allowing developers to choose between different session management strategies, such as URL-based session IDs or cookie-based sessions, based on application requirements and user preferences.
Configuration Options: URL rewriting frameworks and libraries offer various configuration options and customization features, allowing developers to fine-tune URL rewriting Behaviour and optimize performance.
Cross-Site Communication
Cross-Domain Integration: URL rewriting facilitates cross-domain integration and communication between different web applications or services by enabling the sharing of data and session context through URLs.
Single Sign-On (SSO): URL rewriting can be used to implement single sign-on (SSO) solutions, allowing users to authenticate once and access multiple related websites or services without having to log in again.
Security
Session Security: URL rewriting can enhance session security by incorporating session identifiers directly into URLs, making them less susceptible to certain types of session-based attacks such as session fixation.
Encryption Compatibility: URL rewriting is compatible with HTTPS encryption, allowing session identifiers and other sensitive information to be transmitted securely over encrypted connections.

Considerations
When implementing URL rewriting in advanced Java web development, developers should consider various factors to ensure its effectiveness, security, and compatibility with the application requirements. Here are some key considerations:
Security
Session ID Protection: Ensure that session IDs embedded in URLs are sufficiently random and unpredictable to prevent session prediction attacks. Use secure random number generators and cryptographic techniques to generate session IDs.

HTTPS Usage: Transmit URLs with session IDs over HTTPS connections to encrypt data and protect against interception or tampering by attackers. HTTPS encryption ensures the confidentiality and integrity of sensitive information.
Sensitive Information: Avoid embedding sensitive information, such as user credentials or personal data, in URLs to prevent security risks associated with exposure or unauthorized access.
Compatibility
Cross-Browser Support: Test URL rewriting across different web browsers and client-side technologies to ensure compatibility and consistency in Behaviour. Consider browser-specific quirks or limitations that may affect URL parsing or handling.
Fallback Mechanisms: Implement fallback mechanisms to handle scenarios where URL rewriting is not supported or disabled by the client's browser. Provide alternative session management strategies, such as cookie-based sessions, as fallback options.
Performance
URL Length: Consider the impact of URL length on performance and usability, especially for dynamic URLs with appended session IDs or query parameters. Minimize unnecessary URL components and ensure that URLs remain within reasonable length limits.
Caching Optimization: Configure web servers and caching mechanisms to optimize caching of rewritten URLs and associated content. Leverage caching strategies to reduce server load and improve response times for frequently accessed resources.
SEO Considerations
Canonicalization: Implement canonical URLs to specify the preferred version of a web page to search engines and prevent duplicate content issues. Ensure that URL rewriting does not inadvertently create multiple URLs for the same content.
Keyword Inclusion: Incorporate relevant keywords and phrases into rewritten URLs to improve search engine visibility and ranking. Use descriptive and user-friendly URLs that accurately reflect the content and context of web pages.
Maintenance and Scalability
URL Structure: Design a consistent and predictable URL structure that reflects the hierarchy and organization of the website's content. Maintain clear and logical URL patterns to facilitate navigation and management of URLs.
Session Expiration: Implement mechanisms to expire and clean up expired session IDs and associated session data to prevent resource exhaustion and ensure scalability. Consider using short-lived session IDs to minimize server-side storage requirements.
Testing and Monitoring
Testing Coverage: Conduct comprehensive testing of URL rewriting functionality, including unit tests, integration tests, and user acceptance tests, to validate Behaviour and identify potential issues or regressions.
Monitoring and Logging: Implement logging and monitoring mechanisms to track URL rewriting activities, including session ID generation, URL parsing, and session management. Monitor server logs and application metrics for abnormal Behaviour or suspicious activities.

9.4 Session Destruction

Session destruction is a pivotal aspect of session management in advanced Java web development, pivotal for maintaining the integrity and security of user sessions. When a user interacts with a web application, a session is typically created to maintain state information between the client (browser) and the server. This session allows the server to associate subsequent requests from the same client with the appropriate user context. However, once a session is no longer needed or expires, it must be effectively destroyed to release resources and ensure that sensitive session data is not retained longer than necessary.
The process of session destruction can be triggered by various events, including user logout, session timeout, or explicit termination by the server. When a user logs out of the application, perhaps by clicking a "Logout" button or link, the server initiates the session destruction process. This involves invalidating the session associated with the user's session ID and removing any session-related data stored on the server. The server-side application container, such as Apache Tomcat or Jetty, handles the session destruction process, releasing resources allocated for the session, such as memory or database connections, and removing the session entry from its session management system.
During session destruction, the server marks the session as invalid or expired, indicating that it is no longer active or usable. This prevents further access to the session data and ensures that subsequent requests from the same session ID are treated as new sessions. Additionally, session destruction involves releasing any resources

associated with the session, such as cached data, locks, or temporary files. This helps free up server resources and prevents resource leaks or contention issues, particularly in high-traffic or multi-user environments.

Moreover, session destruction is paramount for security purposes in web applications. It ensures that sensitive session data, such as user credentials or access tokens, is promptly erased from server-side storage. Proper session destruction prevents unauthorized access to session state and mitigates the risk of session hijacking or fixation attacks. Furthermore, web frameworks and application containers often provide mechanisms for registering session destruction listeners or callbacks. Developers can leverage these callbacks to execute custom logic or cleanup tasks when a session is destroyed, such as logging out of external services or updating user activity logs.

In addition to user-initiated session destruction, sessions may be automatically destroyed after a predefined period of inactivity, known as the session timeout. This proactive measure helps protect against session hijacking and resource exhaustion by limiting the lifespan of sessions that are no longer actively used. Overall, session destruction plays a pivotal role in session management, ensuring the secure and efficient termination of user sessions in advanced Java web applications. By properly handling session destruction, developers can safeguard sensitive session data, optimize resource usage, and enhance the overall security and reliability of their web applications.

Here's a detailed explanation of session destruction

User Interaction

Session destruction can occur through various user interactions, such as logging out of the application, explicitly terminating the session, or closing the browser window. Additionally, sessions may be automatically destroyed after a period of inactivity to enforce security and resource management policies.

Logout Process

When a user initiates the logout process, typically by clicking on a "Logout" button or link, the web application triggers the session destruction process. This involves invalidating the session associated with the user's session ID and removing any session-related data stored on the server.

Server-Side Cleanup

Upon receiving the logout request, the server-side application container, such as Apache Tomcat or Jetty, handles the session destruction process. It releases any resources allocated for the session, such as memory or database connections, and removes the session entry from its session management system.

Session Invalidation

During session destruction, the server marks the session as invalid or expired, indicating that it is no longer active or usable. This prevents further access to the session data and ensures that subsequent requests from the same session ID are treated as new sessions.

Resource Release

Session destruction also involves releasing any resources associated with the session, such as cached data, locks, or temporary files. This helps free up server resources and prevents resource leaks or contention issues, especially in high-traffic or multi-user environments.

Event Handling

Web frameworks and application containers often provide mechanisms for registering session destruction listeners or callbacks. Developers can use these callbacks to execute custom logic or cleanup tasks when a session is destroyed, such as logging out of external services or updating user activity logs.

Security Considerations

Session destruction is critical for maintaining security in web applications, as it ensures that sensitive session data, such as user credentials or access tokens, is not retained longer than necessary. Proper session destruction prevents unauthorized access to session state and mitigates the risk of session hijacking or session fixation attacks.

Session Timeout

In addition to user-initiated session destruction, sessions may be automatically destroyed after a predefined period of inactivity, known as the session timeout. This helps protect against session hijacking and resource exhaustion by limiting the lifespan of sessions that are no longer actively used.

9.4.1 Importance of Session Destruction

Session destruction holds significant importance in advanced Java web development for several key reasons

Security: Proper session destruction is crucial for maintaining the security of web applications. When a user logs out or their session expires, session destruction ensures that sensitive information, such as user credentials or access tokens, is promptly erased from server-side storage. This prevents unauthorized access to session state and mitigates the risk of session hijacking or fixation attacks.

Resource Management: Sessions consume server-side resources, such as memory, database connections, and temporary storage. Session destruction releases these resources, helping to free up server capacity and prevent resource leaks or contention issues, especially in high-traffic or multi-user environments. Effective resource management is essential for maintaining application performance and scalability.
Data Privacy: Session data may contain sensitive or personally identifiable information (PII) about users. By destroying sessions when they are no longer needed, web applications adhere to data privacy regulations and protect user privacy. Session destruction ensures that session data is not retained longer than necessary, reducing the risk of data breaches or unauthorized access.
Compliance Requirements: Many data protection regulations, such as the General Data Protection Regulation (GDPR) and the California Consumer Privacy Act (CCPA), require organizations to implement measures to secure and manage user data effectively. Proper session destruction is essential for compliance with these regulations, as it helps ensure the secure handling and disposal of session data in accordance with legal requirements.
Prevention of Session Hijacking: Session hijacking occurs when an attacker gains unauthorized access to a user's session ID and impersonates the user. By promptly destroying sessions after logout or inactivity, web applications reduce the window of opportunity for attackers to exploit stolen session IDs. This enhances the overall security posture of the application and protects users from identity theft or unauthorized access to their accounts.
User Experience: Session destruction contributes to a positive user experience by ensuring that users can safely end their sessions and log out of the application securely. By providing clear feedback to users when sessions are terminated, web applications instil confidence and trust in their security measures, fostering a positive relationship with users.

9.4.2 Scenarios for Session Destruction

Session destruction occurs in various scenarios within advanced Java web applications, each serving a specific purpose to ensure security, resource optimization, and compliance with user privacy regulations. Here are some common scenarios for session destruction along with examples:
User Logout
Scenario: When a user actively logs out of the application, either by clicking a "Logout" button or following a logout link.
Example: A user navigates to the account settings page and selects the "Logout" option. Upon confirmation, the server invalidates the user's session, clears session-related data, and redirects the user to the login page.
Session Timeout
Scenario: When a user remains inactive for a specified period, typically defined by the session timeout configuration.
Example: A user logs into an online banking application but becomes inactive for 30 minutes. After the configured session timeout period elapses without any user activity, the server automatically destroys the user's session, ensuring that sensitive banking data is not exposed if the user leaves their computer unattended.
Application Restart or Server Shutdown
Scenario: When the web application undergoes maintenance, updates, or server shutdowns, all active sessions are terminated to ensure data consistency and prevent unauthorized access.
Example: The administrator initiates a server restart to apply security patches. Before restarting the server, the application gracefully shuts down all active sessions, ensuring that users are logged out and session data is safely discarded. Upon server restart, users must log in again to access the application.
Session Expiration on Account Deactivation or Suspension
Scenario: When a user account is deactivated, suspended, or terminated due to policy violations or administrative actions.
Example: An administrator suspends a user account for violating the terms of service. As part of the account suspension process, the server immediately invalidates the user's session, preventing further access to the application. The user is notified of the account suspension upon their next login attempt.
Explicit Session Termination by Administrator
Scenario: When an administrator manually terminates a user's session, typically in response to security incidents, user complaints, or compliance requirements.
Example: An administrator detects suspicious activity associated with a user's session and decides to terminate the session preemptively. Using administrative tools or a dedicated interface, the administrator identifies the user's session and terminates it, forcing the user to log in again to access the application.
Session Revocation Due to Security Breach

Scenario: When a security breach or unauthorized access is detected, all affected sessions are immediately invalidated to prevent further exploitation and protect user data.
Example: The security team identifies unusual login attempts originating from multiple geographic locations, indicating a potential credential stuffing attack. To mitigate the threat, the server revokes all active sessions associated with the compromised credentials, forcing affected users to reset their passwords and reauthenticate to regain access.

9.5 Techniques for Session Destruction

Invalidate the Session
Identify the Session: Before invalidating a session, it's essential to identify the session associated with the user's request. In Java servlets, the HttpSession object provides access to session-related information and allows developers to manipulate session attributes.
Access the HttpSession Object: Obtain a reference to the HttpSession object representing the user's session. This object can be obtained from the HttpServletRequest object using the getSession() method. For example:
HttpSession session = request.getSession();
Clean Up Resources: Optionally, perform any additional cleanup tasks or release resources associated with the session. This may include closing database connections, releasing locks, or deleting temporary files created during the session.
Redirect or Notify User: After invalidating the session, redirect the user to a designated page, such as the login page, to prompt them to authenticate again. Alternatively, provide feedback to the user indicating that their session has been terminated and instruct them on how to proceed.
Example Servlet Code

```
import java.io.IOException;
import javax.servlet.ServletException;
import javax.servlet.annotation.WebServlet;
import javax.servlet.http.HttpServlet;
import javax.servlet.http.HttpServletRequest;
import javax.servlet.http.HttpServletResponse;
import javax.servlet.http.HttpSession;

@WebServlet("/logout")
public class LogoutServlet extends HttpServlet {
  protected void doPost(HttpServletRequest request, HttpServletResponse response)
        throws ServletException, IOException {
     HttpSession session = request.getSession(false);
     if (session != null) {
        session.invalidate();
        response.sendRedirect("login.jsp");
     }
  }
}
```

In this example, the servlet handles a logout request by invalidating the user's session using the invalidate() method. If a session exists (session != null), it is immediately terminated, and the user is redirected to the login page ("login.jsp").

Setting a Timeout
Setting a timeout for session destruction is another essential technique in advanced Java web development. It allows developers to specify a duration of inactivity after which a user's session will be automatically invalidated and destroyed. This helps ensure that sessions are not kept open indefinitely, reducing the risk of security vulnerabilities and resource exhaustion. Here's how to implement session timeout in Java web applications:
Configure Session Timeout
In Java servlets, the session timeout can be configured in the web application's deployment descriptor (web.xml) or programmatically within the servlet code.
To configure the session timeout in web.xml, add the following session-config element

```
<session-config>
```

```xml
<session-timeout>30</session-timeout> <!-- Timeout in minutes -->
</session-config>
```

Alternatively, the session timeout can be set programmatically using the setMaxInactiveInterval() method of the HttpSession object:

```java
HttpSession session = request.getSession();
session.setMaxInactiveInterval(1800); // Timeout in seconds (30 minutes)
```

Monitor User Activity

Once the session timeout is configured, the application should monitor user activity to determine when a session becomes inactive.

User activity can be tracked using JavaScript to detect mouse movements, keyboard inputs, or AJAX requests, which can then be used to reset the session timeout on the server side.

Handle Timeout Events

When a session exceeds the configured timeout duration without any user activity, the servlet container automatically invalidates the session.

Developers can provide custom logic to handle session timeout events, such as redirecting the user to a timeout page or displaying a message indicating that the session has expired.

Example Servlet Code

```java
import java.io.IOException;
import javax.servlet.ServletException;
import javax.servlet.annotation.WebServlet;
import javax.servlet.http.HttpServlet;
import javax.servlet.http.HttpServletRequest;
import javax.servlet.http.HttpServletResponse;
import javax.servlet.http.HttpSession;
@WebServlet("/timeout")
public class TimeoutServlet extends HttpServlet
 {
    protected void doGet(HttpServletRequest request, HttpServletResponse response)
            throws ServletException, IOException {
        HttpSession session = request.getSession(false);
        if (session == null) {
            // Session has already expired or was invalidated
            response.sendRedirect("login.jsp");
        } else {
            // Reset session timeout
            session.setMaxInactiveInterval(1800); // Timeout in seconds (30 minutes)
            // Proceed with request handling
        }
    }
}
```

In this example, the servlet detects whether a session exists for the user. If a session exists, the servlet resets the session timeout to 30 minutes (1800 seconds). If the session has already expired or was invalidated, the user is redirected to the login page.

Logout Mechanisms

Implementing logout mechanisms is a critical technique for session destruction in advanced Java web development. Logout mechanisms allow users to securely end their session and terminate their access to the application, ensuring the protection of sensitive data and enhancing overall security. Here's an explanation of logout mechanisms and how they can be implemented:

User Initiated Logout

One of the most common logout mechanisms is a user-initiated logout, where users explicitly request to end their session and log out of the application.

This can be achieved through a "Logout" button or link in the application's user interface, typically located in a navigation bar or user profile menu.

Clear Session Data

When a user initiates a logout, the server-side application should clear any session-related data associated with the user's session.

This includes removing session attributes, such as user credentials or session-specific preferences, and invalidating the user's session to prevent further access.

Redirect to Login Page

After clearing session data and invalidating the session, the application should redirect the user to the login page or another designated landing page.

This ensures that the user is directed to the appropriate starting point for the authentication process when they attempt to access the application again.

Session Invalidation

Once the logout process is complete, the server should invalidate the user's session using methods provided by the HttpSession object.

This marks the session as no longer valid and ensures that any subsequent requests using the same session ID are treated as new sessions.

Handle Redirects and Notifications

During the logout process, developers can provide feedback to the user to confirm that their logout request was successful.

This can be achieved through notification messages, such as "You have been successfully logged out," or by displaying a confirmation page after the logout process is complete.

Example Servlet Code

```
import java.io.IOException;
import javax.servlet.ServletException;
import javax.servlet.annotation.WebServlet;
import javax.servlet.http.HttpServlet;
import javax.servlet.http.HttpServletRequest;
import javax.servlet.http.HttpServletResponse;
import javax.servlet.http.HttpSession;
@WebServlet("/logout")
public class LogoutServlet extends HttpServlet {
  protected void doGet(HttpServletRequest request, HttpServletResponse response)
        throws ServletException, IOException {
    HttpSession session = request.getSession(false);
    if (session != null) {
      // Clear session data
      session.invalidate();
    }
    // Redirect to login page
    response.sendRedirect("login.jsp");
  }
}
```

In this example, the servlet handles a logout request by clearing session data and invalidating the user's session. If a session exists (session != null), it is immediately terminated. The user is then redirected to the login page ("login.jsp") to authenticate again when they attempt to access the application.

Best Practices for Session Destruction

Use Explicit Logout Mechanisms

Provide users with a clear and accessible way to log out of the application, typically through a "Logout" button or link in the user interface.

Implementing explicit logout mechanisms ensures that users can securely end their sessions when they're done using the application, reducing the risk of unauthorized access to their accounts.

Set Session Timeout

Configure a reasonable session timeout value based on the sensitivity of the application and user Behaviour. A shorter timeout duration reduces the window of opportunity for unauthorized access by limiting the lifespan of idle sessions.

Regularly review and adjust session timeout settings based on security assessments, user feedback, and compliance requirements to strike a balance between security and user convenience.

Implement Inactivity Timeout
Supplement session timeout with an inactivity timeout mechanism that automatically logs out users after a period of inactivity.
Monitor user activity and reset the session timeout whenever user interactions are detected, ensuring that sessions remain active only when users are actively engaged with the application.
Clear Session Data Securely
Ensure that all session-related data is promptly cleared from server-side storage when a user logs out or their session expires. This includes removing session attributes such as user credentials, preferences, or temporary data to prevent unauthorized access or data leakage.
Use secure methods, such as HttpSession.invalidate(), to invalidate sessions on the server side, ensuring that sessions are terminated securely and completely.
Handle Session Termination Events
Implement custom logic to handle session termination events, such as logout or session timeout, gracefully. Provide clear feedback to users confirming that their session has been successfully terminated.
Redirect users to a designated landing page, such as the login page, after session termination to guide them through the reauthentication process and maintain a seamless user experience.
Protect Against Session Fixation Attacks
Mitigate the risk of session fixation attacks by generating new session identifiers upon login or session creation. Invalidate existing session identifiers and issue new ones when users authenticate or transition between authentication states.
Employ secure random number generators or cryptographic techniques to generate session identifiers, making it difficult for attackers to predict or manipulate session identifiers.
Regularly Audit Session Management
Conduct periodic audits of session management practices to identify vulnerabilities, misconfigurations, or outdated session handling mechanisms.
Review server logs, security reports, and compliance assessments to ensure that session destruction is implemented effectively and in accordance with best practices.
Stay informed about emerging security threats and best practices in session management to continuously improve the security posture of your application.
Securely Redirect after Logout: After invalidating the session, redirect the user to a page that confirms they are logged out or to the application's public home page.
Clear Cookies: If your application uses cookies for session management, ensure to clear relevant cookies during the logout process.
Revisit Session Timeout: Regularly review and adjust session timeout settings based on the application's use case and security requirements.

Exercise

Exercise 1 - MCQ

1. What is the primary purpose of using sessions in web applications?
a) to store data on the client-side
b) to enhance the security of web applications
c) to maintain state between client and server
d) to increase the loading speed of web pages
2. Sessions allow for which of the following?
a) Temporary data storage only on the server-side
b) Permanent data storage on the client-side
c) Data storage that is accessible across multiple servers
d) None of the above
3. Which mechanism allows session tracking across multiple requests?
a) SSL encryption
b) POST data
c) Cookies
d) AJAX requests
4. How do cookies work for session management?
a) By encrypting session data

b) By storing session identifiers on the client-side
c) By storing all session data on the client-side
d) By sending session data with every request header
5. What is a disadvantage of using cookies for session management?
a) They can only store a limited amount of data
b) They are stored on the server, consuming memory
c) They make web applications slower
d) They require additional plugins
6. URL rewriting helps in session tracking by
a) Encrypting the URL
b) Appending the session ID to the URL
c) Redirecting all requests to a secure server
d) Changing the protocol from HTTP to HTTPS
7. Which is a benefit of using cookies for session management?
a) They reduce server load by storing all session data on the client-side
b) They provide a seamless user experience across multiple requests
c) They are more secure than server-side sessions
d) They do not require any server resources
8. Session destruction can be initiated by
a) The user closing the browser
b) The server after a timeout period
c) A successful logout operation
d) All of the above
9. Which of the following is true about session timeouts?
a) They are only applicable to cookie-based sessions
b) They help in freeing up server resources
c) They cannot be configured by the web developer
d) They extend the session lifetime indefinitely
10. To prevent session hijacking, it is recommended to
a) Store all session data on the client-side
b) Use URL rewriting exclusively for session tracking
c) Regenerate the session ID after login
d) Avoid using HTTPS

Exercise 2 - True/False

1. A session is a way to preserve user data across multiple HTTP requests.
2. Sessions are stored on the client-side.
3. Cookies are a server-side session management mechanism.
4. URL rewriting can bypass browser cookie restrictions.
5. Cookies must be enabled in the user's browser for sessions to work.
6. Session data is shared across all users of an application.
7. The HttpSession object in Java Servlets is used to track session information.
8. URL rewriting appends the session ID to every link within the web application.
9. Sessions can be used to store sensitive information securely.
10. Using cookies for session management is more secure than URL rewriting.

Exercise 3 - Fill in the blanks

1. A session allows a server to store data to uniquely identify users across ______ requests.
2. For session management, ______ are commonly used to store a unique session ID on the client's browser.
3. URL ______ involves appending the session ID to the URL path to maintain the session across requests.
4. The method invalidate() is used within a servlet to programmatically ______ a session.
5. Cookies set with the HttpOnly attribute help prevent ______ by not allowing the cookies to be accessed through client-side scripts.
6. Session fixation attacks can be mitigated by generating new session identifiers upon ________ or session creation.
7. It's important to configure session timeout values appropriately to balance ________ with user convenience.

8. Session tracking mechanisms in Java can be based on ________ or URL rewriting, allowing the server to associate multiple requests with the same session.
9. One common method for session creation in Java web applications is to obtain the HttpSession object using the ________ method of the HttpServletRequest object.
10. HttpSession objects in Java servlets allow developers to store and manage ________ between multiple requests from the same client.

Exercise 4 – Match case
1. Maintains user data across multiple requests
2. Securely stores session IDs
3. Appends session ID to URL
4. Method to programmatically end a session

A. URL Rewriting
B. Cookies
C. Session Destruction
D. HttpOnly attribute

Exercise 5 - One word answer
1. Default method for session tracking in Java EE applications?
2. Secure attribute setting for cookies?

Exercise 6 – Small answer
1. What method is commonly used to end a user session in Java web applications?
2. Which attribute prevents a cookie from being accessed via JavaScript?

Exercise 7- Long answer
1. Explain how cookies are used for session management in web applications.
2. Describe the process and significance of URL rewriting in session management.
Answers-
Exercise 1- 1) c 2) a 3) c 4) b 5) a 6) b 7) b 8) d 9) b 10) c
Exercise 2 – 1) True 2) False 3) False 4) True 5) False 6) False 7) True 8) True 9) False 10) True
Exercise 3 – 1) multiple 2) cookies 3) rewriting 4) destroy 5) session hijacking 6) login 7) security 8) cookies 9) getSession() 10) session attributes
Exercise 4 – 1 - B. Cookies 2 – D. HttpOnly attribute 3 – A. URL Rewriting 4 – C. Session Destruction
Exercise 5 – 1) HttpSession 2) HttpOnly

Online Resources

Online Practice Paper

Link: https://forms.gle/QL58iXQTLuEDL6N96
QR Code:

YouTube Video Link
Link: https://www.youtube.com/playlist?list=PLzlh_31VWEFrqnmvicr5j-5aIQOHLGgb7
QR Code:

CHAPTER 10 - Java Server Pages (JSP)

10.1 Understanding to JSP

Understanding JSP for Advanced Java" is a comprehensive guide that explores the intricacies of JavaServer Pages (JSP), a powerful technology for building dynamic and interactive web applications in the Java ecosystem. This book delves into the architecture and lifecycle of JSP, offering an in-depth look at how JSP pages are translated, compiled, and executed by the server. It begins by introducing JSP in the context of web development, highlighting its advantages and comparing it with other technologies like Servlets and ASP.NET. Readers are then guided through the fundamental syntax of JSP, including the use of scriptlets, expressions, and declarations, which are essential for embedding Java code within HTML pages.

The book emphasizes the importance of JSP directives, such as page, include, and taglib, which control various aspects of the JSP environment and facilitate the inclusion of reusable components and libraries. It covers the role of implicit objects predefined variables that provide access to various scopes (page, request, session, application)—and how they simplify web application development by providing a seamless interface to interact with client data, server responses, and session management.

A significant portion of the book is dedicated to JSP actions and the JSP Standard Tag Library (JSTL), which standardizes common tasks like iteration, conditionals, and XML manipulation, making JSP development more efficient and less error-prone. The creation and usage of custom tag libraries are also thoroughly explored, enabling developers to extend JSP functionality by defining custom tags tailored to their specific needs.

Advanced topics include robust error handling mechanisms, configuring custom error pages, and employing best practices for debugging JSP applications. The book also introduces the Expression Language (EL), a powerful feature that simplifies the accessibility of data stored in JavaBeans components and various scopes, making JSP code cleaner and more readable.

The integration of JSP with databases using JDBC is covered in detail, including connection pooling techniques for optimizing database interactions. Security is another critical aspect addressed, with chapters on implementing authentication and authorization, as well as secure coding practices to protect against common vulnerabilities.

"Understanding JSP for Advanced Java" goes beyond the basics to discuss performance optimization strategies and best practices for writing efficient, maintainable code. The book concludes with discussions on integrating JSP with AJAX for creating dynamic, asynchronous web applications, and implementing the Model-View-Controller (MVC) architecture, which is a cornerstone of modern web application design. Through comprehensive coverage and practical examples, this book equips advanced Java developers with the knowledge and skills needed to harness the full potential of JSP in their web applications.

10.1.1 JSP Lifecycle

The JSP (JavaServer Pages) lifecycle is a series of steps that a JSP page goes through from its creation to its destruction. Understanding the JSP lifecycle is crucial for advanced Java developers as it helps in optimizing the performance, managing resources, and debugging issues effectively. The lifecycle can be broken down into several distinct phases translation, compilation, initialization, execution, and cleanup. Here is a detailed explanation of each phase with an example to illustrate the process.

Translation Phase

In this phase, the JSP engine (a part of the web server or servlet container) translates the JSP page into a servlet. This involves converting the JSP file into a Java servlet source file. The servlet source file will have the same name as the JSP file but with a .java extension.

Example: Consider a simple JSP page hello.jsp:

```
<%@ page language="java" contentType="text/html; charset=UTF-8" %>
<html>
<head>
  <title>Hello JSP</title>
</head>
<body>
  <h1>Hello, <%= request.getParameter("name") %>!</h1>
</body>
</html>
```

During the translation phase, the JSP engine translates hello.jsp into a Java servlet source file, typically something like hello_jsp.java.

Compilation Phase

The translated servlet source file is then compiled into a servlet class file. This phase involves compiling the Java code generated during the translation phase into bytecode that can be executed by the Java Virtual Machine (JVM).

Example: The translated hello_jsp.java is compiled into hello_jsp.class.

Initialization Phase

Before a JSP page can process requests, it must be initialized. This phase corresponds to the init method in servlets. The jspInit method is called by the container to perform any necessary initialization tasks, such as resource allocation or setting up database connections.

Example: If hello.jsp needs to initialize some resources, it can override the jspInit method

```
public void jspInit() {
    // Initialization code, e.g., loading configuration settings
}
```

Execution Phase

During this phase, the JSP page processes client requests and generates responses. The container invokes the _jspService method, passing the request and response objects. This method is responsible for handling all HTTP requests, processing input data, invoking business logic, and generating the HTML output.

Example: The main logic of hello.jsp is executed within the _jspService method

```
public void _jspService(HttpServletRequest request, HttpServletResponse response)
        throws ServletException, IOException {
    response.setContentType("text/html;charset=UTF-8");
    PrintWriter out = response.getWriter();
    String name = request.getParameter("name");
    out.println("<html><head><title>Hello JSP</title></head>");
    out.println("<body><h1>Hello, " + name + "!</h1></body></html>");
}
```

Cleanup Phase

When the JSP page is no longer needed, the container calls the jspDestroy method to release any resources that were allocated during the initialization or execution phases. This phase is similar to the destroy method in servlets and ensures that any cleanup tasks are performed to free up resources.

Example: If hello.jsp needs to release resources, it can override the jspDestroy method

```
public void jspDestroy() {
    // Cleanup code, e.g., closing database connections
}
```

Complete Example

To summarize the lifecycle, here is how the hello.jsp might look during different phases:

hello.jsp

```
<%@ page language="java" contentType="text/html; charset=UTF-8" %>
<html>
<head>
    <title>Hello JSP</title>
</head>
<body>
    <h1>Hello, <%= request.getParameter("name") %>!</h1>
</body>
</html>
```

Translated hello_jsp.java (simplified)

```
public class hello_jsp extends HttpJspBase {
    public void jspInit() {
        // Initialization code
    }
```

```
    public void _jspService(HttpServletRequest request, HttpServletResponse response)
            throws ServletException, IOException {
        response.setContentType("text/html;charset=UTF-8");
        PrintWriter out = response.getWriter();
        String name = request.getParameter("name");
        out.println("<html><head><title>Hello JSP</title></head>");
        out.println("<body><h1>Hello, " + name + "!</h1></body></html>");
    }
    public void jspDestroy() {
        // Cleanup code
    }
}
```

10.1.2 Key Points in JSP Lifecycle

Translation and Compilation are One-Time Processes

Translation Phase

Translation: When a JSP page is requested for the first time, the JSP engine translates the JSP file into a Java servlet source file.

One-Time: This translation happens only once, unless the JSP file is modified. If the file is modified, the JSP engine will retranslate the file into a new servlet source file.

Example: For a hello.jsp file, the JSP engine generates a hello_jsp.java file.

Compilation Phase

Compilation: After translation, the servlet source file (hello_jsp.java) is compiled into a Java bytecode class file (hello_jsp.class).

One-Time: Like translation, this compilation occurs only once unless the JSP file changes, necessitating a re-translation and recompilation.

Benefits: This ensures that the translation and compilation overhead is minimized, as it only happens when changes are made to the JSP file.

Thread Safety and the _jspService() Method

jspService() Method

Purpose: The _jspService() method is automatically generated and called by the JSP container to handle each request. It processes the request and generates the response.

Not Overridable: Developers cannot override this method as it is crucial for handling the core request-response cycle.

Thread Safety

Concurrency: JSP pages can handle multiple requests concurrently, meaning the _jspService() method is executed by multiple threads simultaneously.

Thread Safety Concerns: Developers must ensure that the code within JSPs is thread-safe. This involves avoiding the use of instance variables and ensuring that shared resources are properly synchronized.

Example: Using local variables within the _jspService() method instead of instance variables to avoid concurrency issues.

Custom Initialization and Cleanup

jspInit() Method

Initialization: The jspInit() method is called by the JSP container when the JSP is first loaded into memory and instantiated. It is used to perform one-time initialization tasks.

Custom Code: Developers can override this method to include code that sets up resources such as database connections, reading configuration files, or initializing application-wide variables.

Example

```
public void jspInit() {
// Initialization code, e.g., setting up a database connection
}
```

jspDestroy() Method

Cleanup: The jspDestroy() method is called when the JSP is being unloaded from memory, usually when the web application is stopping or the server is shutting down.

Resource Release: This method is used to release resources like closing database connections, freeing up memory, or saving state information.
Custom Code: Developers can override this method to include cleanup code.
Example
```
public void jspDestroy() {
// Cleanup code, e.g., closing a database connection
}
```

JSP Elements
Directives
Purpose: Directives provide global information about the JSP page and control the overall structure of the servlet generated from the JSP.
Types:
Page Directive: Sets page-level instructions such as content type, language, error pages, etc.
```
<%@ page language="java" contentType="text/html; charset=UTF-8" %>
```
Include Directive: Includes a file during the translation phase
```
<%@ include file="header.jsp" %>
```
Taglib Directive: Declares a tag library that contains custom tags
```
<%@ taglib uri="http://java.sun.com/jsp/jstl/core" prefix="c" %>
```

Scriptlets
Purpose: Embed Java code within the HTML content. Code within scriptlets is executed every time the JSP page is requested.
Example
```
<%
   String name = request.getParameter("name");
%>
```

Expressions
Purpose: Embed Java expressions directly into the HTML content. The result of the expression is converted to a string and included in the output.
Example
```
    <h1>Hello, <%= request.getParameter("name") %>!</h1>
```

Declarations
Purpose: Declare variables and methods that can be used within the JSP page. These are inserted into the servletclass generated from the JSP page.
Example
```
<%!
   private int counter = 0;
   public int getCounter() {
      return counter++;
   }
%>
```

Actions
Purpose: Use predefined JSP tags to perform actions like instantiating JavaBeans, setting/getting properties, and including other resources at request time.
Examples
```
<jsp:useBean id="person" class="com.example.Person" scope="request" />
<jsp:setProperty name="person" property="name" value="John Doe" />
<jsp:getProperty name="person" property="name" />
```

10.1.3 Scriptlets

Scriptlets are a way to embed Java code directly within a JSP page, allowing developers to dynamically generate content based on business logic or user input. However, their use has become less favored with the advent of more sophisticated and cleaner alternatives like JSP Standard Tag Library (JSTL) and Expression Language (EL). Nonetheless, understanding scriptlets is crucial for maintaining and understanding legacy code.

Usage: Purpose

Embed Java Code: Scriptlets allow you to write Java code within the HTML content of a JSP page.

Dynamic Content Generation: They enable dynamic content generation based on runtime conditions.

Syntax

Scriptlet Syntax: Enclosed within <% and %> tags

```
<% Java code %>
```

Code:

Basic Example

A simple scriptlet that prints the current date and time.

```
<%@ page language="java" contentType="text/html; charset=UTF-8" %>
<html>
<head>
  <title>Current Date and Time</title>
</head>
<body>
  <h1>Current Date and Time:</h1>
  <p>
    <%
      java.util.Date date = new java.util.Date();
      out.println(date.toString());
    %>
  </p>
</body>
</html>
```

Using Scriptlets for Conditional Logic

Scriptlets can be used to include conditional logic directly in the JSP.

```
<%@ page language="java" contentType="text/html; charset=UTF-8" %>
<html>
<head>
  <title>Greeting</title>
</head>
<body>
  <%
    String name = request.getParameter("name");
    if (name == null || name.isEmpty()) {
      out.println("<h1>Hello, Guest!</h1>");
    } else {
      out.println("<h1>Hello, " + name + "!</h1>");
    }
  %>
</body>
</html>
```

Looping with Scriptlets

Scriptlets can be used to loop over collections or arrays.

```
<%@ page language="java" contentType="text/html; charset=UTF-8" %>
<html>
<head>
  <title>Loop Example</title>
</head>
<body>
```

```
  <ul>
    <%
      String[] fruits = {"Apple", "Banana", "Cherry"};
      for (String fruit : fruits) {
        out.println("<li>" + fruit + "</li>");
      }
    %>
  </ul>
</body>
</html>
```

Considerations: Readability and Maintainability
Code Complexity: Embedding Java code within HTML can make JSP pages difficult to read and maintain, especially as the complexity of the logic increases.
Separation of Concerns: Scriptlets violate the principle of separation of concerns by mixing business logic with presentation logic. This can lead to less modular and harder-to-maintain code.

Thread Safety
Thread Safety Issues: JSP pages can handle multiple requests simultaneously. Scriptlets that use instance variables can lead to concurrency issues.
Example of Unsafe Code

```
<%! int counter = 0; %>
<%
  counter++;
  out.println("Counter: " + counter);
%>
```

Safe Alternative: Use local variables instead

```
<%
  int localCounter = 0;
  localCounter++;
  out.println("Counter: " + localCounter);
%>
```

Performance
Compilation Overhead: Every time a JSP page containing scriptlets is updated, the JSP container must retranslate and recompile the page, which can affect performance during deployment.
Efficiency: Overuse of scriptlets can lead to inefficient and bloated JSP pages.

Alternatives to Scriptlets
Expression Language (EL)
Simpler Syntax: EL provides a simpler syntax for accessing data stored in JavaBeans, request, session, and application scopes without using scriptlets.

```
<h1>Hello, ${param.name}!</h1>
```

JSP Standard Tag Library (JSTL)
Standardized Tags: JSTL provides a set of standardized tags for common tasks like iteration, conditionals, and internationalization, which can replace scriptlets for these operations.

```
<c:choose>
  <c:when test="${empty param.name}">
    <h1>Hello, Guest!</h1>
  </c:when>
  <c:otherwise>
    <h1>Hello, ${param.name}!</h1>
  </c:otherwise>
</c:choose>
```

10.1.4 Expressions

JSP expressions provide a way to embed Java expressions directly within HTML content in a JSP page. They are a concise and convenient mechanism for evaluating a Java expression and inserting the result into the response output. Expressions are particularly useful for simple computations and data retrieval from request parameters or attributes.

Usage: Purpose

Embed Java Expressions: JSP expressions allow embedding of Java expressions within the HTML content.

Output Result: The result of the expression is automatically converted to a string and included in the output sent to the client.

Syntax

Expression Syntax: Enclosed within <%= and %> tags

```
<%= Java expression %>
```

Example

A simple example that displays the current date and time using JSP expressions.

```
<%@ page language="java" contentType="text/html; charset=UTF-8" %>
<html>
<head>
   <title>Current Date and Time</title>
</head>
<body>
   <h1>Current Date and Time:</h1>
   <p>
      <%= new java.util.Date() %>
   </p>
</body>
</html>
```

Using Expressions for Request Parameters

JSP expressions can be used to retrieve and display request parameters.

```
<%@ page language="java" contentType="text/html; charset=UTF-8" %>
<html>
<head>
   <title>Greeting</title>
</head>
<body>
   <h1>Hello, <%= request.getParameter("name") %>!</h1>
</body>
</html>
```

Performing Calculations

Expressions can be used for performing simple calculations.

```
<%@ page language="java" contentType="text/html; charset=UTF-8" %>
<html>
<head>
   <title>Calculation Example</title>
</head>
<body>
   <h1>Result of 2 + 3 is: <%= 2 + 3 %></h1>
</body>
</html>
```

This code snippet would output the value of the name variable, where name is a Java variable defined in a scriptlet or elsewhere in the JSP.

Considerations: Readability and Maintainability
Concise and Readable: JSP expressions are concise and can improve readability for simple expressions, especially when compared to scriptlets.
Limited Complexity: Best suited for simple expressions. Complex logic should be avoided as it can decrease readability and maintainability.

Separation of Concerns
Maintain Separation: Use JSP expressions for simple data retrieval and output operations. Avoid embedding complex business logic to maintain a clear separation between business logic and presentation.

Performance
Compilation and Execution: Expressions are evaluated and included in the response each time the page is requested, but this is generally efficient for simple operations.
Minimal Overhead: The overhead associated with using expressions is minimal, making them suitable for frequent use in JSP pages.

Alternatives to Expressions
Expression Language (EL)
Simpler and More Powerful: JSP Expression Language (EL) offers a simpler and more powerful way to access data stored in JavaBeans components, request, session, and application scopes.

```
<h1>Hello, ${param.name}!</h1>
```

Implicit Objects: EL provides a set of implicit objects and predefined functions that can be used to access and manipulate data without the need for explicit Java code.

JSP Standard Tag Library (JSTL)
Standardized Tags: JSTL provides standardized tags for common tasks, including data access and manipulation, which can often replace the need for expressions.

```
<c:out value="${param.name}" />
```

10.1.5 Declarations
Definition: JSP declarations allow developers to define variables and methods that become part of the generated servlet class. Declarations are used to declare fields and methods that need to be accessible across multiple requests and from different parts of the JSP page.
Usage: Purpose
Define Class-Level Variables and Methods: Declarations are used to define variables and methods that are part of the servlet class generated from the JSP page.
Scope: Unlike scriptlets and expressions, which are embedded in the _jspService method, declarations are placed outside this method, making them accessible throughout the servlet class.
Syntax
Declaration Syntax: Enclosed within <%! and %> tags

```
<%! Java code %>
```

Example
Declaring Variables
You can declare class-level variables using JSP declarations. These variables are initialized when the servlet is instantiated and can maintain state across multiple requests.

```
<%@ page language="java" contentType="text/html; charset=UTF-8" %>
<html>
<head>
   <title>Page Visit Counter</title>
</head>
<body>
   <%! private int visitCounter = 0; %>
   <%
      visitCounter++;
```

```
  %>
  <h1>Page visits: <%= visitCounter %></h1>
</body>
</html>
```

Defining Methods

Methods can also be defined using declarations, making them reusable within the JSP page.

```
<%@ page language="java" contentType="text/html; charset=UTF-8" %>
<html>
<head>
  <title>Greeting</title>
</head>
<body>
  <%!
    public String getGreeting(String name) {
      if (name == null || name.isEmpty()) {
        return "Hello, Guest!";
      } else {
        return "Hello, " + name + "!";
      }
    }
  %>
  <h1><%= getGreeting(request.getParameter("name")) %></h1>
</body>
</html>
```

Considerations: Scope and Lifetime

Class-Level Scope**:** Variables declared in declarations have class-level scope and are shared across all instances of the servlet. This means they retain their values between requests and can lead to concurrency issues.

Initialization and Cleanup**:** Declarations are initialized when the servlet is loaded and destroyed when the servlet is unloaded. Use the jspInit and jspDestroy methods for any initialization and cleanup code.

Thread Safety

Concurrency Issues**:** Since declared variables have class-level scope, they can be accessed by multiple threads simultaneously, leading to potential concurrency issues. Synchronization or the use of local variables within the _jspService method is recommended to avoid these issues.

Example of Unsafe Code**:**

```
<%! private int counter = 0; %>
<%
  counter++;
  out.println("Counter: " + counter);
%>
```

Safe Alternative

```
<%
  synchronized(this) {
    counter++;
    out.println("Counter: " + counter);
  }
%>
```

Code Readability and Maintenance

Complexity: Declarations can make the code more complex and harder to read if overused or used for complex logic.

Separation of Concerns**:** To maintain a clear separation of concerns, business logic should ideally be placed in separate Java classes (JavaBeans or other helper classes) rather than in JSP declarations.

Alternatives to Declarations
JavaBeans
Encapsulation**:** JavaBeans provide a way to encapsulate business logic and state management in reusable components.
Usage

```
<jsp:useBean id="person" class="com.example.Person" scope="session" />
<jsp:setProperty name="person" property="name" value="John Doe" />
<jsp:getProperty name="person" property="name" />
```

Custom Tags and JSTL
Custom Tags**:** Define custom tags to encapsulate complex logic that can be reused across different JSP pages.
JSTL: Use JSTL for common tasks like iteration, conditionals, and data formatting, reducing the need for Java code within JSP pages.

Example of Best Practices
Here is a refined example using JavaBeans instead of JSP declarations for a cleaner approach:
Person.java (JavaBean)

```
package com.example;
public class Person {
   private String name;
   public String getName() {
      return name;
   }
   public void setName(String name) {
      this.name = name;
   }
   public String getGreeting() {
      if (name == null || name.isEmpty()) {
         return "Hello, Guest!";
      } else {
         return "Hello, " + name + "!";
      }
   }
}
```

greeting.jsp

```
<%@ page language="java" contentType="text/html; charset=UTF-8" %>
<jsp:useBean id="person" class="com.example.Person" scope="request" />
<jsp:setProperty name="person" property="name" param="name" />
<html>
<head>
   <title>Greeting</title>
</head>
<body>
   <h1><%= person.getGreeting() %></h1>
</body>
</html>
```

10.2 Directives in JSP: Page, Include, Taglib

JSP directives are special instructions to the JSP container that affect the overall structure and Behaviour of the JSP page and the resulting servlet. They are used to set global values such as the scripting language, the content type, and to include files or tag libraries. There are three main types of JSP directives: page, include, and taglib.

Page Directive

Purpose

The page directive is used to define various attributes that affect the overall Behaviour of the JSP page. It provides a way to set page-level instructions such as importing classes, setting content types, and specifying error handling.

Syntax

```
<%@ page attribute="value" %>
```

Common Attributes

Specifies the scripting language used in the page. The default and most commonly used value is "java".

```
<%@ page language="java" %>
```

contentType: Sets the MIME type and character encoding of the response. The default is text/html; charset=ISO-8859

```
<%@ page contentType="text/html; charset=UTF-8" %>
```

import: Imports Java classes and packages, similar to the import statement in Java.

```
<%@ page import="java.util.*, java.text.SimpleDateFormat" %>
```

session: Specifies whether the JSP page participates in HTTP sessions. The default is true

```
<%@ page session="false" %>
```

buffer: Defines the buffer size for the output stream. The default is 8kb.

```
<%@ page buffer="16kb" %>
```

autoFlush: Specifies whether the buffer should be automatically flushed when it is full. The default is true.

```
<%@ page autoFlush="false" %>
```

errorPage: Indicates the URL of another JSP page that will handle any exceptions thrown by the current page.

```
<%@ page errorPage="error.jsp" %>
```

isErrorPage: Specifies whether the current page is an error handling page. The default is false.

```
<%@ page isErrorPage="true" %>
```

isELIgnored: Indicates whether the JSP container should ignore Expression Language (EL) expressions within the page. The default is false.

```
<%@ page isELIgnored="true" %>
```

Example

```
<%@ page language="java" contentType="text/html; charset=UTF-8" import="java.util.*, java.text.*" session="true" buffer="8kb" autoFlush="true" errorPage="error.jsp" %>
<html>
<head>
  <title>Page Directive Example</title>
</head>
<body>
  <h1>Current Date and Time: <%= new java.util.Date() %></h1>
</body>
</html>
```

Include Directive

Purpose

The include directive is used to include the content of another file (usually a JSP file or static HTML file) during the translation phase. This means the content is included before the JSP page is compiled, making it part of the generated servlet.

Syntax

```
<%@ include file="relativeURL" %>
```

How It Works

Static Inclusion: The content of the included file is statically inserted into the including JSP page during translation. Changes to the included file require recompilation of the including JSP page.

Example

Including a header and footer in a JSP page.

```
<%@ include file="header.jsp" %>
<html>
<head>
  <title>Include Directive Example</title>
```

```
</head>
<body>
  <h1>Main Content of the Page</h1>
  <%@ include file="footer.jsp" %>
</body>
</html>
```

header.jsp

```
<div class="header">
  <h2>This is the header section</h2>
</div>
```

footer.jsp

```
<div class="footer">
  <h2>This is the footer section</h2>
</div>
```

Taglib Directive

Purpose

The taglib directive is used to declare a custom tag library that the JSP page will use. This allows developers to use custom tags defined in tag libraries, which can encapsulate complex functionality in simple, reusable tags.

Syntax

```
<%@ taglib uri="uri" prefix="prefix" %>
```

Attributes

uri: Specifies the URI that uniquely identifies the tag library.

prefix: Defines a prefix that will be used to distinguish the custom tags within the JSP page.

Example

Using JSTL (JavaServer Pages Standard Tag Library) core tags

```
<%@ taglib uri="http://java.sun.com/jsp/jstl/core" prefix="c" %>
<html>
<head>
  <title>Taglib Directive Example</title>
</head>
<body>
  <c:set var="message" value="Hello, JSTL!" />
  <h1><c:out value="${message}" /></h1>
</body>
</html>
```

Key Attributes

language: Specifies the scripting language used in the JSP page. The default is Java.

contentType: Defines the MIME type and character encoding of the response from the JSP page.

import: Allows importing Java packages and classes.

session: Indicates whether the page participates in a session.

errorPage: Specifies a URL to another JSP page for handling exceptions.

isErrorPage: Marks the current page as an error page.

10.3 JSP Standard Actions

JSP Standard Actions are predefined tags in JSP that provide a way to interact with the server-side objects, control the Behaviour of the JSP container, and dynamically include or forward requests to other resources. These actions are used to manage JavaBeans components, include content, forward requests, and create HTML forms, among other functionalities. They simplify the process of writing server-side logic within JSP pages.

Key JSP Standard Actions

<jsp:useBean>

<jsp:setProperty>

<jsp:getProperty>

<jsp:include>
<jsp:forward>
<jsp:param>
<jsp:plugin>

<jsp:useBean>
Purpose
The <jsp:useBean> action is used to instantiate or locate an existing JavaBean. This allows for the use of JavaBeans within a JSP page to encapsulate and reuse business logic.
Syntax
<jsp:useBean id="beanInstanceName" class="fullyQualifiedClassName" scope="page|request|session|application" />
Attributes
id: The identifier used to reference the bean instance in the JSP page.
class: The fully qualified class name of the JavaBean.
scope: Specifies the scope of the bean. Possible values are page, request, session, and application.
Example
<jsp:useBean id="person" class="com.example.Person" scope="session" />
<jsp:setProperty name="person" property="name" value="John Doe" />
<jsp:getProperty name="person" property="name" />

<jsp:setProperty>
Purpose
The <jsp:setProperty> action is used to set the properties of a JavaBean. It can set properties based on request parameters or fixed values.

Syntax
<jsp:setProperty name="beanInstanceName" property="propertyName" value="value" />

Attributes
name: The identifier of the bean instance.
property: The name of the property to be set. Use * to set multiple properties from request parameters.
value: The value to set for the property. If not specified, it uses the request parameter with the same name as the property.
Example
<jsp:setProperty name="person" property="name" value="Jane Doe" />
<jsp:setProperty name="person" property="age" value="30" />

Using Request Parameters
<jsp:setProperty name="person" property="*" />

<jsp:getProperty>
Purpose
The <jsp:getProperty> action retrieves the value of a property from a JavaBean and inserts it into the output stream.
Syntax
<jsp:getProperty name="beanInstanceName" property="propertyName" />
Attributes
name: The identifier of the bean instance.
property: The name of the property to be retrieved.
Example
<jsp:getProperty name="person" property="name" />

<jsp:include>
Purpose
The <jsp:include> action includes the content of another resource (e.g., another JSP page or an HTML file) at request processing time. This is known as dynamic inclusion.
Syntax
```
<jsp:include page="relativeURL" flush="true|false" />
```
Attributes
page: The relative URL of the resource to be included.
flush: Indicates whether to flush the buffer before including the resource. The default is false.
Example
```
<jsp:include page="header.jsp" />
<jsp:include page="footer.jsp" />
```

<jsp:forward>
Purpose
The <jsp:forward> action forwards the request to another resource (e.g., another JSP page, a servlet). The control is transferred to the specified resource, and the response from the current JSP page is discarded.
Syntax
```
<jsp:forward page="relativeURL" />
```
Attributes
page: The relative URL of the resource to which the request is forwarded.
Example
```
<jsp:forward page="nextPage.jsp" />
```

<jsp:param>
Purpose
The <jsp:param> action is used to add parameters to a request when using <jsp:include> or <jsp:forward> actions.
Syntax
```
<jsp:param name="parameterName" value="parameterValue" />
```
Attributes
name: The name of the parameter.
value: The value of the parameter.
Example
```
<jsp:forward page="nextPage.jsp">
   <jsp:param name="user" value="John Doe" />
   <jsp:param name="age" value="30" />
</jsp:forward>
```

1. <jsp:plugin>
Purpose
The <jsp:plugin> action is used to embed a Java applet or a JavaBean in the generated HTML page. It helps in generating the appropriate HTML code for the client browser to load Java components.
Syntax
```
<jsp:plugin type="bean|applet" code="classFile" codebase="url" width="width" height="height">
   <jsp:param name="parameterName" value="parameterValue" />
</jsp:plugin>
```

Attributes
type: Specifies whether the component is a bean or an applet.
code: The name of the class file containing the applet or bean.
codebase: The base URL of the applet or bean class file.
width: The width of the applet or bean.
height: The height of the applet or bean.

Example

```
<jsp:plugin type="applet" code="MyApplet.class" codebase="applets" width="300" height="200">
  <jsp:param name="param1" value="value1" />
</jsp:plugin>
```

Considerations

Readability and Maintainability

Encapsulation: Using JavaBeans with <jsp:useBean>, <jsp:setProperty>, and <jsp:getProperty> encapsulates business logic, making the JSP page more readable and maintainable.

Reusability: Including content with <jsp:include> allows for modular, reusable components such as headers, footers, and navigation bars.

Performance

Dynamic Inclusion: The <jsp:include> action is performed at request time, which can affect performance if the included resource is resource-intensive or involves complex processing.

Forwarding Requests: Using <jsp:forward> transfers control to another resource, which can streamline request processing by centralizing logic in a single resource.

Best Practices

Avoid Overuse: Excessive use of standard actions can make the JSP page cluttered. Balance the use of these actions with custom tags and beans to maintain clean and readable code.

Thread Safety: When using beans, ensure thread safety by properly managing bean scopes and avoiding shared mutable state.

10.4 Introduction to Expression Language (EL) and JSTL

JavaServer Pages (JSP) technology provides a powerful way to build dynamic web content by using Java within HTML. To simplify JSP development and reduce the amount of embedded Java code, two significant advancements were introduced: Expression Language (EL) and JavaServer Pages Standard Tag Library (JSTL). These technologies promote cleaner, more maintainable code by separating business logic from presentation.

Expression Language (EL)

Purpose: Expression Language (EL) is a scripting language used in JSP to access and manipulate data stored in JavaBeans components, request attributes, session attributes, and other objects. EL simplifies the retrieval and display of dynamic content by using concise and intuitive syntax.

Syntax

EL expressions are enclosed within ${}

```
${expression}
```

Key Features

Implicit Objects: EL provides several implicit objects for easy data access:

pageScope: Access attributes stored in the page scope.

requestScope: Access attributes stored in the request scope.

sessionScope: Access attributes stored in the session scope.

applicationScope: Access attributes stored in the application scope.

param: Access request parameters.

paramValues: Access request parameter values as an array.

header: Access request headers.

headerValues: Access request header values as an array.

cookie: Access cookies.

initParam: Access context initialization parameters.

Property and Collection Access: EL can access properties of JavaBeans and elements of collections.

```
${user.name}
${user.address.city}
${users[0].name}
```

Operators: EL supports a range of operators, including arithmetic, relational, logical, and conditional operators.

```
${1 + 1}
```

```
${price > 100}
${user.active && user.role == 'admin'}
${user.name ?: 'Guest'}
```

Functions**:** EL supports functions defined in tag libraries, allowing for more complex operations.

Example

```
<%@ taglib uri="http://java.sun.com/jsp/jstl/core" prefix="c" %>
<html>
<head>
   <title>Expression Language Example</title>
</head>
<body>
   <h1>Welcome, ${user.name}!</h1>
   <p>Your role is: ${user.role}</p>
   <p>The price with tax is: ${price * 1.1}</p>
</body>
</html>
```

Features and Syntax

Simplicity**:** EL provides a simple and efficient way to access data stored in the request, session, and application scopes.

Syntax**:** It uses ${expression} syntax to evaluate expressions, which can access beans' properties, implicit objects, and more. ${user.name}

Implicit Objects**:** EL has implicit objects for easy access to request, session, application scopes, parameters, headers, etc. ${param.username}

10.5 JSTL (JavaServer Pages Standard Tag Library)

The JavaServer Pages Standard Tag Library (JSTL) is a collection of custom tags that provide core functionalities common to many JSP applications. JSTL tags encapsulate reusable functionality, allowing developers to write less code and avoid embedding complex Java logic directly in JSP pages.

Tag Libraries: JSTL is divided into several functional areas, each provided by a different tag library.

Core Tags (c): Provides essential tags for common tasks like iteration, conditionals, and URL management.

Formatting Tags (fmt): Supports internationalization and localization, including number and date formatting.

SQL Tags (sql): Simplifies database access and query execution within JSP pages.

XML Tags (x): Facilitates XML data manipulation and transformation.

Functions Tags (fn): Defines common functions for string manipulation.

Core Tags (c Tag Library)

Iteration

<c:forEach>: Iterates over a collection of items

```
<c:forEach var="item" items="${items}">
   ${item.name}
</c:forEach>
```

Conditional

<c:if>: Evaluates a test condition and displays content if true.

```
<c:if test="${user.admin}">
   <p>Welcome, Admin!</p>
</c:if>
```

<c:choose>: Similar to a switch statement, it allows multiple conditions.

```
<c:choose>
   <c:when test="${user.role == 'admin'}">
      <p>Welcome, Admin!</p>
   </c:when>
   <c:otherwise>
      <p>Welcome, User!</p>
```

```
    </c:otherwise>
</c:choose>
```

URL Management

<c:url>: Constructs a URL with optional query parameters

```
<c:url var="logoutUrl" value="/logout" />
<a href="${logoutUrl}">Logout</a>
```

Formatting Tags (fmt Tag Library)

Internationalization and Localization

<fmt:message>: Retrieves a localized message based on a key.

```
<fmt:message key="welcome.message" />
```

Number and Date Formatting

<fmt:formatNumber>: Formats numerical values.

```
<fmt:formatNumber value="${price}" type="currency" />
```

<fmt:formatDate>: Formats date values.

```
<fmt:formatDate value="${now}" pattern="yyyy-MM-dd" />
```

SQL Tags (sql Tag Library)

Database Access

<sql:query>: Executes a SQL query

```
<sql:query var="result" dataSource="${dataSource}">
    SELECT * FROM users
</sql:query>
<c:forEach var="row" items="${result.rows}">
    ${row.username}
</c:forEach>
```

XML Tags (x Tag Library)

XML Manipulation

<x:parse>: Parses XML data.

```
<x:parse var="doc" xml="${xmlData}" />
```

<x:transform>: Applies an XSLT transformation.

```
<x:transform xml="${doc}" xslt="${xsltFile}" />
```

Functions Tags (fn Tag Library)

String Manipulation

fn:length: Returns the length of a string.

```
${fn:length(user.name)}
```

fn:toUpperCase: Converts a string to upper case.

```
${fn:toUpperCase(user.name)}
```

Example Usage

Combining EL and JSTL to create a dynamic, maintainable JSP page.

```
<%@ taglib uri="http://java.sun.com/jsp/jstl/core" prefix="c" %>
<%@ taglib uri="http://java.sun.com/jsp/jstl/fmt" prefix="fmt" %>
<%@ taglib uri="http://java.sun.com/jsp/jstl/functions" prefix="fn" %>
<html>
<head>
    <title>EL and JSTL Example</title>
</head>
<body>
    <h1>Welcome, ${user.name}!</h1>
    <p>Your role is: ${user.role}</p>
    <p>Items in your cart:</p>
```

```
    <ul>
        <c:forEach var="item" items="${cart.items}">
            <li>${item.name} - <fmt:formatNumber value="${item.price}" type="currency" /></li>
        </c:forEach>
    </ul>
    <p>Total Price: <fmt:formatNumber value="${cart.totalPrice}" type="currency" /></p>
    <p>Message: ${fn:toUpperCase('hello, world!')}</p>
</body>
</html>
```

Using EL and JSTL Together

Expression Language (EL) and JavaServer Pages Standard Tag Library (JSTL) are essential tools for advanced Java developers working with JSP. EL simplifies data access and manipulation, while JSTL provides a rich set of tags for common tasks, enhancing code readability, maintainability, and efficiency. By leveraging EL and JSTL, developers can create cleaner, more maintainable JSP pages that separate business logic from presentation, promoting better design practices and easier maintenance. Understanding and effectively using EL and JSTL are crucial skills for advanced Java web application development.

Exercise

Exercise 1 – MCQ

1. What is the purpose of JSP scriptlets?
a) To define a JSP page attribute
b) To include another resource in the JSP page
c) To insert Java code into the HTML
d) To declare JSP tag libraries
2. Which of the following JSP elements allows you to insert Java variables into the HTML?
a) Scriptlets
b) Declarations
c) Expressions
d) Directives
3. Which directive is used to include a file at the time the JSP page is requested?
a) <%@ page %>
b) <%@ include %>
c) <%@ taglib %>
d) None of the above
4. JSP declarations are used for:
a) Defining Java methods
b) Instantiating Java objects
c) Declaring variables
d) Both a and c
5. Which of the following is true about the JSP page directive?
a) It includes a file during the JSP translation phase
b) It declares a page-specific attribute
c) It is used to write Java code inside a JSP page
d) It defines a tag library
6. Expression Language (EL) is primarily used for:
a) Simplifying the access to application data
b) Including files in a JSP page
c) Declaring JSP-specific variables
d) Writing complex Java code in JSP
7. Which JSTL core tag is used to iterate over a collection?
a) <c:set>
b) <c:forEach>
c) <c:if>
d) <c:choose>
8. The taglib directive in JSP is used to:

a) Define Java variables
b) Import Java classes
c) Include another JSP file
d) Declare the use of a tag library
9. Which of the following is NOT a feature of JSP?
a) Ability to include servlets directly
b) Direct access to Java classes and libraries
c) Built-in session management
d) Automatic garbage collection
10. The JSTL <c:if> tag is used for:
a) Iterating over collections
b) Conditional processing
c) Setting variables
d) Handling exceptions

Exercise 2 –True/False
1. JSP scriptlets are used to include Java code that is executed every time a JSP page is requested.
2. The JSP include directive is processed at request time.
3. Expression Language (EL) can be used to directly call Java methods within a JSP page.
4. JSP declarations are used to declare variables that are local to the JSP page.
5. The page directive is used to define page-specific attributes like error pages and buffer sizes.
6. In JSP, EL expressions are enclosed in #{} brackets.
7. The JSTL <c:out> tag automatically escapes HTML and XML special characters.
8. You can mix EL and JSTL tags within the same JSP page to build dynamic content.
9. The JSP taglib directive is used at compile time to link to a library of custom tags.
10. EL is disabled in JSP pages by default for security reasons.

Exercise 3 – Fill in the blanks
1. To execute Java code within a JSP page, developers use ___ to insert scriptlets.
2. The ___ directive in JSP is used to import classes and packages.
3. Expression Language (EL) expressions are enclosed in ___ brackets.
4. The ___ tag in JSTL is used for conditional processing based on the evaluation of an expression.
5. JSP pages use the ___ directive to include content from other files at the time the page is requested.
6. Expression Language (EL) simplifies data access and manipulation by providing a concise syntax for accessing ____________ objects and properties.
7. JSP pages can include ____________ from other resources using directives like <jsp:include> and <jsp:forward>.
8. JSP ____________ are custom tags that provide pre-defined functionality for common tasks such as iteration, conditionals, and formatting.
9. JSP pages are translated into ____________ by the JSP container during deployment.
10. The ____________ method is the main entry point for processing requests in a JSP page.

Exercise 4 – Match Case
1. Inserts Java code into the JSP page
2. Used to format and parse text
3. Directive for declaring page dependencies
4. Accesses bean properties and collections

A. <%@ taglib %>
B. <%@ include %>
C. Scriptlets
D. JSTL and EL

Exercise 5 – One word answer
1. Which JSP element is used to write Java expressions inside HTML?
2. What is the JSP standard action for forwarding a request to another resource?

Exercise 6 – Small answer
1. What JSP directive is used to include a file at page translation time?
2. Which JSTL core tag is used to iterate over a collection of objects?

Exercise 7 - Long answer
1. Explain how JSP scriptlets, expressions, and declarations differ from each other.
2. Describe how EL and JSTL work together in JSP pages to simplify web application development.

Answer-
Exercise 1 – 1) c 2) c 3) b 4) d 5) b 6) a 7) b 8) d 9) a 10) b
Exercise 2 – 1) True 2) False 3) False 4) False 5) True 6) False 8) True 9) True 10) True 11) False
Exercise 3 – 1) <% %> 2) page 3) ${ } 4) <c:if> 5) include 6) JavaBeans 7) content 8) Standard Actions 9) Java servlets 10) jspService()
Exercise 4 – 1 – C. Scriptlets 2 – D. JSTL and EL 3 – B. <%@ include %> 4 – A. <%@ taglib %>
Exercise 5 – 1) Expressions 2) forward

Online Resources

Online Practice Paper

Link: https://forms.gle/39U3C5Fwqjo8ebBq7
QR Code:

YouTube Video Link
Link: https://www.youtube.com/playlist?list=PLzlh_31VWEFoytSDG1lrWRVbsPlnvvG3z
QR Code:

CHAPTER 11 - Struts Framework (version 2.x)

11.1 Introduction

Struts 2 is an evolution of the original Struts framework, merging concepts from Web work, another popular MVC framework. It introduces several enhancements:
Simpler Configuration: Uses annotations and conventions to reduce the complexity of configuration.
POJO Actions: Action classes are simple POJOs, making them easier to write and test.
Improved Tag Support: Provides more flexible and powerful tag libraries.
AJAX Support: Built-in support for AJAX to create dynamic web applications.

Key Components
Model: Represents the application's data and business logic. In Struts, the model is usually composed of JavaBeans, Enterprise JavaBeans (EJBs), or Plain Old Java Objects (POJOs).
View: Defines the presentation layer. Struts uses JavaServer Pages (JSPs) or other view technologies like Velocity or FreeMarker to create the user interface.
Controller: Manages the flow of the application. Struts provides a centralized controller called ActionServlet that processes user requests and routes them to the appropriate Action classes.

Key Features of Struts 2
MVC Framework: Struts 2 implements the MVC pattern, promoting a clear separation of concerns which enhances application maintainability.
Convention Over Configuration: Struts 2 favours convention over configuration, reducing the need for extensive XML configuration.
Tag Support: Provides a rich set of tags for form handling, data rendering, and more, which reduces the scripting needed in JSP files.
Integration: Offers easy integration with other Java frameworks and technologies, such as Spring, Hibernate, and JPA.
Interceptors: Uses an interceptor stack for request processing, allowing for customizable request handling and preprocessing.

11.2 Basics of MVC

The Model-View-Controller (MVC) architecture is a software design pattern commonly used for developing user interfaces that divide the related program logic into three interconnected elements. This separation helps to manage complex applications by organizing the code in a more modular way, promoting code reuse, and facilitating ease of maintenance.

Components of MVC
Model
View
Controller

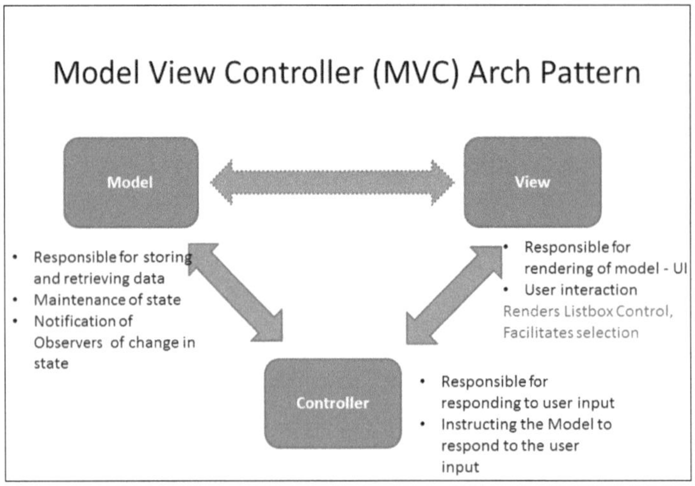

Figure 11.1

Model

The Model represents the data and the business logic of the application. It is responsible for directly managing the data, logic, and rules of the application.

Responsibilities

Data Management: It encapsulates the application's data and provides methods to retrieve, update, and manipulate the data.

Business Logic: Implements the core functionality and business rules of the application.

Notification: Notifies the view of any changes in the data, allowing the view to update accordingly.

Examples

JavaBeans/POJOs: Standard Java objects used to represent the application's data.

Data Access Objects (DAOs): Classes that provide an abstract interface to the database or other persistence mechanisms.

View

The View represents the presentation layer of the application. It is responsible for displaying the data to the user and sending user commands to the Controller.

Responsibilities

Rendering UI: Generates the user interface and presents the data to the user.

Receiving User Input: Captures user input from various UI elements (like forms, buttons) and forwards it to the Controller.

Update from Model: Subscribes to changes in the Model and refreshes the UI when the data changes.

Examples

JavaServer Pages (JSP): Technology used to create dynamically generated web pages based on HTML, XML, or other document types.

JavaFX/Swing: Frameworks used for building graphical user interfaces in Java.

Controller

The Controller acts as an intermediary between the Model and the View. It processes user input, interacts with the Model to perform operations, and determines the next view to display.

Responsibilities

Request Handling: Receives and handles all user requests and actions.

Input Processing: Processes input data, performs validation, and applies business logic.

Model Update: Interacts with the Model to update the state based on user actions.

View Selection: Determines which view should be rendered based on the outcome of the operations.

Examples

Servlets: Java classes that handle HTTP requests and responses in web applications.

Struts Action Classes: Part of the Struts framework, these classes handle the user actions and interact with the Model.

MVC Interaction Flow
User Interaction**:** The user interacts with the View by performing some action (e.g., clicking a button, submitting a form).
Controller Processing: The Controller receives the input from the View, processes it (e.g., validating the data, invoking business logic), and interacts with the Model.
Model Update: The Controller updates the Model if necessary (e.g., saving data to the database, updating the state).
View Update**:** The Model notifies the View of any changes, prompting the View to refresh and display the updated data to the user.
Response to User**:** The View presents the updated data or the outcome of the user action back to the user.

Advantages of MVC
Separation of Concerns: Each component (Model, View, Controller) has distinct responsibilities, making the application more modular and easier to manage.
Reusability: Components can be reused across different parts of the application or in different projects.
Maintainability: Clear separation of concerns makes it easier to maintain and extend the application. Changes in one component have minimal impact on others.
Testability: Isolated components are easier to test, allowing for more effective unit testing and debugging.

MVC in Java
Java provides various frameworks and tools that implement the MVC architecture, making it easier to develop web and desktop applications. Some popular MVC frameworks in the Java ecosystem include:
Struts: An open-source framework for building web applications using the MVC design pattern.
Spring MVC: Part of the Spring Framework, it provides a comprehensive approach to building web applications with an MVC architecture.
JavaServer Faces (JSF)**:** A Java specification for building component-based user interfaces for web applications.

11.3 Basic Struts Architecture

ActionServlet
The core controller component in Struts.
It handles all incoming requests and determines the appropriate action to process the request.
Configured in the web.xml deployment descriptor file.
struts-config.xml
A configuration file where you define the mapping between URLs and Action classes, form beans, global forwards, and other settings.
This file is critical for the Struts framework as it dictates the routing and handling of requests.
ActionForm
A JavaBean that represents the form inputs from the user.
It encapsulates the form data and performs basic validation.
This form bean is automatically populated by the Struts framework based on the incoming request parameters.
Action Class
Contains the business logic to process the user request.
Each Action class extends org.apache.struts.action.Action and overrides the execute method.
The execute method processes the request, interacts with the model, and returns an ActionForward to determine the next view.
ActionForward
Represents the next resource (such as a JSP) to forward or redirect the user to after processing the request.
Can be global or specific to an Action class.
ActionMapping
Defines the mapping between a user request and an Action class.
Configured in the struts-config.xml file.

Example Workflow
User Request**:** A user submits a form or clicks a link, sending an HTTP request to the server.

ActionServlet: The ActionServlet intercepts the request and consults the struts-config.xml file to determine the appropriate Action class to handle the request.
ActionForm: If the request involves a form, the corresponding ActionForm is populated with the request parameters.
Action Class: The ActionServlet then forwards the request to the specified Action class. The Action class executes the business logic.
Model Interaction: The Action class may interact with the model (database operations, business logic processing, etc.).
ActionForward: Based on the outcome of the processing, the Action class returns an ActionForward to the ActionServlet.
View Rendering: The ActionServlet uses the ActionForward to dispatch the request to the appropriate view (JSP), which renders the response to the user.

11.4 Developing a Simple Struts 2 Application

Struts 2 is an elegant, extensible framework for creating enterprise-ready Java web applications. The framework is designed to streamline the full development cycle, from building, to deploying, to maintaining applications over time. This guide will walk you through developing a simple Struts 2 application.

Prerequisites
Basic knowledge of Java and web development
JDK installed on your system
A servlet container like Apache Tomcat
An integrated development environment (IDE) like Eclipse or IntelliJ IDEA

Step-by-Step Guide
Setting Up the Project
Create a New Dynamic Web Project
Open your IDE and create a new Dynamic Web Project named SimpleStruts2App.
Set the target runtime to Apache Tomcat.
Add Struts 2 Libraries
Download the Struts 2 distribution from the official website.
Extract the contents and copy the necessary JAR files from the lib directory to the WEB-INF/lib directory of your project.
Configuring web.xml
Create and configure the web.xml file in the WEB-INF directory

```
<?xml version="1.0" encoding="UTF-8"?>
<web-appxmlns="http://xmlns.jcp.org/xml/ns/javaee"xmlns:xsi="http://www.w3.org/2001/XMLSchema-instance"        xsi:schemaLocation="http://xmlns.jcp.org/xml/ns/javaeehttp://xmlns.jcp.org/xml/ns/javaee/web-app_3_1.xsd" version="3.1">
  <display-name>SimpleStruts2App</display-name>
  <!-- Struts 2 Filter Configuration -->
  <filter>
    <filter-name>struts2</filter-name>
    <filter-class>org.apache.struts2.dispatcher.filter.StrutsPrepareAndExecuteFilter</filter-class>
  </filter>
  <filter-mapping>
    <filter-name>struts2</filter-name>
    <url-pattern>/*</url-pattern>
  </filter-mapping>
  <welcome-file-list>
    <welcome-file>index.jsp</welcome-file>
  </welcome-file-list>
</web-app>
```

Creating the Struts Configuration File
Create a struts.xml file in the src directory to define the configuration for your Struts application

```
<?xml version="1.0" encoding="UTF-8" ?>
```

```
<!DOCTYPE struts PUBLIC "-//Apache Software Foundation//DTD Struts Configuration 2.3//EN"
"http://struts.apache.org/dtds/struts-2.3.dtd">
<struts>
  <package name="default" extends="struts-default">
    <action name="helloWorld" class="com.example.action.HelloWorldAction">
      <result name="success">/hello.jsp</result>
    </action>
  </package>
</struts>
```

Creating the Action Class

Create an Action class named HelloWorldAction in the src/com/example/action directory

```
package com.example.action;
import com.opensymphony.xwork2.ActionSupport;
public class HelloWorldAction extends ActionSupport {
  private String message;
  public String execute() {
    message = "Hello, Struts 2!";
    return SUCCESS;
  }
  public String getMessage() {
    return message;
  }
}
```

1. Creating the View

Create a JSP file named hello.jsp in the WebContent directory to display the message

```
<%@ taglib uri="/struts-tags" prefix="s" %>
<html>
<head>
  <title>Hello World</title>
</head>
<body>
  <h1><s:property value="message"/></h1>
</body>
</html>
```

Create another JSP file named index.jsp in the WebContent directory to serve as the entry point:

```
<html>
<head>
  <title>Simple Struts 2 Application</title>
</head>
<body>
  <h2>Welcome to Struts 2</h2>
  <a href="helloWorld">Say Hello</a>
</body>
</html>
```

Running the Application

Deploy the Application

Right-click on your project in the IDE and select Run As > Run on Server.

Choose your Apache Tomcat server and click Finish.

Access the Application

Open a web browser and navigate to http://localhost:8080/SimpleStruts2App.

Click on the “Say Hello” link to trigger the HelloWorldAction and view the message.

11.5 Struts 2 Architecture

Apache Struts 2 is a robust, extensible framework for building enterprise-ready Java web applications. It follows the Model-View-Controller (MVC) design pattern to separate the application logic, user interface, and control flow. Understanding the architecture of Struts 2 is crucial for developers aiming to leverage its full potential in creating scalable, maintainable web applications.

11.5.1 Core Components of Struts 2 Architecture

Action: The central component where business logic is executed.
Interceptor: Objects that provide cross-cutting functionalities like logging, validation, and file upload.
ValueStack/Ognl: Manages the data and state of the application, facilitating data transfer between the Model and the View.
Result: Represents the outcome of an action and determines the view to render.
ActionContext: Provides access to various application data like request parameters, session, and application data.
Configuration Files: Include struts.xml for action mappings and struts.properties for framework settings.

Struts 2 architecture is built around a few core components that interact with each other to process user requests and generate responses. These components include Actions, Interceptors, Results, and the Value Stack. Here's how they work together within the MVC pattern

Action

Definition: An Action is a class that implements the com.opensymphony.xwork2.Action interface or extends ActionSupport.

Role: Executes the business logic and returns a String result, which is mapped to a view

```
package com.example.action;
import com.opensymphony.xwork2.ActionSupport;
public class HelloWorldAction extends ActionSupport {
   private String message;
   public String execute() {
      message = "Hello, Struts 2!";
      return SUCCESS;
   }
   public String getMessage() {
      return message;
   }
}
```

Interceptor

Definition: Interceptors are invoked before and after the execution of an Action.

Role: Provide cross-cutting functionalities such as validation, file upload handling, logging, and more.

```
<interceptors>
   <interceptor name="myInterceptor" class="com.example.interceptor.MyInterceptor"/>
</interceptors>
<default-interceptor-ref name="myInterceptorStack"/>.
```

ValueStack/Ognl

ValueStack: A storage mechanism that holds all the data related to the request, including the action and the objects created by the action.

OGNL (Object-Graph Navigation Language): A powerful expression language used to manipulate and access data on the ValueStack.

```
<s:property value="message"/>
```

Result

Definition: A result defines the view that should be rendered after an Action is executed.
Types: Common types include dispatcher (forward to a JSP), redirect, redirectAction, etc.

```
<action name="helloWorld" class="com.example.action.HelloWorldAction">
   <result name="success">/hello.jsp</result>
</action>
```

ActionContext

Definition: ActionContext is a container that holds the context data for a particular action execution.

Role: Provides access to request parameters, session attributes, and application scope data.

```
Map<String, Object> session = ActionContext.getContext().getSession();
```

Configuration Files

struts.xml: Main configuration file that defines action mappings, interceptors, and result paths.

```
<?xml version="1.0" encoding="UTF-8" ?>
<!DOCTYPE struts PUBLIC "-//Apache Software Foundation//DTD Struts Configuration 2.3//EN"
"http://struts.apache.org/dtds/struts-2.3.dtd">

<struts>
  <package name="default" extends="struts-default">
    <action name="helloWorld" class="com.example.action.HelloWorldAction">
      <result name="success">/hello.jsp</result>
    </action>
  </package>
</struts>
```

struts.properties: Optional file for configuring Struts 2 settings, such as error messages and logging levels.

Request Flow in Struts 2

Client Request: The client sends an HTTP request to the server.

FilterDispatcher: The request is intercepted by the FilterDispatcher (or StrutsPrepareAndExecuteFilter in newer versions).

Action Mapping: The FilterDispatcher consults struts.xml to find the appropriate action mapping for the request URL.

Interceptors: Before invoking the Action, configured interceptors are executed.

Action Execution: The mapped Action is executed, performing the business logic.

Result Selection: Based on the return value of the Action, the corresponding result (view) is selected.

View Rendering: The selected result is rendered and returned to the client.

Advantages of Struts 2

Simplified Action Classes: Actions are simple POJOs, making them easier to write and test.

Powerful Interceptor Mechanism: Provides a clean way to add cross-cutting concerns without cluttering the Action code.

Flexible Configuration: Uses XML and annotations for configuration, offering flexibility and reducing boilerplate code.

Rich Tag Library: Simplifies the creation of dynamic and interactive user interfaces.

11.5.2 Workflow of a Struts 2 Application

Struts 2 is a popular Java web application framework that implements the Model-View-Controller (MVC) design pattern. The workflow of a Struts 2 application involves a series of steps that handle user requests, process business logic, and render views. Understanding this workflow is crucial for advanced Java developers to effectively utilize Struts 2 in their projects.

Struts 2 Request Processing Workflow

Client Request: A user initiates a request by interacting with the web application (e.g., clicking a link, submitting a form).

FilterDispatcher: The request is intercepted by the FilterDispatcher (or StrutsPrepareAndExecuteFilter in newer versions), which is configured in the web.xml file.

Action Mapping: The FilterDispatcher consults the struts.xml configuration file to determine the appropriate Action class to handle the request.

Interceptors: Before the Action class is executed, a series of interceptors are invoked to provide cross-cutting functionalities like validation, logging, and file upload handling.

Action Execution: The mapped Action class is executed, where the business logic is processed.

Result Selection: Based on the return value of the Action, the corresponding result (usually a view) is selected.

View Rendering: The selected view (e.g., a JSP page) is rendered and the response is sent back to the client.

Detailed Steps in the Workflow

Client Request

When a user interacts with the web application by submitting a form, clicking a link, or performing another action, an HTTP request is sent to the server.

FilterDispatcher

Definition: The FilterDispatcher (or StrutsPrepareAndExecuteFilter) is a servlet filter that acts as the front controller in Struts 2.

Role: It intercepts incoming requests and forwards them to the appropriate action based on the configuration defined in struts.xml.

```
<filter>
  <filter-name>struts2</filter-name>
  <filter-class>org.apache.struts2.dispatcher.filter.StrutsPrepareAndExecuteFilter</filter-class>
</filter>
<filter-mapping>
  <filter-name>struts2</filter-name>
  <url-pattern>/*</url-pattern>
</filter-mapping>
```

Action Mapping

Definition: Action mappings are defined in the struts.xml configuration file. This file maps URLs to specific Action classes.

Role: Determines which Action class should handle the incoming request

```
<struts>
  <package name="default" extends="struts-default">
    <action name="helloWorld" class="com.example.action.HelloWorldAction">
      <result name="success">/hello.jsp</result>
    </action>
  </package>
</struts>
```

Interceptors

Definition: Interceptors are objects that provide pre-processing and post-processing functionality to actions.

Role: They handle common concerns such as input validation, logging, and file upload handling before and after the Action class is executed.

```
<interceptors>
  <interceptor name="myInterceptor" class="com.example.interceptor.MyInterceptor"/>
</interceptors>
<default-interceptor-ref name="myInterceptorStack"/>
```

Action Execution

Definition: An Action class contains the business logic for handling a specific request.

Role: The Action class processes the request, interacts with the model to retrieve or update data, and returns a result string indicating the outcome.

```
package com.example.action;
import com.opensymphony.xwork2.ActionSupport;
public class HelloWorldAction extends ActionSupport {
  private String message;
  public String execute() {
    message = "Hello, Struts 2!";
    return SUCCESS;
  }
  public String getMessage() {
    return message;
  }
}
```

Result Selection

Definition: A result is a mapping from a logical result name (e.g., "success") to a specific view (e.g., a JSP page).

Role: Based on the result string returned by the Action class, the framework selects the appropriate view to render.

```
<action name="helloWorld" class="com.example.action.HelloWorldAction">
  <result name="success">/hello.jsp</result>
</action>
```

View Rendering

Definition: The view is the presentation layer that displays the data to the user.

Role: Renders the response, typically using JSP, FreeMarker, or Velocity templates, and sends it back to the client.

```
<%@ taglib uri="/struts-tags" prefix="s" %>
<html>
<head>
  <title>Hello World</title>
</head>
<body>
  <h1><s:property value="message"/></h1>
</body>
</html>
```

Advantages of Struts 2 Workflow

Decoupling: The separation of concerns between the model, view, and controller promotes a cleaner and more maintainable codebase.

Extensibility: Interceptors provide a flexible mechanism for adding cross-cutting concerns without modifying the core business logic.

Configuration: The struts.xml file provides a centralized configuration for defining action mappings, making the application easier to manage.

11.5.3 Configuration

Configuring Struts 2 involves setting up your development environment, defining application-specific settings, and configuring the core components like Actions, Interceptors, and Results. This chapter will guide you through the configuration steps necessary to get a Struts 2 application up and running.

Setting Up the Development Environment

Install Java Development Kit (JDK)**:** Ensure you have the latest JDK installed on your system. Struts 2 requires JDK 1.7 or higher.

Install a Servlet Container: You need a servlet container such as Apache Tomcat to run your web application.

Integrated Development Environment (IDE)**:** An IDE like Eclipse, IntelliJ IDEA, or NetBeans simplifies the development process.

Download Struts 2**:** Download the Struts 2 distribution from the official Apache Struts website.

Project Structure

Create a new dynamic web project with the following structure:

```
SimpleStruts2App/
├── src/
│   └── com/
│       └── example/
│           └── action/
│               └── HelloWorldAction.java
├── WebContent/
│   ├── WEB-INF/
│   │   ├── lib/
│   │   ├── web.xml
│   │   └── struts.xml
│   └── hello.jsp
└── index.jsp
```

Configuration Files

web.xml

The web.xml file is the deployment descriptor for the web application. It configures the Struts 2 filter and defines URL patterns.

```
<?xml version="1.0" encoding="UTF-8"?>
<web-app xmlns="http://xmlns.jcp.org/xml/ns/javaee"
        xmlns:xsi="http://www.w3.org/2001/XMLSchema-instance"
        xsi:schemaLocation="http://xmlns.jcp.org/xml/ns/javaee
        http://xmlns.jcp.org/xml/ns/javaee/web-app_3_1.xsd"
        version="3.1">
  <display-name>SimpleStruts2App</display-name>

  <!-- Struts 2 Filter Configuration -->
  <filter>
    <filter-name>struts2</filter-name>
    <filter-class>org.apache.struts2.dispatcher.filter.StrutsPrepareAndExecuteFilter</filter-class>
  </filter>
  <filter-mapping>
    <filter-name>struts2</filter-name>
    <url-pattern>/*</url-pattern>
  </filter-mapping>
  <welcome-file-list>
    <welcome-file>index.jsp</welcome-file>
  </welcome-file-list>
</web-app>
```

struts.xml

The struts.xml file is the main configuration file for Struts 2. It maps actions to classes and defines result views.

```
<?xml version="1.0" encoding="UTF-8"?>
<!DOCTYPE struts PUBLIC "-//Apache Software Foundation//DTD Struts Configuration 2.3//EN"
"http://struts.apache.org/dtds/struts-2.3.dtd">
<struts>
  <package name="default" extends="struts-default">
    <!-- Action Mapping -->
    <action name="helloWorld" class="com.example.action.HelloWorldAction">
      <result name="success">/hello.jsp</result>
    </action>
  </package>
</struts>
```

Core Components Configuration

Actions

Actions are the core of Struts 2's MVC implementation. They process user input, interact with the model, and determine the appropriate view to render.

Example Action Class:

```
package com.example.action;
import com.opensymphony.xwork2.ActionSupport;
public class HelloWorldAction extends ActionSupport {
  private String message;
  public String execute() {
    message = "Hello, Struts 2!";
    return SUCCESS;
  }
  public String getMessage() {
    return message;
  }
```

```
}
```
In struts.xml, you define how this action is mapped
```
<action name="helloWorld" class="com.example.action.HelloWorldAction">
   <result name="success">/hello.jsp</result>
</action>
```

Interceptors

Interceptors are used for cross-cutting concerns like validation, logging, and file upload handling. They are executed before and after the action.

Custom Interceptor Example

Create an interceptor by implementing the Interceptor interface
```
package com.example.interceptor;
import com.opensymphony.xwork2.interceptor.AbstractInterceptor;
import com.opensymphony.xwork2.ActionInvocation;
public class MyInterceptor extends AbstractInterceptor {
   @Override
   public String intercept(ActionInvocation invocation) throws Exception {
      // Pre-processing logic
      System.out.println("Before action execution");
      // Proceed to the next interceptor or action
      String result = invocation.invoke();
      // Post-processing logic
      System.out.println("After action execution");
      return result;
   }
}
```
Configure the interceptor in struts.xml
```
<package name="default" extends="struts-default">
   <interceptors>
      <interceptor name="myInterceptor" class="com.example.interceptor.MyInterceptor"/>
      <interceptor-stack name="myStack">
         <interceptor-ref name="myInterceptor"/>
         <interceptor-ref name="defaultStack"/>
      </interceptor-stack>
   </interceptors>
   <default-interceptor-ref name="myStack"/>
   <action name="helloWorld" class="com.example.action.HelloWorldAction">
      <result name="success">/hello.jsp</result>
   </action>
</package>
```

Results

Results define the view to render based on the action's outcome. Common result types include dispatcher, redirect, and redirectAction.

Dispatcher Result Example

In the struts.xml configuration file
```
<action name="helloWorld" class="com.example.action.HelloWorldAction">
   <result name="success">/hello.jsp</result>
</action>
```

Value Stack and OGNL

Struts 2 uses the Value Stack to store all data related to the current request. OGNL (Object-Graph Navigation Language) is used to access and manipulate data in the Value Stack.

Using OGNL in JSP
```
<%@ taglib uri="/struts-tags" prefix="s" %>
```

```
<html>
<head>
  <title>Hello World</title>
</head>
<body>
  <h1><s:property value="message"/></h1>
</body>
</html>
```

Advanced Configuration

Annotation-Based Configuration

Struts 2 supports annotations as an alternative to XML configuration.

Action Class with Annotations

```
package com.example.action;
import com.opensymphony.xwork2.ActionSupport;
import org.apache.struts2.convention.annotation.Action;
import org.apache.struts2.convention.annotation.Result;
public class HelloWorldAction extends ActionSupport {
  private String message;
  @Action(value = "helloWorld", results = {
    @Result(name = "success", location = "/hello.jsp")
  })
  public String execute() {
    message = "Hello, Struts 2!";
    return SUCCESS;
  }
  public String getMessage() {
    return message;
  }
}
```

Enable annotation scanning in struts.xml

```
<constant name="struts.convention.action.packages" value="com.example.action"/>
```

Custom Interceptor Stacks

Create custom interceptor stacks to apply specific interceptors to different actions.

```
<interceptor-stack name="customStack">
  <interceptor-ref name="myInterceptor"/>
  <interceptor-ref name="defaultStack"/>
</interceptor-stack>
<default-interceptor-ref name="customStack"/>
```

11.5.4 Struts 2 vs. Struts 1

Struts 2 is not just an evolution of Struts 1; it's a complete rewrite that offers significant improvements

Action Class

Struts 1: Actions are tightly coupled to the framework and require extending the Action class.

Struts 2: Actions are simple POJOs, making them more flexible and easier to test.

Form Handling

Struts 1: Uses ActionForm classes to handle form data, which adds boilerplate code.

Struts 2: Form data is handled directly by action properties, reducing redundancy.

Validation

Struts 1: Validation logic is placed in ActionForm classes and configured via validation.xml.

Struts 2: Uses interceptors for validation, with options for XML configuration or annotations.

Configuration

Struts 1: Configuration is primarily XML-based, using struts-config.xml.

Struts 2: Supports both XML-based (struts.xml) and annotation-based configuration.
Interceptors
Struts 1: No built-in interceptor support, requiring custom implementations for cross-cutting concerns.
Struts 2: Built-in support for interceptors, providing a clean and flexible way to handle cross-cutting concerns.
Tag Libraries
Struts 1: Uses the Struts Tag Library (Struts-EL) for form elements and error messages.
Struts 2: Provides a richer and more flexible tag library that integrates well with OGNL.
Architecture
Struts 1: Utilizes a central ActionServlet controller.
Struts 2: Uses a FilterDispatcher (or StrutsPrepareAndExecuteFilter) as the central controller.
Result Types
Struts 1: Limited result types such as dispatcher, forward, and redirect.
Struts 2: More flexible result types including dispatcher, redirect, chain, and stream.
Type Conversion
Struts 1: Requires manual type conversion.
Struts 2: Automatic type conversion using OGNL simplifies data handling.
Testability
Struts 1: Harder to test due to tight coupling with the framework.
Struts 2: Easier to test because actions are POJOs and support dependency injection.
Ajax Support
Struts 1: Limited and requires manual implementation.
Struts 2: Built-in support for Ajax with the Struts2-Dojo plugin.
Plugins
Struts 1: Fewer plugins available.
Struts 2: Extensive plugin support enhances functionality and integration options.
Internationalization
Struts 1: Requires manual implementation.
Struts 2: Built-in support for internationalization using properties files.
Annotations
Struts 1: Does not support annotations.
Struts 2: Supports annotations, reducing the need for extensive XML configuration.
Zero Configuration
Struts 1: Not available.
Struts 2: Supported with the convention-plugin, allowing for zero-configuration setups.
Modularization
Struts 1: Limited modularization capabilities.
Struts 2: Better modularization and integration with frameworks like Spring.
Documentation
Struts 1: Older and less detailed documentation.
Struts 2: More extensive and updated documentation available.
Community Support
Struts 1: Smaller and older community.
Struts 2: Larger and more active community providing better support and resources.

11.5.5 Setting up and Configuring Struts 2 Project

Struts 2 is a powerful framework for building Java EE web applications. This chapter will guide you through the steps of setting up and configuring a Struts 2 project, from creating a new project to configuring essential components like actions, interceptors, and results.

Prerequisites
Java Development Kit (JDK): Ensure you have JDK 1.7 or higher installed.
Servlet Container: Install a servlet container like Apache Tomcat.
Integrated Development Environment (IDE): Use an IDE such as Eclipse, IntelliJ IDEA, or NetBeans.
Struts 2 Libraries: Download the Struts 2 distribution from the official Apache Struts website.

Project Structure
Create a new dynamic web project in your IDE with the following structure

```
SimpleStruts2App/
├── src/
│   └── com/
│       └── example/
│           └── action/
│               └── HelloWorldAction.java
├── WebContent/
│   ├── WEB-INF/
│   │   ├── lib/
│   │   ├── web.xml
│   │   └── struts.xml
│   └── hello.jsp
└── index.jsp
```

Adding Struts 2 Libraries
Copy the necessary Struts 2 libraries into the WEB-INF/lib directory. The essential libraries include:
struts2-core-*.jar
xwork-core-*.jar
ognl-*.jar
commons-fileupload-*.jar
commons-io-*.jar
freemarker-*.jar
javassist-*.jar
log4j-*.jar

Configuring web.xml
The web.xml file is the deployment descriptor for the web application. It configures the Struts 2 filter and defines URL patterns

```
<?xml version="1.0" encoding="UTF-8"?>
<web-app xmlns="http://xmlns.jcp.org/xml/ns/javaee"
       xmlns:xsi="http://www.w3.org/2001/XMLSchema-instance"
       xsi:schemaLocation="http://xmlns.jcp.org/xml/ns/javaee
       http://xmlns.jcp.org/xml/ns/javaee/web-app_3_1.xsd"
       version="3.1">
   <display-name>SimpleStruts2App</display-name>

   <!-- Struts 2 Filter Configuration -->
   <filter>
      <filter-name>struts2</filter-name>
      <filter-class>org.apache.struts2.dispatcher.filter.StrutsPrepareAndExecuteFilter</filter-class>
   </filter>
   <filter-mapping>
      <filter-name>struts2</filter-name>
      <url-pattern>/*</url-pattern>
   </filter-mapping>
   <welcome-file-list>
      <welcome-file>index.jsp</welcome-file>
   </welcome-file-list>
</web-app>
```

Configuring struts.xml
The struts.xml file is the main configuration file for Struts 2. It maps actions to classes and defines result views.

```
<?xml version="1.0" encoding="UTF-8"?>
```

```
<!DOCTYPE struts PUBLIC "-//Apache Software Foundation//DTD Struts Configuration 2.3//EN"
"http://struts.apache.org/dtds/struts-2.3.dtd">
<struts>
  <package name="default" extends="struts-default">
    <!-- Action Mapping -->
    <action name="helloWorld" class="com.example.action.HelloWorldAction">
      <result name="success">/hello.jsp</result>
    </action>
  </package>
</struts>
```

Creating an Action Class

Create a simple action class that processes user input and returns a result.

HelloWorldAction.java**:**

```
package com.example.action;
import com.opensymphony.xwork2.ActionSupport;
public class HelloWorldAction extends ActionSupport {
  private String message;
  public String execute() {
    message = "Hello, Struts 2!";
    return SUCCESS;
  }
  public String getMessage() {
    return message;
  }
  public void setMessage(String message) {
    this.message = message;
  }
}
```

Creating a JSP Page

Create a JSP page to display the result of the action.

hello.jsp**:**

```
<%@ taglib uri="/struts-tags" prefix="s" %>
<html>
<head>
  <title>Hello World</title>
</head>
<body>
  <h1><s:property value="message"/></h1>
</body>
</html>
```

Testing the Application

Deploy the Application: Deploy the application to your servlet container (e.g., Apache Tomcat).

Access the application**:** Open a web browser and navigate to http://localhost:8080/SimpleStruts2App/helloWorld.action.

Advanced Configurations

Using Annotations

Struts 2 supports annotations for configuration, reducing the need for XML configuration.

HelloWorldAction.java with annotations:

```
package com.example.action;
import com.opensymphony.xwork2.ActionSupport;
import org.apache.struts2.convention.annotation.Action;
```

```java
import org.apache.struts2.convention.annotation.Result;
public class HelloWorldAction extends ActionSupport {
    private String message;
    @Action(value = "helloWorld", results = {
        @Result(name = "success", location = "/hello.jsp")
    })
    public String execute() {
        message = "Hello, Struts 2!";
        return SUCCESS;
    }
    public String getMessage() {
        return message;
    }
    public void setMessage(String message) {
        this.message = message;
    }
}
```

Enable annotation scanning in struts.xml

```xml
<constant name="struts.convention.action.packages" value="com.example.action"/>
```

Configuring Interceptors

Interceptors in Struts 2 are powerful mechanisms for handling cross-cutting concerns such as logging, validation, and exception handling.

Custom Interceptor

Create a custom interceptor by extending AbstractInterceptor.

```java
package com.example.interceptor;
import com.opensymphony.xwork2.interceptor.AbstractInterceptor;
import com.opensymphony.xwork2.ActionInvocation;
public class LoggingInterceptor extends AbstractInterceptor {
    @Override
    public String intercept(ActionInvocation invocation) throws Exception {
        System.out.println("Before action execution");
        String result = invocation.invoke();
        System.out.println("After action execution");
        return result;
    }
}
```

Configure the interceptor in struts.xml

```xml
<package name="default" extends="struts-default">
    <interceptors>
        <interceptor name="loggingInterceptor" class="com.example.interceptor.LoggingInterceptor"/>
        <interceptor-stack name="loggingStack">
            <interceptor-ref name="loggingInterceptor"/>
            <interceptor-ref name="defaultStack"/>
        </interceptor-stack>
    </interceptors>
    <default-interceptor-ref name="loggingStack"/>
    <action name="helloWorld" class="com.example.action.HelloWorldAction">
        <result name="success">/hello.jsp</result>
    </action>
</package>
```

11.6 Interceptors

Interceptors in Struts 2 are a core feature that facilitate the handling of cross-cutting concerns such as logging, validation, authentication, and more, in a clean, modular, and reusable manner. They act as a layer that intercepts incoming requests and outgoing responses, allowing developers to add pre-processing and post-processing logic around the invocation of actions. This design pattern ensures that repetitive tasks can be centralized, reducing code duplication and enhancing maintainability. Struts 2 includes a variety of built-in interceptors, such as those for parameter population (params), type conversion (conversion), model-driven actions (modelDriven), validation (validation), and exception handling (exception). Each of these interceptors addresses common needs in web application development, allowing developers to focus on business logic rather than boilerplate code. Additionally, developers can create custom interceptors by implementing the Interceptor interface or, more commonly, by extending the AbstractInterceptor class, thus leveraging the lifecycle methods to insert their custom logic before and after the action execution.

Configuration of interceptors is done in the struts.xml file, where they can be applied to individual actions or grouped into interceptor stacks for reuse across multiple actions. This configuration flexibility allows for fine-grained control over which interceptors are applied and when. For example, an interceptor stack can be defined that includes logging, exception handling, and parameter population, and this stack can then be applied to a set of actions. Developers can also exclude specific interceptors from a stack for particular actions if needed. Parameters can be passed to interceptors to customize their Behaviour, enhancing their flexibility and adaptability to different scenarios.

By using interceptors, developers can significantly improve the modularity of their applications. Cross-cutting concerns are isolated in interceptors rather than being scattered throughout the codebase, promoting a clear separation of concerns. This not only makes the code more readable and maintainable but also simplifies debugging and testing. Furthermore, the extensibility provided by interceptors allows for easy integration of new functionalities without altering the core business logic. For example, adding a new security check or a logging mechanism can be done by simply introducing a new interceptor and configuring it appropriately. Overall, interceptors in Struts 2 provide a robust mechanism for enhancing the scalability, maintainability, and modularity of web applications, making them an indispensable tool for advanced Java developers.

11.6.1 How Interceptors Work

Interceptors in Struts 2 function as a layer that intercepts requests and responses, allowing developers to encapsulate common functionality such as logging, validation, and authentication in a reusable and maintainable way. Here's a detailed explanation of how interceptors work within the Struts 2 framework

Interceptor Invocation

Request Flow

When a client sends a request, it first hits the Struts 2 filter (StrutsPrepareAndExecuteFilter), which is configured in the web.xml file. This filter prepares the necessary context and then delegates the request processing to the ActionProxy.

The ActionProxy is responsible for creating the action invocation and determining the appropriate action to execute based on the request.

Interceptor Stack

Each action in Struts 2 can have an associated interceptor stack. An interceptor stack is a collection of interceptors configured in a specific order.

The configuration of these interceptors is typically done in the struts.xml file, where they can be applied globally, to specific packages, or to individual actions.

Execution Order

When the ActionProxy prepares to invoke the action, it first traverses through the configured interceptor stack.

Each interceptor in the stack has an intercept method, which is called in the order they are configured. This method can execute logic before and after the action execution.

Pre-processing

Before Action Execution

During pre-processing, interceptors can perform tasks such as setting up resources, validating input, logging requests, or altering request parameters.

For example, the params interceptor populates the action properties with the parameters from the HTTP request.

Action Execution

After all pre-processing interceptors have been executed, the action method itself is invoked. The result of this method is typically a string representing the outcome of the action (e.g., "success", "error").

The ActionInvocation object, which represents the context of the action invocation, is passed through the interceptors and ultimately used to invoke the action.
Post-processing
After Action Execution
Once the action method has executed, the control flow returns through the interceptors in the reverse order. This is where post-processing logic can be applied.
Interceptors can perform tasks such as cleaning up resources, logging the response, or handling exceptions.
Result Processing
Result Rendering
After all interceptors have completed their post-processing, the framework determines the appropriate result view to render based on the action's return value and the result mappings in struts.xml.
The response is then generated and sent back to the client.

Example of Interceptor Workflow
Consider a scenario where we have an interceptor stack with a logging interceptor, a validation interceptor, and a parameter population interceptor.
Request Handling
The client sends a request to login.action.
The StrutsPrepareAndExecuteFilter intercepts the request and creates an ActionProxy.
Interceptor Stack Execution
The ActionProxy starts executing the interceptor stack.
The loggingInterceptor logs the incoming request details.
The validationInterceptor validates the input parameters against defined rules.
The paramsInterceptor populates the action's properties with request parameters.
Action Execution
After pre-processing by the interceptors, the LoginAction's execute method is called.
The method processes the login logic and returns a result string, e.g., "success".
Post-processing
The control flow returns through the interceptors in reverse order.
The paramsInterceptor might clean up any resources if needed.
The validationInterceptor does nothing specific during post-processing.
The loggingInterceptor logs the response details.
Result Rendering
The result string "success" is used to determine the appropriate JSP page to render as configured in struts.xml.
The JSP page is rendered and sent back to the client.

11.6.2 Common Uses of Interceptors

Interceptors in Struts 2 are versatile components that allow developers to handle various cross-cutting concerns effectively. Here are some of the most common uses of interceptors
Logging
Logging is a fundamental use of interceptors. By creating a logging interceptor, developers can record details about incoming requests, action executions, and responses. This helps in monitoring the application's Behaviour, debugging issues, and maintaining audit trails.
Example

```
public class LoggingInterceptor extends AbstractInterceptor {
  @Override
  public String intercept(ActionInvocation invocation) throws Exception {
    System.out.println("Before action execution: " + invocation.getAction().getClass().getName());
    String result = invocation.invoke();
    System.out.println("After action execution: " + invocation.getAction().getClass().getName());
    return result;
  }
}
```

Authentication and Authorization

Interceptors are widely used for handling authentication and authorization. An authentication interceptor can check if the user is logged in, while an authorization interceptor can verify if the user has the necessary permissions to access a particular action.

Example:

```
public class AuthenticationInterceptor extends AbstractInterceptor {
   @Override
   public String intercept(ActionInvocation invocation) throws Exception {
      Map<String, Object> session = ActionContext.getContext().getSession();
      if (session.get("user") == null) {
         return "login"; // Redirect to login page
      }
      return invocation.invoke();
   }
}
```

Input Validation

Validation interceptors ensure that user inputs meet certain criteria before the action method is executed. Struts 2 provides a built-in validation interceptor that works in conjunction with XML or annotation-based validation rules.

Example:

```
<action name="submitForm" class="com.example.action.FormAction">
   <interceptor-ref name="validation"/>
   <interceptor-ref name="workflow"/>
   <result name="input">/form.jsp</result>
   <result name="success">/success.jsp</result>
</action>
```

File Upload Handling

Interceptors can be used to handle file uploads. The fileUpload interceptor processes multipart HTTP requests and maps file data to action properties.

Example:

```
<action name="uploadFile" class="com.example.action.FileUploadAction">
   <interceptor-ref name="fileUpload">
      <param name="maximumSize">2097152</param> <!-- 2MB -->
   </interceptor-ref>
   <interceptor-ref name="defaultStack"/>
   <result name="success">/uploadSuccess.jsp</result>
</action>
```

Internationalization (i18n)

The i18n interceptor automatically handles locale changes and makes internationalized messages available to the action and views. This simplifies the development of multi-language applications.

Example

```
<interceptor-stack name="i18nStack">
   <interceptor-ref name="i18n"/>
   <interceptor-ref name="defaultStack"/>
</interceptor-stack>
```

Exception Handling

Exception handling interceptors catch exceptions thrown by actions and provide a centralized way to handle errors, such as logging them or redirecting to error pages.

Example:

```
public class ExceptionHandlingInterceptor extends AbstractInterceptor {
   @Override
   public String intercept(ActionInvocation invocation) throws Exception {
```

```
        try {
            return invocation.invoke();
        } catch (Exception e) {
            // Log the exception and redirect to an error page
            e.printStackTrace();
            return "error";
        }
    }
}
```

Performance Monitoring

Interceptors can be used to measure the performance of action executions by recording the time taken to process requests. This helps in identifying and optimizing slow actions.

Example:

```
public class PerformanceMonitoringInterceptor extends AbstractInterceptor {
    @Override
    public String intercept(ActionInvocation invocation) throws Exception {
        long startTime = System.currentTimeMillis();
        String result = invocation.invoke();
        long endTime = System.currentTimeMillis();
        System.out.println("Execution time: " + (endTime - startTime) + "ms");
        return result;
    }
}
```

Custom Pre- and Post-processing

Developers often need to perform custom pre-processing (e.g., setting up resources) and post-processing (e.g., cleaning up resources). Custom interceptors can be created for these purposes.

Example:

```
public class ResourceManagementInterceptor extends AbstractInterceptor {
    @Override
    public String intercept(ActionInvocation invocation) throws Exception {
        // Pre-processing: Setup resources
        Resource resource = ResourceManager.getResource();
        ActionContext.getContext().put("resource", resource);
        String result = invocation.invoke();
        // Post-processing: Cleanup resources
        ResourceManager.releaseResource(resource);
        return result;
    }
}
```

11.6.3 Configuring Interceptors

Configuring interceptors in Struts 2 involves defining them in the struts.xml configuration file, associating them with action classes, and potentially creating custom interceptor stacks. This section provides a detailed guide on how to configure interceptors effectively.

Basic Configuration

Interceptors are defined within the <interceptors> element in struts.xml. Each interceptor has a unique name and a class that implements the interceptor logic.

Example of Defining an Interceptor:

```
<interceptors>
    <interceptor name="loggingInterceptor" class="com.example.interceptor.LoggingInterceptor"/>
</interceptors>
```

This defines an interceptor named loggingInterceptor which uses the LoggingInterceptor class.

Associating Interceptors with Actions

Once defined, interceptors can be associated with actions. This is done using the <interceptor-ref> element within an <action> element.

Example of Associating an Interceptor with an Action:

```
<package name="default" extends="struts-default">
  <action name="login" class="com.example.action.LoginAction">
    <interceptor-ref name="loggingInterceptor"/>
    <interceptor-ref name="defaultStack"/>
    <result name="success">/home.jsp</result>
    <result name="error">/login.jsp</result>
  </action>
</package>
```

In this example, the login action uses the loggingInterceptor followed by the defaultStack.

Creating and Using Interceptor Stacks

Interceptor stacks group multiple interceptors together. This is useful for applying a common set of interceptors to multiple actions.

Example of Defining an Interceptor Stack:

```
<interceptors>
  <interceptor name="loggingInterceptor" class="com.example.interceptor.LoggingInterceptor"/>
  <interceptor name="authenticationInterceptor" class="com.example.interceptor.AuthenticationInterceptor"/>
  <interceptor-stack name="customStack">
    <interceptor-ref name="loggingInterceptor"/>
    <interceptor-ref name="authenticationInterceptor"/>
    <interceptor-ref name="defaultStack"/>
  </interceptor-stack>
</interceptors>
```

Here, customStack includes loggingInterceptor, authenticationInterceptor, and defaultStack.

Example of Using an Interceptor Stack with an Action:

```
<package name="default" extends="struts-default">
  <default-interceptor-ref name="customStack"/>
  <action name="dashboard" class="com.example.action.DashboardAction">
    <result name="success">/dashboard.jsp</result>
  </action>
</package>
```

The dashboard action uses the customStack by default.

Excluding Interceptors

Specific interceptors can be excluded from an interceptor stack for certain actions.

Example of Excluding an Interceptor:

```
<action name="publicPage" class="com.example.action.PublicPageAction">
  <interceptor-ref name="customStack">
    <exclude name="authenticationInterceptor"/>
  </interceptor-ref>
  <result name="success">/public.jsp</result>
</action>
```

In this example, publicPage action excludes the authenticationInterceptor from the customStack.

Passing Parameters to Interceptors

Interceptors can be customized by passing parameters in the configuration. This allows for flexible and dynamic Behaviour based on specific needs.

Example of Passing Parameters to an Interceptor:

```
<interceptor name="loggingInterceptor" class="com.example.interceptor.LoggingInterceptor">
  <param name="logLevel">DEBUG</param>
</interceptor>
```

```
<action name="dataProcessing" class="com.example.action.DataProcessingAction">
   <interceptor-ref name="loggingInterceptor"/>
   <result name="success">/result.jsp</result>
</action>
```

In this example, logLevel is passed to the loggingInterceptor, enabling debug-level logging.

Built-in Interceptor Stacks

Struts 2 provides several predefined interceptor stacks, such as defaultStack and basicStack. These stacks include commonly used interceptors and can be extended or customized as needed.

Example of Using a Built-in Interceptor Stack:

```
<package name="default" extends="struts-default">
   <action name="userProfile" class="com.example.action.UserProfileAction">
      <interceptor-ref name="defaultStack"/>
      <result name="success">/profile.jsp</result>
   </action>
</package>
```

11.7 Tag Library in Struts 2

Struts 2 provides a robust tag library that simplifies the development of web applications by offering a set of custom tags for creating dynamic web pages. These tags encapsulate complex logic and interactions, making it easier for developers to work with forms, control flow, internationalization, and more. This chapter explores the various tags available in the Struts 2 tag library and demonstrates their usage with examples.

Introduction to Struts 2 Tags

Struts 2 tags are JSP custom tags that provide a way to interact with the Struts framework's features directly within JSP pages. They help in creating interactive and dynamic web pages without writing Java code in JSP files. The Struts 2 tag library is divided into several categories

Control Tags
Data Tags
Form Tags
UI Tags
Ajax Tags

Control Tags

Control tags manage the control flow and data manipulation in JSP pages. Some of the key control tags are

<s:if>: Evaluates its body content if the supplied condition is true.

Example:

```
<s:if test="%{#user != null}">
Welcome, <s:property value="%{#user.username}"/>!
</s:if>
```

<s:else>: Used in conjunction with <s:if> to render content when the condition is false.

Example:

```
<s:if test="%{#user != null}">
Welcome, <s:property value="%{#user.username}"/>!
</s:if>
<s:else>
Please <a href="login.jsp">login</a>.
</s:else>
```

<s:iterator>: Iterates over a collection of objects.

Example:

```
<s:iterator value="items" var="item">
<s:property value="#item.name"/> - <s:property value="#item.price"/><br/>
</s:iterator>
```

Data Tags

Data tags help in manipulating and accessing data within the JSP page.

<s:property>: Prints the value of an expression, useful for displaying action properties.

Example:

```
<s:property value="username"/>
```

<s:set>: Sets a value in the value stack.

Example:

```
<s:set name="welcomeMessage" value="'Welcome to Struts 2!'"/>
<s:property value="#welcomeMessage"/>2
```

<s:date>: Formats a Date object.

Example:

```
<s:date name="currentDate" format="yyyy-MM-dd"/>
```

Form Tags

Form tags simplify the creation and handling of HTML forms. They automatically bind form fields to action properties.

<s:form>: Creates an HTML form.

Example:

```
<s:form action="login">
  <s:textfield name="username" label="Username"/>
  <s:password name="password" label="Password"/>
  <s:submit value="Login"/>
</s:form>
```

<s:textfield>: Creates an HTML text field.

Example:

```
<s:textfield name="username" label="Username"/>
```

<s:password>: Creates an HTML password field.

Example:

```
<s:password name="password" label="Password"/>
```

<s:submit>: Creates an HTML submit button.

Example:

```
<s:submit value="Submit"/>
```

UI Tags

UI tags provide a higher level of abstraction for creating user interface elements. They often generate complex HTML, JavaScript, and CSS code.

<s:div>: Creates a div element.

Example:

```
<s:div theme="ajax" id="contentDiv">
  <s:property value="content"/>
</s:div>
```

3<s:a>: Creates a hyperlink.

Example:

```
<s:a href="%{details.action?id=1}">View Details</s:a>
```

<s:select>: Creates a dropdown list.

Example:

```
<s:select name="country" list="{'USA', 'Canada', 'Mexico'}" label="Country"/>
```

Ajax Tags

Ajax tags enhance the user experience by enabling partial page updates without a full page refresh. These tags integrate with AJAX (Asynchronous JavaScript and XML) functionality.

<sx:div>: Creates a div element that can be dynamically updated using AJAX.

Example:

```
<sx:div href="dynamicContent.action" listenTopics="refreshDiv">
  Loading content...
</sx:div>
```

<sx:submit>: Creates a submit button that submits the form using AJAX.

Example:

```
<sx:submit value="Submit" targets="resultDiv"/>
```

Example Usage of Struts 2 Tags

Here is a simple example demonstrating the use of various Struts 2 tags to create a user registration form.

JSP Page (register.jsp):

```
<%@ taglib prefix="s" uri="/struts-tags" %>
<html>
<head>
  <title>Register</title>
</head>
<body>
  <h2>Register</h2>
  <s:form action="register">
    <s:textfield name="username" label="Username"/>
    <s:password name="password" label="Password"/>
    <s:textfield name="email" label="Email"/>
    <s:select name="country" list="{'USA', 'Canada', 'Mexico'}" label="Country"/>
    <s:submit value="Register"/>
  </s:form>
</body>
</html>
```

Action Class (RegisterAction.java):

```
package com.example.action;
import com.opensymphony.xwork2.ActionSupport;
public class RegisterAction extends ActionSupport {
  private String username;
  private String password;
  private String email;
  private String country;
  // Getters and Setters
  @Override
  public String execute() {
    // Registration logic
    return SUCCESS;
  }
}
```

struts.xml Configuration:

```
<struts>
  <package name="default" extends="struts-default">
    <action name="register" class="com.example.action.RegisterAction">
      <result name="success">/welcome.jsp</result>
      <result name="input">/register.jsp</result>
    </action>
  </package>
</struts>
```

11.7.1 Validations in Struts 2

Validation is a crucial aspect of any web application to ensure that the data entered by users is accurate and meets the required criteria. Struts 2 provides a robust validation framework that allows developers to perform validations on action properties before the action method is executed. This chapter covers the different types of validations in Struts 2, including XML-based validations, annotation-based validations, and custom validations.

XML-Based Validation

XML-based validation in Struts 2 involves defining validation rules in an XML file associated with an action. The XML file should be named using the convention <action-class-name>-validation.xml and placed in the same package as the action class.

Example:

```
< <!-- RegisterAction-validation.xml -->
<!DOCTYPE validators PUBLIC "-//OpenSymphony Group//XWork Validator 1.0.3//EN"
                    "http://www.opensymphony.com/xwork/xwork-validator-1.0.3.dtd">
<validators>
   <field name="username">
      <field-validator type="requiredstring">
         <message>Username is required</message>
      </field-validator>
   </field>
   <field name="password">
      <field-validator type="requiredstring">
         <message>Password is required</message>
      </field-validator>
      <field-validator type="stringlength">
         <param name="minLength">6</param>
         <param name="maxLength">12</param>
         <message>Password must be between 6 and 12 characters</message>
      </field-validator>
   </field>
   <field name="email">
      <field-validator type="requiredstring">
         <message>Email is required</message>
      </field-validator>
      <field-validator type="email">
         <message>Invalid email format</message>
      </field-validator>
   </field>
</validators>
```

In this example, validation rules are defined for the username, password, and email fields of the RegisterAction class. If any of these validations fail, the user is redirected back to the input page, and error messages are displayed.

Annotation-Based Validation

Annotation-based validation in Struts 2 allows developers to define validation rules directly in the action class using Java annotations. This approach keeps the validation logic close to the business logic and can make the code more readable.

Example:

```
package com.example.action;
import com.opensymphony.xwork2.ActionSupport;
import com.opensymphony.xwork2.validator.annotations.RequiredStringValidator;
import com.opensymphony.xwork2.validator.annotations.StringLengthFieldValidator;
import com.opensymphony.xwork2.validator.annotations.EmailValidator;
public class RegisterAction extends ActionSupport {
   private String username;
   private String password;
   private String email;
   @RequiredStringValidator(message = "Username is required")
   public void setUsername(String username) {
      this.username = username;
   }
   @RequiredStringValidator(message = "Password is required")
```

```java
    @StringLengthFieldValidator(minLength = "6", maxLength = "12", message = "Password must be between 6 and 12 characters")
    public void setPassword(String password) {
        this.password = password;
    }
    @RequiredStringValidator(message = "Email is required")
    @EmailValidator(message = "Invalid email format")
    public void setEmail(String email) {
        this.email = email;
    }
    // Getters and business logic here
    @Override
    public String execute() {
        // Registration logic
        return SUCCESS;
    }
}
```

In this example, validation annotations are used to specify the validation rules for the username, password, and email fields. The validation framework will automatically enforce these rules when the action is invoked.

Custom Validation

Sometimes, built-in validators are not sufficient for specific validation requirements. In such cases, custom validators can be created by implementing the Validator interface or extending one of the existing validator classes.

Example:

```java
package com.example.validator;
import com.opensymphony.xwork2.validator.ValidationException;
import com.opensymphony.xwork2.validator.validators.FieldValidatorSupport;
public class CustomValidator extends FieldValidatorSupport {
    @Override
    public void validate(Object object) throws ValidationException {
        String fieldName = getFieldName();
        String value = (String) getFieldValue(fieldName, object);
        if (value != null && value.length() < 5) {
            addFieldError(fieldName, object);
        }
    }
}
```

Usage in Action Class (XML-based)

```xml
<!-- RegisterAction-validation.xml -->
<validators>
    <field name="customField">
        <field-validator type="customValidator">
            <message>Custom field must be at least 5 characters long</message>
        </field-validator>
    </field>
</validators>
```

Usage in Action Class (Annotation-based)

```java
import com.example.validator.CustomValidator;
import com.opensymphony.xwork2.validator.annotations.CustomValidator;
public class RegisterAction extends ActionSupport {
    private String customField;
    @CustomValidator(type = "customValidator", message = "Custom field must be at least 5 characters long")
    public void setCustomField(String customField) {
        this.customField = customField;
    }
```

```
    // Other fields, getters, and setters
}
```

11.8 Tiles Framework in Struts 2

The Tiles framework is a powerful templating system used in Struts 2 to create reusable layouts for web applications. It allows developers to define consistent look-and-feel templates for different pages, thereby enhancing modularity and maintainability. This chapter delves into the Tiles framework, explaining its architecture, configuration, and usage in Struts 2 applications.

Introduction to Tiles Framework

Tiles is a layout framework that enables the creation of reusable templates for web applications. It allows the definition of common page elements (like headers, footers, and navigation menus) in one place and their reuse across multiple pages. By breaking pages into smaller, reusable components, Tiles promotes a cleaner separation of concerns and a more maintainable codebase.

Architecture of Tiles

The Tiles framework is based on three main concepts

Definitions: A definition specifies the layout of a page and includes references to the various components (tiles) that make up the page.

Templates: A template is a reusable layout that defines placeholders for content. These placeholders are filled by the components specified in the definitions.

Components: Components are the individual pieces of content that populate the placeholders in a template. These can be JSP fragments, static content, or other templates.

Configuring Tiles in Struts 2

To use Tiles in a Struts 2 application, you need to configure the Tiles plugin and define your templates and definitions.

Step 1: Adding Dependencies

Ensure that you have the required dependencies in your pom.xml file if you are using Maven:

```
<dependency>
    <groupId>org.apache.struts</groupId>
    <artifactId>struts2-tiles-plugin</artifactId>
    <version>2.5.x</version>
</dependency>
<dependency>
    <groupId>org.apache.tiles</groupId>
    <artifactId>tiles-core</artifactId>
    <version>3.0.8</version>
</dependency>
<dependency>
    <groupId>org.apache.tiles</groupId>
    <artifactId>tiles-api</artifactId>
    <version>3.0.8</version>
</dependency>
<dependency>
    <groupId>org.apache.tiles</groupId>
    <artifactId>tiles-jsp</artifactId>
    <version>3.0.8</version>
</dependency>
```

Step 2: Configuring struts.xml

Modify your struts.xml to include the Tiles result type and set up the default package to extend the Tiles plugin.

```
<struts>
    <constant name="struts.custom.i18n.resources" value="messages"/>
    <constant name="struts.tiles.definition" value="/WEB-INF/tiles.xml"/>

    <package name="default" extends="struts-default,tiles-default">
        <action name="home" class="com.example.action.HomeAction">
            <result name="success" type="tiles">home.page</result>
```

```
        </action>
    </package>
</struts>
```

Step 3: Defining Tiles Configuration

Create a tiles.xml file in the WEB-INF directory to define your templates and layout.

```
<!DOCTYPE tiles-definitions PUBLIC "-//Apache Software Foundation//DTD Tiles Configuration 3.0//EN"
"http://tiles.apache.org/dtds/tiles-config_3_0.dtd">
<tiles-definitions>
    <definition name="baseLayout" template="/WEB-INF/layouts/baseLayout.jsp">
        <put-attribute name="title" value="Default Title"/>
        <put-attribute name="header" value="/WEB-INF/layouts/header.jsp"/>
        <put-attribute name="footer" value="/WEB-INF/layouts/footer.jsp"/>
        <put-attribute name="menu" value="/WEB-INF/layouts/menu.jsp"/>
        <put-attribute name="body" value=""/>
    </definition>
    <definition name="home.page" extends="baseLayout">
        <put-attribute name="title" value="Home"/>
        <put-attribute name="body" value="/WEB-INF/content/home.jsp"/>
    </definition>
</tiles-definitions>
```

Step 4: Creating Layout Templates

Create the layout template baseLayout.jsp and include placeholders for the header, footer, menu, and body content.

```
<!-- baseLayout.jsp -->
<%@ taglib uri="http://tiles.apache.org/tags-tiles" prefix="tiles" %>
<html>
<head>
    <title><tiles:getAsString name="title"/></title>
</head>
<body>
    <div id="header">
        <tiles:insertAttribute name="header"/>
    </div>
    <div id="menu">
        <tiles:insertAttribute name="menu"/>
    </div>
    <div id="body">
        <tiles:insertAttribute name="body"/>
    </div>
    <div id="footer">
        <tiles:insertAttribute name="footer"/>
    </div>
</body>
</html>
```

Step 5: Creating Component JSPs

Create the component JSPs that will be included in the layout, such as header.jsp, footer.jsp, menu.jsp, and home.jsp.

```
<!-- header.jsp -->
<div>
    <h1>My Application Header</h1>
</div>

<!-- footer.jsp -->
<div>
    <p>My Application Footer</p>
</div>
```

```
<!-- menu.jsp -->
<div>
  <ul>
    <li><a href="home.action">Home</a></li>
    <!-- Other menu items -->
  </ul>
</div>

<!-- home.jsp -->
<div>
  <h2>Welcome to the Home Page</h2>
  <p>This is the home page content.</p>
</div>
```

Using Tiles in Struts 2 Actions

In your Struts 2 actions, you can specify the result type as tiles and refer to the Tiles definition name.

Example Action Class:

```
package com.example.action;
import com.opensymphony.xwork2.ActionSupport;
public class HomeAction extends ActionSupport {
  @Override
  public String execute() {
    return SUCCESS;
  }
}
```

Example struts.xml Entry**:**

```
<package name="default" extends="struts-default,tiles-default">
  <action name="home" class="com.example.action.HomeAction">
    <result name="success" type="tiles">home.page</result>
  </action>
</package>
```

Exercise

Exercise 1- MCQ

1. What pattern does Struts 2 framework implement to separate concerns in web application development?
a) DAO
b) MVC
c) Observer
d) Singleton
2. Which component in Struts 2 serves as the 'Controller'?
a) ActionMapper
b) ActionSupport
c) Interceptor
d) FilterDispatcher
3. What is the primary role of an Interceptor in Struts 2?
a) To update the model
b) To render the view
c) To intercept and process requests before they reach the action
d) To manage database connections
4. Which Struts 2 component is responsible for rendering the UI?
a) Action
b) Result
c) Interceptor
d) ValueStack

5. How are business logic errors typically reported back to the user in a Struts 2 application?
a) Through exceptions
b) Using ActionErrors
c) By logging errors to a file
d) Using HTTP status codes
6. Which feature of Struts 2 allows developers to create reusable UI components?
a) OGNL
b) Tag Library
c) Interceptors
d) ValueStack
7. What is the Tiles framework used for in Struts 2?
a) Data validation
b) Request processing
c) Creating dynamic forms
d) Managing page layouts
8. In Struts 2, which file typically contains the application's navigation rules?
a) web.xml
b) struts.properties
c) struts.xml
d) tiles.xml
9. Which of the following is a common use of Interceptors in Struts 2?
a) Validating user input
b) Encrypting data
c) Connecting to a database
d) Writing logs
10. How is OGNL (Object-Graph Navigation Language) used in Struts 2?
a) For database mapping
b) To bind data from the view to the action classes
c) To configure the web server
d) To compile Java source code

Exercise 2- True/ False

1. Struts 2 is based on the Model-View-Controller (MVC) design pattern.
2. In Struts 2, actions are the model component of the MVC pattern.
3. Struts 2 uses Front Controller pattern to centralize the request handling.
4. Interceptors in Struts 2 can modify the request before it reaches the action.
5. The Struts 2 framework provides tags for working directly with JDBC in JSP pages.
6. Tiles in Struts 2 is used for managing complex layouts with reusable template components.
7. Struts 2 actions must extend a specific base class to be executed by the framework.
8. The Struts 2 tag library is used to eliminate the need for Java code in JSP pages.
9. Struts 2 supports automatic type conversion for action properties.
10. In Struts 2, the framework's configuration is primarily done via annotations in the action classes.

Exercise 3- Fill in the blanks

1. In Struts 2, the ______ interceptor is responsible for populating the values of form fields into the action class properties.
2. The Struts 2 framework implements the ______ design pattern to separate the application logic, user interface, and control flow.
3. To define a reusable page layout in Struts 2, the ______ framework can be utilized.
4. Struts 2 actions can return a(n) ______ result to dynamically choose the next resource to navigate to.
5. The ______ tag in Struts 2 is used to render HTML form elements that are bound to action class properties.
6. Struts 2 is based on the ________ design pattern, which separates the application's logic, user interface, and data.
7. The core component that manages the request processing in Struts 2 is called the ________.
8. To handle form submissions in Struts 2, you typically use the ________ tag library, which simplifies the creation of form elements.

9. The Tiles framework in Struts 2 uses the ________ file to specify templates and definitions for the layout of web pages.
10. The primary configuration file for Struts 2 is named ________ and it resides in the WEB-INF directory.

Exercise 4- Match Case
1. Manages navigation and workflows in Struts 2
2. Used for defining UI components in Struts 2
3. Central concept in Struts 2 for handling data
4. Architectural pattern implemented by Struts 2

A. MVC Pattern
B. Tiles Framework
C. Interceptors
D. Tag Library

Exercise 5- One-word answer
1. What is the core component of Struts 2 that enables the MVC architecture?
2. Which framework is integrated with Struts 2 for managing complex web page layouts?

Exercise 6- Small answer
1. What Struts 2 component is responsible for mapping requests to action classes?
2. Which Struts 2 tag is used to display a text field in a form?

Exercise 7- Long answer
1. Explain the role of Interceptors in Struts 2 and how they influence the request processing lifecycle.
2. Describe how the Tiles framework integrates with Struts 2 to manage web page layouts and provide an example of its usage.

Answer-
Exercise 1- 1) b 2) d 3) c 4) b 5) b 6) b 7) d 8) c 9) a 10) b
Exercise 2- 1) True 2) False 3) True 4) True 5) False 6) True 7) False 8) True 9) True 10) False
Exercise 3- 1) params 2) MVC 3) Tiles 4) dynamic 5) s:form 6) Model-View-Controller (MVC) 7) FilterDispatcher 8) Struts form 9) tiles.xml 10)struts.xml
Exercise 4- 1 – C. Interceptors 2 – D. Tag Library 3 – B. Tiles Framework 4 – A. MVC Pattern
Exercise 5- 1) Action 2) Tiles

Online Resources

Online Practice Paper

Link: https://forms.gle/ZqG9phCXhVWTS6478
QR Code:

YouTube Video Link

Link: https://www.youtube.com/playlist?list=PLzlh_31VWEFpYOL6QX-brDP98qKT15VMX
QR Code:

CHAPTER 12 - Hibernate Framework (version 3.x)

12.1 Introduction to ORM

Object-Relational Mapping (ORM) is a programming technique used to convert data between incompatible type systems in object-oriented programming languages. In the context of advanced Java applications, ORM serves as a bridge between the object-oriented domain model and relational databases, enabling developers to manipulate database records using the same principles they apply to their Java objects. This chapter introduces the concepts, benefits, and key components of ORM, with a focus on its implementation in Java using frameworks like Hibernate.

Key Concepts of ORM

Mapping: ORM maps Java classes to database tables and Java objects to rows in those tables. This mapping allows developers to interact with the database using Java objects rather than SQL queries.

Configuration: The mapping configuration is typically defined in XML files or using annotations within the Java classes. This configuration specifies how Java class fields correspond to database columns.

Session Management: ORM frameworks provide a session or entity manager that handles the interaction between the Java application and the database. This session manages the lifecycle of persistent objects, including their retrieval, storage, and deletion.

Common ORM Frameworks in Java

Hibernate: Hibernate is one of the most widely used ORM frameworks in Java. It offers robust mapping capabilities, support for complex queries, and a powerful caching mechanism.

Java Persistence API (JPA): JPA is a standard specification for ORM in Java. It provides a set of annotations and interfaces for ORM, and various implementations like Hibernate, EclipseLink, and OpenJPA adhere to this standard.

MyBatis: MyBatis, unlike full ORM frameworks, focuses on mapping SQL queries to Java methods. It offers more control over SQL execution while still providing the benefits of mapping.

How ORM Works

Configuration: Define the mapping between Java classes and database tables. This can be done using XML configuration files or annotations.

XML Configuration:

```
<hibernate-mapping>
  <class name="com.example.Customer" table="CUSTOMER">
    <id name="id" column="CUSTOMER_ID">
      <generator class="native"/>
    </id>
    <property name="name" column="NAME"/>
    <property name="email" column="EMAIL"/>
  </class>
</hibernate-mapping>
```

Annotation Configuration:

```
@Entity
@Table(name = "CUSTOMER")
public class Customer {
  @Id
  @GeneratedValue(strategy = GenerationType.IDENTITY)
  @Column(name = "CUSTOMER_ID")
  private Long id;
  @Column(name = "NAME")
  private String name;
  @Column(name = "EMAIL")
  private String email;
  // Getters and setters
}
```

Session Management: Use the ORM framework's session or entity manager to perform CRUD operations.
Example with Hibernate:

```
Session session = HibernateUtil.getSessionFactory().openSession();
session.beginTransaction();
// Create
Customer customer = new Customer();
customer.setName("John Doe");
customer.setEmail("john.doe@example.com");
session.save(customer);
session.getTransaction().commit();
session.close();
```

Queries: ORM frameworks provide ways to write queries using an object-oriented approach. Hibernate uses HQL (Hibernate Query Language), which is similar to SQL but works with Java objects.
Example HQL Query

```
Session session = HibernateUtil.getSessionFactory().openSession();
Query query = session.createQuery("from Customer where name = :name");
query.setParameter("name", "John Doe");
List<Customer> customers = query.list();
session.close();
```

Key Benefits of ORM
Productivity: By automating the repetitive task of data conversion and SQL generation, ORM allows developers to focus more on the business logic rather than boilerplate code.
Maintainability: ORM promotes a cleaner separation of concerns, making the application easier to understand, modify, and maintain.
Performance Optimization: Modern ORM frameworks offer sophisticated caching, eager loading, and lazy loading techniques to optimize application performance.
Vendor Independence: ORM frameworks abstract the underlying database system, making it easier to switch between different database vendors with minimal changes to the application code.

12.2 Introduction to Hibernate 3.x

Hibernate 3.x is a robust and highly efficient Object-Relational Mapping (ORM) framework widely used in the Java ecosystem for managing relational data in enterprise applications. As an open-source framework, Hibernate 3.x bridges the gap between Java applications and relational databases, facilitating seamless persistence and retrieval of Java objects. This version of Hibernate introduces several powerful features that enhance its flexibility and performance, making it a preferred choice for developers. At its core, Hibernate 3.x allows developers to define mappings between Java classes and database tables, automating the conversion of Java data types to SQL data types and vice versa. This capability eliminates the need for extensive JDBC code, simplifying database interactions and reducing the risk of errors. Hibernate 3.x supports advanced query capabilities through Hibernate Query Language (HQL), which is similar to SQL but operates on Java objects rather than database tables. This abstraction allows for more intuitive query construction and manipulation of persistent data.
Moreover, Hibernate 3.x includes features such as caching mechanisms to optimize database access, lazy loading to defer fetching of related entities until needed, and sophisticated transaction management to ensure data integrity and consistency. It also supports the Java Persistence API (JPA), providing a standardized approach to ORM in Java applications. By leveraging Hibernate 3.x, developers can significantly boost productivity, maintainability, and scalability of their applications, focusing more on business logic rather than intricate database management tasks. Overall, Hibernate 3.x stands as a cornerstone in the Java development landscape, empowering developers to build efficient, scalable, and maintainable enterprise applications with ease.
Core Components of Hibernate
Hibernate 3.x is a comprehensive framework for object-relational mapping in Java, providing various core components that facilitate the interaction between Java applications and relational databases. Understanding these core components is essential for leveraging the full power of Hibernate in developing enterprise-level applications. This chapter delves into the key components of Hibernate 3.x, explaining their roles and functionalities in detail.

Configuration

The Configuration class is the starting point for any Hibernate application. It is responsible for bootstrapping Hibernate and building the session factory. The Configuration object is used to specify the location of the Hibernate configuration file (hibernate.cfg.xml or equivalent) and mapping files. It allows the application to configure settings such as database connection parameters, cache settings, and other Hibernate properties.

```
Configuration configuration = new Configuration().configure();
SessionFactory sessionFactory = configuration.buildSessionFactory();
```

SessionFactory

The SessionFactory is a thread-safe, immutable object that serves as a factory for Session instances. It is created once during application initialization and provides access to Session objects, which are the primary interfaces for database operations. The SessionFactory is a heavyweight object and should be created only once per application.

```
SessionFactory sessionFactory = new Configuration().configure().buildSessionFactory();
```

Session

The Session interface represents a single unit of work with the database. It is a lightweight, non-thread-safe object that provides methods for CRUD (Create, Read, Update, Delete) operations, query execution, and transaction management. A Session object is typically opened when needed and closed when the unit of work is completed.

```
Session session = sessionFactory.openSession();
session.beginTransaction();
// Perform database operations
session.getTransaction().commit();
session.close();
```

Transaction

The Transaction interface is used to demarcate transaction boundaries. It abstracts the underlying transaction management mechanism, whether it be JDBC, JTA, or some other transaction management API. Transactions ensure data consistency and integrity by allowing multiple operations to be executed as a single atomic unit.

```
Transaction transaction = session.beginTransaction();
try {
// Perform database operations
transaction.commit();
} catch (Exception e) {
transaction.rollback();
}
```

Query and Criteria

Hibernate 3.x provides the Query interface for executing HQL (Hibernate Query Language) queries and the Criteria API for building type-safe, programmatic queries. HQL is an object-oriented query language similar to SQL but operates on persistent objects rather than database tables. The Criteria API allows dynamic query construction without the need for HQL strings.

```
// HQL query
Query query = session.createQuery("from Customer where name = :name");
query.setParameter("name", "John Doe");
List<Customer> customers = query.list();
// Criteria query
Criteria criteria = session.createCriteria(Customer.class);
criteria.add(Restrictions.eq("name", "John Doe"));
List<Customer> customers = criteria.list();
```

Persistent Objects and POJOs

In Hibernate, entities or persistent objects are simple Java objects, also known as Plain Old Java Objects (POJOs). These objects are mapped to database tables using annotations or XML configuration. Hibernate manages the persistence lifecycle of these objects, including their creation, retrieval, updating, and deletion from the database.

```
@Entity
@Table(name = "CUSTOMER")
public class Customer {
    @Id
    @GeneratedValue(strategy = GenerationType.IDENTITY)
    @Column(name = "CUSTOMER_ID")
```

```java
    private Long id;
    @Column(name = "NAME")
    private String name;
    @Column(name = "EMAIL")
    private String email;
    // Getters and setters
}
```

Mapping Files and Annotations

Hibernate supports two ways to define the mapping between Java classes and database tables: XML configuration files and JPA annotations. Mapping files specify how class properties correspond to database columns, define relationships between entities, and configure various ORM settings.

```xml
<!-- XML Mapping -->
<hibernate-mapping>
    <class name="com.example.Customer" table="CUSTOMER">
        <id name="id" column="CUSTOMER_ID">
            <generator class="native"/>
        </id>
        <property name="name" column="NAME"/>
        <property name="email" column="EMAIL"/>
    </class>
</hibernate-mapping>
```

Caching

Hibernate 3.x supports both first-level and second-level caching. First-level cache is associated with the Session object and is used to cache objects within a session. Second-level cache is associated with the SessionFactory and is used to cache objects across sessions. Caching improves performance by reducing the number of database hits for frequently accessed data.

```xml
<!-- Example Cache Configuration in hibernate.cfg.xml -->
<property name="hibernate.cache.use_second_level_cache">true</property>
<property
name="hibernate.cache.region.factory_class">org.hibernate.cache.ehcache.EhCacheRegionFactory</property>
```

Configuration and Mapping

Setting up Hibernate involves configuring the SessionFactory and defining mappings that tell Hibernate how to map domain model objects to database tables.

Configuration

To configure Hibernate, you typically need to define properties related to database connectivity and specify the mappings between Java classes and database tables. The configuration can be done using either an XML file (hibernate.cfg.xml) or programmatically using the Configuration class in Hibernate i.e., hibernate.cfg.xml

This is the most common way to configure Hibernate. Here's an example of what hibernate.cfg.xml might look like:

```xml
<!DOCTYPE hibernate-configuration PUBLIC
    "-//Hibernate/Hibernate Configuration DTD 3.0//EN"
    "http://hibernate.sourceforge.net/hibernate-configuration-3.0.dtd">
<hibernate-configuration>
    <session-factory>
        <!-- Database connection settings -->
        <property name="hibernate.connection.driver_class">com.mysql.cj.jdbc.Driver</property>
        <property name="hibernate.connection.url">jdbc:mysql://localhost:3306/your_database</property>
        <property name="hibernate.connection.username">your_username</property>
        <property name="hibernate.connection.password">your_password</property>

        <!-- JDBC connection pool settings -->
        <property name="hibernate.c3p0.min_size">5</property>
        <property name="hibernate.c3p0.max_size">20</property>
        <property name="hibernate.c3p0.timeout">300</property>
        <property name="hibernate.c3p0.max_statements">50</property>
```

```
        <property name="hibernate.c3p0.idle_test_period">3000</property>

        <!-- SQL dialect -->
        <property name="hibernate.dialect">org.hibernate.dialect.MySQLDialect</property>
        <!-- Enable Hibernate's automatic session context management -->
        <property name="hibernate.current_session_context_class">thread</property>
        <!-- Echo all executed SQL to stdout -->
        <property name="hibernate.show_sql">true</property>
        <!-- Drop and re-create the database schema on startup -->
        <property name="hibernate.hbm2ddl.auto">update</property>

        <!-- Specify annotated entity classes -->
        <mapping class="com.example.model.YourEntityClass" />
        <!-- OR specify mapping files -->
        <!-- <mapping resource="com/example/model/YourEntityClass.hbm.xml" /> -->
    </session-factory>
</hibernate-configuration>
```

Programmatic Configuration

You can also configure Hibernate programmatically using the Configuration class:

```
import org.hibernate.SessionFactory;
import org.hibernate.cfg.Configuration;
Configuration configuration = new Configuration();
configuration.setProperty("hibernate.connection.driver_class", "com.mysql.cj.jdbc.Driver");
configuration.setProperty("hibernate.connection.url", "jdbc:mysql://localhost:3306/your_database");
configuration.setProperty("hibernate.connection.username", "your_username");
configuration.setProperty("hibernate.connection.password", "your_password");
configuration.setProperty("hibernate.dialect", "org.hibernate.dialect.MySQLDialect");
configuration.setProperty("hibernate.show_sql", "true");
configuration.setProperty("hibernate.hbm2ddl.auto", "update");
// Add annotated classes
configuration.addAnnotatedClass(YourEntityClass.class);
SessionFactory sessionFactory = configuration.buildSessionFactory();
```

Mapping

Mapping defines how Java classes are mapped to database tables. Hibernate supports both XML-based mapping and annotation-based mapping.

XML-based Mapping

This involves creating an XML mapping file (e.g., YourEntityClass.hbm.xml):

```
<!DOCTYPE hibernate-mapping PUBLIC "-//Hibernate/Hibernate Mapping DTD 3.0//EN"
  "http://hibernate.sourceforge.net/hibernate-mapping-3.0.dtd">
<hibernate-mapping>
  <class name="com.example.model.YourEntityClass" table="your_entity_table">
    <id name="id" column="id">
      <generator class="native" />
    </id>
    <property name="propertyName" column="property_column" />
    <!-- Other properties and mappings -->
  </class>
</hibernate-mapping>
```

Annotation-based Mapping

Annotations can be used directly in the Java classes to define the mapping. Here's an example:

```
import javax.persistence.Entity;
import javax.persistence.Id;
import javax.persistence.GeneratedValue;
import javax.persistence.GenerationType;
```

```java
@Entity
public class YourEntityClass {
   @Id
   @GeneratedValue(strategy = GenerationType.IDENTITY)
   private Long id;
   private String propertyName;
   // Getters and setters
}
```

Putting It All Together

Here is a step-by-step summary of setting up Hibernate:

Add Hibernate Dependencies: Ensure you have Hibernate and a database connector (e.g., MySQL Connector/J) in your project dependencies.

Create Configuration File: Create hibernate.cfg.xml with database connection details and entity mappings.

Define Entity Classes: Create Java classes representing your database tables. Annotate these classes or create corresponding XML mapping files.

Build SessionFactory: Use the Configuration class to read the configuration and build a SessionFactory.

Use Hibernate in Your Application: Obtain sessions from the SessionFactory and use them to perform database operations.

Example

Entity Class

```java
import javax.persistence.Entity;
import javax.persistence.Id;
import javax.persistence.GeneratedValue;
import javax.persistence.GenerationType;
@Entity
public class Product {
   @Id
   @GeneratedValue(strategy = GenerationType.IDENTITY)
   private Long id;
   private String name;
   private Double price;
   // Getters and setters
}
```

Configuration File (hibernate.cfg.xml)

```xml
<hibernate-configuration>
   <session-factory>
      <property name="hibernate.connection.driver_class">com.mysql.cj.jdbc.Driver</property>
      <property name="hibernate.connection.url">jdbc:mysql://localhost:3306/your_database</property>
      <property name="hibernate.connection.username">your_username</property>
      <property name="hibernate.connection.password">your_password</property>
      <property name="hibernate.dialect">org.hibernate.dialect.MySQLDialect</property>
      <property name="hibernate.show_sql">true</property>
      <property name="hibernate.hbm2ddl.auto">update</property>
      <mapping class="com.example.model.Product" />
   </session-factory>
</hibernate-configuration>
```

Main Application

```java
import org.hibernate.Session;
import org.hibernate.SessionFactory;
import org.hibernate.cfg.Configuration;
public class MainApp {
   public static void main(String[] args) {
```

```
        // Create configuration
        Configuration configuration = new Configuration().configure();
        // Build session factory
        SessionFactory sessionFactory = configuration.buildSessionFactory();
        // Obtain session and begin transaction
        Session session = sessionFactory.openSession();
        session.beginTransaction();
        // Create a new product
        Product product = new Product();
        product.setName("Laptop");
        product.setPrice(999.99);
        // Save the product
        session.save(product);
        // Commit transaction
        session.getTransaction().commit();
        // Close session
        session.close();
        sessionFactory.close();
    }
}
```

12.3 Hibernate Architecture

Hibernate is a powerful, high-performance Object-Relational Mapping (ORM) framework for Java applications. It facilitates the management of relational data in Java applications by bridging the gap between object-oriented domain models and relational database systems. Understanding Hibernate's architecture is crucial for developers looking to leverage its full potential in building efficient and scalable data access layers.

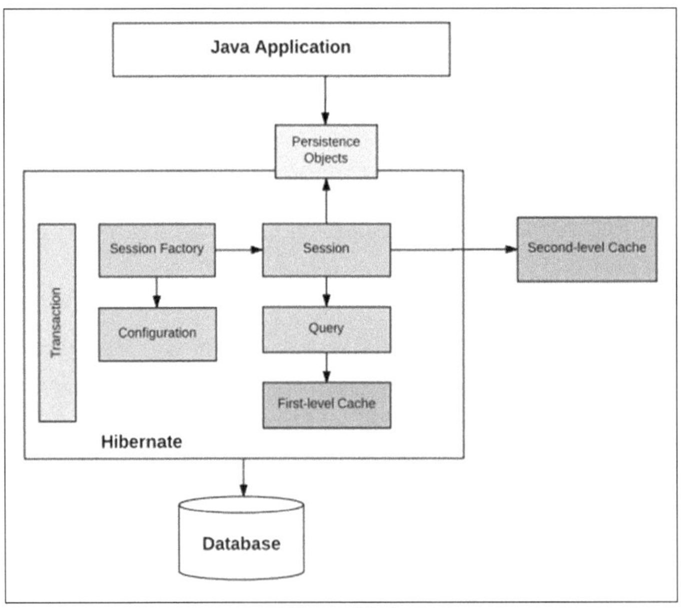

Figure 12.1

Hibernate's architecture is designed to provide a flexible, efficient, and scalable solution for Java applications interacting with relational databases. The key components include:
Configuration: Loads and manages configuration settings.
SessionFactory: A thread-safe, immutable factory for creating sessions.
Session: A single-threaded, short-lived object for CRUD operations.
Transaction: Provides a consistent API for transaction management.
Query and Criteria API: Tools for retrieving data using HQL and a programmatic approach.

Persistent Objects and Collections: Java objects managed by Hibernate.
Connection Provider and Transaction Management: Abstracts the details of database connectivity and transaction management.

Core Components of Hibernate Architecture

Hibernate's architecture is designed around several key components that work together to provide a robust ORM solution. These components include:

Configuration Object

The Configuration object is the starting point of a Hibernate application. It is responsible for the following
Loading configuration settings from the hibernate.cfg.xml file or programmatically setting them.
Specifying database connection details, Hibernate-specific properties, and mappings between Java classes and database tables.

Example: Configuration configuration = new Configuration().configure();

SessionFactory

The SessionFactory is a thread-safe, immutable object created during the application startup. It is built from the Configuration object and serves as a factory for Session objects. It holds the compiled mappings for a specific database.

Thread-safe: It can be shared by all application threads.
Immutable: Once created, its state cannot be changed.
Singleton: Typically, only one instance is created per application.
Example: SessionFactory sessionFactory = configuration.buildSessionFactory();

Session

The Session object is a single-threaded, short-lived object that represents a conversation between the application and the database. It wraps a JDBC connection and is used to perform CRUD (Create, Read, Update, Delete) operations.

Short-lived: Should be created and destroyed with each unit of work.
Not thread-safe: Each thread/transaction should use a separate session.
Example: Session session = sessionFactory.openSession();

Transaction

The Transaction interface in Hibernate abstracts the underlying transaction management system. It provides a consistent programming model for handling transactions across different databases and application servers.

Optional: Transactions are not mandatory, but they help manage units of work.
Consistent API: Provides a uniform way to handle transactions, whether using JDBC, JTA, or other transaction management systems.

Example

```
Transaction transaction = session.beginTransaction();
transaction.commit();
```

Query and Criteria API

Hibernate provides two ways to retrieve data from the database:
HQL (Hibernate Query Language): An object-oriented query language similar to SQL but operates on persistent objects and their properties.
Criteria API: A programmatic way to create queries. It allows for dynamic query creation with a fluent API.

HQL Example

```
List results = session.createQuery("FROM Product").list();
```

Criteria API Example:

```
CriteriaBuilder builder = session.getCriteriaBuilder();
CriteriaQuery<Product> query = builder.createQuery(Product.class);
Root<Product> root = query.from(Product.class);
query.select(root);
List<Product> results = session.createQuery(query).getResultList();
```

Persistent Objects and Collections

Persistent objects are Java objects that Hibernate manages. These objects are associated with database rows. When a session is active, changes to these objects are automatically synchronized with the database.

Transient: Objects not associated with any database row.
Persistent: Objects associated with a database row within a session.
Detached: Persistent objects that have been disconnected from the session.

Example

```
Product product = new Product();
product.setName("Laptop");
session.save(product);
```

Connection Provider and Transaction Management

Hibernate abstracts the details of obtaining JDBC connections and managing transactions. This abstraction allows Hibernate to integrate with different application servers and transaction management strategies.

Connection Provider: Abstracts the strategy for obtaining JDBC connections.

Transaction Management: Abstracts the transaction management strategies, allowing Hibernate to use different mechanisms such as JDBC transactions, JTA, or CMT.

Example

```
configuration.setProperty("hibernate.connection.provider_class",
"org.hibernate.connection.C3P0ConnectionProvider");
configuration.setProperty("hibernate.transaction.factory_class",
"org.hibernate.transaction.JTATransactionFactory");
```

How Hibernate Works

Configuration and SessionFactory Creation: Upon application startup, Hibernate is configured, and a SessionFactory is created.

Session Opening: When database access is needed, a new Session is opened from the SessionFactory.

Transaction Management: A Transaction is started, and database operations are executed within the context of this transaction.

Query Execution: Queries or updates are executed using HQL, Criteria API, or native SQL.

Transaction Commit/Rollback: The transaction is committed, saving changes to the database, or rolled back if there are errors.

Session Closing: The Session is closed, releasing database connections and other resources.

12.4 CRUD Operations with Hibernate

CRUD operations refer to the four basic functions implemented in database applications: Create, Read, Update, and Delete. Hibernate, a prominent Object-Relational Mapping (ORM) framework, simplifies these operations in Java, allowing developers to interact with databases using high-level object manipulation rather than low-level SQL queries. This chapter explores how to perform CRUD operations with Hibernate, providing essential knowledge for students and developers.

12.4.1 Configuring Hibernate

Before diving into CRUD operations, ensure your Hibernate environment is set up correctly. This includes configuring the SessionFactory, typically done in a hibernate.cfg.xml file or programmatically in your application's startup logic. The SessionFactory should know about your entity classes and database connection details.

12.4.2 CRUD Operations in Detail

Create (Inserting Data)

Creating or inserting data into the database involves creating an instance of your entity class, setting its properties, and persisting it using a Hibernate session.

Code:

```
import org.hibernate.Session;
import org.hibernate.SessionFactory;
import org.hibernate.Transaction;
import org.hibernate.cfg.Configuration;
public class HibernateCreateExample {
public static void main(String[] args) {
// Load configuration and build session factory
Configuration configuration = new Configuration().configure();
SessionFactory sessionFactory = configuration.buildSessionFactory();
// Open a session
Session session = sessionFactory.openSession();
```

```
// Begin a transaction
Transaction transaction = session.beginTransaction();
// Create a new product
Product product = new Product();
product.setName("Smartphone");
product.setPrice(299.99);
// Save the product
session.save(product);
// Commit the transaction
transaction.commit();
// Close the session
session.close();
sessionFactory.close();
   }
     }
```

In this example
A SessionFactory is created using the configuration.
A new session is opened.
A transaction is begun.
A new Product object is created and populated.
The save method is called to persist the object to the database.
The transaction is committed, and the session is closed.

Read (Fetching Data)

Reading data can be performed in several ways, including loading an entity by its primary key, querying the database using HQL (Hibernate Query Language), or using the Criteria API for more complex retrievals.

Loading by Primary Key

Code:

```
Session session = sessionFactory.openSession();
Product product = session.get(Product.class, productId);
session.close();
```

Using HQL

Code:

```
public class HibernateHQLExample {
public static void main(String[] args) {
SessionFactory sessionFactory = new Configuration().configure().buildSessionFactory();
 Session session = sessionFactory.openSession();
 // Create an HQL query
 String hql = "FROM Product WHERE price > :price";
 List<Product> products = session.createQuery(hql, Product.class)
                         .setParameter("price", 100.00)
                         .getResultList();
 for (Product product : products) {
    System.out.println("Product Name: " + product.getName());
    System.out.println("Product Price: " + product.getPrice());
 }
 session.close();
 sessionFactory.close();
 }
}
```

Update (Modifying Data)

Updating data involves retrieving an entity, making changes to its properties, and committing the transaction. Hibernate automatically tracks changes to persistent entities and updates the database upon transaction commit.

Code:

```
public class HibernateUpdateExample {
public static void main(String[] args) {
 SessionFactory sessionFactory = new Configuration().configure().buildSessionFactory();
 Session session = sessionFactory.openSession();
 // Begin a transaction
 Transaction transaction = session.beginTransaction();
 // Retrieve a product by primary key
 Long productId = 1L;
 Product product = session.get(Product.class, productId);
 if (product != null) {
    // Update product properties
    product.setPrice(349.99);
    // Save the changes
    session.update(product);
    // Commit the transaction
    transaction.commit();
 } else {
    System.out.println("Product not found!");
    transaction.rollback();
 }
 session.close();
 sessionFactory.close();
 }
}
```

Delete (Removing Data)

Deleting data requires fetching the entity to be deleted and then calling the delete method on the session.

Code:

```
public class HibernateDeleteExample {
public static void main(String[] args) {
 SessionFactory sessionFactory = new Configuration().configure().buildSessionFactory();
 Session session = sessionFactory.openSession();
 // Begin a transaction
 Transaction transaction = session.beginTransaction();
 // Retrieve a product by primary key
 Long productId = 1L;
 Product product = session.get(Product.class, productId);
 if (product != null) {
    // Delete the product
    session.delete(product);
    // Commit the transaction
    transaction.commit();
 } else {
    System.out.println("Product not found!");
    transaction.rollback();
 }
 session.close();
 sessionFactory.close();
  }
 }
```

Best Practices for CRUD Operations

Effective transaction management is crucial for maintaining data integrity, consistency, and performance in applications using Hibernate. Here are best practices for managing transactions in Hibernate

Wrap CRUD Operations in Transactions

Always Use Transactions

Ensure all CRUD operations (Create, Read, Update, Delete) are wrapped in transactions. This guarantees that the operations are atomic, consistent, isolated, and durable (ACID properties).

Example:

```
Session session = HibernateUtil.getSessionFactory().openSession();
Transaction transaction = null;
try {
    transaction = session.beginTransaction();
    // Perform CRUD operations
    Product product = new Product();
    product.setName("Laptop");
    product.setPrice(1000.00);
    session.save(product);
    transaction.commit();
} catch (Exception e) {
    if (transaction != null) transaction.rollback();
    e.printStackTrace();
} finally {
    session.close();
}
```

Use Programmatic Transaction Management

Programmatic Transactions

Manage transactions programmatically using the beginTransaction, commit, and rollback methods. This provides fine-grained control over transaction boundaries.

Example:

```
public void saveProduct(Product product) {
    Session session = HibernateUtil.getSessionFactory().openSession();
    Transaction transaction = null;
    try {
        transaction = session.beginTransaction();
        session.save(product);
        transaction.commit();
    } catch (Exception e) {
        if (transaction != null) transaction.rollback();
        e.printStackTrace();
    } finally {
        session.close();
    }
}
```

Handle Transactions in a Declarative Manner

Use Spring Transaction Management

When using Spring, leverage its declarative transaction management to simplify transaction handling and reduce boilerplate code. Use annotations like @Transactional.

Example:

```
@Service
public class ProductService {
    @Autowired
    private ProductRepository productRepository;
    @Transactional
    public void saveProduct(Product product) {
        productRepository.save(product);
    }
}
```

Configure Transaction Management in Spring

Ensure Spring's transaction management is configured correctly in the application context.

Example:

```xml
<!-- Enable annotation-driven transaction management -->
<tx:annotation-driven transaction-manager="transactionManager"/>

<!-- Define the transaction manager -->
<bean id="transactionManager" class="org.springframework.orm.hibernate5.HibernateTransactionManager">
   <property name="sessionFactory" ref="sessionFactory"/>
</bean>
```

Rollback Transactions on Exceptions

Rollback on Exceptions

Always rollback transactions in case of exceptions to avoid partial updates and maintain data consistency.

Example:

```java
try {
   transaction = session.beginTransaction();
   // Perform operations
   transaction.commit();
} catch (Exception e) {
   if (transaction != null) transaction.rollback();
   e.printStackTrace();
} finally {
   session.close();
}
```

Use @Transactional Rollback Mechanism

In Spring, specify rollback rules for @Transactional methods to handle specific exceptions.

Example:

```java
@Transactional(rollbackFor = Exception.class)
public void saveProduct(Product product) {
   productRepository.save(product);
}
```

Transaction Propagation and Isolation Levels

Choose Appropriate Propagation Levels

Use different propagation levels (e.g., REQUIRED, REQUIRES_NEW, MANDATORY) based on the business requirements to manage nested transactions and ensure correct transaction boundaries.

Example:

```java
@Transactional(propagation = Propagation.REQUIRES_NEW)
public void saveProduct(Product product) {
   productRepository.save(product);
}
```

Set Isolation Levels

Configure appropriate isolation levels (e.g., READ_COMMITTED, REPEATABLE_READ, SERIALIZABLE) to handle concurrency issues and ensure data consistency.

Example

```java
@Transactional(isolation = Isolation.REPEATABLE_READ)
public void updateProductPrice(Long productId, Double newPrice) {
   Product product = productRepository.findById(productId);
   product.setPrice(newPrice);
   productRepository.save(product);
}
```

Use Optimistic and Pessimistic Locking

Optimistic Locking

Use versioning to handle concurrent updates and detect conflicts using @Version.

Example:

```java
@Entity
public class Product {
```

```
    @Id
    @GeneratedValue(strategy = GenerationType.IDENTITY)
    private Long id;
    @Version
    private int version;
    // other fields, getters, and setters
}
```

Pessimistic Locking
Use pessimistic locking when conflicts are expected frequently, ensuring exclusive access to a resource.
Example:

```
Product product = session.get(Product.class, productId, LockMode.PESSIMISTIC_WRITE);
```

Manage Long-Running Transactions
Avoid Long-Running Transactions
Avoid keeping transactions open for long periods to prevent resource contention and potential deadlocks. Break long-running operations into smaller, manageable transactions if possible.
Use Detached Objects
Use detached objects for long-running business processes. Reattach them to a new session when needed.
Example:

```
public void longRunningOperation(Product product) {
    Session session = HibernateUtil.getSessionFactory().openSession();
    Transaction transaction = session.beginTransaction();
    try {
        session.saveOrUpdate(product);
        transaction.commit();
    } catch (Exception e) {
        if (transaction != null) transaction.rollback();
        e.printStackTrace();
    } finally {
        session.close();
    }
}
```

12.5 Mapping Collections and Associations

In the realm of database applications, complex relationships between entities are common. Hibernate, as a comprehensive Object-Relational Mapping (ORM) framework, offers robust support for mapping collections and associations between entities. This capability allows developers to model intricate data structures in an object-oriented manner, facilitating data manipulation and retrieval. This chapter delves into the essentials of mapping collections and associations in Hibernate, illuminating the path for students to master these critical concepts.
Understanding Associations
Associations in Hibernate represent the relationships between different entities in a relational database. Understanding and effectively managing these associations is crucial for designing a robust and efficient data model. This section explains the various types of associations in Hibernate and how to map them:
Types of Associations
There are four primary types of associations in Hibernate:
One-to-One Association
One-to-Many Association
Many-to-One Association
Many-to-Many Association
Each type of association maps to a different kind of relationship between entities.
One-to-One Association
A one-to-one association maps a single entity to another single entity. This is useful when each instance of an entity is associated with one and only one instance of another entity.
Example:

```
@Entity
public class User {
```

```
    @Id
    @GeneratedValue(strategy = GenerationType.IDENTITY)
    private Long id;
    private String username;
    @OneToOne(cascade = CascadeType.ALL)
    @JoinColumn(name = "profile_id")
    private UserProfile profile;
    // getters and setters
}

@Entity
public class UserProfile {
    @Id
    @GeneratedValue(strategy = GenerationType.IDENTITY)
    private Long id;
    private String address;
    @OneToOne(mappedBy = "profile")
    private User user;
    // getters and setters
}
```

In this example, each User has one UserProfile, and each UserProfile is associated with one User. The @OneToOne annotation is used to specify this relationship.

One-to-Many Association

A one-to-many association maps a single entity to a collection of other entities. This is useful when each instance of an entity is associated with multiple instances of another entity.

Example:

```
@Entity
public class Category {
    @Id
    @GeneratedValue(strategy = GenerationType.IDENTITY)
    private Long id;
    private String name;
    @OneToMany(mappedBy = "category", cascade = CascadeType.ALL, orphanRemoval = true)
    private List<Product> products = new ArrayList<>();
    // getters and setters
}

@Entity
public class Product {
    @Id
    @GeneratedValue(strategy = GenerationType.IDENTITY)
    private Long id;
    private String name;
    @ManyToOne
    @JoinColumn(name = "category_id")
    private Category category;
    // getters and setters
}
```

In this example, each Category can have multiple Products, and each Product belongs to one Category. The @OneToMany annotation is used on the collection side, and the @ManyToOne annotation is used on the single side.

Many-to-One Association

A many-to-one association maps multiple entities to a single entity. This is useful when many instances of an entity are associated with one instance of another entity.

Example:

```
@Entity
```

```
public class Order {
   @Id
   @GeneratedValue(strategy = GenerationType.IDENTITY)
   private Long id;
   private String orderNumber;
   @ManyToOne
   @JoinColumn(name = "customer_id")
   private Customer customer;
   // getters and setters
}

@Entity
public class Customer {
   @Id
   @GeneratedValue(strategy = GenerationType.IDENTITY)
   private Long id;
   private String name;
   @OneToMany(mappedBy = "customer", cascade = CascadeType.ALL, orphanRemoval = true)
   private List<Order> orders = new ArrayList<>();
   // getters and setters
}
```

In this example, many Orders can be associated with one Customer, and each Customer can have multiple Orders. The @ManyToOne annotation is used on the many side, and the @OneToMany annotation is used on the one side.

Many-to-Many Association

A many-to-many association maps multiple entities to multiple entities. This is useful when instances of both entities can have multiple relationships with instances of the other entity.

Example:

```
@Entity
public class Student {
   @Id
   @GeneratedValue(strategy = GenerationType.IDENTITY)
   private Long id;
   private String name;
   @ManyToMany(cascade = CascadeType.ALL)
   @JoinTable(
      name = "student_course",
      joinColumns = @JoinColumn(name = "student_id"),
      inverseJoinColumns = @JoinColumn(name = "course_id")
   )
   private Set<Course> courses = new HashSet<>();
   // getters and setters
}
@Entity
public class Course {
   @Id
   @GeneratedValue(strategy = GenerationType.IDENTITY)
   private Long id;
   private String name;
   @ManyToMany(mappedBy = "courses")
   private Set<Student> students = new HashSet<>();
   // getters and setters
}
```

In this example, each Student can enroll in multiple Courses, and each Course can have multiple Students. The @ManyToMany annotation is used on both sides of the relationship, and a join table is specified to manage the association.

Bidirectional vs. Unidirectional Associations
Unidirectional Associations
Unidirectional associations are defined on one side of the relationship only.
Example:
```
@Entity
public class Order {
    @Id
    @GeneratedValue(strategy = GenerationType.IDENTITY)
    private Long id;
    private String orderNumber;
    @ManyToOne
    @JoinColumn(name = "customer_id")
    private Customer customer;
    // getters and setters
}
```
Bidirectional Associations
Bidirectional associations are defined on both sides of the relationship. This allows navigation from both entities.
Example:
```
@Entity
public class Customer {
    @Id
    @GeneratedValue(strategy = GenerationType.IDENTITY)
    private Long id;
    private String name;
    @OneToMany(mappedBy = "customer", cascade = CascadeType.ALL, orphanRemoval = true)
    private List<Order> orders = new ArrayList<>();
    // getters and setters
}

@Entity
public class Order {
    @Id
    @GeneratedValue(strategy = GenerationType.IDENTITY)
    private Long id;
    private String orderNumber;
    @ManyToOne
    @JoinColumn(name = "customer_id")
    private Customer customer;
    // getters and setters
}
```
Cascading Operations
Cascading operations allow operations to be propagated to associated entities automatically. Common cascading operations include PERSIST, MERGE, REMOVE, REFRESH, DETACH.
Example:
```
@Entity
public class Customer {
    @Id
    @GeneratedValue(strategy = GenerationType.IDENTITY)
    private Long id;
    private String name;
    @OneToMany(mappedBy = "customer", cascade = CascadeType.ALL, orphanRemoval = true)
    private List<Order> orders = new ArrayList<>();
    // getters and setters
}
```
In this example, if a Customer is saved, updated, or deleted, the same operations will be applied to its associated Orders.

Mapping Associations

Hibernate supports different types of associations between entities: one-to-one, one-to-many, many-to-one, and many-to-many. Here's how to map these associations:

One-to-One Association

A one-to-one association maps a single entity to another single entity. This is typically mapped using @OneToOne.

Example:

```
@Entity
public class User {
   @Id
   @GeneratedValue(strategy = GenerationType.IDENTITY)
   private Long id;
   private String username;
   @OneToOne(cascade = CascadeType.ALL)
   @JoinColumn(name = "profile_id")
   private UserProfile profile;
   // getters and setters
}

@Entity
public class UserProfile {
   @Id
   @GeneratedValue(strategy = GenerationType.IDENTITY)
   private Long id;
   private String address;
   @OneToOne(mappedBy = "profile")
   private User user;
   // getters and setters
}
```

One-to-Many Association

A one-to-many association maps a single entity to a collection of other entities. This is typically mapped using @OneToMany.

Example:

```
@Entity
public class Category {
   @Id
   @GeneratedValue(strategy = GenerationType.IDENTITY)
   private Long id;
   private String name;
   @OneToMany(mappedBy = "category", cascade = CascadeType.ALL, orphanRemoval = true)
   private List<Product> products = new ArrayList<>();
   // getters and setters
}

@Entity
public class Product {
   @Id
   @GeneratedValue(strategy = GenerationType.IDENTITY)
   private Long id;
   private String name;
   @ManyToOne
   @JoinColumn(name = "category_id")
   private Category category;
   // getters and setters
}
```

Many-to-One Association

A many-to-one association maps multiple entities to a single entity. This is typically mapped using @ManyToOne.

Example:

```
@Entity
public class Order {
   @Id
   @GeneratedValue(strategy = GenerationType.IDENTITY)
   private Long id;
   private String orderNumber;
   @ManyToOne
   @JoinColumn(name = "customer_id")
   private Customer customer;
   // getters and setters
}

@Entity
public class Customer {
   @Id
   @GeneratedValue(strategy = GenerationType.IDENTITY)
   private Long id;
   private String name;
   @OneToMany(mappedBy = "customer", cascade = CascadeType.ALL, orphanRemoval = true)
   private List<Order> orders = new ArrayList<>();
   // getters and setters
}
```

Many-to-Many Association

A many-to-many association maps multiple entities to multiple entities. This is typically mapped using @ManyToMany.

Example:

```
@Entity
public class Student {
   @Id
   @GeneratedValue(strategy = GenerationType.IDENTITY)
   private Long id;
   private String name;
   @ManyToMany(cascade = CascadeType.ALL)
   @JoinTable(
      name = "student_course",
      joinColumns = @JoinColumn(name = "student_id"),
      inverseJoinColumns = @JoinColumn(name = "course_id")
   )
   private Set<Course> courses = new HashSet<>();
   // getters and setters
}

@Entity
public class Course {
   @Id
   @GeneratedValue(strategy = GenerationType.IDENTITY)
   private Long id;
   private String name;
   @ManyToMany(mappedBy = "courses")
   private Set<Student> students = new HashSet<>();
   // getters and setters
}
```

Mapping Collections
Hibernate supports mapping collections such as List, Set, Map, and Bag. Here's how to map these collections in Hibernate:
List
A List is an ordered collection that allows duplicate elements. Hibernate maps a List to a database table with an additional column for the list index.
Example:
```
@Entity
public class Product {
   @Id
   @GeneratedValue(strategy = GenerationType.IDENTITY)
   private Long id;

   private String name;
   @ElementCollection
   @CollectionTable(name = "product_images", joinColumns = @JoinColumn(name = "product_id"))
   @Column(name = "image_url")
   @OrderColumn(name = "list_index")
   private List<String> images = new ArrayList<>();
   // getters and setters
}
```
Set
A Set is an unordered collection that does not allow duplicate elements. Hibernate maps a Set to a database table without an additional index column.
Example:
```
@Entity
public class Product {
   @Id
   @GeneratedValue(strategy = GenerationType.IDENTITY)
   private Long id;
   private String name;
   @ElementCollection
   @CollectionTable(name = "product_tags", joinColumns = @JoinColumn(name = "product_id"))
   @Column(name = "tag")
   private Set<String> tags = new HashSet<>();
   // getters and setters
}
```
Map
A Map is a collection of key-value pairs. Hibernate maps a Map to a database table with separate columns for the keys and values.
Example:
```
@Entity
public class Product {
   @Id
   @GeneratedValue(strategy = GenerationType.IDENTITY)
   private Long id;
   private String name;
   @ElementCollection
   @CollectionTable(name = "product_attributes", joinColumns = @JoinColumn(name = "product_id"))
   @MapKeyColumn(name = "attribute_key")
   @Column(name = "attribute_value")
   private Map<String, String> attributes = new HashMap<>();
   // getters and setters
}
```
Bag

A Bag is an unordered collection that allows duplicates and is similar to a List but without an index column.
Example:

```
@Entity
public class Product {
   @Id
   @GeneratedValue(strategy = GenerationType.IDENTITY)
   private Long id;
   private String name;
   @ElementCollection
   @CollectionTable(name = "product_features", joinColumns = @JoinColumn(name = "product_id"))
   @Column(name = "feature")
   private Collection<String> features = new ArrayList<>();
   // getters and setters
}
```

12.6 Hibernate Annotations

Hibernate Annotations provide a streamlined approach to configuring and mapping Java objects (entities) to relational database tables, offering an alternative to XML-based configuration. These annotations are metadata tags embedded within entity classes, enhancing code readability and reducing configuration overhead. Key annotations include @Entity, which marks a class as an entity that corresponds to a database table, and @Table, which specifies the table details like name and schema.

The @Id annotation designates the primary key of an entity, while @GeneratedValue determines its generation strategy, such as identity, sequence, or table-based. Relationships between entities are defined using annotations like @OneToOne, @OneToMany, @ManyToOne, and @ManyToMany, which specify the cardinality and type of association between entities. @JoinColumn complements these annotations by defining the foreign key column in database tables. For field-level mapping, @Column links entity attributes to table columns, enabling customization of column names, types, and constraints. Hibernate also supports @Transient, indicating fields that should not be persisted. Querying is facilitated through @NamedQuery and @NamedQueries, allowing developers to predefine JPQL queries for reuse. These annotations collectively simplify the development of Java applications using Hibernate, promoting cleaner code and efficient database interactions by embedding configuration details directly into entity classes.

12.6.1 The Role of Annotations in Hibernate

Annotations in Hibernate play a pivotal role in simplifying and enhancing the configuration and mapping of Java objects (entities) to relational database tables. They serve as metadata tags that are directly embedded within entity classes, replacing or complementing the traditional XML-based configuration. Here's how annotations contribute to the effectiveness of Hibernate in Java enterprise applications:

Declarative Mapping

Annotations provide a declarative way to define the mapping between entities and database tables. Instead of maintaining separate XML configuration files, developers annotate entity classes directly with metadata that describes how each entity attribute maps to a table column.

Improved Readability and Maintainability

By embedding metadata within the entity classes themselves, annotations enhance code readability and maintainability. Developers can easily understand the database schema and mappings by examining the entity class, rather than switching between Java code and external XML configuration files.

Reduced Configuration Overhead

Annotations significantly reduce configuration overhead compared to XML-based configuration. They eliminate the need for verbose XML files and simplify the setup process, making it easier to get started with Hibernate and reducing the chance of configuration errors.

Integration with Java Language Features

Annotations leverage Java language features such as annotations processing and reflection, which facilitate dynamic runtime processing of metadata. This integration allows Hibernate to introspect entity classes at runtime and automatically generate SQL queries based on the annotations present.

Enhanced Development Productivity

With annotations, developers can focus more on business logic and application development rather than configuration management. Annotations streamline the mapping of complex relationships (such as one-to-one, one-to-many, many-to-one, and many-to-many) and provide convenient shortcuts for defining primary keys, generated values, and query mappings.

Support for ORM Best Practices

Hibernate annotations support Object-Relational Mapping (ORM) best practices by providing annotations like @Entity, @Table, @Id, @GeneratedValue, @Column, and various relationship annotations (@OneToOne, @OneToMany, @ManyToOne, @ManyToMany). These annotations enforce database constraints, optimize database interactions, and ensure data integrity.

Example Usage

```
@Entity
@Table(name = "employees")
public class Employee {
   @Id
   @GeneratedValue(strategy = GenerationType.IDENTITY)
   @Column(name = "employee_id")
   private Long id;
   @Column(name = "first_name")
   private String firstName;
   @Column(name = "last_name")
   private String lastName;
   @ManyToOne
   @JoinColumn(name = "department_id")
   private Department department;
   // Constructors, getters, setters
}
```

In this example, @Entity marks the Employee class as an entity, @Table specifies the database table details, @Id and @GeneratedValue define the primary key and its generation strategy, @Column maps attributes to table columns, and @ManyToOne with @JoinColumn establishes a many-to-one relationship with the Department entity.

Overall, annotations in Hibernate streamline development, improve code maintainability, and enhance the integration of Java applications with relational databases, making Hibernate a powerful ORM framework in Java enterprise development.

Key Hibernate Annotations

Hibernate provides a set of key annotations that are essential for mapping Java objects (entities) to relational database tables and defining various aspects of persistence Behaviour. Here are some of the key Hibernate annotations along with their roles and usage

@Entity

Role: Marks a Java class as an entity, indicating that instances of this class will be persisted to the database.

Usage: Applied to entity classes, typically placed at the class level.

```
@Entity
public class Product {
// entity attributes, constructors, getters/setters
}
```

@Table

Role: Specifies the details of the database table that corresponds to the annotated entity.

Usage: Applied to entity classes, allows configuration of table name, schema, and other attributes.

```
@Entity
@Table(name = "products")
public class Product {
// entity attributes, constructors, getters/setters
}
```

@Id
Role: Marks a field as the primary key of the entity.
Usage: Applied to the primary key field of the entity class.

```
@Id
@GeneratedValue(strategy = GenerationType.IDENTITY)
@Column(name = "product_id")
private Long id;
```

@GeneratedValue
Role: Specifies the generation strategy for the values of the primary key.
Usage: Applied to the primary key field, determines how primary key values are generated (e.g., IDENTITY, SEQUENCE, TABLE).

```
@GeneratedValue(strategy = GenerationType.IDENTITY)
```

@Column
Role: Maps an entity attribute to a database column.
Usage: Applied to fields or getter methods of entity attributes, allows customization of column name, type, length, and other attributes.

```
@Column(name = "product_name", nullable = false, length = 100)
private String name;
```

@ManyToOne, @OneToMany, @OneToOne, @ManyToMany
Role: Defines different types of associations between entities (e.g., many-to-one, one-to-many, one-to-one, many-to-many).
Usage: Applied to fields representing associations between entities, specifies the type and direction of the relationship.

```
@ManyToOne
@JoinColumn(name = "category_id")
private Category category;
@OneToMany(mappedBy = "category")
private List<Product> products;
@ManyToOne
@JoinColumn(name = "category_id")
private Category category;
@OneToMany(mappedBy = "category")
private List<Product> products;
```

@JoinColumn
Role: Specifies the column used for joining an entity association or collection.
Usage: Applied with association annotations (@OneToOne, @ManyToOne, @OneToMany, @ManyToMany), defines the foreign key column in the database.

```
@ManyToOne
@JoinColumn(name = "category_id")
private Category category;
```

@Transient
Role: Marks a field or property as not persistent, indicating that it should not be mapped to any database column.
Usage: Applied to fields or methods that should be excluded from database mapping.

```
@Transient
private transientField;
```

@NamedQuery, @NamedQueries
Role: Defines named queries using JPQL (Java Persistence Query Language), which can be reused across the application.
Usage: Applied at the entity class level, allows pre-definition of JPQL queries for efficient query management.

```
@NamedQuery(
name = "findProductsByCategory",
query = "SELECT p FROM Product p WHERE p.category = :category"
)
```

@NamedNativeQuery, @NamedNativeQueries
Role: Similar to @NamedQuery but for native SQL queries.

Usage: Allows defining native SQL queries using database-specific SQL syntax.

```
@NamedNativeQuery(
name = "findProductsByCategoryNative",
query = "SELECT * FROM products WHERE category_id = :categoryId",
resultClass = Product.class
)
```

12.6.2 Advantages of Using Hibernate Annotations

Simplified Configuration

Hibernate Annotations simplify the configuration process by embedding metadata directly within entity classes. This eliminates the need for separate XML configuration files, reducing configuration overhead and making the codebase more compact and easier to manage.

Enhanced Readability

Annotations improve code readability by colocating metadata with the entity definitions. Developers can easily understand the database mappings, relationships, and persistence details by examining the annotated entity classes directly, without needing to refer to external configuration files.

Reduced Development Time

By eliminating the need for verbose XML configurations and providing a more intuitive way to define mappings and relationships, Hibernate Annotations accelerate development time. Developers can focus more on business logic and application functionality rather than spending time on configuration management.

Compile-Time Checking and Validation

Annotations provide compile-time checking and validation of mappings and relationships. This helps catch errors early in the development cycle, reducing the likelihood of runtime exceptions and database inconsistencies.

Integration with Java Language Features

Annotations leverage Java language features such as annotations processing and reflection. This integration allows Hibernate to dynamically process metadata at runtime, generate SQL queries, and manage database interactions efficiently.

Support for Object-Relational Mapping (ORM) Best Practices

Hibernate Annotations support OR best practices by offering annotations like (@Entity, @Table, @Id, @GeneratedValue, @Column, @ManyToOne, @JoinColumn). These annotations enforce database constraints, optimize database interactions, and ensure data integrity.

Query Management and Optimization

Annotations like @NamedQuery and @NamedNativeQuery allow developers to predefine JPQL and native SQL queries, respectively, within entity classes. This improves query management, promotes code reuse, and enhances query performance through Hibernate's query caching mechanisms.

Flexibility and Customization

While annotations provide convenient defaults for common scenarios, they also offer flexibility for customization. Developers can override default Behaviours and configure advanced settings using annotation attributes and Hibernate-specific features.

Example Usage

```
@Entity
@Table(name = "products")
public class Product {
   @Id
   @GeneratedValue(strategy = GenerationType.IDENTITY)
   @Column(name = "product_id")
   private Long id;
   @Column(name = "product_name", nullable = false, length = 100)
   private String name;
   @ManyToOne
   @JoinColumn(name = "category_id")
   private Category category;
   // Constructors, getters, setters
}
```

In this example, annotations (@Entity, @Table, @Id, @GeneratedValue, @Column, @ManyToOne, @JoinColumn) are used to define the Product entity and its mappings. These annotations improve code clarity, reduce boilerplate configuration, and facilitate efficient persistence operations.

12.7 Transitioning from XML to Annotations

Understanding the Context

Current XML Configuration

In XML-based Hibernate configuration, entity mappings, database table definitions, primary key generation strategies, and relationships are defined in separate XML files (hibernate.cfg.xml, mapping files).

Move to Annotations

Hibernate Annotations allow developers to embed metadata directly within entity classes using Java annotations (@Entity, @Table, @Id, @GeneratedValue, etc.), replacing or complementing XML configurations.

Steps to Transition

Familiarize with Hibernate Annotations

Start by understanding key Hibernate annotations and their usage. Learn how annotations define entity mappings, relationships (@OneToOne, @OneToMany, @ManyToOne, @ManyToMany), primary keys (@Id, @GeneratedValue), and column mappings (@Column, @JoinColumn).

Identify Entities for Migration

Begin with new entities or less complex mappings to gain familiarity with annotations. Choose entities that will benefit most from annotation-based configuration, such as those requiring frequent updates or complex mappings.

Convert XML Configurations to Annotations

Entity Declaration **(**@Entity**,** @Table**):** Replace <class> and <subclass> declarations with @Entity and @Table annotations.

Primary Key (@Id, @GeneratedValue): Replace <id> and <composite-id> mappings with @Id and @GeneratedValue annotations for primary key definitions.

Properties (@Column, @ManyToOne, etc.): Replace <property>, <many-to-one>, <one-to-many>, and other property mappings with appropriate annotations (@Column, @ManyToOne, @OneToMany, etc.).

Named Queries (@NamedQuery, @NamedNativeQuery): Migrate named queries defined in hbm.xml files to @NamedQuery or @NamedNativeQuery annotations in entity classes.

Validate and Test

After converting each entity, thoroughly test database interactions to ensure mappings are correctly implemented and database operations behave as expected. Verify that annotations accurately reflect the intended mappings and relationships.

Refactor and Optimize

Refactor existing code and optimize annotations based on feedback and performance testing. Use Hibernate-specific optimizations like batch processing, caching strategies, and lazy loading to enhance application performance.

Document and Train

Document the transition process, including annotations used, best practices, and potential pitfalls. Conduct knowledge transfer sessions or workshops to educate team members on annotation-based configuration in Hibernate.

Example of Transition:

Before (XML-based configuration)

```
<class name="com.example.Product" table="products">
  <id name="id" column="product_id">
    <generator class="identity"/>
  </id>
  <property name="name" column="product_name"/>
  <many-to-one name="category" class="com.example.Category" column="category_id"/>
</class>
```

After (using annotations)

```
@Entity
@Table(name = "products")
public class Product {
```

```
    @Id
    @GeneratedValue(strategy = GenerationType.IDENTITY)
    @Column(name = "product_id")
    private Long id;
    @Column(name = "product_name")
    private String name;
    @ManyToOne
    @JoinColumn(name = "category_id")
    private Category category;
    // Constructors, getters, setters
}
```

Benefits of Transition

Simplified Configuration: Annotations reduce configuration overhead by embedding metadata directly within entity classes, eliminating the need for separate XML files.

Enhanced Readability: Colocating metadata with entity definitions improves code readability and maintenance, making database mappings easier to understand.

Improved Development Efficiency: Annotations streamline development by providing a more intuitive way to define mappings and relationships, allowing developers to focus on application logic rather than configuration management.

Exercise

Exercise 1 – MCQ

1. What is Hibernate in Java?
a) A web server
b) A design pattern
c) An object-relational mapping (ORM) framework
d) A version control system
2. Which component in Hibernate is responsible for managing the session objects?
a) Configuration
b) SessionFactory
c) Transaction
d) Query
3. In Hibernate architecture, which interface acts as a factory for Transaction objects?
a) Configuration
b) Session
c) SessionFactory
d) ConnectionProvider
4. Which operation is not directly supported by Hibernate's Session interface?
a) save()
b) update()
c) delete()
d) merge()
5. How are many-to-one relationships represented in Hibernate?
a) Using the @ManyToOne annotation
b) With a foreign key
c) Through the use of a mapping file
d) All of the above
6. What does the inverse="true" attribute specify in a Hibernate mapping file?
a) That the relationship is bidirectional
b) That Hibernate should ignore the mapping
c) That the child entity owns the relationship
d) That the parent entity owns the relationship
7. Which is the correct way to configure a Hibernate mapping file?
a) Using XML files
b) Annotations in the Java class

c) Programmatically in the Java code
d) All of the above are correct
8. What is the purpose of the <generator> element in a Hibernate mapping file?
a) To specify the database generator
b) To generate the primary key values
c) To define the version of Hibernate used
d) To configure the session factory
9. Which statement about Hibernate's lazy loading feature is true?
a) It loads all associated objects immediately.
b) It can be turned off globally.
c) It loads associated objects on demand.
d) It requires manual activation for each query.
10. How does Hibernate achieve data query and retrieval?
a) Using JDBC
b) Through HQL (Hibernate Query Language)
c) With native SQL queries
d) All of the above

Exercise 2 – True/False
1. Hibernate is exclusively used for relational databases.
2. The SessionFactory in Hibernate is a thread-safe object used to create Session instances.
3. Hibernate ORM directly supports JSON column types in relational databases.
4. Lazy loading in Hibernate means that data is fetched from the database as soon as the entity is accessed for the first time.
5. In Hibernate, the @Entity annotation is used to mark a class as a Hibernate entity.
6. Hibernate requires XML mapping files to operate.
7. The primary key in a Hibernate entity can be auto-generated using the @GeneratedValue annotation.
8. Hibernate's Session interface represents a physical connection with the database.
9. Cascade="all" in a Hibernate mapping file means that all operations (save, update, delete) are cascaded from parent to child.
10. Hibernate Query Language (HQL) allows for database-independent queries.

Exercise 3 – Fill in the blanks
1. To map a Java class to a database table, Hibernate uses the ___ annotation.
2. Hibernate's ___ interface is the main runtime interface between a Java application and Hibernate.
3. For generating schema-independent IDs, Hibernate can use the ___ strategy in the @GeneratedValue annotation.
4. The ___ method of the Session interface is used to retrieve an entity by its primary key.
5. To define a one-to-many relationship in Hibernate, the ___ annotation is used on the collection property in the entity class.
6. Hibernate uses ____to map Java objects to database tables.
7. Hibernate Query Language (HQL) allows developers to write ________________ queries.
8. The ________________ in Hibernate manages database connections and provides session management.
9. Hibernate simplifies the interaction between Java applications and databases through its ________________.
10. Mapping files or annotations are used to define the ________________ between Java objects and database tables.

Exercise 4 – Match case
1. Manages transactions in Hibernate
2. Design pattern separating concerns in applications
3. Responsible for creating Session objects in Hibernate
4. Annotation for mapping collection relationships

A. @OneToMany
B. SessionFactory
C. Transaction

D. MVC

Exercise 5 – One word answer
1. What Hibernate annotation is used to mark a class as an entity?
2. Which design pattern does Struts 2 implement to separate business logic from user interface?

Exercise 6 – Small answer
1. Which annotation in Hibernate is used to define the primary key of an entity?
2. In MVC architecture, what component is responsible for handling user input?

Exercise 7 – Long answer
1. Explain how the SessionFactory in Hibernate works and why it is considered important in Hibernate applications.
2. Describe the interceptor mechanism in Struts 2 and its role in web application development.

Answer-
Exercise 1 – 1) c 2) b 3) b 4) d 5) d 6) c 7) d 8) b 9) c 10) d
Exercise 2 – 1) False 2) True 3) False 4) False 5) True 6) False 7) True 8) False 9) True 10) True
Exercise 3 – 1) @Entity 2) Session 3) GenerationType.AUTO 4) get 5) @OneToMany 6) object-relational mapping (ORM) 7) database-independent 8) SessionFactory 9) Object-Relational Mapping (ORM) 10) mapping
Exercise 4 – 1 – C. Transaction 2 – D. MVC 3 – B. SessionFactory 4 – A. @OneToMany
Exercise 5 – 1) @Entity 2) MVC

Online Resources

Online Practice Paper

Link: https://forms.gle/YmxduHMXhcv5u3ft6
QR Code:

YouTube Video Link

Link: https://www.youtube.com/playlist?list=PLzlh_31VWEFqTDh51DnkscBdYCozNemEp
QR Code:

CHAPTER 13 - Spring Framework (version 3.x)

13.1 Introduction to Spring and DI

Spring is a powerful and widely used open-source framework for building Java applications. It provides comprehensive infrastructure support for developing Java applications, making it easier to create robust, scalable, and maintainable applications.

Dependency Injection (DI) in Spring

Dependency Injection (DI) is a core principle in the Spring framework that facilitates loose coupling between components in a Java application. In traditional programming, classes instantiate their dependencies directly using new keyword, which creates tight coupling and makes testing and maintenance challenging.

DI in Spring allows objects to be injected with their dependencies rather than creating them internally. This inversion of control (IoC) allows for better modularization and reusability of code, as components are more independent and easier to manage.

Key Concepts in DI

Dependency: A class (or object) that another class relies on to perform its functions.

Injection: The process of supplying a dependency to a class that requires it, typically through constructor injection, setter injection, or field injection.

Benefits of DI

Reduced Coupling: Dependencies are managed externally, reducing the direct dependency between classes.

Easier Testing: Dependencies can be mocked or stubbed easily during unit testing, allowing for more comprehensive and isolated testing.

Flexible Configuration: Dependencies can be configured externally, making it easier to change the Behaviour of an application without modifying code.

How Spring Implements DI

In Spring, DI is primarily achieved through:

Constructor Injection: Dependencies are provided via the constructor of a class.

Setter Injection: Dependencies are set through setter methods.

Field Injection: Dependencies are injected directly into fields of a class (though this is less recommended due to testing and maintainability concerns).

Example

Consider a service class UserService that requires a UserRepository dependency to perform database operations. Using DI in Spring, you would define these components as follows:

```
public class UserService {
   private final UserRepository userRepository;
   public UserService(UserRepository userRepository) {
      this.userRepository = userRepository;
   }
   // Service methods using userRepository
}
```

In the Spring configuration file (often XML or Java configuration), you would declare the beans and specify how dependencies are wired together

```
<bean id="userRepository" class="com.example.repository.UserRepositoryImpl" />
<bean id="userService" class="com.example.service.UserService">
   <constructor-arg ref="userRepository" />
</bean>
```

13.1.1 Core Concepts of Spring

Spring is a comprehensive framework for building Java applications. It provides a wide range of features that facilitate easier development and management of enterprise applications. The core concepts of Spring include:

Inversion of Control (IoC)

IoC is a design principle where the control of object creation and lifecycle is inverted from the application code to the framework.

In Spring, IoC is implemented through Dependency Injection (DI), where objects are provided with their dependencies rather than creating them internally.

Dependency Injection (DI)

DI is a technique used in Spring to achieve IoC.

It allows objects to be injected with their dependencies, typically through constructor injection, setter injection, or field injection.

This promotes loose coupling between components, making the code more modular, reusable, and easier to test.

Aspect-Oriented Programming (AOP)

AOP complements OOP (Object-Oriented Programming) by providing a way to modularize cross-cutting concerns.

In Spring, AOP allows you to define aspects (common functionality) separately from the core business logic.

Typical uses include logging, transaction management, security, and performance monitoring.

Spring Container

The core of the Spring framework is the Spring Container, which manages the lifecycle of Spring beans (objects).

It creates and manages the beans, and it applies DI to inject dependencies into beans as specified in the configuration.

The Spring Container is typically implemented as ApplicationContext, which loads bean definitions from XML, Java annotations, or Java-based configuration classes.

Spring Beans

Spring beans are Java objects managed by the Spring Container.

They are configured and managed through metadata (XML, annotations, or Java configuration) that describes how beans should be created, wired, and managed.

Beans are typically singleton by default, but can be scoped as prototype, request, session, etc., depending on the application's needs.

Spring Modules

Spring provides various modules that cater to different aspects of application development, such as data access (Spring JDBC, ORM with Spring), web development (Spring MVC, Spring WebFlux), security (Spring Security), and more.

Each module offers specialized features and integrates seamlessly with the core Spring framework.

Spring MVC (Model-View-Controller)

Spring MVC is a popular web framework built on top of the Spring framework.

It follows the MVC design pattern where Model represents the application data and business rules, View renders the user interface, and Controller handles user input and responds accordingly.

Spring MVC provides robust support for building web applications and RESTful services.

Example

```
// Example of a Spring bean with dependency injection
@Component
public class UserService {
   private final UserRepository userRepository;
   @Autowired
   public UserService(UserRepository userRepository) {
      this.userRepository = userRepository;
   }
   // Service methods using userRepository
}
```

13.1.2 Understanding Dependency Injection (DI)

Dependency Injection is at the heart of Spring's functionality, allowing for loose coupling between classes and their dependencies. With DI, objects are provided with their dependencies at runtime rather than compile-time, facilitating more flexible, testable, and maintainable code.

Types of Dependency Injection in Spring

Constructor Injection

Constructor Injection is a type of DI where dependencies are provided through the object's constructor.

In Spring, you declare dependencies as constructor arguments in the bean definition.

This type of injection ensures that all mandatory dependencies are provided at the time of object creation, making the object immutable once instantiated.

It is often considered the preferred method as it makes dependencies explicit and immutable.

Example

```
public class UserService {
   private final UserRepository userRepository;
   public UserService(UserRepository userRepository) {
      this.userRepository = userRepository;
   }
   // Service methods using userRepository
}
```

Setter Injection

Setter Injection is a type of DI where dependencies are provided through setter methods.

In Spring, you define setter methods for each dependency, and Spring injects the dependencies after creating the bean instance.

Setter Injection allows flexibility by providing optional dependencies and allowing changes to dependencies after object creation.

```
public class UserService {
   private UserRepository userRepository;
   public void setUserRepository(UserRepository userRepository) {
      this.userRepository = userRepository;
   }
   // Service methods using userRepository
}
```

Field Injection

Field Injection is a type of DI where dependencies are directly injected into fields of the bean class.

In Spring, you annotate the fields with @Autowired or @Resource annotations to indicate dependencies.

Field Injection is convenient but can lead to tight coupling and makes it difficult to mock dependencies for unit testing.

Example

```
public class UserService {
   @Autowired
   private UserRepository userRepository;

   // Service methods using userRepository
}
```

Choosing the Right Injection Type

Constructor Injection is generally recommended as it ensures that dependencies are injected once and are immutable, promoting thread safety and clearer object initialization.

Setter Injection is useful for optional dependencies or when there are many dependencies, allowing for flexibility in configuration.

Field Injection is convenient for rapid development but should be used cautiously to avoid tight coupling and to ensure testability.

Configuring Spring Beans

In Spring, beans are Java objects managed by the Spring IoC (Inversion of Control) container. They are configured using metadata that describes how beans should be created, wired, and managed. There are several approaches to configure beans in Spring

XML Configuration

XML-based configuration is one of the traditional ways to configure beans in Spring.

You define beans in an XML file (applicationContext.xml or any other name), specifying their class, dependencies, and other configuration details.

Example

```
<beans xmlns="http://www.springframework.org/schema/beans"
      xmlns:xsi="http://www.w3.org/2001/XMLSchema-instance"
      xsi:schemaLocation="http://www.springframework.org/schema/beans
                  http://www.springframework.org/schema/beans/spring-beans.xsd">
```

```
    <!-- Define a bean -->
    <bean id="userService" class="com.example.service.UserService">
        <property name="userRepository" ref="userRepository" />
    </bean>
    <!-- Define another bean -->
    <bean id="userRepository" class="com.example.repository.UserRepositoryImpl" />
</beans>
```

Java-based Configuration:

Java-based configuration allows you to define beans using Java configuration classes annotated with @Configuration.

Beans and their dependencies are declared as methods within the configuration class, using @Bean annotations.

Example

```
@Configuration
public class AppConfig {
    @Bean
    public UserService userService() {
        return new UserService(userRepository());
    }
    @Bean
    public UserRepository userRepository() {
        return new UserRepositoryImpl();
    }
}
```

Component Scanning

Spring supports component scanning, where it automatically detects classes annotated with @Component, @Service, @Repository, or other stereotype annotations.

Beans are registered in the Spring IoC container based on the packages specified for scanning.

Example

```
// Service class annotated with @Service
@Service
public class UserService {
    private final UserRepository userRepository;
    @Autowired
    public UserService(UserRepository userRepository) {
        this.userRepository = userRepository;
    }
    // Service methods using userRepository
}
```

Choosing the Configuration Approach

XML Configuration is suitable for legacy applications or when you prefer a centralized configuration approach.

Java-based Configuration is recommended for modern applications as it promotes type safety, refactoring, and easier integration with Java-based tools.

Component Scanning is convenient for discovering and registering beans automatically, reducing explicit bean configuration.

13.2 Spring MVC

Spring MVC (Model-View-Controller) is a robust web framework built on top of the Spring framework, designed to simplify the development of web applications in Java. At its core, Spring MVC follows the MVC architectural pattern, which divides an application into three interconnected components: the Model, the View, and the Controller.

In Spring MVC, the Model represents the application data and business logic, encapsulated within Java objects (POJOs) or Spring beans. These objects are typically retrieved from a database or other data sources.

The View is responsible for rendering the response to the client. In Spring MVC, views are often implemented using JSP (JavaServer Pages), Thymeleaf, or other template engines. Views are responsible for presenting data to users in a readable format.

The Controller acts as an intermediary between the Model and the View, handling user input and directing the flow of the application. Controllers are implemented as Spring beans and are responsible for processing incoming requests, invoking appropriate business logic (from the Model), and selecting the appropriate view to render the response.

Spring MVC provides robust features for building scalable and maintainable web applications, including support for request mapping, data binding, validation, and exception handling. It promotes clean separation of concerns, making it easier to manage and test each component independently. Additionally, Spring's dependency injection (DI) and aspect-oriented programming (AOP) capabilities seamlessly integrate with Spring MVC, enhancing modularity and extensibility. Overall, Spring MVC is widely adopted in enterprise environments for its flexibility, performance, and comprehensive tooling support, making it an ideal choice for developing Java-based web applications

Core Concepts of Spring MVC

Spring MVC (Model-View-Controller) is a powerful web framework built on top of the Spring framework, designed to facilitate the development of flexible and maintainable web applications in Java. The core concepts of Spring MVC include

DispatcherServlet

The DispatcherServlet is the heart of the Spring MVC framework. It acts as a front controller that receives all incoming requests and dispatches them to the appropriate handlers (controllers) based on URL mappings.

Controller

Controllers in Spring MVC are responsible for processing user requests, executing business logic, and preparing data for rendering. They handle different types of requests (GET, POST, etc.) mapped to specific URLs using @RequestMapping or other specialized annotations.

Example

```
@Controller
public class HomeController {
   @RequestMapping("/")
   public String home(Model model) {
      model.addAttribute("message", "Welcome to our website!");
      return "home"; // returns the logical view name
   }
}
```

Handler Mapping

Handler mappings define how requests are mapped to controllers and their methods. Spring MVC provides various handler mapping strategies, such as @RequestMapping, @GetMapping, @PostMapping, and more.

Model

The Model in Spring MVC represents the data that is exposed to the view for rendering. It is populated by the controller and typically consists of Java objects (POJOs) or collections.

Example

```
public class User {
   private String name;
   private int age;
   // getters and setters
}
```

ViewResolver

View resolvers in Spring MVC resolve logical view names returned by controllers to actual view implementations (JSP, Thymeleaf templates, etc.). They facilitate the rendering of the model data to produce the final response sent to the client.

View

Views are responsible for presenting the model data to the user in a user-friendly format (HTML, XML, JSON, etc.). They interact with the model to access the data and generate the appropriate response.

Interceptor

Interceptors are used to preprocess incoming requests or postprocess outgoing responses before or after the execution of a controller handler method. They provide cross-cutting concerns such as logging, authorization, or validation.

HandlerAdapter

Handler adapters are responsible for invoking controller methods and managing their lifecycle. They adapt the request and response objects to the controller methods and facilitate method invocation.

Setting Up Spring MVC

Setting up a Spring MVC project involves configuring the Spring MVC dispatcher servlet, setting up controllers, views, and resolving view names. Here's a basic setup process

Project Setup

Maven/Gradle: Start by setting up a Maven or Gradle project. Include dependencies for Spring MVC, such as spring-webmvc, in your pom.xml or build.gradle file.

```
<!-- Maven dependency for Spring MVC -->
<dependency>
   <groupId>org.springframework</groupId>
   <artifactId>spring-webmvc</artifactId>
   <version>${spring.version}</version>
</dependency>
```

Web Deployment Descriptor (web.xml)

Configure the DispatcherServlet in your web.xml. This servlet acts as the front controller for Spring MVC and handles all incoming requests.

```
<servlet>
   <servlet-name>dispatcher</servlet-name>
   <servlet-class>org.springframework.web.servlet.DispatcherServlet</servlet-class>
   <init-param>
      <param-name>contextConfigLocation</param-name>
      <param-value>/WEB-INF/spring-mvc-config.xml</param-value>
   </init-param>
   <load-on-startup>1</load-on-startup>
</servlet>
<servlet-mapping>
   <servlet-name>dispatcher</servlet-name>
   <url-pattern>/</url-pattern>
</servlet-mapping>
```

Spring Configuration (spring-mvc-config.xml)

Create a Spring configuration file (spring-mvc-config.xml) where you define beans, view resolvers, and other MVC-specific configurations.

```
     <beans xmlns="http://www.springframework.org/schema/beans"
     xmlns:xsi="http://www.w3.org/2001/XMLSchema-instance"
     xmlns:context="http://www.springframework.org/schema/context"
     xsi:schemaLocation="http://www.springframework.org/schema/beans
                    http://www.springframework.org/schema/beans/spring-beans.xsd
                    http://www.springframework.org/schema/context
                    http://www.springframework.org/schema/context/spring-context.xsd">

   <!-- Enable component scanning for Spring MVC controllers -->
   <context:component-scan base-package="com.example.controllers" />
   <!-- Configure view resolver -->
   <bean class="org.springframework.web.servlet.view.InternalResourceViewResolver">
      <property name="prefix" value="/WEB-INF/views/" />
      <property name="suffix" value=".jsp" />
   </bean>
</beans>
```

Create Controllers

Create Spring MVC controllers by annotating classes with @Controller and defining handler methods annotated with @RequestMapping.

Create Views

Create view files (JSP, Thymeleaf templates, etc.) in /WEB-INF/views/ directory or as specified in your view resolver configuration.

```
<!-- home.jsp -->
<html>
<body>
  <h1>${message}</h1>
</body>
</html>
```

Run the Application

Deploy your application to a servlet container (Tomcat, Jetty, etc.) and access it using the defined URL patterns (/ in the above example).

13.2.1 Understanding the Request Processing Flow

Client Sends Request

A client (typically a web browser) sends an HTTP request to the web application. The request is directed to a specific URL mapped to a controller in the Spring MVC application.

DispatcherServlet Receives Request

The DispatcherServlet, configured in the web.xml, acts as the front controller for Spring MVC. It receives all incoming requests and acts as the central hub for handling requests.

Handler Mapping

The DispatcherServlet consults the configured HandlerMapping to determine which controller (handler) should process the request based on the URL mapping (@RequestMapping annotations).

Controller Handling

Once the appropriate controller is determined, the DispatcherServlet delegates the request to the corresponding controller method (handler method).

Controllers are typically annotated with @Controller and define handler methods annotated with @RequestMapping or other request mapping annotations (@GetMapping, @PostMapping, etc.).

Controller Executes Business Logic

The controller method executes the business logic necessary to process the request. It may interact with services, repositories, or other components to retrieve data or perform operations.

Model Preparation

During the execution of the controller method, the controller prepares a Model object that holds data to be displayed or processed by the view.

The Model can be populated with attributes using model.addAttribute() or similar methods.

View Resolution

After executing the controller method and populating the Model, the DispatcherServlet needs to determine which view should render the response.

The DispatcherServlet consults the configured ViewResolver (defined in spring-mvc-config.xml or Java configuration) to map the logical view name returned by the controller to an actual view implementation (JSP, Thymeleaf template, etc.).

View Rendering

The selected view renders the response using the data provided by the Model. It generates the HTML, XML, JSON, or other content types to be sent back to the client.

Response Sent to Client

Finally, the DispatcherServlet sends the rendered view back to the client as an HTTP response.

13.2.2 Advantages of Spring MVC

Modular and Extensible Architecture

Spring MVC follows the MVC (Model-View-Controller) architectural pattern, promoting a clean separation of concerns between different components of the application.

This modular architecture allows developers to focus on specific aspects of the application (business logic, presentation, data access) independently, enhancing maintainability and scalability.

Flexible URL Mapping and Request Handling

Spring MVC provides flexible and powerful mechanisms for mapping URLs to controller methods using annotations like @RequestMapping, @GetMapping, @PostMapping, etc.
This allows developers to define clear and concise URL structures and handle various types of HTTP requests (GET, POST, PUT, DELETE) efficiently.
Powerful Data Binding and Validation
Spring MVC supports robust data binding and validation mechanisms, simplifying the process of binding HTTP request parameters to Java objects (@ModelAttribute, @RequestParam, etc.).
It integrates seamlessly with validation frameworks like Hibernate Validator, enabling easy validation of user input and error handling.
Integrated with Spring Ecosystem
Spring MVC is part of the larger Spring framework ecosystem, benefiting from features such as dependency injection (DI), aspect-oriented programming (AOP), transaction management, and more.
This integration enhances the capabilities of Spring MVC, making it easier to leverage other Spring modules and libraries for additional functionality.
Support for Multiple Views and Templating Engines
Spring MVC supports various view technologies, including JSP (JavaServer Pages), Thymeleaf, Freemarker, and others.
Developers can choose the most suitable templating engine based on project requirements and preferences, facilitating the development of dynamic and responsive user interfaces.
Testability and Tightly Integrated Testing Support
Spring MVC promotes test-driven development (TDD) and facilitates unit testing and integration testing of controllers and other components.
It provides built-in support for testing using mock objects (MockMvc), making it easier to write and execute tests without requiring a full application server.
Enhanced Security Features
Spring MVC integrates seamlessly with Spring Security, providing comprehensive security features such as authentication, authorization, CSRF protection, and more.
This helps developers implement robust security measures to protect applications against common security vulnerabilities.
Community Support and Active Development
Spring MVC benefits from a large and active community of developers and contributors.
The framework is continuously evolving with updates, improvements, and new features, ensuring long-term support and keeping up-to-date with industry standards and best practices.

13.3 Spring AOP

Spring AOP (Aspect-Oriented Programming) in the context of Spring Framework provides a powerful mechanism to modularize cross-cutting concerns in Java applications. It allows developers to encapsulate behaviours that cut across multiple modules into reusable components called aspects. This separation promotes cleaner, more maintainable code by reducing code duplication and improving the separation of concerns.
In Spring AOP, aspects are implemented using regular Java classes annotated with @Aspect. These aspects define pointcuts, which specify where and when advice (additional behaviour) should be applied in the application's execution flow. Types of advice include @Before (executed before a method call), @After (executed after a method call), @Around (wraps a method call), @AfterReturning (executed after a method returns a value), and @AfterThrowing (executed when a method throws an exception).
Spring AOP integrates seamlessly with Spring's IoC (Inversion of Control) container and supports various pointcut expressions to target specific join points in the application. It enhances modularity, promotes code reusability, and simplifies maintenance by allowing developers to add or modify application behaviours without altering the core application logic. Overall, Spring AOP is instrumental in achieving cleaner architecture and more manageable Java applications.

13.3.1 Core Concepts of Spring AOP

Aspect
An aspect is a modular unit that encapsulates cross-cutting concerns.
In Spring AOP, aspects are implemented using regular classes annotated with @Aspect.
Aspects contain advice (code to be executed) and pointcuts (definitions of where the advice should be applied).
Join Point

A join point is a point in the execution of the application where an aspect can be plugged in.
Common join points include method execution, method invocation, exception handling, field access, etc.
Advice
Advice is the action taken by an aspect at a particular join point.
Types of advice include @Before (executed before a method execution), @After (executed after a method execution), @Around (wraps a method execution), @AfterReturning (executed after a method returns a value), and @AfterThrowing (executed if a method throws an exception).
Pointcut
A pointcut is a predicate that matches join points.
It specifies where advice should be applied in the application.
Pointcuts are defined using expressions or annotations in Spring AOP.
Introduction
Introduction allows adding new methods or attributes to existing classes.
It helps in enhancing the capabilities of existing classes without modifying their code directly.

13.3.2 Implementing Spring AOP

Spring AOP is implemented using runtime proxies, meaning it's not as powerful as compile-time frameworks like AspectJ, but it provides enough capability for most enterprise applications without requiring special compilation steps.
Declaring Aspects
Aspects in Spring can be declared using regular classes annotated with @Aspect. This makes it clear that the class is not just a regular class but has aspects that will be applied to other parts of the application.

```
@Aspect
@Component
public class LoggingAspect {
  @Before("execution(* com.example.service.*.*(..))")
  public void beforeMethodExecution(JoinPoint joinPoint) {
    String methodName = joinPoint.getSignature().getName();
    System.out.println("Before executing method " + methodName);
  }

  @AfterReturning(pointcut = "execution(* com.example.service.*.*(..))", returning = "result")
  public void afterMethodExecution(JoinPoint joinPoint, Object result) {
    String methodName = joinPoint.getSignature().getName();
    System.out.println("After executing method: " + methodName + ", Result: " + result);
  }
}
```

Types of Advice
Spring AOP supports five types of advice annotations:
@Before: Run before the method execution.
@AfterReturning: Run after the method returns a result.
@AfterThrowing: Run after the method exits by throwing an exception.
@After: Run after the method execution regardless of its outcome.
@Around: Surrounds a method execution, allowing pre- and post-execution customization.

Pointcut Expressions
Pointcuts determine the join points of interest, and Spring uses the AspectJ pointcut expression language by default. Expressions can match method execution join points based on various criteria, including method names, annotations, or parameter types.

```
@Pointcut("execution(* com.example.service.*.*(..))")
public void serviceLayer() {}
```

Integrating Aspects with Spring Beans

To integrate aspects with Spring-managed beans, ensure that your aspect class is detected during the component scan, or declare it explicitly in your configuration. Spring will automatically proxy beans that match the pointcut expressions defined in your aspects.

Integrate with Spring Beans:
Ensure that your aspect class is managed as a Spring bean (@Component or registered in XML configuration) to be picked up by Spring's component scanning.

Testing and Validation
Validate the implementation by writing unit tests to ensure that aspects intercept method calls and execute advice as expected.
Use mock testing frameworks like Mockito alongside Spring's testing utilities (MockMvc, TestRestTemplate) to validate aspect behaviour.

Advantages of Using Spring AOP
Simplified Code: By externalizing cross-cutting concerns, business logic becomes cleaner and more focused on its purpose.
Improved Modularity: AOP helps in organizing system-wide concerns into separate modules, improving the modularity of the application.
Easy Configuration: Spring AOP can be easily configured using annotations or XML configuration, making it accessible without requiring deep AOP knowledge.

13.4 Setting up Spring Project and Configuring Dependencies

Spring Framework has become an integral part of developing robust Java applications, offering a comprehensive programming and configuration model. Setting up a Spring project properly and managing dependencies efficiently are foundational steps that ensure the smooth development and scalability of Java applications. This chapter guides you through initiating a Spring project, configuring its dependencies, and laying the groundwork for a flexible and maintainable application.

13.4.1 Setting Up a Spring Project

Setting up a Spring project involves configuring the necessary components and dependencies to leverage the Spring Framework for building Java applications. Here's a comprehensive guide suitable for an advanced Java book

Setting Up a Spring Project
Project Initialization
Start by initializing a new Java project using a build tool such as Maven or Gradle. These tools simplify dependency management and project configuration.
Maven Example (pom.xml)

```
<project xmlns="http://maven.apache.org/POM/4.0.0"
      xmlns:xsi="http://www.w3.org/2001/XMLSchema-instance"
      xsi:schemaLocation="http://maven.apache.org/POM/4.0.0              http://maven.apache.org/xsd/maven-
4.0.0.xsd">
  <modelVersion>4.0.0</modelVersion>
  <groupId>com.example</groupId>
  <artifactId>spring-project</artifactId>
  <version>1.0-SNAPSHOT</version>
  <packaging>jar</packaging>
  <properties>
    <spring.version>5.3.9.RELEASE</spring.version>
  </properties>
  <dependencies>
    <!-- Spring Core & Context -->
    <dependency>
      <groupId>org.springframework</groupId>
      <artifactId>spring-context</artifactId>
```

```
        <version>${spring.version}</version>
      </dependency>
      <!-- Other dependencies as needed (e.g., Spring Web, Spring AOP, etc.) -->
    </dependencies>
</project>
```

Gradle Example (build.gradle)

```
plugins {
   id 'java'
}
group 'com.example'
version '1.0-SNAPSHOT'
repositories {
   mavenCentral()
}
dependencies {
   implementation 'org.springframework:spring-context:5.3.9.RELEASE'
   // Other dependencies as needed
}
```

Spring Configuration

Create a Spring configuration file (applicationContext.xml for XML-based configuration or Java configuration classes annotated with @Configuration).

XML-based Configuration (applicationContext.xml):

```
<!-- applicationContext.xml -->
<beans xmlns="http://www.springframework.org/schema/beans"
      xmlns:xsi="http://www.w3.org/2001/XMLSchema-instance"
      xsi:schemaLocation="http://www.springframework.org/schema/beans
                  http://www.springframework.org/schema/beans/spring-beans.xsd">
   <!-- Define Spring beans and their configurations -->
   <bean id="userService" class="com.example.service.UserServiceImpl">
      <!-- Bean properties and dependencies -->
   </bean>
</beans>
```

Java-based Configuration (AppConfig.java):

```
@Configuration
@ComponentScan(basePackages = "com.example")
public class AppConfig {
   // Define beans and configurations using Java annotations
}
```

Add Spring Dependencies

Include Spring dependencies relevant to your project's requirements (spring-context, spring-web, spring-jdbc, etc.) in your build configuration file (pom.xml or build.gradle).

Develop Spring Components

Develop service classes, DAOs (Data Access Objects), controllers, and other components using Spring annotations (@Service, @Repository, @Controller, etc.) to leverage Spring's dependency injection and other features.

Run and Test

Deploy your Spring application to a servlet container (Tomcat, Jetty, etc.) or run it as a standalone application.

Write unit tests using frameworks like JUnit, Mockito, and Spring's testing utilities (MockMvc, TestRestTemplate) to validate functionality and integration.

Using Spring Initializer

Navigate to Spring Initializer: A web-based tool for generating Spring Boot projects.

Project Metadata: Fill in the details such as Project, Language (Java), Spring Boot version, Project Metadata (Group, Artifact, Name, Description, Package name), and Packaging (Jar or War).

Dependencies: Add the necessary Spring Boot Starter dependencies based on the requirements of your project. Common starters include Spring Web, Spring Data JPA, Spring Security, etc.
Generate: Click on the generate button to download the project template as a zip file.
Import: Extract the zip file and import the project into your preferred IDE (Eclipse, IntelliJ IDEA, VS Code, etc.).

Configuring Dependencies
Managing dependencies is a crucial part of setting up a Spring project. Dependencies can be managed manually, but it is highly recommended to use a build tool like Maven or Gradle for this purpose.
Maven Configuration
For projects using Maven, dependencies are configured in the pom.xml file. Here's how you can add Spring Boot dependencies to your Maven project
Parent Configuration: Define the Spring Boot starter parent in your pom.xml. This parent project provides dependency and plugin management for applications built with Spring Boot.

```
<parent>
  <groupId>org.springframework.boot
</groupId>
  <artifactId>spring-boot-starter-parent
</artifactId>
  <version>2.4.5
</version>
</parent>
```

Dependencies: Add Spring Boot starter dependencies to the <dependencies> section of your pom.xml. Each starter dependency simplifies the inclusion of a particular set of related technologies.

```
<dependencies>
  <dependency>
    <groupId>org.springframework.boot
</groupId>
    <artifactId>spring-boot-starter-web
</artifactId>
  </dependency>
  <!-- Add more dependencies as needed -->
</dependencies>
```

Build Configuration: Optionally, configure the Spring Boot Maven plugin for packaging and running your application.

```
<build>
  <plugins>
    <plugin>
      <groupId>org.springframework.boot
</groupId>
      <artifactId>spring-boot-maven-plugin
</artifactId>
    </plugin>
  </plugins>
</build>
```

Gradle Configuration: For projects using Gradle, dependencies are configured in the build.gradle file. Similar to Maven, Spring Boot provides a plugin for Gradle that simplifies dependency management:
Plugin Application: Apply the Spring Boot plugin and define the Spring Boot version

```
Plugins
 {
id 'org.springframework.boot' version '2.4.5'
id 'java'
}
```

Dependencies: Add dependencies by including them in the dependencies block of your build.gradle.

```
dependencies
{
  implementation 'org.springframework.boot:spring-boot-starter-web'
```

```
    // Additional dependencies
}
```

Common Dependency Types: Compile Dependencies: Required for compiling and running the application.
Provided Dependencies: Used when the dependency is provided by the runtime environment (e.g., servlet APIs in a web container).
Test Dependencies: Used only for testing purposes (JUnit, Mockito, etc.).
Transitive Dependencies: Dependencies may have their own dependencies (transitive dependencies), which are automatically resolved by build tools like Maven and Gradle.
Use dependency management plugins or configurations (<dependencyManagement> in Maven) to manage version conflicts and ensure consistency across dependencies.
Repository Management: Repositories (<repositories> in Maven, repositories {} in Gradle) specify where to find dependencies (e.g., Maven Central, custom repositories).
Ensure repositories are accessible and include necessary dependencies for your project.
Versioning and Updates: Regularly update dependency versions to leverage bug fixes, security patches, and new features.
Use tools like Maven's versions:update plugin or Gradle's dependency update task to automate version management.

Exercise

Exercise 1- MCQ

1. What does DI stand for in Spring Framework?
a) Direct Injection
b) Dependency Injection
c) Detailed Injection
d) Data Injection
2. Which feature of Spring Framework makes it easy to manage application components and services?
a) JDBC Template
b) Dependency Injection
c) Model-View-Controller
d) Aspect-Oriented Programming
3. What is the primary purpose of Spring MVC?
a) To support direct access to databases
b) To implement cross-cutting concerns
c) To simplify the development of web applications
d) To manage security configurations
4. Which of the following is a core concept in Spring AOP?
a) Joinpoint
b) JDBC Template
c) DispatcherServlet
d) ViewResolver
5. How can you define beans in a Spring application?
a) Using XML configuration files
b) With Java-based configuration
c) Through annotations
d) All of the above
6. What annotation is commonly used to mark a class as a Spring component?
a) @Component
b) @Service
c) @Repository
d) All of the above are correct
7. Which Spring module provides support for creating RESTful web services?
a) Spring MVC
b) Spring Boot
c) Spring Security
d) Spring Data

8. In Spring AOP, what defines when an advice should be executed?
a) Joinpoint
b) Pointcut
c) Advice
d) Aspect
9. Which file is typically used to declare Spring beans in XML configuration?
a) pom.xml
b) applicationContext.xml
c) web.xml
d) spring-config.xml
10. For a Spring project, which build tool is used to manage dependencies?
a) Maven
b) Gradle
c) Ant
d) Make

Exercise 2- True/False

1. Spring Framework is an application framework and inversion of control container for the Java platform.
2. Dependency Injection (DI) in Spring can only be achieved through XML configuration.
3. Spring MVC is a design pattern used to separate model logic from user interface code.
4. In Spring AOP, aspects cannot be applied to beans defined in the Spring context.
5. @Autowired annotation in Spring is used for automatic dependency injection.
6. Spring Boot is required to run any Spring application.
7. AOP stands for Aspect-Oriented Programming and is used to increase modularity by allowing the separation of cross-cutting concerns.
8. Spring MVC stands for Spring Model-View-Controller.
9. In Spring, the @Controller annotation is used to mark a class as a Spring MVC controller.
10. Spring Security is a framework that provides comprehensive security services for Java EE-based enterprise software applications.

Exercise 3- Fill in the blanks

1. To inject bean dependencies in Spring without using XML configuration, one can use the ___ annotation.
2. Spring MVC follows the ___ design pattern to separate the application logic from the user interface.
3. In Spring, ___ is used to create a web application context for Spring MVC applications.
4. ___ in Spring AOP allows developers to execute advice on specified join points.
5. To manage project dependencies in Spring, the build tool ___ is often used.
6. Spring Transactions facilitate declarative transaction management using annotations like .
7. Spring Framework is a comprehensive framework for building ____
8. Inversion of Control (IoC) is the principle where objects receive their dependencies from an _____rather than creating them internally.
9. Aspect-Oriented Programming (AOP) in Spring allows developers to modularize ____
10. Spring MVC provides a structured approach to ____

Exercise 4- Match Case

1. Framework for simplifying configuration and integration of Spring applications
2. Simplifies the development of web applications with Spring
3. Allows defining cross-cutting concerns such as logging and transaction management
4. Technique to manage object creation and wiring in Spring

A. Spring AOP
B. Spring Boot
C. Spring MVC
D.Dependency Injection

Exercise 5- One word answer

1. What Spring annotation is used to automatically inject dependencies?

2. Which Spring framework module simplifies aspect-oriented programming?

Exercise 6 – Small answer

1. Which interface in Spring is used for transaction management?
2. What annotation defines a Spring bean in the application context without XML configuration?

Exercise 7 – Long answer

1. Explain how Spring's Dependency Injection (DI) facilitates loose coupling in application components.
2. Describe the process of setting up a basic Spring Boot application and its advantages for developers new to Spring.

Answer-

Exercise 1- 1) b 2) b 3) c 4) a 5) d 6) d 7) a 8) b 9) b 10) a
Exercise 2- 1) True 2) False 3) False 4) False 5) True 6) False 7) True 8) True 9) True 10) True
Exercise 3- 1) @Autowired 2) MVC 3) DispatcherServlet 4) Pointcut 5) Maven 6) @Transactional 7) enterprise Java applications 8) external source 9) cross-cutting concerns 10) building web applications.
Exercise 4- 1 – B. Spring Boot 2 – C. Spring MVC 3 – A. Spring AOP 4 – D. Dependency Injection
Exercise 5- 1) @Autowired 2) AOP

Online Resources

Online Practice Paper

Link: https://forms.gle/zAM6PsYA23s2GdQ78
QR Code:

YouTube Video Link

Link: https://www.youtube.com/playlist?list=PLzlh_31VWEFrvrBakYUPoVKhin4X9vhG2
QR Code:

CHAPTER 14 - Spring Boot Framework (Version 2.x)

14.1 Introduction to Spring Boot

Spring Boot represents a paradigm shift in the Spring ecosystem, offering a radical approach to developing Spring applications with minimal fuss. Designed to simplify the bootstrapping and development of new Spring projects, Spring Boot makes it easier than ever to create stand-alone, production-grade Spring-based applications. This chapter provides a comprehensive introduction to Spring Boot, detailing its core features, benefits, and the philosophy behind its design.

14.1.1 What is Spring Boot?

Spring Boot is a revolutionary framework in the Java ecosystem designed to simplify the development and deployment of production-grade applications. It builds upon the robust foundations of the Spring Framework while eliminating much of the boilerplate code and configuration overhead traditionally associated with Java development. Here's an in-depth explanation suitable for an advanced Java book

Streamlined Development and Configuration

Spring Boot fundamentally changes how developers approach Java application development by providing a convention-over-configuration paradigm. This means that Spring Boot makes sensible assumptions about the configuration based on the dependencies and environment detected at runtime. Developers can start new projects quickly using Spring Boot's starters—pre-packaged dependencies for common tasks like web applications, data access, messaging, and more.

Key Features and Benefits

Opinionated Defaults and Auto-Configuration: Spring Boot embraces opinionated defaults to minimize configuration. It automatically configures the application based on classpath dependencies, reducing the need for manual setup. For example, adding spring-boot-starter-web brings in everything needed to build a web application using Spring MVC and an embedded server like Tomcat or Jetty. Developers can override these configurations using application properties or YAML files.

Embedded Servers: One of the hallmark features of Spring Boot is its support for embedded servers. Applications can be packaged as executable JARs containing an embedded server, allowing them to be deployed and run with a simple java -jar command. This approach simplifies deployment and promotes consistency across development, testing, and production environments.

Production-Ready Features with Spring Boot Actuator: Spring Boot Actuator provides production-ready features out of the box, such as health checks, metrics, auditing, and environment inspection. Actuator endpoints expose operational information about the application via HTTP or JMX, facilitating monitoring and management without additional coding effort.

Spring Boot Starters: Starters are a set of convenient dependency descriptors that simplify the inclusion of specific sets of dependencies in applications. For instance, spring-boot-starter-data-jpa includes dependencies to set up Spring Data JPA with Hibernate, while spring-boot-starter-security includes Spring Security for authentication and authorization.

Microservices and Cloud-Native Development: Spring Boot's lightweight and opinionated approach makes it ideal for microservices architecture and cloud-native development. It integrates seamlessly with cloud platforms like AWS, Azure, and Google Cloud, offering features like cloud-native configuration management and service discovery.

Spring Boot CLI: For rapid prototyping and scripting, the Spring Boot CLI allows developers to create Spring-powered applications using Groovy scripts. This command-line tool provides a lightweight and interactive environment to develop and test ideas quickly.

14.1.2 Philosophy Behind Spring Boot

Spring Boot is built upon several core principles and philosophies that distinguish it from traditional Java application development frameworks. Understanding these principles provides insights into why and how Spring Boot simplifies and accelerates the development of Java applications:

Convention over Configuration: Spring Boot follows the principle of convention over configuration. This means that it provides sensible defaults and configurations based on conventions, reducing the need for developers to specify every configuration detail manually. By adhering to well-established conventions, Spring Boot minimizes boilerplate code and allows developers to focus more on writing business logic rather than configuring infrastructure.

Simplify Dependency Management: Managing dependencies in Java projects can be complex and time-consuming. Spring Boot simplifies dependency management by offering a curated set of "starters." These starters are opinionated sets of dependencies that are pre-configured to work together seamlessly for common use cases, such as web applications, data access, messaging, and more. Developers can easily include starters in their projects with a single dependency declaration, streamlining the setup process and ensuring compatibility between dependencies.

Embedded Servers and Production-Ready Features: Spring Boot promotes the use of embedded servers (like Tomcat, Jetty, or Undertow) as part of its opinionated approach. Embedding servers within the application JAR simplifies deployment and eliminates the need for external server setups. Additionally, Spring Boot Actuator provides out-of-the-box production-ready features, including health checks, metrics, auditing, and environment inspection. These features enable developers to monitor and manage applications efficiently without requiring additional configuration or coding effort.

Facilitate Microservices Architecture: In the era of microservices and cloud-native applications, Spring Boot offers robust support for building microservices architectures. Its lightweight nature, coupled with support for containerization and cloud platforms, makes it an ideal choice for developing and deploying microservices. Spring Boot's ability to integrate seamlessly with cloud services and its built-in support for distributed tracing, service discovery, and configuration management further enhances its suitability for microservices-based projects.

Developer Productivity: Spring Boot prioritizes developer productivity by providing tools like the Spring Boot CLI (Command Line Interface) for rapid application development and prototyping. The CLI allows developers to create Spring-powered applications using Groovy scripts, offering a streamlined and interactive development experience. Additionally, Spring Boot's comprehensive documentation, community support, and ecosystem of plugins and extensions contribute to enhancing developer efficiency and accelerating project timelines.

Opportunity for Customization: Despite its opinionated approach, Spring Boot provides ample opportunities for customization. Developers can override default configurations, add additional dependencies, and fine-tune application settings using properties files or YAML configuration. This flexibility ensures that Spring Boot can adapt to a wide range of project requirements and architectural preferences while still benefiting from its simplified setup and productivity-enhancing features.

14.1.3 Getting Started with Spring Boot

Starting with Spring Boot involves setting up a new project, understanding its key components, and leveraging its powerful features to quickly build robust Java applications. Here's a comprehensive guide suitable for an advanced Java book:

Setting Up a Spring Boot Project

To begin with Spring Boot, follow these steps

Choose a Build Tool: Spring Boot projects are typically managed using Maven or Gradle. Both tools simplify dependency management and project setup.

Initialize a Project: Use Spring Initializer (https://start.spring.io/) or your IDE to generate a new Spring Boot project. Specify dependencies such as Spring Web for web applications, Spring Data JPA for data access, or Spring Security for security features.

Project Structure: A typical Spring Boot project has a standardized structure with main application class in the root package (@SpringBootApplication annotated class), configuration files in src/main/resources, and Java source code in src/main/java.

Understanding Key Components

Application Class: The main class annotated with @SpringBootApplication serves as the entry point. It combines @Configuration, @EnableAutoConfiguration, and @ComponentScan annotations.

Configuration: Spring Boot uses sensible defaults for configuration, which can be overridden using application.properties or application.yml files. Configuration properties can be used to customize application Behaviour, database connections, logging, etc.

Dependencies and Starters: Spring Boot starters (spring-boot-starter-*) simplify dependency management by bundling commonly used libraries. For example, spring-boot-starter-web includes everything needed to build a web application.

Developing with Spring Boot

Controller: Use @RestController or @Controller annotations to define RESTful endpoints or MVC controllers. Handle HTTP requests and responses using methods annotated with @GetMapping, @PostMapping, etc.

Data Access: Spring Boot integrates seamlessly with Spring Data, making it easy to set up repositories (@Repository) and data access objects (DAOs). Use @Entity and @Repository annotations to define entities and repositories.

Service Layer: Implement business logic in service classes (@Service) that are injected into controllers and other components using @Autowired.

Testing: Spring Boot supports unit testing with frameworks like JUnit and integration testing with Spring's testing utilities (@SpringBootTest, @MockBean, etc.).

Running and Deploying

Embedded Servers: Spring Boot applications are packaged as executable JAR files with embedded servers (Tomcat, Jetty, or Undertow). Run the application using java -jar command or directly from the IDE.

Deployment: Deploy Spring Boot applications to cloud platforms (AWS, Azure, Google Cloud) or traditional servers. Configure deployment settings in application.properties or cloud-specific configurations.

Monitoring and Management

Actuator: Include Spring Boot Actuator dependency to gain production-ready features like health checks (/actuator/health), metrics (/actuator/metrics), and environment details (/actuator/env).

Continuous Integration and Deployment (CI/CD)

Integrate Spring Boot applications with CI/CD pipelines using tools like Jenkins, GitLab CI, or AWS CodePipeline. Automate build, test, and deployment processes to streamline development workflows.

14.2 Creating and Deploying Spring Boot Projects

Spring Boot simplifies the process of creating and deploying Spring applications by providing a comprehensive platform that requires minimal configuration and setup. It is designed to get your Spring applications up and running as quickly as possible, with an opinionated setup for a quick and straightforward start. This chapter explores the steps involved in creating, configuring, and deploying Spring Boot projects, ensuring developers have the knowledge to bring their applications from conception to production efficiently.

Creating a Spring Boot Project

Creating and deploying Spring Boot projects involves several detailed steps, from initial setup to deployment strategies. Here's a comprehensive guide suitable for an advanced Java book:

Creating and Deploying Spring Boot Projects

Setting Up the Development Environment

Choose a Build Tool: Spring Boot projects are typically managed using Maven or Gradle. Ensure the build tool is installed and configured properly on your development machine.

Using Spring Initialiser: Start a new project using Spring Initialiser, a web-based tool that generates Spring Boot projects with specified dependencies. Configure project metadata such as group, artifact, and dependencies like Spring Web, Spring Data JPA, Spring Security, etc.

Project Structure: A typical Spring Boot project follows a standard structure:

```
/src
  /main
    /java      <-- Java source code
      /com/example/myproject   <-- Application package
        /controller   <-- Spring MVC controllers
        /service      <-- Business services
        /repository   <-- Data repositories (Spring Data)
        /model        <-- Entity classes
        MyProjectApplication.java  <-- Main application class
    /resources   <-- Configuration files
      application.properties (or .yml)  <-- Application-specific properties
      /static    <-- Static resources (HTML, CSS, JS)
      /templates  <-- Template files (Thymeleaf, FreeMarker)
```

Development with Spring Boot

Main Application Class: The entry point of a Spring Boot application is a class annotated with @SpringBootApplication. This annotation combines @Configuration, @EnableAutoConfiguration, and @ComponentScan—enabling auto-configuration and component scanning.

Controller Layer: Define RESTful APIs or MVC controllers using annotations like @RestController or @Controller. Map HTTP requests to handler methods annotated with @GetMapping, @PostMapping, etc., to process requests and return responses.
Service Layer: Implement business logic in service classes annotated with @Service. Services encapsulate application logic and are typically injected into controllers and other components using @Autowired.
Data Access Layer: Use Spring Data repositories (@Repository) to interact with databases. Define entity classes annotated with @Entity and corresponding repositories extending JpaRepository or other Spring Data interfaces.
Configuration: Customize application Behaviour using application.properties or application.yml files. Configure database connections, logging levels, server ports, and other settings specific to your application requirements.

Running and Testing

Embedded Servers: Spring Boot applications are packaged as executable JAR files with embedded servers (Tomcat, Jetty, or Undertow). Run the application locally using the command java -jar <application-name>.jar or directly from the IDE.
Unit and Integration Testing: Use frameworks like JUnit and Spring's testing utilities (@SpringBootTest, @MockBean) for unit testing and integration testing. Test application components, controllers, and services to ensure functionality and reliability.

Packaging and Deployment

Packaging: Build an executable JAR file using Maven (mvn clean package) or Gradle (./gradlew clean build). Spring Boot's build plugins automatically package dependencies and configure the main class for execution.
Deployment Strategies:
Standalone JAR: Deploy the generated JAR file to any server or cloud platform capable of running Java applications. Execute the JAR using java -jar <application-name>.jar.
Containerization: Package the application as a Docker image and deploy it to container orchestration platforms like Kubernetes. Use Docker files and Kubernetes deployment manifests to define and manage application deployments.
Cloud Deployment: Deploy Spring Boot applications to cloud providers (AWS, Azure, Google Cloud) using platform-specific services like AWS Elastic Beanstalk, Azure App Service, or Google App Engine. Configure environment-specific properties and credentials for cloud integration.

Monitoring and Management

Spring Boot Actuator: Include Spring Boot Actuator in your project to expose production-ready endpoints (/actuator/health, /actuator/metrics, etc.) for monitoring application health, metrics, and environment details. Customize Actuator endpoints and security settings as needed.

Continuous Integration and Delivery (CI/CD)

Implement CI/CD pipelines using tools like Jenkins, GitLab CI/CD, or AWS Code Pipeline. Automate build, test, and deployment processes to ensure consistent and reliable application delivery.

14.3 Spring Boot AOP and Database Integration

Aspect-Oriented Programming (AOP) in Spring Boot allows developers to modularize cross-cutting concerns, such as logging, transaction management, security, and performance monitoring, into reusable components known as aspects. AOP enhances modularity by separating concerns that cut across multiple parts of the application. Here's how AOP works in Spring Boot:

Key Concepts of AOP

Aspect: An aspect is a modularization of a concern that cuts across multiple classes. It encapsulates cross-cutting concerns (e.g., logging) and provides reusable solutions.
Advice: Advice is the action taken by an aspect at a particular join point. It defines what action is to be taken and when it should be applied.
Join Point: A join point is a specific point in the execution of the application where an aspect can be applied. In Spring Boot, join points are typically method executions or field access points.
Pointcut: A pointcut is a predicate that matches join points. It specifies where in the application's execution an aspect should be applied.
Weaving: Weaving is the process of applying aspects to a target object to create an advised object. This can be done at compile time, load time, or runtime.

Using AOP in Spring Boot

Dependency: Include spring-boot-starter-aop dependency in your pom.xml or build.gradle file to enable AOP support in your Spring Boot project.

Aspect Definition: Define an aspect using the @Aspect annotation on a regular Java class. Inside the aspect, use annotations like @Before, @After, @Around, @AfterReturning, and @AfterThrowing to define advice methods that execute at specific join points.
Pointcut Expression: Use pointcut expressions with annotations like @Pointcut to define where advice should be applied. Pointcut expressions use language similar to regular expressions to match method executions based on their signatures, annotations, or package names.
Example Scenarios
Logging: Create an aspect to log method executions across the application.
Transaction Management: Implement declarative transaction management using @Transactional annotation and aspects to handle transaction boundaries.
Security: Apply method-level security checks using aspects to enforce access control rules.
Performance Monitoring: Measure method execution times and performance metrics using aspects.
Benefits
Modularity: AOP promotes modularity by separating cross-cutting concerns from the main application logic.
Reusability: Aspects are reusable components that can be applied across different parts of the application.
Maintainability: Centralizing cross-cutting concerns improves code maintainability by reducing duplication and ensuring consistent behaviour.
Database Integration in Spring Boot
Spring Boot simplifies database integration by providing seamless support for relational databases through Spring Data and JDBC templates. Here’s how to integrate databases into a Spring Boot application
Data Source Configuration
Define database connection properties (e.g., URL, username, password) in application.properties or application.yml.
Configure a data source bean using @Configuration and @Bean annotations. Spring Boot auto-configures a data source if database-specific properties are provided.
Spring Data JPA Integration
Include spring-boot-starter-data-jpa dependency to enable Spring Data JPA support.
Define entity classes annotated with @Entity, specifying table mappings and relationships.
Create repository interfaces extending JpaRepository or other Spring Data interfaces. Spring Boot auto-generates implementation classes for these interfaces at runtime.
JDBC Template Integration
Use JdbcTemplate for low-level JDBC operations if not using Spring Data JPA.
Define a JdbcTemplate bean and inject it into service classes for executing SQL queries and updates.
Transaction Management
Use @Transactional annotation to enable declarative transaction management on service methods. Spring Boot manages transaction boundaries, rollback rules, and isolation levels automatically.
Configure transaction management properties in application.properties for fine-tuning transaction behaviour.
Database Migration
Use tools like Flyway or Liquibase to manage database schema evolution and versioning.
Define SQL migration scripts in the db/migration directory or specify them in application.properties for automatic execution during application startup.
Testing and Mocking
Use embedded databases (e.g., H2, HSQLDB) or configure test-specific data sources for unit and integration testing.
Mock database interactions using frameworks like Mockito for unit testing service and repository classes.
Transactional Testing
Use @Transactional annotation with test methods to roll back database changes after each test execution, ensuring test data consistency.

14.3.1 Spring Boot and Aspect-Oriented Programming (AOP)

AOP complements OOP by providing a means to separate cross-cutting concerns from business logic. Spring Boot simplifies AOP implementation, allowing developers to focus on application logic rather than boilerplate code.
Enabling AOP in Spring Boot
To use AOP in Spring Boot, include the spring-boot-starter-aop dependency in your pom.xml or build.gradle file.
Maven

```
<dependency>
   <groupId>org.springframework.boot</groupId>
   <artifactId>spring-boot-starter-aop</artifactId>
</dependency>
```
Gradle
```
implementation 'org.springframework.boot:spring-boot-starter-aop'
```

Defining Aspects

Aspects are defined using the @Aspect annotation. Within aspects, you can define pointcuts to specify where advice should be applied and advice methods that indicate what action should be taken.

Declare an Aspect
```
@Aspect
@Component
public class LoggingAspect {
   // Aspect methods here
}
```
Pointcut Declaration: Pointcuts determine the join points where advice should be applied, using expression language to match methods.
```
@Pointcut("execution(* com.example.service.*.*(..))")
private void serviceLayerExecution() {}
```

Advice Types: Spring AOP supports various types of advice annotations, including @Before, @AfterReturning, @AfterThrowing, @After, and @Around.
```
@Before("serviceLayerExecution()")
public void logBeforeServiceMethod(JoinPoint joinPoint) {
   // Logging logic here
}
```

14.4 Database Integration in Spring Boot

Spring Boot provides seamless integration with relational and non-relational databases through auto-configuration, simplifying connection setup, entity management, and transaction control.

Configuring a Data Source

Spring Boot auto-configures a data source if it detects database drivers and Spring Data dependencies on the classpath. Further customization can be achieved through properties defined in application.properties or application.yml.

Example Configuration (application.properties)
```
spring.datasource.url=jdbc:mysql://localhost:3306/mydb
spring.datasource.username=dbuser
spring.datasource.password=dbpass
spring.datasource.driver-class-name=com.mysql.cj.jdbc.Driver
```

Using Spring Data JPA

pring Boot simplifies database integration by providing seamless support for relational databases through Spring Data JPA. Spring Data JPA is a part of the larger Spring Data project, which aims to provide a consistent and easy way to access data in Java applications.

Key Concepts of Spring Data JPA

Entity: An entity represents a table in a relational database. It is typically annotated with @Entity and may include additional annotations (@Table, @Column, etc.) to define mapping details like table name, column names, relationships, etc.

Repository: A repository is an interface that extends JpaRepository (or a derived interface like CrudRepository or PagingAndSortingRepository). Spring Data JPA auto-generates implementation code at runtime based on method signatures defined in the repository interface.

EntityManager and Session: EntityManager (or Hibernate Session) manages entity objects and their lifecycle in the context of JPA. It provides methods for CRUD operations (Create, Read, Update, Delete), querying entities, and managing transactions.

JPQL (Java Persistence Query Language): JPQL is a query language similar to SQL but operates on JPA entity objects rather than database tables. It allows developers to write database queries in a platform-independent manner.

Steps to Integrate Spring Data JPA in Spring Boot

Dependency Configuration

Include spring-boot-starter-data-jpa dependency in your project's build configuration (pom.xml or build.gradle). This includes dependencies for Spring Data JPA, Hibernate (JPA implementation), and database drivers (e.g., H2, MySQL, PostgreSQL).

Entity Definition

Define entity classes using @Entity annotation. An entity class represents a database table, and its attributes represent table columns.

Example

```
@Entity
public class User {
  @Id
  @GeneratedValue(strategy = GenerationType.IDENTITY)
  private Long id;
  @Column(name = "username")
  private String username;
  @Column(name = "email")
  private String email;
  // Getters and setters
}
```

Repository Definition

Create a repository interface extending JpaRepository and specifying the entity type (User) and primary key type (Long). Spring Data JPA provides methods like findById, save, findAll, etc., out of the box.

Example

```
public interface UserRepository extends JpaRepository<User, Long> {
// Additional custom query methods can be defined here
}
```

Configuration Properties

Configure database connection properties(spring.datasource.url spring.datasource.username)

Example (application.properties)

```
spring.datasource.url=jdbc:mysql://localhost:3306/mydb
spring.datasource.username=root
spring.datasource.password=password
spring.datasource.driver-class-name=com.mysql.jdbc.Driver
spring.jpa.database-platform=org.hibernate.dialect.MySQL5Dialect
spring.jpa.hibernate.ddl-auto=update
```

Transactional Management

Use @Transactional annotation on service methods to manage database transactions automatically. Spring Boot ensures that each method is executed within a transaction boundary, handling commit and rollback based on method outcomes.

Query Methods

Define custom query methods in the repository interface using method naming conventions (findBy..., deleteBy..., etc.) or JPQL queries (@Query annotation). Spring Data JPA translates method names into corresponding SQL queries at runtime.

Testing and Mocking

Unit Testing: Use embedded databases (e.g., H2) for unit testing to isolate database interactions and ensure consistent test results.

Mocking: Use Mockito or similar frameworks to mock repository interfaces in service layer tests, focusing on business logic without depending on database connectivity.

Advanced Features
Auditing: Automatically populate fields (@CreatedBy, @CreatedDate, @LastModifiedDate) using Spring Data JPA auditing capabilities.
Pagination and Sorting: Leverage PagingAndSortingRepository for pagination (findAll(Pageable pageable)) and sorting (findAll(Sort sort)) of query results.

14.5 Spring Boot View and Caching

In Spring Boot, views are used to render the user interface for web applications. Typically, Spring Boot supports several view technologies out of the box, such as Thymeleaf, FreeMarker, and JSP (JavaServer Pages). Views in Spring Boot are responsible for presenting data to users in a format that can be rendered by web browsers.
Key Concepts of Spring Boot Views
View Resolver: A view resolver in Spring Boot maps view names returned by controllers to actual view templates. It resolves logical view names to physical view resources.
View Technologies
Thymeleaf: A modern server-side Java template engine for web and standalone environments. It provides a natural way to create HTML templates using expressions (th:text, th:if, etc.) embedded in HTML.
FreeMarker: A template engine that generates HTML web pages. It uses templates and data models to produce text output.
JSP (JavaServer Pages): A technology for developing web pages that support dynamic content. JSP files are compiled into servlets and executed on the server.
View Resolving Configuration: Configure view resolvers in Spring Boot's application configuration (application.properties or application.yml) to specify the prefix and suffix for view templates.
Example of Configuring Thymeleaf in Spring Boot
To configure Thymeleaf in a Spring Boot application
Dependency Configuration: Ensure that spring-boot-starter-thymeleaf dependency is included in your pom.xml or build.gradle file.
View Resolver Configuration: By default, Spring Boot configures Thymeleaf with sensible defaults, so minimal configuration is required. You can customize the template prefix, suffix, and other settings if needed.
Template Creation: Create Thymeleaf HTML templates (.html files) in the src/main/resources/templates directory. Use Thymeleaf expressions to bind data from the model to the view.
Example hello.html Thymeleaf template

```
<!DOCTYPE html>
<html xmlns:th="http://www.thymeleaf.org">
<head>
  <title>Spring Boot Thymeleaf Example</title>
</head>
<body>
  <h1>Hello, <span th:text="${name}">User</span>!</h1>
</body>
</html>
```

Controller Configuration: Create Spring MVC controllers that handle requests and return view names mapped to Thymeleaf templates.
Example controller:

```
@Controller
public class HelloController
{
  @GetMapping("/hello")
  public String hello(Model model)
{
    model.addAttribute("name", "John Doe");
    return "hello";
  }
}
```

Accessing Views: When a request is made to /hello, Spring Boot resolves the logical view name "hello" to hello.html Thymeleaf template and renders it with data from the model.

Spring Boot Caching

Caching in Spring Boot improves application performance by temporarily storing data that is frequently accessed or computationally expensive to retrieve. Spring Boot provides support for integrating caching mechanisms seamlessly into applications.

Key Concepts of Spring Boot Caching

Cache Abstraction: Spring Boot's cache abstraction provides a consistent way to use various caching solutions (EhCache, Redis, Caffeine, etc.) in Spring applications.

Annotations: Use caching annotations (@Cacheable, @CachePut, @CacheEvict, @Caching) to define caching behaviour at method level in service classes. These annotations allow developers to specify caching logic declaratively.

Cache Managers: Configure cache managers in Spring Boot application configuration (application.properties or application.yml) to define caching providers and their properties.

Example of Configuring Caching in Spring Boot

To configure caching in a Spring Boot application:

Dependency Configuration: Include dependencies such as spring-boot-starter-cache and a caching provider (spring-boot-starter-cache-caffeine, spring-boot-starter-cache-ehcache, etc.) in your project's build configuration.

Cache Manager Configuration: Define cache manager properties in application.properties or application.yml to specify caching provider settings.

Example application.properties configuration for Caffeine cache:

```
spring.cache.type=caffeine
spring.cache.caffeine.spec=maximumSize=100
```

Service Layer Configuration: Annotate methods in service classes with caching annotations (@Cacheable, @CachePut, etc.) to enable caching for specific methods.

Example service method using @Cacheable:

```
@Service
public class ProductService
 {
   @Cacheable("products")
   public Product getProductById(Long id)
{
      // Method implementation to fetch product by id from database
   }
}
```

Accessing Cached Data: When a method annotated with @Cacheable is called with the same arguments, Spring Boot checks the cache first. If the data is found in the cache, it is returned without executing the method. If not found, the method is executed, and the result is stored in the cache for future access.

14.5.1 Spring Boot and View Resolution

In Spring Boot, view resolution is the process of mapping logical view names returned by controllers to actual view templates that render the user interface for web applications. Spring Boot supports various view technologies out of the box, such as Thymeleaf, FreeMarker, and JSP (JavaServer Pages), making it flexible for developers to choose based on their preferences and project requirements.

Key Concepts of View Resolution in Spring Boot

ViewResolver Interface: In Spring Boot, the ViewResolver interface resolves the logical view names returned by controllers to actual view templates. It allows developers to define how view names are translated into view objects that render the response.

Supported View Technologies

Thymeleaf: A modern server-side Java template engine that supports natural template creation using expressions embedded in HTML. It is widely used for building web applications.

FreeMarker: A template engine that generates HTML web pages using templates and data models. It provides flexibility and extensibility for template customization.

JSP (JavaServer Pages): A technology for developing dynamic web pages that support both HTML and Java code. It integrates well with Java EE applications.

ViewResolver Configuration: Spring Boot simplifies view resolver configuration by providing sensible defaults for common scenarios. Developers can customize view resolver Behaviour through configuration properties or programmatically in Java configuration classes.

Example of Configuring Thymeleaf View Resolver in Spring Boot
To configure Thymeleaf as a view resolver in a Spring Boot application
Dependency Configuration: Include spring-boot-starter-thymeleaf dependency in your project's build configuration (pom.xml or build.gradle). This dependency includes Thymeleaf and its dependencies required for integration.
Template Directory Structure: Create Thymeleaf HTML templates (.html files) under the src/main/resources/templates directory. Thymeleaf templates use expressions (th:text, th:if, etc.) to bind data from the model to the view.
Example hello.html Thymeleaf template:

```
<!DOCTYPE html>
<html xmlns:th="http://www.thymeleaf.org">
<head>
   <title>Spring Boot Thymeleaf Example</title>
</head>
<body>
   <h1>Hello, <span th:text="${name}">User</span>!</h1>
</body>
</html>
```

Controller Configuration: Create Spring MVC controllers that handle requests and return view names mapped to Thymeleaf templates. The controller method populates model attributes used by the view.
Example controller

```
@Controller
public class HelloController {
   @GetMapping("/hello")
   public String hello(Model model)
  {
       model.addAttribute("name", "John Doe");
       return "hello"; // "hello" is the logical view name mapped to hello.html
   }
}
```

ViewResolver Properties: Optionally, customize Thymeleaf view resolver properties in application.properties or application.yml to configure template caching, prefix, suffix, etc.
Example application.properties configuration:

```
spring.thymeleaf.prefix=classpath:/templates/
spring.thymeleaf.suffix=.html
spring.thymeleaf.cache=false
```

Accessing Views: When a request is made to /hello, Spring Boot resolves the logical view name "hello" returned by the controller to hello.html Thymeleaf template. Thymeleaf processes the template, replaces expressions with actual data, and renders the HTML response.

Advanced View Resolution
Internationalization (i18n): Spring Boot supports internationalization of views by resolving locale-specific message bundles (messages.properties, messages_en.properties, etc.) and rendering localized content.
Error Handling: Customize error pages and views for handling exceptions and HTTP error responses (404 Not Found, 500 Internal Server Error, etc.) in Spring Boot applications.

14.5.2 Configuring a View Resolver

In Spring Boot, a view resolver is responsible for translating logical view names (returned by controllers) into actual view objects that render the response sent back to the client's browser. Spring Boot supports various view technologies like Thymeleaf, FreeMarker, JSP (JavaServer Pages), and others. Configuring a view resolver involves setting up the appropriate dependencies and configuring properties to define how views are resolved.

Steps to Configure a View Resolver:
Choose a View Technology: Decide which view technology you want to use (e.g., Thymeleaf, FreeMarker, JSP).
Dependency Configuration

Include the appropriate starter dependency for your chosen view technology in your project's build configuration (pom.xml for Maven or build.gradle for Gradle).

For example, to configure Thymeleaf, include spring-boot-starter-thymeleaf:

```
<!-- For Maven -->
<dependency>
  <groupId>org.springframework.boot</groupId>
  <artifactId>spring-boot-starter-thymeleaf</artifactId>
</dependency>
```

Template Directory Structure

For most view technologies, place your view templates (HTML, JSP, or FreeMarker templates) under the src/main/resources/templates directory. This directory is automatically picked up by Spring Boot for template resolution.

Configure View Resolver Properties

Spring Boot typically auto-configures view resolvers based on sensible defaults. However, you can customize view resolver properties in application.properties or application.yml if needed.

Example configuration for Thymeleaf in application.properties:

```
# Thymeleaf configuration
spring.thymeleaf.prefix=classpath:/templates/
spring.thymeleaf.suffix=.html
spring.thymeleaf.cache=false
```

Explanation:
spring.thymeleaf.prefix: Specifies the prefix that should be added to view names when building a URL to the template file.
spring.thymeleaf.suffix: Specifies the suffix that should be added to view names when building a URL to the template file.
spring.thymeleaf.cache: Specifies whether templates should be cached (set to false for development to see changes without restarts).

Controller Configuration
Create Spring MVC controllers that handle requests and return logical view names mapped to actual view templates.

```
@Controller
public class HomeController {
  @GetMapping("/home")
  public String home(Model model) {
    model.addAttribute("message", "Hello, Spring Boot!");
    return "home"; // "home" is the logical view name mapped to home.html
  }
}
```

Accessing Views
When a request is made to /home, Spring Boot resolves the logical view name "home" returned by the controller to home.html Thymeleaf template (assuming Thymeleaf is configured).
Thymeleaf processes the template, replaces expressions with actual data (like "Hello, Spring Boot!" in this case), and renders the HTML response sent to the client's browser.

Advanced View Resolution
Internationalization (i18n): Configure message bundles (messages.properties, messages_cn.properties, etc.) for internationalization support in views.
Error Handling: Customize error pages and views for handling exceptions and HTTP error responses (404 Not Found, 500 Internal Server Error, etc.).

14.5.3 Customizing View Resolution

In Spring Boot, view resolution customization involves configuring view resolvers to translate logical view names into actual view templates that render the user interface. This customization can include specifying template locations, view naming conventions, and integrating with different view technologies.

Steps to Customize View Resolution

Understanding View Resolvers

View resolvers in Spring Boot implement the ViewResolver interface, which resolves logical view names returned by controllers to actual view objects (templates).

By default, Spring Boot provides auto-configuration for common view technologies like Thymeleaf, FreeMarker, and JSP.

Custom View Resolver Configuration

To customize view resolution, you can define and configure your own view resolver beans in Spring Boot's application configuration.

Example: Custom Thymeleaf View Resolver

If you want to customize Thymeleaf view resolution, you can create a custom configuration class annotated with @Configuration and define a ViewResolver bean.

```
import org.springframework.context.annotation.Bean;
import org.springframework.context.annotation.Configuration;
import org.springframework.web.servlet.ViewResolver;
import org.thymeleaf.spring5.view.ThymeleafViewResolver;
import org.thymeleaf.spring5.templateresolver.SpringResourceTemplateResolver;
@Configuration
public class CustomThymeleafViewResolverConfig {
   @Bean
   public ViewResolver thymeleafViewResolver() {
      ThymeleafViewResolver resolver = new ThymeleafViewResolver();
      resolver.setTemplateEngine(templateEngine());
      resolver.setCharacterEncoding("UTF-8");
      resolver.setOrder(1); // Set view resolver order if multiple resolvers are configured
      return resolver;
   }
   @Bean
   public SpringResourceTemplateResolver templateResolver() {
      SpringResourceTemplateResolver resolver = new SpringResourceTemplateResolver();
      resolver.setPrefix("classpath:/templates/"); // Set template prefix
      resolver.setSuffix(".html"); // Set template suffix
      resolver.setTemplateMode("HTML");
      resolver.setCharacterEncoding("UTF-8");
      resolver.setCacheable(false); // Disable template caching for development
      return resolver;
   }
   // Other Thymeleaf template engine configurations, if needed
}
```

In this example

thymeleafViewResolver() method configures a ThymeleafViewResolver bean with a custom templateEngine() (not shown) and sets properties like character encoding and order.

templateResolver() method configures a SpringResourceTemplateResolver bean with properties such as template prefix (classpath:/templates/), suffix (.html), caching settings, and encoding.

Controller and View Usage

Create controllers that return logical view names mapped to actual view templates. Ensure that the logical view names match the configured prefixes and suffixes in your custom view resolver.

```
@Controller
public class HomeController {
   @GetMapping("/home")
   public String home(Model model) {
      model.addAttribute("message", "Hello, Spring Boot!");
      return "home"; // "home" is the logical view name mapped to home.html
```

```
    }
}
```

Advanced Customization

Integrating with Custom View Technologies: Extend Spring Boot's ViewResolver interface to integrate with custom view technologies or existing frameworks not supported out of the box.

Multi-View Resolver Configuration: Configure multiple view resolvers with different orders to handle specific view resolution scenarios (e.g., fallback views).

Benefits of Customizing View Resolution

Flexibility: Customize view resolution to fit specific project requirements, such as customizing template locations, naming conventions, and integrating with specialized view technologies.

Performance: Optimize view resolution performance by fine-tuning caching settings, template resolution strategies, and resource handling.

Integration: Seamlessly integrate Spring Boot with existing infrastructure and third-party libraries by extending or customizing view resolution mechanisms.

Best Practices for View Templates

Use of Template Engines

Choose a Suitable Template Engine: Select a template engine (e.g., Thymeleaf, FreeMarker) based on your project requirements and familiarity.

Leverage Template Features: Utilize template engine features like expression languages (th:, #{}, ${} in Thymeleaf) for dynamic content rendering and conditional display.

Organize Directory Structure

Standardize Template Locations: Place templates in a consistent directory structure (e.g., src/main/resources/templates/) to ease maintenance and navigation.

Separate Concerns: Maintain separate directories for different types of templates (e.g., layouts/, fragments/, partials/) to manage layout, partials, and reusable components.

Layouts and Fragments

Use Layout Templates: Implement layout templates (e.g., header, footer) to maintain a consistent user interface across pages.

Create Reusable Fragments: Extract reusable fragments (e.g., navigation bar, sidebar) into separate templates and include them across multiple pages.

Internationalization (i18n)

Externalize Textual Content: Externalize static textual content into message bundles (messages.properties, messages_en.properties) for easy localization and internationalization.

Utilize Message Resolution: Leverage template engine features (e.g., Thymeleaf's #{} or ${}) to resolve messages based on the current locale.

Template Inheritance and Composition

Use Template Inheritance: Employ template inheritance mechanisms provided by the template engine (e.g., Thymeleaf's th:replace, th:include) for modularization and reusability.

Avoid Redundancy: Refactor common code segments into parent templates and extend them in child templates to avoid duplication.

Optimize Performance

Enable Template Caching: Configure template caching (if applicable) to improve performance by reducing template parsing overhead.

Minimize Template Complexity: Keep templates lightweight and avoid excessive logic or business processing in views to maintain responsiveness.

Security Considerations

Escape User Input: Sanitize and escape user inputs rendered in templates to prevent cross-site scripting (XSS) vulnerabilities.

Avoid Dynamic Template Generation: Minimize dynamic template generation based on user input to mitigate security risks.

Testing and Validation

Unit Test Templates: Write unit tests to validate template rendering and Behaviour using testing frameworks like JUnit.

Integrate with UI Testing: Integrate template testing with end-to-end UI testing frameworks (e.g., Selenium) to ensure functional correctness.
Version Control and Collaboration
Use Version Control: Manage templates and related resources (e.g., CSS, JavaScript) using version control systems (e.g., Git) for versioning and collaboration.
Code Reviews: Conduct code reviews to ensure adherence to coding standards, template organization, and best practices.
Documentation and Maintenance
Document Template Structure: Document template structure, naming conventions, and usage guidelines to facilitate onboarding and maintenance for new team members.
Monitor and Refactor: Regularly monitor template performance and refactor as needed to optimize rendering speed and maintainability.

14.6 Caching in Spring Boot

Caching in Spring Boot involves storing and retrieving data from an in-memory cache to improve application performance. It leverages the cache abstraction provided by Spring Framework, which supports integration with various caching providers like EhCache, Redis, Caffeine, and others.
Key Concepts of Caching in Spring Boot
Cache Abstraction: Spring Boot's cache abstraction provides a consistent way to use different caching solutions without tying the application code to a specific implementation.
Annotations: Developers can annotate methods in Spring components (e.g., service classes, repository methods) with caching annotations to control caching Behaviour.
@Cacheable: Indicates that the result of invoking a method can be cached. Subsequent calls with the same arguments return the cached result without executing the method.
@CachePut: Updates the cache with the result of the method execution. It always executes the method and updates the cache with its result.
@CacheEvict: Removes entries from the cache, either before or after the method invocation, based on specified conditions.
Cache Managers: Spring Boot supports multiple cache managers (e.g., ConcurrentMapCacheManager for in-memory caching, EhCacheCacheManager for EhCache, RedisCacheManager for Redis) that manage the cache storage and retrieval process.
Configuration: Caching configuration in Spring Boot can be customized through properties in application.properties or application.yml, where developers define cache names, cache types, eviction policies, and TTL (time-to-live) settings.

Example of Using Caching in Spring Boot
Dependency Configuration: Include the appropriate caching starter dependency (spring-boot-starter-cache) in your project's build configuration (pom.xml or build.gradle).

```
<!-- For Maven -->
<dependency>
<groupId>org.springframework.boot</groupId>
<artifactId>spring-boot-starter-cache</artifactId>
</dependency>
```

Cache Manager Configuration: Configure a cache manager in application.properties or application.yml. Below is an example configuration for using the default ConcurrentMapCacheManager:

```
spring.cache.type=caffeine
spring.cache.caffeine.spec=maximumSize=100
```

Service Layer Example: Annotate methods in service classes with caching annotations to enable caching for specific methods.

```
import org.springframework.cache.annotation.Cacheable;
import org.springframework.stereotype.Service;
@Service
public class BookService {
   @Cacheable(value = "books", key = "#isbn")
   public Book findBookByIsbn(String isbn) {
      // Method implementation to fetch book details from database or external service
```

```
        return bookRepository.findByIsbn(isbn);
    }
}
```

In this example
@Cacheable(value = "books", key = "#isbn") annotates the findBookByIsbn method to cache results with key "books" and a dynamic key based on isbn parameter.
Subsequent calls to findBookByIsbn with the same isbn value retrieve cached results without executing the method, improving performance.
Accessing Cached Data: When findBookByIsbn is called with a new isbn, Spring Boot checks the cache (books) for a matching key. If found, it returns the cached Book object; otherwise, it executes the method to fetch data, stores it in the cache, and returns.

Benefits of Caching in Spring Boot
Improved Performance: Reduces response times by serving cached data instead of retrieving it from slower data sources.
Scalability: Handles increased application loads efficiently by reducing the number of database or external API calls.
Simplicity: Integrates caching seamlessly with existing Spring components using declarative annotations, minimizing boilerplate code.
Configurability: Allows customization of cache providers, eviction policies, and cache TTL to align with application requirements.

Using Cache Annotations
Spring Boot provides several cache annotations from the org.springframework.cache.annotation package, which simplify the implementation of caching logic in service methods or any Spring-managed beans.
Key Cache Annotations
@Cacheable Annotation
Use @Cacheable on a method to cache its results based on the method parameters.
Syntax: @Cacheable(value = "cacheName", key = "#parameter")
Parameters:
value: Specifies the name of the cache where results should be stored.
key: Defines the cache key. It can be a constant or a SpEL (Spring Expression Language) expression based on method parameters.

```
import org.springframework.cache.annotation.Cacheable;
import org.springframework.stereotype.Service;
@Service
public class BookService {
    @Cacheable(value = "booksCache", key = "#isbn")
    public Book findBookByIsbn(String isbn) {
        // Method implementation to fetch book details from database or external service
        return bookRepository.findByIsbn(isbn);
    }
}
```

In this example, the findBookByIsbn method caches the result in a cache named "booksCache" with a cache key based on the isbn parameter. Subsequent calls with the same isbn value retrieve the cached Book object without executing the method again.
@CachePut Annotation
Use @CachePut to update the cache with the result of the method execution.

Unlike @Cacheable, @CachePut always executes the method and updates the cache with its return value.

Syntax: @CachePut(value = "cacheName", key = "#parameter")

```
import org.springframework.cache.annotation.CachePut;
```

```
import org.springframework.stereotype.Service;
@Service
public class BookService {
  @CachePut(value = "booksCache", key = "#book.isbn")
  public Book updateBook(Book book) {
    // Method implementation to update book details in database or external service
    return bookRepository.save(book);
  }
}
```

In this example, the updateBook method updates the Book object in the database or external service and ensures that the updated object is also stored or updated in the "booksCache" cache.

@CacheEvict Annotation
Use @CacheEvict to remove one or more entries from the cache.
It can be applied before or after a method invocation, depending on the beforeInvocation attribute.
Syntax: @CacheEvict(value = "cacheName", key = "#parameter", allEntries = true/false, beforeInvocation = true/false)

```
import org.springframework.cache.annotation.CacheEvict;
import org.springframework.stereotype.Service;
@Service
public class BookService {
  @CacheEvict(value = "booksCache", key = "#isbn")
  public void evictBook(String isbn) {
    // Method implementation to delete book details from database or external service
    bookRepository.deleteByIsbn(isbn);
  }
}
```

In this example, the evictBook method removes the cached Book object with the specified isbn from the "booksCache" cache. The method's execution can be configured to occur beforeInvocation (default) or afterInvocation.

Additional Considerations
Conditional Caching: Use SpEL expressions (#result, #root.args, etc.) in cache annotations to customize cache keys dynamically based on method parameters or return values.
Cache Configuration: Configure cache providers (ConcurrentMapCacheManager, EhCacheCacheManager, etc.) and cache settings (expiration, eviction policies) in application.properties or application.yml.
Testing: Write unit tests to validate caching Behaviour using testing frameworks like JUnit, ensuring expected cache hits and misses.

Benefits of Using Cache Annotations
Simplicity: Declarative cache annotations reduce boilerplate code and simplify caching logic implementation.
Performance: Improves application performance by reducing the need to repeatedly fetch data from slower data sources.
Flexibility: Allows fine-grained control over caching Behaviour with options for caching, updating, and evicting entries based on method executions.

Exercise

Exercise 1- MCQ

1. What is the primary goal of Spring Boot?
a) To make it easier to deploy Spring applications on application servers.
b) To provide a comprehensive programming and configuration model for Java-based enterprise applications.
c) To simplify the development of new Spring applications with minimal configuration.
d) To enhance the security features of Spring applications.
2. Which file is commonly used to configure application properties in Spring Boot?
a) pom.xml
b) application.properties

c) web.xml
d) config.xml
3. How can you run a Spring Boot application?
a) By deploying it to a web server like Tomcat.
b) Using the java -jar command with the application's jar file.
c) Only through an IDE with a Spring Boot plugin.
d) Compiling the source code manually and running the main class.
4. What does AOP stand for in the context of Spring Boot?
a) Application Object Programming
b) Aspect-Oriented Programming
c) Advanced Option Processing
d) Application Oriented Protocol
5. Which annotation is used to mark a main class as a Spring Boot application?
a) @SpringBootApplication
b) @EnableAutoConfiguration
c) @SpringBootConfiguration
d) @ApplicationRunner
6. For database integration, Spring Boot prefers which approach to configure the data source?
a) XML configuration files
b) Java-based configuration
c) Automatically configuring DataSource using application properties
d) Manual configuration in each controller
7. Which of the following is a feature of Spring Boot?
a) Requires extensive XML configuration for setup.
b) Does not support embedded servers.
c) Automatic configuration based on classpath settings.
d) Limited support for RESTful services.
8. What is the role of @Repository in Spring Boot?
a) Marks a class as a service.
b) Indicates a DAO component in the persistence layer.
c) Specifies a class that performs CRUD operations on entities.
d) Both b and c are correct.
9. Which cache abstraction does Spring Boot provide by default?
a) EhCache
b) JCache
c) Caffeine
d) Spring's cache abstraction
10. How does Spring Boot simplify database migrations?
a) By using JDBC templates for database operations.
b) Through the integration with database migration tools like Flyway or Liquibase.
c) Requiring manual SQL scripts for each database change.
d) Database migrations are not supported in Spring Boot.

Exercise 2- True/False

1. Spring Boot eliminates the need for XML configuration.
2. Spring Boot applications can only be deployed on traditional web servers.
3. @EnableAutoConfiguration in Spring Boot automatically configures your application based on the dependencies you have added.
4. Spring Boot requires the manual setup of a DataSource bean for database operations.
5. Spring Boot AOP (Aspect-Oriented Programming) can only be applied to beans managed by the Spring container.
6. Spring Boot supports both SQL and NoSQL databases out of the box. True/False.
7. Properties in application.properties or application.yml can be overridden at runtime via environment variables.
8. Spring Boot's embedded server feature only supports Tomcat.
9. Spring Boot automatically enables caching for your application if it detects a cache provider on the classpath.

10. Database migrations in Spring Boot can be automated using tools like Flyway or Liquibase without additional configuration.

Exercise 3- Fill in the blanks

1. In Spring Boot, the primary file for externalizing configuration properties is named ___.
2. To enable the automatic configuration of Spring MVC in a Spring Boot application, use the annotation ___.
3. For integrating Aspect-Oriented Programming (AOP) in Spring Boot, one must include the dependency ___ in the project.
4. Spring Boot supports database migrations through tools like ___, which can be easily integrated.
5. To cache method results in Spring Boot, you can use the annotation ___ on the methods you want to cache.
6. Spring Boot is a framework that simplifies ________________ by providing pre-configured templates and auto-configuration.
7. The main advantages of using Spring Boot include rapid ________________ and reduced boilerplate code.
8. ___________ is a widely used caching provider that integrates seamlessly with Spring Boot applications.
9. Spring Boot applications can be easily deployed as ________________ or deployed in cloud environments using services like AWS or Azure.
10. Dependency injection in Spring Boot is facilitated through annotations like ________________, which automatically wires dependencies.

Exercise 4- Match Case

1. Simplifies application development by providing default configurations
2. Enables aspect-oriented programming support in Spring Boot applications
3. Framework used for seamless database integration in Spring Boot
4. Automatically configures your Spring application based on the dependencies present in the classpath

Exercise 5- One word answer

1. What Spring Boot annotation is used to automatically configure a web application based on dependencies?
2. Which Spring Boot feature simplifies the addition of a persistence layer?

Exercise 6- Small answer

1. Which Spring Boot annotation is used for dependency injection?
2. What is the name of the Spring Boot starter for using Spring MVC?

Exercise 7–Long answer

1. Explain how Spring Boot simplifies the deployment of web applications.
2. Describe the role of Spring Data JPA in Spring Boot applications and how it enhances data access layers.

Answer-

Exercise 1- 1) c 2) b 3) b 4) b 5) a 6) c 7) c 8) d 9) d 10) b
Exercise 2- 1) True 2) False 3) True 4) False 5) True 6) True 7) True 8) False 9) True 10) False
Exercise3-1) application.properties or application.yml 2) @EnableAutoConfiguration or SpringBootApplication 3) spring-boot-starter-aop 4) Flyway or Liquibase 5) @Cacheable 6) J ava-based enterprise 7) application development 8) EhCache 9) standalone executables (JAR files) 10) @Autowired
Exercise 4- 1 – C. Spring Boot
2 – D. @EnableAspectJAutoProxy
3 – B. Spring Data
4 – A. @EnableAutoConfiguration
Exercise 5- 1) @SpringBootApplication, 2) Spring Data JPA

Online Resources

Online Practice Paper

Link: https://forms.gle/pz5cTmGhH6c3Z4MK7
QR Code:

YouTube Video Link

Link: https://www.youtube.com/playlist?list=PLzlh_31VWEFqDZjADGB6Qv7N_VyGpuzXh
QR Code:

CHAPTER 15 - Advanced Web Services and Messaging

15.1 RESTful Web Services

RESTful Web Services represent a fundamental approach to designing APIs that are efficient, scalable, and interoperable in advanced Java applications. At its core, REST (Representational State Transfer) employs a resource-based architecture where every resource is uniquely identified by a URI (Uniform Resource Identifier). These resources are manipulated using standard HTTP methods:

GET to retrieve resource representations, POST to create new resources, PUT to update existing ones, and DELETE to remove them. This adherence to HTTP methods not only simplifies the API design but also ensures that operations align with the semantics of the web. RESTful services are stateless, meaning each request from a client to a server contains all necessary information for the server to fulfill it, promoting scalability and reliability in distributed systems.

The representation of resources in RESTful APIs commonly uses lightweight formats such as JSON (JavaScript Object Notation) or XML (eXtensible Markup Language), allowing for efficient data exchange between clients and servers. This choice of format optimizes network bandwidth usage and facilitates easy parsing and manipulation of data in client applications. Furthermore, REST encourages the use of hypermedia to drive application state (HATEOAS - Hypermedia as the Engine of Application State), where responses include links to related resources. This feature enables clients to dynamically navigate and discover available actions within the API without prior knowledge of the URIs, enhancing flexibility and usability.

In practical terms, designing a RESTful API involves defining clear and meaningful URIs that represent resources and their relationships. For instance, a banking application might have URIs like /accounts for managing accounts, /transactions for transaction history, and so forth. Each URI path should correspond to a resource, and HTTP methods should be chosen based on the desired operation:

GET for retrieving data, POST for creating new data, PUT for updating existing data, and DELETE for removing data.

The benefits of RESTful Web Services extend beyond simplicity and scalability. They promote loose coupling between clients and servers, enabling independent evolution and deployment of both components. This architecture is particularly suitable for microservices-based applications where each service can expose its functionality as a RESTful API, facilitating modularity, scalability, and ease of maintenance. Moreover, the use of standard HTTP methods and formats ensures broad compatibility with various client platforms, from traditional web applications to mobile devices and IoT (Internet of Things) devices.

Understanding RESTful principles and their application is crucial for developers working with advanced Java frameworks like Spring Boot. Such frameworks provide robust support for building and consuming RESTful APIs, offering features like annotation-driven controllers, automatic serialization/deserialization of JSON data, and integration with various testing and documentation tools. Mastery of RESTful concepts empowers developers to design APIs that are not only efficient and scalable but also capable of supporting the complex requirements of modern distributed applications.

15.1.1 Principles of RESTful Architecture

REST (Representational State Transfer) is an architectural style for designing networked applications. It emphasizes simplicity, scalability, and the use of standard protocols and formats. Understanding the principles of RESTful architecture is essential for designing efficient and interoperable APIs in advanced Java applications.

Client-Server Architecture

Principle: Separation of concerns between the client and server components.

Explanation: In RESTful architecture, the client and server are independent entities that interact through a uniform interface. The client initiates requests to the server, which processes them and returns responses. This separation allows clients and servers to evolve independently, enabling scalability and enhancing the overall system's flexibility.

Statelessness

Principle: Each request from a client to the server must contain all the information necessary to understand and fulfill the request.

Explanation: Servers do not store client state between requests. Instead, each request from the client must include all required data, such as authentication credentials or session information. This statelessness simplifies server implementation, improves reliability, and supports scalability in distributed systems.

Uniform Interface
Principle: A uniform and well-defined interface between clients and servers based on standard HTTP methods and resource representations.
Explanation: RESTful APIs use standard HTTP methods (GET, POST, PUT, DELETE) to perform operations on resources. Each resource is uniquely identified by a URI (Uniform Resource Identifier), and representations of resources are exchanged using standard formats like JSON (JavaScript Object Notation) or XML (eXtensible Markup Language). This uniformity simplifies client-server communication, enhances interoperability, and allows for the decoupling of clients and servers.
Resource-Based
Principle: Resources are key abstractions in RESTful architecture, and each resource is uniquely identified by a URI.
Explanation: Resources represent entities or concepts within the application, such as users, products, or data objects. Clients interact with these resources using CRUD (Create, Read, Update, Delete) operations through the appropriate HTTP methods. The use of URIs to identify resources promotes a hierarchical and logical organization of the API, facilitating navigation and discovery of available resources.
Representation of Resources
Principle: Resources are represented in a standardized format (e.g., JSON, XML) that can be exchanged between clients and servers.
Explanation: Representations of resources define their state and structure, allowing clients to understand and manipulate them. JSON has become the predominant format due to its simplicity, readability, and widespread support in web development. APIs provide representations of resources in responses, and clients send representations in requests, enabling data exchange in a consistent and interoperable manner.
Hypermedia as the Engine of Application State (HATEOAS)
Principle: Responses in RESTful APIs should include hypermedia links that allow clients to navigate and interact with related resources dynamically.
Explanation: HATEOAS enhances the flexibility and discoverability of APIs by including links to related resources within responses. Clients can navigate through the API by following these links, eliminating the need for prior knowledge of URI structures. This feature enables servers to evolve their APIs over time without breaking client implementations, promoting loose coupling and facilitating the integration of new functionality.

Benefits of RESTful Architecture
Simplicity: RESTful principles promote a straightforward design that is easy to understand and implement.
Scalability: Stateless communication and resource-based interactions support scalability in distributed systems.
Interoperability: Standardized interfaces and representations facilitate integration with diverse clients and platforms.
Flexibility: HATEOAS enhances API flexibility by allowing dynamic navigation and interaction with related resources.

15.2 Implementing RESTful Web Services in Java

RESTful Web Services in Java are typically implemented using frameworks like **Spring Boot**, which provide comprehensive support for building and deploying REST APIs efficiently. Here's a step-by-step explanation of how to implement RESTful services:
Choose a Framework
Spring Boot: It simplifies the setup and configuration of RESTful services with its auto-configuration features, embedded server support, and extensive libraries for handling HTTP requests, serialization, and more.
Define Resource Representation
POJOs (Plain Old Java Objects): Represent resources using Java classes annotated with frameworks like Jackson for JSON serialization. For example, a Product class might represent a product with attributes like id, name, and price.
Mapping URLs to Methods
Controller Annotations: Use annotations like @RestController and @RequestMapping to map HTTP requests to Java methods. For instance, @GetMapping("/products/{id}") maps a GET request to fetch a product by its ID.
Handle HTTP Methods
CRUD Operations: Implement methods annotated with @GetMapping, @PostMapping, @PutMapping, and @DeleteMapping for handling GET, POST, PUT, and DELETE operations respectively.

Data Persistence (Optional)
Database Integration: Use frameworks like Spring Data JPA or Hibernate to persist data to relational databases. Entities are mapped to database tables, and repositories provide CRUD operations.
Error Handling
Exception Handling: Implement @ControllerAdvice to handle exceptions gracefully and return appropriate HTTP status codes and error messages.
Testing
Unit Testing: Use tools like JUnit and Mockito to write unit tests for controller methods, ensuring correct Behaviour and error handling.
Example: Implementing a Product API with Spring Boot

```
@RestController
@RequestMapping("/api/products")
public class ProductController {
    @Autowired
    private ProductService productService;
    @GetMapping
    public List<Product> getAllProducts() {
        return productService.getAllProducts();
    }
    @GetMapping("/{id}")
    public ResponseEntity<Product> getProductById(@PathVariable Long id) {
        Product product = productService.getProductById(id);
        if (product != null) {
            return ResponseEntity.ok(product);
        } else {
            return ResponseEntity.notFound().build();
        }
    }
    @PostMapping
    public ResponseEntity<Product> createProduct(@RequestBody Product product) {
        Product createdProduct = productService.createProduct(product);
        return ResponseEntity.status(HttpStatus.CREATED).body(createdProduct);
    }
    @PutMapping("/{id}")
    public ResponseEntity<Product> updateProduct(@PathVariable Long id, @RequestBody Product product) {
        Product updatedProduct = productService.updateProduct(id, product);
        if (updatedProduct != null) {
            return ResponseEntity.ok(updatedProduct);
        } else {
            return ResponseEntity.notFound().build();
        }
    }
    @DeleteMapping("/{id}")
    public ResponseEntity<Void> deleteProduct(@PathVariable Long id) {
        productService.deleteProduct(id);
        return ResponseEntity.noContent().build();
    }
}
```

In this example, the ProductController class defines endpoints (/api/products) for CRUD operations on products. Annotations like @GetMapping, @PostMapping, @PutMapping, and @DeleteMapping map HTTP methods to Java methods, handling requests to fetch, create, update, and delete products.

Best Practices
Use DTOs (Data Transfer Objects): Transfer data between client and server to avoid exposing internal entity structures.

Versioning: Implement versioning strategies (e.g., URI versioning, request headers) to manage API changes over time.
Security: Secure APIs using mechanisms like HTTPS, OAuth, and role-based access control.

15.3 Building RESTful Services in Java

RESTful services in Java are commonly implemented using frameworks like **Spring Boot** due to their robust support for creating scalable and maintainable APIs. Below are the key steps and considerations when building RESTful services:
Setup and Configuration
Choose a Framework**:** Select a framework that supports RESTful service development. Spring Boot is widely used for its simplicity and extensive feature set, including auto-configuration and embedded server capabilities.
Project Setup**:** Initialize a new Spring Boot project using tools like Maven or Gradle. Include dependencies for web, data access (if needed), and JSON serialization libraries like Jackson.
Define Resource Representation
POJOs (Plain Old Java Objects): Define Java classes to represent resources in your application. These classes encapsulate data fields and may include annotations for JSON serialization/deserialization.

```
public class Product {
private Long id;
private String name;
private double price;
// Getters and setters
}
```

Create Controller Classes
RestController Annotation: Annotate controller classes with @RestController to mark them as RESTful controllers. Use @RequestMapping and HTTP method annotations (@GetMapping, @PostMapping, @PutMapping, @DeleteMapping) to define endpoint mappings.

```
@RestController
@RequestMapping("/api/products")
public class ProductController {
  @Autowired
  private ProductService productService;
  @GetMapping
  public List<Product> getAllProducts() {
    return productService.getAllProducts();
  }
  @GetMapping("/{id}")
  public ResponseEntity<Product> getProductById(@PathVariable Long id) {
    Product product = productService.getProductById(id);
    if (product != null) {
      return ResponseEntity.ok(product);
    } else {
      return ResponseEntity.notFound().build();
    }
  }
  @PostMapping
  public ResponseEntity<Product> createProduct(@RequestBody Product product) {
    Product createdProduct = productService.createProduct(product);
    return ResponseEntity.status(HttpStatus.CREATED).body(createdProduct);
  }
  @PutMapping("/{id}")
  public ResponseEntity<Product> updateProduct(@PathVariable Long id, @RequestBody Product product) {
    Product updatedProduct = productService.updateProduct(id, product);
    if (updatedProduct != null) {
      return ResponseEntity.ok(updatedProduct);
    } else {
```

```
            return ResponseEntity.notFound().build();
        }
    }
    @DeleteMapping("/{id}")
    public ResponseEntity<Void> deleteProduct(@PathVariable Long id) {
        productService.deleteProduct(id);
        return ResponseEntity.noContent().build();
    }
}
```

Service Layer

Business Logic: Implement service classes (ProductService in the example above) to encapsulate business logic and interact with data repositories or external systems.

```
@Service
public class ProductService {
    @Autowired
    private ProductRepository productRepository;
    public List<Product> getAllProducts() {
        return productRepository.findAll();
    }
    public Product getProductById(Long id) {
        return productRepository.findById(id).orElse(null);
    }
    public Product createProduct(Product product) {
        return productRepository.save(product);
    }
    public Product updateProduct(Long id, Product product) {
        if (productRepository.existsById(id)) {
            product.setId(id);
            return productRepository.save(product);
        }
        return null;
    }
    public void deleteProduct(Long id) {
        productRepository.deleteById(id);
    }
}
```

Data Access (Optional)

Repository Layer: Use Spring Data repositories or Hibernate/JPA for data access and persistence. Repositories provide CRUD operations and query methods to interact with databases.

```
@Repository
public interface ProductRepository extends JpaRepository<Product, Long> {
// Custom query methods if needed
}
```

Error Handling

Exception Handling: Implement global exception handlers (@ControllerAdvice) to manage and return appropriate HTTP status codes and error messages for different scenarios.

Testing

Unit Testing: Write unit tests using frameworks like JUnit and Mockito to validate controller methods, service layer logic, and repository interactions.

Best Practices

Use DTOs (Data Transfer Objects)**:** Transfer data between client and server to avoid exposing internal entity structures.

Security: Implement security measures such as HTTPS, OAuth, and input validation to protect APIs from unauthorized access and malicious attacks.

Documentation: Use tools like Swagger to generate API documentation automatically, ensuring clarity and ease of use for API consumers.

15.3.1 Understanding RESTful Principles

REST (Representational State Transfer) is an architectural style for designing networked applications. It relies on a stateless, client-server, cacheable communications protocol -- the HTTP. RESTful applications use HTTP requests to perform CRUD (Create, Read, Update, Delete) operations on resources.

Resources and Resource Identification

Resources: In REST, resources are the key abstractions. A resource is an object or representation of something, which has data, relationships to other resources, and methods that operate on it. Examples include users, orders, and products.

Resource Identification: Each resource is identified by a URI (Uniform Resource Identifier). For example:
GET /users/{userId}

HTTP Methods

REST uses standard HTTP methods to perform operations on resources:

GET: Retrieve a resource.
POST: Create a new resource.
PUT: Update an existing resource.
DELETE: Remove a resource.
PATCH: Partially update an existing resource.

Statelessness

Each HTTP request from a client to the server must contain all the information the server needs to fulfill the request. The server should not store any context information from previous requests. This makes RESTful applications scalable and easier to maintain.

Client-Server Architecture

The client and server are independent. Clients interact with the resources by using URIs, and servers handle the requests. This separation of concerns allows for the independent evolution of client and server components.

Cacheability

Responses from the server must explicitly state whether they are cacheable or not. If a response is cacheable, clients can reuse that response data for subsequent requests, reducing the need for repeated fetching from the server.

Layered System

A RESTful system can have multiple layers, such as security layers, load balancing layers, and gateways. Each layer interacts only with the adjacent layer, allowing for better scalability and manageability.

Uniform Interface

The uniform interface simplifies the architecture and decouples the implementation of clients and servers. It includes:

Identification of resources: URIs.
Manipulation of resources through representations: Using JSON or XML.
Self-descriptive messages: Including metadata to describe how to process the message.
Hypermedia as the engine of application state (HATEOAS): Clients interact with resources entirely through hypermedia provided dynamically by applications.

Implementing RESTful Services with Spring Framework

Setting Up Spring REST Controller

In Spring, you can use the @RestController annotation to create RESTful web services.

```
import org.springframework.web.bind.annotation.*;
@RestController
@RequestMapping("/users")
public class UserController {
  @GetMapping("/{id}")
  public User getUser(@PathVariable Long id) {
    // Retrieve user by id
  }
  @PostMapping
  public User createUser(@RequestBody User user) {
```

```
        // Create a new user
    }
    @PutMapping("/{id}")
    public User updateUser(@PathVariable Long id, @RequestBody User user) {
        // Update existing user
    }
    @DeleteMapping("/{id}")
    public void deleteUser(@PathVariable Long id) {
        // Delete user by id
    }
}
```

Handling JSON Responses

Spring uses the Jackson library by default to handle JSON data. You can configure it further if needed.

```
import com.fasterxml.jackson.annotation.JsonProperty;
public class User {
    @JsonProperty("id")
    private Long id;
    @JsonProperty("name")
    private String name;
    // Getters and setters
}
```

Integrating Hibernate for Persistence

To integrate Hibernate for database operations, define your entities and repositories.

Entity Definition

```
import javax.persistence.*;
@Entity
@Table(name = "users")
public class User
{
    @Id
    @GeneratedValue(strategy = GenerationType.IDENTITY)
    private Long id;
    @Column(name = "name")
    private String name;
    // Getters and setters
}
```

Repository Definition

```
import org.springframework.data.jpa.repository.JpaRepository;
public interface UserRepository extends JpaRepository<User, Long> {
}
```

Service Layer

```
import org.springframework.beans.factory.annotation.Autowired;
import org.springframework.stereotype.Service;
import java.util.List;
@Service
public class UserService {
    @Autowired
    private UserRepository userRepository;
    public User getUser(Long id) {
        return userRepository.findById(id).orElse(null);
    }
    public User createUser(User user) {
```

```
        return userRepository.save(user);
    }
    public User updateUser(Long id, User user) {
        if (userRepository.existsById(id)) {
            user.setId(id);
            return userRepository.save(user);
        }
        return null;
    }
    public void deleteUser(Long id) {
        userRepository.deleteById(id);
    }
}
```

15.3.2 Choosing a Framework

Frameworks simplify application development by providing pre-built functionalities, enforcing best practices, and facilitating code reuse. When choosing a framework, consider the following factors:

Project Requirements

Complexity: Assess the complexity of the project. For simple applications, lightweight frameworks like Spring Boot may be sufficient. For complex enterprise applications, you might need the full Spring Framework or Java EE.

Domain: Different frameworks excel in different domains. For web applications, consider Spring MVC or JSF. For data-intensive applications, Hibernate might be more appropriate.

Community and Support

Community Size: A large and active community can be a significant advantage, providing access to a wealth of shared knowledge, third-party tools, and extensions.

Documentation: Comprehensive and well-maintained documentation is crucial for smooth development.

Support: Evaluate the availability of professional support if required.

Learning Curve

Ease of Learning: Consider how steep the learning curve is for the framework. This can affect development time and the ease of onboarding new developers.

Existing Skills: Assess the existing skills of your team. Leveraging a framework that your team is already familiar with can save significant training time.

Performance and Scalability

Performance: Analyze the performance characteristics of the framework. For high-performance requirements, investigate frameworks known for their efficiency.

Scalability: Ensure the framework supports scalable architecture to accommodate future growth.

Integration and Compatibility

Integration: Check how well the framework integrates with other tools and technologies you plan to use (e.g., databases, messaging systems, front-end frameworks).

Compatibility: Ensure compatibility with existing systems and libraries you might need to integrate.

Popular Java Frameworks

Spring Framework

Overview: Spring is a comprehensive framework for enterprise Java development. It provides extensive support for building web applications, managing security, and handling transactions.

Modules: Includes Spring MVC for web applications, Spring Boot for simplified configuration, Spring Data for data access, and Spring Security for security.

Advantages

Large ecosystem with extensive third-party support.

Modular and flexible, allowing you to use only the parts you need.

Excellent documentation and community support.

Disadvantages

Can be complex and have a steep learning curve.

Configuration can be verbose, although Spring Boot helps alleviate this.

Hibernate

Overview: Hibernate is an ORM (Object-Relational Mapping) framework that simplifies database interactions by mapping Java objects to database tables.

Features

Automatic SQL generation.

Caching support for performance optimization.

HQL (Hibernate Query Language) for object-oriented querying.

Advantages

Simplifies database operations and reduces boilerplate code.

Supports complex queries and relationships.

Integrates well with Spring.

Disadvantages

Can introduce performance overhead.

Learning curve for mastering ORM concepts and performance tuning.

JavaServer Faces (JSF)

Overview: JSF is a component-based framework for building user interfaces for web applications.

Features

UI components with event-driven programming model.

Integrated with Java EE for enterprise features.

Advantages

Simplifies the development of complex UIs.

Rich set of UI components.

Disadvantages

Can be heavy-weight for simple applications.

Less popular than some other frameworks, leading to fewer resources and community support.

Play Framework

Overview: Play is a reactive web framework that uses a stateless architecture and is built on Akka.

Features

Asynchronous I/O for high scalability.

Hot-reloading for quick development cycles.

Advantages

High performance and scalability.

Modern development practices.

Disadvantages

Smaller community compared to Spring.

Can be overkill for simple applications.

Micronaut

Overview: Micronaut is a modern JVM-based framework designed for building modular and microservice-based applications.

Features

Low memory footprint and fast startup time.

Built-in support for service discovery, distributed configuration, and client-side load balancing.

Advantages

Ideal for microservices and serverless applications.

Annotation-driven, similar to Spring but with improved performance.

Disadvantages

Newer and less mature than Spring.

Smaller ecosystem and community.

Decision-Making Process

Define Requirements: Clearly outline the project requirements, including performance, scalability, and complexity.

Evaluate Options: Compare frameworks based on the factors discussed above.

Prototype: Develop a small prototype using the shortlisted frameworks to assess their suitability.
Feedback and Iteration: Gather feedback from the team and iterate on the decision if necessary.
Make an Informed Decision: Choose the framework that best aligns with your project's needs and your team's expertise.

15.3.3 Building RESTful Services with Spring Boot

Building RESTful services with Spring Boot is an essential skill for modern Java developers. Spring Boot simplifies the creation of production-ready applications by providing a convention-over-configuration approach. Here's a detailed guide for your advanced Java book:

Building RESTful Services with Spring Boot

Introduction to Spring Boot

Spring Boot is a framework built on top of the Spring Framework. It simplifies the development of Java applications by providing a set of conventions and reducing the need for boilerplate code. Key features include:
Auto-configuration: Automatically configures Spring applications based on the dependencies you add.
Embedded servers: Comes with embedded Tomcat, Jetty, or Undertow servers, eliminating the need for external server configuration.
Production-ready features: Includes metrics, health checks, and externalized configuration.

Setting Up a Spring Boot Project

You can create a Spring Boot project using Spring Initialiser, which is an online tool for generating Spring Boot projects.
Using Spring Initialiser:
Go to Spring Initialiser.
Select your project settings (e.g., Maven Project, Java, and the desired Spring Boot version).
Add dependencies like Spring Web, Spring Data JPA, and H2 Database.
Generate the project and download the ZIP file.
Unzip the file and import it into your IDE (e.g., IntelliJ IDEA, Eclipse).

Creating a RESTful Web Service

Let's build a simple RESTful service for managing a list of users.
Project Structure

```
src/
├── main/
│   ├── java/
│   │   └── com/example/demo/
│   │       ├── DemoApplication.java
│   │       ├── controller/
│   │       │   └── UserController.java
│   │       ├── model/
│   │       │   └── User.java
│   │       ├── repository/
│   │       │   └── UserRepository.java
│   │       └── service/
│   │           └── UserService.java
│   └── resources/
│       ├── application.properties
│       └── data.sql
└── test/
    └── java/
        └── com/example/demo/
            └── DemoApplicationTests.java
```

DemoApplication.java

```
package com.example.demo;
import org.springframework.boot.SpringApplication;
import org.springframework.boot.autoconfigure.SpringBootApplication;
@SpringBootApplication
public class DemoApplication {
```

```
    public static void main(String[] args) {
        SpringApplication.run(DemoApplication.class, args);
    }
}
```

User.java (Model)

```
package com.example.demo.model;
import javax.persistence.*;
@Entity
public class User {
    @Id
    @GeneratedValue(strategy = GenerationType.IDENTITY)
    private Long id;
    private String name;
    private String email;
    // Getters and setters
}
```

UserRepository.java

```
package com.example.demo.repository;
import com.example.demo.model.User;
import org.springframework.data.jpa.repository.JpaRepository;
public interface UserRepository extends JpaRepository<User, Long> {
}
```

UserService.java

```
package com.example.demo.service;
import com.example.demo.model.User;
import com.example.demo.repository.UserRepository;
import org.springframework.beans.factory.annotation.Autowired;
import org.springframework.stereotype.Service;
import java.util.List;
@Service
public class UserService {
    @Autowired
    private UserRepository userRepository;

    public List<User> getAllUsers() {
        return userRepository.findAll();
    }
    public User getUserById(Long id) {
        return userRepository.findById(id).orElse(null);
    }
    public User createUser(User user) {
        return userRepository.save(user);
    }
    public User updateUser(Long id, User user) {
        if (userRepository.existsById(id)) {
            user.setId(id);
            return userRepository.save(user);
        }
        return null;
    }
    public void deleteUser(Long id) {
        userRepository.deleteById(id);
    }
}
```

UserController.java

```
package com.example.demo.controller;
import com.example.demo.model.User;
import com.example.demo.service.UserService;
import org.springframework.beans.factory.annotation.Autowired;
import org.springframework.http.ResponseEntity;
import org.springframework.web.bind.annotation.*;
import java.util.List;
@RestController
@RequestMapping("/users")
public class UserController {
   @Autowired
   private UserService userService;
   @GetMapping
   public List<User> getAllUsers() {
      return userService.getAllUsers();
   }
   @GetMapping("/{id}")
   public ResponseEntity<User> getUserById(@PathVariable Long id) {
      User user = userService.getUserById(id);
      if (user == null) {
         return ResponseEntity.notFound().build();
      }
      return ResponseEntity.ok(user);
   }
   @PostMapping
   public User createUser(@RequestBody User user) {
      return userService.createUser(user);
   }
   @PutMapping("/{id}")
   public ResponseEntity<User> updateUser(@PathVariable Long id, @RequestBody User user) {
      User updatedUser = userService.updateUser(id, user);
      if (updatedUser == null) {
         return ResponseEntity.notFound().build();
      }
      return ResponseEntity.ok(updatedUser);
   }
   @DeleteMapping("/{id}")
   public ResponseEntity<Void> deleteUser(@PathVariable Long id) {
      userService.deleteUser(id);
      return ResponseEntity.noContent().build();
   }
}
```

Configuration

application.properties**:**

```
spring.datasource.url=jdbc:h2:mem:testdb
spring.datasource.driverClassName=org.h2.Driver
spring.datasource.username=sa
spring.datasource.password=password
spring.jpa.database-platform=org.hibernate.dialect.H2Dialect
spring.h2.console.enabled=true
```

Database Initialization

data.sql**:**

```
INSERT INTO USER (NAME, EMAIL) VALUES ('John Doe', 'john.doe@example.com');
INSERT INTO USER (NAME, EMAIL) VALUES ('Jane Smith', 'jane.smith@example.com');
```

Running the Application
Run the DemoApplication class as a Java application. Spring Boot will start the embedded Tomcat server and initialize the database with the data provided in data.sql.
Testing the RESTful Service
Use tools like curl, Postman, or a web browser to test the endpoints.
Create a User:

```
POST /users
Content-Type: application/json
{
  "name": "Alice Johnson",
  "email": "alice.johnson@example.com"
}
```

15.3 Java Message Service (JMS)

Java Message Service (JMS) is a Java API that allows applications to create, send, receive, and read messages in a reliable and asynchronous manner. It provides a way for Java applications to communicate with each other and with non-Java applications using messaging systems. JMS is part of the Java Platform, Enterprise Edition (Java EE), and facilitates the integration of heterogeneous enterprise systems by enabling loosely coupled, reliable, and scalable communication.
JMS supports two primary messaging models: point-to-point (PTP) and publish/subscribe (Pub/Sub). In the point-to-point model, messages are sent to a specific queue, where they are held until the receiving application retrieves them. This model is useful for scenarios where each message must be processed by a single consumer, such as order processing systems. The publish/subscribe model, on the other hand, allows messages to be broadcast to multiple subscribers via topics. This is ideal for applications where messages need to be distributed to multiple consumers, such as news feeds or stock price updates.
JMS ensures reliable communication through several key features. It supports synchronous and asynchronous message delivery, ensuring that messages are delivered and processed even in the event of failures. It also provides message persistence, enabling messages to be stored in a message store until they are successfully processed. Additionally, JMS supports transactions, allowing multiple message operations to be grouped into a single unit of work, which can be committed or rolled back together.
JMS is widely used in enterprise applications for integrating various components and systems, enabling event-driven architectures, and decoupling components to improve scalability and flexibility. With JMS, developers can build robust and scalable messaging solutions that facilitate seamless communication across diverse systems and platforms, enhancing the overall efficiency and reliability of enterprise applications.
Core Concepts of JMS
Understanding the core concepts of Java Message Service (JMS) is essential for developing robust messaging solutions in enterprise applications. Here are the key concepts that form the foundation of JMS:
Message-Oriented Middleware (MOM)

JMS is a specification for message-oriented middleware that facilitates communication between different components of a distributed application. MOM allows applications to exchange messages asynchronously, ensuring loose coupling and reliable communication.

MS Providers and Clients
JMS Provider: A messaging system that implements the JMS interface and manages the communication infrastructure. Examples include Apache ActiveMQ, IBM MQ, and RabbitMQ.
JMS Client: Any Java application or component that produces or consumes messages. JMS clients interact with the JMS provider to send and receive messages.
JMS Destinations

JMS uses destinations to specify the target for messages. There are two types of destinations:

Queue: Used in the point-to-point (PTP) messaging model. A queue holds messages until they are consumed by a single consumer.
Topic: Used in the publish/subscribe (Pub/Sub) messaging model. A topic broadcasts messages to all subscribed consumers.

Messages

JMS messages are objects that consist of three parts:

Header: Contains metadata about the message, such as destination, delivery mode, priority, and expiration.
Properties: Custom name-value pairs that can be used for message filtering and selection.
Body: The actual content of the message. JMS defines five message types based on the body content:
TextMessage: Contains a string.
MapMessage: Contains a set of key-value pairs.
BytesMessage: Contains an array of bytes.
StreamMessage: Contains a stream of Java primitive values.
ObjectMessage: Contains a serialized Java object.

Producers and Consumers

Message Producer: A JMS client that creates and sends messages to a destination.
Message Consumer: A JMS client that receives and processes messages from a destination. Consumers can operate in synchronous mode, where they explicitly fetch messages, or asynchronous mode, where a message listener handles incoming messages.

Connection and Session

Connection: Represents an active connection to the JMS provider. It encapsulates the underlying transport protocol and is used to create sessions.
Session: A single-threaded context for producing and consuming messages. Sessions ensure message ordering and transaction management. They can be transacted or non-transacted, and they provide methods for creating message producers, consumers, and destinations.

Message Acknowledgment

JMS provides different modes for acknowledging message receipt:

AUTO_ACKNOWLEDGE: The session automatically acknowledges the receipt of a message once it has been successfully processed.
CLIENT_ACKNOWLEDGE: The client explicitly acknowledges the receipt of messages.
DUPS_OK_ACKNOWLEDGE: The session lazily acknowledges the receipt of messages, which may result in duplicate messages.
TRANSACTED: Messages are acknowledged as part of a transaction, ensuring that all messages are processed successfully before acknowledgment.

Durable and Non-Durable Subscriptions

In the Pub/Sub model, subscriptions can be durable or non-durable:

Durable Subscription: Ensures that a subscriber receives all messages published to a topic, even if the subscriber is temporarily disconnected.
Non-Durable Subscription: The subscriber only receives messages while it is actively subscribed.

Message Selectors

Message selectors are SQL-like expressions that allow consumers to filter messages based on message headers and properties. This enables selective message processing based on specific criteria.

Transactions

JMS supports transactions, allowing multiple message operations to be grouped into a single unit of work. Transactions ensure that all operations are either committed successfully or rolled back in case of failure, providing reliability and consistency.

15.4.1 JMS Messaging Models

Java Message Service (JMS) supports two primary messaging models: point-to-point (PTP) and publish/subscribe (Pub/Sub). These models define how messages are produced, delivered, and consumed, catering to different use cases and communication patterns in distributed applications.

1. Point-to-Point (PTP) Model

In the point-to-point (PTP) messaging model, messages are sent to a specific queue, and each message is consumed by exactly one receiver. This model is suitable for scenarios where each message needs to be processed by only one consumer, ensuring reliable and ordered delivery of messages.

Key Concepts

Queue: The destination where messages are sent. A queue holds messages until they are consumed by a receiver.
Message Producer: The component that creates and sends messages to a queue.
Message Consumer: The component that receives and processes messages from a queue.

Characteristics
One-to-One Communication: Each message is delivered to a single consumer.
Message Retention: Messages remain in the queue until they are consumed or expire.
Load Balancing: Multiple consumers can be attached to a queue, and the JMS provider distributes the messages among the available consumers, providing load balancing.
Use Cases
Task scheduling systems.
Order processing systems.
Any scenario requiring reliable, one-to-one communication between components.
Example

```
// Creating a queue
Queue queue = session.createQueue("exampleQueue");
// Creating a message producer
MessageProducer producer = session.createProducer(queue);
// Creating a message consumer
MessageConsumer consumer = session.createConsumer(queue);
```

Publish/Subscribe (Pub/Sub) Model
In the publish/subscribe (Pub/Sub) messaging model, messages are sent to a topic, and multiple subscribers can receive the messages. This model is suitable for scenarios where messages need to be broadcast to multiple consumers simultaneously.
Key Concepts
Topic: The destination where messages are sent. A topic broadcasts messages to all subscribed consumers.
Publisher: The component that creates and sends messages to a topic.
Subscriber: The component that receives and processes messages from a topic.
Characteristics
One-to-Many Communication: Each message is delivered to all active subscribers.
Durable Subscriptions: Subscribers can register as durable, ensuring they receive all messages published while they are subscribed, even if they are temporarily disconnected.
Non-Durable Subscriptions: Subscribers receive messages only while they are actively connected to the topic.
Use Cases
News distribution systems.
Stock price updates.
Any scenario requiring broadcast communication to multiple recipients.
Example

```
// Creating a topic
Topic topic = session.createTopic("exampleTopic");
// Creating a publisher
MessageProducer producer = session.createProducer(topic);
// Creating a subscriber
MessageConsumer subscriber = session.createConsumer(topic);
```

15.4.2 Implementing JMS in Java Applications

Implementing Java Message Service (JMS) in Java applications involves setting up the messaging infrastructure, configuring connections, and writing code to produce and consume messages. This section will guide you through the steps necessary to implement JMS in a Java application, using Apache ActiveMQ as the JMS provider.
Setting Up the JMS Provider
First, you need a JMS provider. Apache ActiveMQ is a popular, open-source JMS provider.
Download and Install ActiveMQ:
Download ActiveMQ from the official website.
Extract the downloaded archive.
Start the ActiveMQ server by running the following command from the ActiveMQ directory

```
bin/activemq start
```

The default web console is available at http://localhost:8161/admin (username: admin, password: admin).
Adding JMS Dependencies
Add the necessary dependencies to your pom.xml file if you are using Maven:

```xml
<dependency>
   <groupId>org.apache.activemq</groupId>
   <artifactId>activemq-all</artifactId>
   <version>5.16.3</version>
</dependency>
```

For Gradle, add the following to your build.gradle file:

```
implementation 'org.apache.activemq:activemq-all:5.16.3'
```

Configuring JMS Connection

Create a connection to the JMS provider. The ConnectionFactory class is used to create connections to the JMS provider.

Example Code:

```java
import javax.jms.Connection;
import javax.jms.ConnectionFactory;
import javax.jms.JMSException;
import javax.jms.Session;
import org.apache.activemq.ActiveMQConnectionFactory;
public class JMSConfig {
   private static final String BROKER_URL = "tcp://localhost:61616";
   private static final String USERNAME = "admin";
   private static final String PASSWORD = "admin";
   public static Connection createConnection() throws JMSException {
      ConnectionFactory factory = new ActiveMQConnectionFactory(BROKER_URL);
      Connection connection = factory.createConnection(USERNAME, PASSWORD);
      connection.start();
      return connection;
   }
   public static Session createSession(Connection connection) throws JMSException {
      return connection.createSession(false, Session.AUTO_ACKNOWLEDGE);
   }
}
```

Creating a Message Producer

A message producer sends messages to a specific destination (queue or topic).

Example Code:

```java
import javax.jms.MessageProducer;
import javax.jms.Queue;
import javax.jms.Session;
import javax.jms.TextMessage;
public class JMSProducer {
   public static void main(String[] args) {
      try {
         Connection connection = JMSConfig.createConnection();
         Session session = JMSConfig.createSession(connection);

         Queue queue = session.createQueue("exampleQueue");
         MessageProducer producer = session.createProducer(queue);
         TextMessage message = session.createTextMessage("Hello, JMS!");
         producer.send(message);
         System.out.println("Message sent: " + message.getText());
         session.close();
         connection.close();
      } catch (JMSException e) {
         e.printStackTrace();
      }
   }
}
```

Creating a Message Consumer

A message consumer receives messages from a specific destination.

Example Code:

```
import javax.jms.MessageConsumer;
import javax.jms.Message;
import javax.jms.Queue;
import javax.jms.Session;
import javax.jms.TextMessage;
public class JMSConsumer {
   public static void main(String[] args) {
      try {
         Connection connection = JMSConfig.createConnection();
         Session session = JMSConfig.createSession(connection);
         Queue queue = session.createQueue("exampleQueue");
         MessageConsumer consumer = session.createConsumer(queue);
         Message message = consumer.receive();
         if (message instanceof TextMessage) {
            TextMessage textMessage = (TextMessage) message;
            System.out.println("Message received: " + textMessage.getText());
         }
         session.close();
         connection.close();
      } catch (JMSException e) {
         e.printStackTrace();
      }
   }
}
```

Handling JMS Exceptions

JMS exceptions (JMSException) should be properly handled to ensure the application can recover from errors. Consider implementing retry mechanisms and proper logging.

Example Code

```
public class JMSUtil {
   public static void handleJMSException(JMSException e) {
      e.printStackTrace();
      // Add logging and retry mechanisms here
   }
}
```

Integration with Spring

For a more comprehensive approach, consider integrating JMS with Spring, which simplifies JMS configuration and provides additional features like message converters, JMS templates, and integration with other Spring components.

Example Code:

```
import org.springframework.context.annotation.Bean;
import org.springframework.context.annotation.Configuration;
import org.springframework.jms.annotation.EnableJms;
import org.springframework.jms.core.JmsTemplate;
import org.apache.activemq.ActiveMQConnectionFactory;
@Configuration
@EnableJms
public class JMSConfig {
   private static final String BROKER_URL = "tcp://localhost:61616";
   @Bean
   public ActiveMQConnectionFactory connectionFactory() {
      ActiveMQConnectionFactory factory = new ActiveMQConnectionFactory();
      factory.setBrokerURL(BROKER_URL);
      return factory; }
```

```
    @Bean
    public JmsTemplate jmsTemplate() {
        return new JmsTemplate(connectionFactory());
    }
}
```

15.5 JMS API and Messaging Domains

The Java Message Service (JMS) API is a Java API that enables applications to create, send, receive, and read messages in a reliable and asynchronous manner. It serves as a critical component for building enterprise-level, message-oriented middleware systems. JMS provides a standardized way to implement messaging solutions, ensuring interoperability between different JMS providers and easing the development of robust, scalable applications.

JMS defines two primary messaging domains: point-to-point (PTP) and publish/subscribe (Pub/Sub). The point-to-point domain is based on the concept of queues. In this model, messages are sent to a specific queue and are consumed by a single receiver. Each message is delivered to only one consumer, ensuring reliable, one-to-one communication. This model is ideal for use cases like order processing systems, where each order (message) must be processed by one application instance.

The publish/subscribe domain, on the other hand, is centered around topics. In this model, messages are published to a topic and are consumed by multiple subscribers. Each message can be delivered to multiple consumers, facilitating one-to-many communication. This model is well-suited for scenarios like news distribution systems or stock price updates, where messages need to be broadcast to multiple consumers simultaneously. JMS ensures that all active subscribers receive the published messages, and durable subscriptions can be used to retain messages for subscribers that are temporarily offline.

The JMS API is structured around several core interfaces and classes. Key components include the ConnectionFactory, which creates connections to the JMS provider; Connection, which represents an active connection to the provider; Session, which is a context for producing and consuming messages; and Message, which encapsulates the data being transferred. Producers and consumers interact with queues or topics through these components, enabling the development of flexible, decoupled messaging architectures. The API also supports advanced features like message selectors for filtering, various acknowledgment modes, and transactional message processing, ensuring comprehensive support for complex messaging scenarios.

15.5.1 Core Components of the JMS API

The Java Message Service (JMS) API is built around several key components that enable the development of robust, asynchronous, and reliable messaging applications. These core components facilitate message production, consumption, and management within the JMS framework. Here, we will explore the primary elements that form the foundation of the JMS API.

ConnectionFactory

The ConnectionFactory interface is used to create connections to the JMS provider. It is a factory for Connection objects, which represent an active link to the messaging system. There are two specialized types of connection factories:

QueueConnectionFactory: For creating connections in the point-to-point (PTP) domain.

TopicConnectionFactory: For creating connections in the publish/subscribe (Pub/Sub) domain.

Example:

```
ConnectionFactory connectionFactory = new ActiveMQConnectionFactory("tcp://localhost:61616");
Connection connection = connectionFactory.createConnection();
```

Connection

A Connection represents an active connection to the JMS provider. It encapsulates the client's connection to the JMS provider and is used to create sessions. The connection needs to be started before messages can be sent or received.

Example:

```
connection.start();
```

Session

A Session is a single-threaded context for producing and consuming messages. It is created from a Connection and provides methods to create message producers, consumers, and destinations (queues and topics). Sessions also support transactions and various acknowledgment modes.

Example:

```
Session session = connection.createSession(false, Session.AUTO_ACKNOWLEDGE);
```
Destination

A Destination is the target for messages. It can be either a Queue or a Topic, depending on the messaging model being used (PTP or Pub/Sub). Destinations are created by the JMS provider and used by producers and consumers to send and receive messages.

Example:
```
Queue queue = session.createQueue("exampleQueue");
Topic topic = session.createTopic("exampleTopic");
```
MessageProducer

A MessageProducer is an object created by a session to send messages to a destination. Producers can send various types of messages, including text, bytes, object, and map messages.

Example:
```
MessageProducer producer = session.createProducer(queue);
TextMessage message = session.createTextMessage("Hello, JMS!");
producer.send(message);
```
MessageConsumer

A MessageConsumer is an object created by a session to receive messages from a destination. Consumers can operate in synchronous mode (explicitly fetching messages) or asynchronous mode (using message listeners).

Example:
```
MessageConsumer consumer = session.createConsumer(queue);
Message message = consumer.receive();
```
Message

A Message is the object that encapsulates the data being transferred between JMS clients. JMS defines several types of messages based on the payload:

TextMessage: Contains a string.
BytesMessage: Contains a stream of bytes.
ObjectMessage: Contains a serialized Java object.
MapMessage: Contains a set of key-value pairs.
StreamMessage: Contains a stream of Java primitive values.

Example:
```
TextMessage textMessage = session.createTextMessage("This is a text message");
```
MessageListener

A MessageListener is an interface implemented by objects that asynchronously receive messages. It is used to handle messages in an event-driven manner, allowing applications to process messages without blocking.

Example
```
consumer.setMessageListener(new MessageListener() {
  public void onMessage(Message message) {
    if (message instanceof TextMessage)
{
      try {
        String text = ((TextMessage) message).getText();
        System.out.println("Received: " + text);
      } catch (JMSException e) {
        e.printStackTrace();
      }
    }
  }
});
```
Message Acknowledgment

JMS supports different acknowledgment modes to ensure messages are properly processed:

AUTO_ACKNOWLEDGE: The session automatically acknowledges receipt of a message once it has been successfully received.

CLIENT_ACKNOWLEDGE: The client explicitly acknowledges the receipt of a message.

DUPS_OK_ACKNOWLEDGE: The session lazily acknowledges receipt of messages, which can result in duplicates.

SESSION_TRANSACTED: Messages are acknowledged as part of a transaction.

JMSException
JMSException is the base exception class for all JMS-related errors. Proper handling of these exceptions is crucial for ensuring the robustness and reliability of JMS applications.

15.5.2 Implementing Messaging with the JMS API involves:

Implementing messaging with the JMS API involves several critical steps that enable Java applications to communicate asynchronously and reliably. This section will detail the essential tasks needed to integrate JMS into your applications, providing a comprehensive guide to each stage of the process.

Setting Up the JMS Provider

To start with JMS, you need a JMS provider. For example, Apache ActiveMQ is a popular, open-source JMS provider.

Steps:

Download and Install ActiveMQ

Download ActiveMQ from the official website.

Extract the downloaded archive.

Start the ActiveMQ server by running: bin/activemq start

Access the Web Console

The default web console is available at http://localhost:8161/admin (username: admin, password: admin).

Adding JMS Dependencies

Add the necessary dependencies to your build configuration. For Maven, update your pom.xml:

```
<dependency>
<groupId>org.apache.activemq</groupId>
<artifactId>activemq-all</artifactId>
<version>5.16.3</version>
</dependency>
```

For Gradle, add the following to your build.gradle:

```
implementation 'org.apache.activemq:activemq-all:5.16.3'
```

Creating a Connection Factory

The ConnectionFactory is the starting point for working with JMS. It is used to create connections to the JMS provider.

Example Code:

```
import javax.jms.ConnectionFactory;
import org.apache.activemq.ActiveMQConnectionFactory;
ConnectionFactory connectionFactory = new ActiveMQConnectionFactory("tcp://localhost:61616");
```

Establishing a Connection

Using the ConnectionFactory, establish a connection to the JMS provider.

Example Code:

```
import javax.jms.Connection;
import javax.jms.JMSException;
Connection connection = connectionFactory.createConnection("admin", "admin");
connection.start();
```

Creating a Session

A Session is used to create producers, consumers, and destinations (queues or topics). Sessions can be transacted and support different acknowledgment modes.

Example Code:

```
import javax.jms.Session;
Session session = connection.createSession(false, Session.AUTO_ACKNOWLEDGE);
```

Defining Destinations

Destinations are the targets for messages. They can be Queue (for point-to-point communication) or Topic (for publish/subscribe communication).

Example Code:

```
import javax.jms.Queue;
import javax.jms.Topic;
Queue queue = session.createQueue("exampleQueue");
```

```
Topic topic = session.createTopic("exampleTopic");
```

Creating Message Producers

A MessageProducer is used to send messages to a destination.

Example Code:

```
import javax.jms.MessageProducer;
import javax.jms.TextMessage;
MessageProducer producer = session.createProducer(queue);
TextMessage message = session.createTextMessage("Hello, JMS!");
producer.send(message);
```

Creating Message Consumers

A MessageConsumer is used to receive messages from a destination.

Example Code:

```
import javax.jms.MessageConsumer;
import javax.jms.Message;
import javax.jms.TextMessage;
MessageConsumer consumer = session.createConsumer(queue);
Message receivedMessage = consumer.receive();
if (receivedMessage instanceof TextMessage) {
TextMessage textMessage = (TextMessage) receivedMessage;
System.out.println("Received: " + textMessage.getText());
}
```

Implementing Asynchronous Message Consumption

For asynchronous message processing, implement the MessageListener interface.

Example Code:

```
import javax.jms.MessageListener;
import javax.jms.Message;
public class MyMessageListener implements MessageListener {
   @Override
   public void onMessage(Message message) {
      if (message instanceof TextMessage) {
         try {
            String text = ((TextMessage) message).getText();
            System.out.println("Asynchronously received: " + text);
         } catch (JMSException e) {
            e.printStackTrace();
         }
      }
   }
}
MessageConsumer consumer = session.createConsumer(queue);
consumer.setMessageListener(new MyMessageListener());
```

Handling JMS Exceptions

Properly handle JMSException to ensure robustness and error recovery.

Example Code:

```
try {
   // JMS operations
} catch (JMSException e) {
   e.printStackTrace();
   // Implement retry logic or error handling
}
```

Closing Resources

Always close JMS resources to avoid resource leaks.

Example Code:

```
producer.close();
consumer.close();
```

```
session.close();
connection.close();
```

15.6 Design Patterns in Java

Design patterns represent solutions to common problems in software design. They are best practices refined over time by the developer community to solve recurring design issues, making code more flexible, reusable, and maintainable. In Java, understanding design patterns is crucial for writing well-structured and efficient applications. This chapter will explore several fundamental design patterns, including Singleton, Factory, Observer, and Decorator, providing insights into their implementation and use cases in Java.

Singleton Pattern

Purpose - The Singleton pattern ensures that a class has only one instance and provides a global point of access to it.

Implementation - Singleton in Java is typically implemented by making the constructor private and providing a static method that returns the instance.

Code:

```
public class Singleton {
    private static Singleton instance;

    private Singleton() {}

    public static synchronized Singleton getInstance() {
        if (instance == null) {
            instance = new Singleton();
        }
        return instance;
    }
}
```

Use Cases

Managing a connection to a database.

Implementing a logging class.

Factory Pattern

Purpose- The Factory pattern is used to create objects without specifying the exact class of object that will be created. This is achieved by defining an interface for creating an object and letting subclasses decide which class to instantiate.

Implementation

Code:

```
public interface Product {}
public class ConcreteProductA implements Product {}
public class ConcreteProductB implements Product {}
public class Factory
{
    public Product createProduct(String type)
{
        switch (type)
{
            case "A": return new ConcreteProductA();
            case "B": return new ConcreteProductB();
            default: throw new IllegalArgumentException("Type not supported.");
        }
    }
}
```

Use Cases

Creating objects when there are multiple implementations or classes with the same interface.

Isolating the client code from the implementation classes.

Observer Pattern

Purpose- The Observer pattern defines a one-to-many dependency between objects so that when one object changes state, all its dependents are notified and updated automatically.

Implementation - Java provides built-in support for the Observer pattern with java.util.Observable (now deprecated in favor of the Property Change Listener mechanism) and java.util.Observer.

Code:

```
public class ConcreteSubject extends Observable {
   private int state;
   public void setState(int state) {
      this.state = state;
      setChanged();
      notifyObservers(state);
   }
}
public class ConcreteObserver implements Observer {
   public void update(Observable obj, Object arg) {
      System.out.println("New state: " + arg);
   }
}
```

Use Cases

Implementing distributed event handling systems.

MVC frameworks where the model is the subject, and views are observers.

Decorator Pattern

Purpose - The Decorator pattern allows behaviour to be added to an individual object, either statically or dynamically, without affecting the behaviour of other objects from the same class.

Implementation-

Code-

```
public interface Component {
   void operation();
}
public class ConcreteComponent implements Component
{
   public void operation() {
      // Implementation
   }
}
public abstract class Decorator implements Component {
   protected Component component;
   public Decorator(Component component)
{
      this.component = component;
   }
   public void operation() {
      component.operation();
   }
}
public class ConcreteDecorator extends Decorator {
   public ConcreteDecorator(Component component)
{
      super(component);
   }
   public void operation()
{
      super.operation();
      addedBehaviour();
   }
   private void addedBehaviour()
```

```
{
    // New Behaviour
  }
}
```

Use Cases

Adding responsibilities to objects dynamically.

Implementing cross-cutting concerns such as logging, transaction management, or security in a flexible manner.

Exercise

Exercise 1 – MCQ

1. Which HTTP method is typically used to create a resource in a RESTful web service?
a) GET
b) POST
c) PUT
d) DELETE
2. What is the main purpose of Java Message Service (JMS)?
a) Data serialization
b) Web scraping
c) Messaging between two or more clients
d) Encrypting web traffic
3. Which of the following is a fundamental principle of RESTful architecture?
a) Stateful operations
b) Use of XML only
c) Stateless communication
d) High coupling
4. In RESTful web services, what is idempotency?
a) The ability to modify resources
b) Operations that produce the same results if executed once or multiple times
c) Unique identifiers for resources
d) Authentication mechanism
5. Which design pattern is commonly used to build a RESTful web service?
a) Singleton
b) Factory Method
c) MVC (Model-View-Controller)
d) Observer
6. What does JMS API provide for messaging?
a) TCP/IP protocols
b) A method for synchronous file transfer
c) A way to create, send, receive, and read messages
d) HTML parsing capabilities
7. Which of the following is NOT a messaging domain in JMS?
a) Point-to-Point (Queue)
b) Publish-Subscribe (Topic)
c) Request-Reply
d) Multicast
8. What is a Microservice in Java?
a) A lightweight service that performs a specific task
b) A large monolithic Java application
c) A Java applet
d) A servlet
9. Which pattern is specifically aimed at Microservices Architecture for handling failures?
a) Singleton
b) Circuit Breaker
c) Factory
d) Proxy

10. How do Microservices communicate with each other?
a) Through global variables
b) Using direct class instantiation
c) By invoking static methods
d) Using lightweight protocols like HTTP/REST or messaging

Exercise 2 – True/False

1. RESTful web services use HTTP methods to represent CRUD operations.
2. In a microservices architecture, each service runs in a shared process to reduce resource consumption.
3. The Singleton design pattern ensures that a class has only one instance and provides a global point of access to it.
4. JMS stands for Java Messaging Service, which is a Java API for RESTful web services.
5. Idempotence is a property of any operation that allows it to be applied multiple times without changing the result beyond the initial application.
6. Microservices are designed to be stateful to enhance performance and reliability.
7. The Observer design pattern is used in Java to notify a set of objects about state changes in another object.
8. In JMS, the Point-to-Point messaging domain supports a one-to-many communication model.
9. Implementing RESTful web services in Java requires a servlet container like Apache Tomcat.
10. Circuit Breaker is a design pattern used in microservices to prevent a failure in one service from cascading to other services.

Exercise 3 – Fill in the blanks

1. In RESTful architecture, the primary communication protocol used is ___________.
2. Java Message Service (JMS) provides a standardized way for Java applications to create, send, receive, and read ___________.
3. The ___________ design pattern ensures that a class has only one instance and provides a global point of access to it.
4. Microservices architecture focuses on building applications as a collection of small, ___________ services.
5. Design patterns in Java provide reusable solutions to common ___________ in software design.
6. SON Web Token (JWT) is commonly used in RESTful services for _______ allowing secure exchange of information between parties as a JSON object.
7. WS-AtomicTransaction is a specification that ensures that distributed transactions are completed in an ________ manner.
8. _________ is software or hardware infrastructure supporting sending and receiving messages between distributed systems without requiring the systems to be online at the same time.
9. WSDL (Web Services Description Language) is an XML-based language used for describing the functionality offered by a ________.
10. JMS (Java Message Service) is an API that provides a way to create, send, receive, and read messages in a ________system.

Exercise 4 – Match Case

1. Ensures that a class has only one instance and provides a global point of access to it.
2. Allows an object to publish changes to its state and notifies dependent objects automatically.
3. Defines an interface for creating an object but allows subclasses to alter the type of objects that will be created.
4. Used to construct a complex object step by step.

A. Singleton
B. Observer
C. Factory Method
D. Builder

Exercise 5 – One word answer

1. What is a design pattern?
2. What design pattern ensures that a class has only one instance and provides a global point of access to it?

Exercise 6 – Small answer

1. What is RESTful architecture?
2. What is the purpose of the Singleton design pattern?

Exercise 7 – Long answer
1. Explain the concept of Microservices Architecture.
2. Describe the role of Java Message Service (JMS) in messaging systems.

Answer-

Exercise 1 – 1) b 2) c 3) c 4) b 5) c 6) c 7) d 8) a 9) b 10) d

Exercise 2 –1) True 2) False 3) True 4) False 5) True 6) False 7) True 8) False 9) True 10) True

Exercise 3 –1) HTTP 2) messages 3) Singleton 4) independently deployable 5) problems 6) authentication and authorization 7) atomic 8) Message-oriented middleware (MOM) 9) web service 10) message-oriented middleware

Exercise 4 – 1 – A. Singleton 2 – B. Observer 3 – C. Factory Method 4 – D. Builder

Exercise 5 – 1) Template 2) Singleton

Online Resources

Online Practice Paper

Link: https://forms.gle/yUFUVbBkzn1xnypV6
QR Code:

YouTube Video Link

Link: https://www.youtube.com/playlist?list=PLzlh_31VWEFpHfA7lPmrp4wpmZYRaA6gU
QR Code:

CHAPTER 16 - Viva – Voce of Advanced Java

Q1: What is the difference between ServerSocket and Socket in Java?
Ans: ServerSocket is used to create a server that listens for incoming connections, while Socket is used by a client to establish a connection with a server. Once connected, both can communicate over Input/Output streams.

Q2: What is the significance of the bind(), listen() and accept() methods in socket programming?
Ans: These methods are used in server-side programming. bind() binds the server to a port, listen() makes it ready to accept connections, and accept() waits for a connection from a client.

Q3: What are the steps involved in establishing a connection using JDBC?
Ans: The basic steps are: Load JDBC Driver, Establish a connection using DriverManager.getConnection(), Create a Statement or PreparedStatement, Execute SQL queries, and Close the connection.

Q4: What is the difference between Statement and PreparedStatement in JDBC ?
Ans: Statement is used for executing static SQL queries, while PreparedStatement allows executing precompiled SQL queries with dynamic parameters. PreparedStatement is more efficient and prevents SQL injection.

Q5: What are the core components of Java EE architecture?
Ans: Java EE components include EJB (Enterprise JavaBeans), JSP, Servlets, JPA (Java Persistence API), JMS (Java Message Service), and web services.

Q6: How do EJB components interact in Java EE applications?
Ans: EJBs are server-side components that encapsulate business logic. They are accessed by remote clients or other server components using interfaces, providing services like transactions, security, and concurrency.

Q7: What is the role of JPA in enterprise applications?
Ans: JPA (Java Persistence API) is used to manage relational data in enterprise applications. It allows developers to map Java objects to database tables using annotations and handles data persistence seamlessly.

Q8: What is the importance of transaction management in enterprise applications?
Ans: Transaction management ensures that a group of operations either completes successfully (commit) or fails completely (rollback), maintaining data integrity. This is especially important in distributed systems.

Q9: How do you create a Jar file in Java and what does it contain?
Ans: A JAR (Java Archive) file is created using the jar command. It contains compiled Java classes, resources, and metadata in a compressed format. It's used for packaging libraries and standalone applications.

Q10: How is a WAR file structured and what is it used for?
Ans: A WAR (Web Application Archive) file contains web components such as Servlets, JSPs, static content (HTML, CSS), and configuration files (web.xml). It is used for deploying web applications to a server.

Q11: What is the role of the web.xml file in a java web applications?
Ans: The web.xml file is the deployment descriptor in Java web applications. It defines servlet mappings, filters, session configurations, and context parameters.

Q12: Explain the importance of the MVC architecture in web applications development
Ans: MVC (Model-View-Controller) separates business logic (Model), presentation logic (View), and control flow (Controller). This separation enhances maintainability and scalability of web applications.

Q13: What is a web container and how does it support Servlets and JSPs?
Ans: A web container (e.g., Tomcat) provides an environment for the execution of web components like Servlets and JSPs. It manages their lifecycle, request-response handling, and session management.

Q14: How would you set up a Java web application project using Maven?

Ans: Using Maven, you define the project structure with pom.xml, specifying dependencies like the Servlet API. You can then package the project as a WAR file and deploy it to a web container.

Q15: What is the role of the doGet() and doPost() methods in a Servlet?
Ans: doGet() handles HTTP GET requests, typically used to retrieve data. doPost() handles POST requests, usually to send or submit data. These methods process requests from clients and generate responses.

Q16: Explain the servlet lifecycle methods.
Ans: The servlet lifecycle includes three methods: init() (initializes the servlet), service() (handles requests and responses), and destroy() (cleanup before removal). These are managed by the web container.

Q17: How does session management work in Java Servlets?
Ans: Sessions in Java can be managed using HttpSession, cookies, or URL rewriting. HttpSession stores session data on the server, while cookies store small pieces of data on the client-side.

Q18: What is the difference between cookies and URL rewriting in session management?
Ans: Cookies store session information on the client-side, sent with each request. URL rewriting adds session information to the URL when cookies are disabled or unsupported.

Q19: What is the difference between JSP and servlets?
Ans: JSP is a server-side technology used for generating dynamic content, mainly the presentation layer. Servlets handle business logic and control flow. JSP is compiled into Servlets at runtime.

Q20: What are JSP scriptlets and how are they used?
Ans: JSP scriptlets are blocks of Java code embedded within <% %> tags. They allow you to embed Java logic directly into HTML pages. However, using scriptlets is discouraged in favor of JSTL and EL (Expression Language).

Q21: How does the Struts2 framework implement MVC?
Ans: In Struts 2, the Controller is implemented through actions (classes), the Model handles data, and the View is typically JSP or other presentation technologies. The framework handles request mapping and flow between them.

Q22: What are interceptors in Struts2, and how do they work?
Ans: Interceptors in Struts 2 are objects that can process a request before and after the action executes. They are used for functionalities like validation, logging, and session management.

Q23; What is Hibernate and how does it simplify database interaction in java?
Ans: Hibernate is an ORM (Object-Relational Mapping) framework that maps Java objects to database tables. It simplifies data access by eliminating the need for manual SQL, allowing developers to work with objects instead of SQL queries.

Q24: What is the purpose of the hibernate.cfg.xml file?
Ans: The hibernate.cfg.xml file is used to configure Hibernate settings, such as database connection information (URL, username, password), dialect, and resource mappings.

Q25: What is dependency injections in Spring, and how does it work?
Ans: Dependency injection (DI) in Spring allows objects to be injected into other objects at runtime, rather than being instantiated internally. This promotes loose coupling and easier testing.

Q26: What is the difference between BeanFactory and ApplicationContext in Spring?
Ans: BeanFactory is a simple factory for managing beans, while ApplicationContext extends BeanFactory by providing more advanced features like event propagation, declarative services, and internationalization.

Q27: What is SpringBoot and how does it simplify applications development?

Ans: Spring Boot simplifies Spring-based application development by providing pre-configured templates, auto-configuration, and embedded servers, reducing the need for complex XML configurations.

Q28: How does SpringBoot support microservices architecture?
Ans: Spring Boot supports microservices by providing a lightweight framework for creating independent, self-contained services. Features like embedded servers and simple RESTful web service creation help with microservice development.

Q29: What is the difference between REST and SOAP web services in java?
Ans: REST is an architectural style that uses HTTP for communication and is lightweight. SOAP is a protocol that uses XML for message formatting and provides built-in error handling and security, but is heavier than REST.

Q30: What is JMS(Java Message Service) and how does it work?
Ans: JMS is a messaging API that allows Java applications to send and receive messages asynchronously. It supports both point-to-point messaging (via queues) and publish-subscribe messaging.

YouTube Video Link

Link: https://www.youtube.com/playlist?list=PLzlh_31VWEFoau3kfwhzqUg--UDr5zpHa
QR Code:

ADDITIONAL RESOURCES

Advanced Java Videos Playlist

Link:https://www.youtube.com/playlist?list=PLzlh_31VWEFoZXs-3KLPda_DVlN9IPJyg

QR Code:

Java Interview Playlist:
Link: https://www.youtube.com/playlist?list=PLzlh_31VWEFryjvGNIVtyBVYvddpxKexP

QR Code:

Java EE 7 Application Developer (Paper Code - 1Z0-900) Playlist.
Link: https://www.youtube.com/playlist?list=PLzlh_31VWEFodNsy-MeBm7RdKGWAO4TzF

QR Code:

Oracle Certified Professional Java Programmer OCPJP (Paper Code - 1Z0-809) Playlist.
Link: https://www.youtube.com/playlist?list=PLzlh_31VWEFqzXoVrZjKV6cZQKi7iG2D9

QR Code:

Oracle Certified Master Java Enterprise Architect (OCMJEA)(Paper Code - 1Z0-807) Playlist.
Link: https://www.youtube.com/playlist?list=PLzlh_31VWEFqdceCx1Pivwi5ypdvfVaEs

QR Code:

Oracle Certified Master Java Enterprise Architect (OCMJEA)(Paper Code - 1Z0-807) Playlist.
Link: https://www.youtube.com/playlist?list=PLzlh_31VWEFr90bIgv56c3xabjV50iFLV

QR Code:

Core Java Textbook Playlist.
Link: https://www.youtube.com/playlist?list=PLzlh_31VWEFofK7phOZSB9OO9rP1bkaxB

QR Code: